Understanding Cultural Transmission in Anthropology

Methodology and History in Anthropology

General Editor: David Parkin, Fellow of All Souls College, Oxford

UNDERSTANDING CULTURAL TRANSMISSION IN ANTHROPOLOGY
A Critical Synthesis

Edited by
Roy Ellen, Stephen J. Lycett and Sarah E. Johns

berghahn
NEW YORK · OXFORD
www.berghahnbooks.com

First published in 2013 by

Berghahn Books

www.berghahnbooks.com

Library of Congress Cataloging-in-Publication Data
A catalog record for this book
is available from the Library of Congress

Understanding cultural transmission in anthropology: a critical synthesis /
edited by Roy Ellen, Stephen Lycett, and Sarah Johns. -- First edition.
 pages cm. -- (Methodology and history in anthropology; v. 26)
 Includes bibliographical references and index.
 ISBN 978-0-85745-993-0 (hardback: alk. paper) -- ISBN 978-0-85745-
994-7 (institutional ebook) -- ISBN 978-1-78238-071-9 (pbk.: alk. paper)
-- ISBN 978-1-78238-072-6 (retail ebook)
 1. Human evolution. 2. Social evolution. 3. Social systems. 4. Culture
and communication. 5. Intercultural communication. 6. Ethnobiology.
7. Traditional ecological knowledge. I. Ellen, R. F., 1947-
 GN281.U56 2013
 599.93'8--dc23

2013005578

British Library Cataloguing in Publication Data
A catalogue record for this book is available from the British Library

Printed in the United States on acid-free paper

ISBN 978-0-85745-993-0 (hardback)
ISBN 978-1-78238-071-9 (paperback)
ISBN 978-0-85745-994-7 (institutional ebook)
ISBN 978-1-78238-072-6 (retail ebook)

CONTENTS

LIST OF FIGURES

LIST OF TABLES

PREFACE

As humans, we are social animals who acquire much of our behaviour from other individuals of our species and who innovate new behaviours, which we in turn disseminate. In the process of leading our daily lives, we are constantly influenced by others in the way we behave, what we wear, the technology we use, the way we speak, and the political, moral and religious values that we come to hold. This process of 'transmission' permeates every aspect of human society, and our beliefs, attitudes and customs have come to be the predominant means through which we have adapted and come to occupy our current dominant position in global life systems.

The study of human culture, and the diverse patterns of behaviour it creates, has traditionally defined the discipline of anthropology. In this volume, which has developed out of a seminar series organized by the School of Anthropology and Conservation at the University of Kent, we have drawn together a diverse range of contributors from different disciplines. These span biology, primatology, palaeoanthropology, psychology, social anthropology, ethnobiology and archaeology, and examine social and cultural transmission from a range of perspectives. Anyone who has even tangentially encountered the existing literature on this topic will be well aware of the controversies surrounding the term 'culture' with regard to its definition and its presence (or otherwise) in animals other than humans. Here, for the sake of pragmatism, we and other contributors largely use the terms 'social learning', 'social transmission' and 'cultural transmission' as synonyms, accepting that while animals other than humans undoubtedly learn behaviours via social interaction, the content and mode of transmission (and the resultant behavioural patterns) vary widely from species to species.

The chapters display some radically different – and not always theoretically harmonious – approaches, but all share the conviction that a unifying and central theme in anthropological theory must be the study of cultural transmission. This diversity and inclusivity demonstrates the variety of current research approaches and paradigms dedicated to tackling this problem, while emphasizing how the models we now use are integral to, and are accepted by, a range of different disciplines. Because humans are not the only species to engage in the process of social or cultural transmission, the study of 'culture' has implications for, and is influenced by, research extending beyond the more traditional confines of 'anthropology'. We deliberately wanted to set the issue of human cultural transmission against this wider backdrop in order to reiterate this point. The studies presented are diverse not only in taxonomy, but also in chronology, geography and focus in terms of precisely what behaviours are being transmitted socially in each case. Again, this emphasizes the long-term character of our cultural heritage (at a scale of millions of years), as well as highlighting that whatever our future as a species may hold, cultural transmission will continue to play a strong role in shaping the legacy of humanity's tomorrow.

Roy Ellen, Stephen J. Lycett and Sarah E. Johns
School of Anthropology and Conservation
University of Kent at Canterbury

ON THE CONCEPT OF CULTURAL TRANSMISSION

Roy Ellen and Michael D. Fischer

Introduction

The renaissance of 'big issues' in anthropology (Parkin and Ulijaszek 2007; Allen, Callan, Dunbar and James 2008), and various discussions about how best to integrate theory and approaches across the spectrum of the subject (e.g. Ellen 2010), inevitably draws us towards the notion of cultural transmission. This is because the systems of culturally mediated social relations that anthropologists are evidently so well equipped to study only survive in the long run because they provide the conditions for their own continuity, and more critically, promote biological reproduction and survival. However, although there is increasing interest in the theoretical centrality of cultural transmission, it remains underplayed in many areas of anthropology where it might be thought to have an application.

For present purposes we can begin with the notion of culture (in its most inclusive and extensive sense) as emerging from non-genetic social transmission of information and associated actions or practices as mediated by the brain, other body systems and existing instantiated cultural information. As is now well established, the brain itself has been subjected to cultural selection pressures that have resulted in greater size and complexity (Bonner 1980: 4; Dunbar 2003). As the efficiency of learning depends on memory, so the brain has not only evolved to process cultural input, but has been increasingly moulded by an environment in which cultural transmission has become crucial for survival, especially in humans (Richerson and Boyd 2005).

Thus, in each human lifetime exposure to rich cultural environments reorganizes neural circuitry in ways which stimulate optimal performance in social contexts (Edelman 1992), 'fixing' memorate knowledge through the limbic system and habitual bodily activity. As a resource for adaptation, as part of an 'extended phenotype' (Dawkins 1982) if you will, culture is, therefore, more rapid, focused and flexible than either genetic or physiological adaptation, and is an engine for the production of diversity quite as complex but less predictable than any found in biological systems. In biological systems there are clear chemical and other constraints on information transmission – the structure of DNA, replication speeds, sexual maturation, mate selection and gestation times – but with culture there is a common perception of relatively few constraints, although those constraints deriving from the properties of available channels for acquisition, transmission, storage and expression, together with conformance to fundamental limits as described by information theory (Shannon and Weaver 1949), require much more exploration and consideration. And it is evaluating precisely the impact of these constraints that poses some of the greatest challenges in studying cultural transmission.

In this volume we review and juxtapose current work on the theme of cultural transmission, defined as 'the emergence, acquisition, storage, and communication of ideas and practices' (Cohen 2010: S194). Cultural transmission implies movement of ideas and practices between individuals or groups and is therefore always social, but not all learning is strictly cultural since it may not have been acquired from others, nor subsequently transmitted. Moreover, because learned behaviour is displayed by different individuals does not necessarily mean it has been transmitted, since some practices are so protean that they are constantly re-created, giving only the appearance of having been transmitted.

Cultural transmission is, of course, imperfect. Genetic transmission is subject to many obstacles to fidelity which are resolved by requirements for physical conformance at the molecular level so that the majority of faulty transmissions cannot further reproduce. Cultural transmission is potentially more hazardous, given that socio-cultural output rarely reproduces in a precisely identical form, and there is no physical vehicle of transmission to enforce fidelity. Perhaps this observation provides us with a clue that it is not just 'information' that is transmitted but rather expressions or relations. It is all the more important, therefore, given its evolutionary importance for *Homo sapiens*, that human social systems provide for secure and effective contexts in which transmission can take place, and within which transmitted culture can be refined and edited to enforce sufficient conformance.

Let us start with the idea that cultural transmission is the reproduction of information and practices through social learning, independent of the genes or other biochemical means, and involving one or more motor-sensory system (Heyes 1994). We can then ask, as comparative zoologists have done (Laland and Galef 2009), just how common it is amongst all living animals. For Bonner (1980) it is distributed throughout the animal kingdom, not only evident in classic studies of learned behaviour in birds and various primates (Humle and Newton-Fisher, this volume), but also fish (Laland, this volume). Of the more well-known and anthropologically relevant work, there are − for example − reports of the transmission of chimpanzee material culture, innovated washing of food in managed populations of habituated macaques, and self medication using particular plant species (e.g. Humle and Newton-Fisher, this volume; Nishida 1986; Huffman 1997; Whiten et al. 1999). The repeated discovery of similar cases serves to remind us to avoid teleological definitions of culture, as something that sufficiently defines us as what we are as a species. Clearly, the more complex mental states of which humans are capable − consciousness, higher order intentionality, language, sharing, narrativity − the very features that underpin the Geertzian (1973: 5) idea of culture as 'webs of significance', have a profound influence on how culture is transmitted, but we should not allow these elaborate means to dictate our definitions, or otherwise cross-species comparison becomes impossible (Lycett, Collard and McGrew 2009). In the study of fossil hominins we have the additional challenge of devising frameworks of analysis for long periods of evolutionary history when the role of cultural transmission was itself undergoing significant expansion and transformation (Lycett, this volume).

In studying cultural transmission we have to explore and attempt to synthesize hypotheses and data over a series of levels. We might distinguish the following: (a) the micro-level, applying to bodily and cognitive aspects of processes of learning and innovation, and to interpersonal interaction; (b) the middle-range level, at which social institutions serve as contexts for perpetuating transmission and ensuring its fidelity; and (c) the macro-level, addressing issues of cultural history, adaptation, phylogeny, diversification and spatial diffusion.

One persistent problem in anthropological theorizing of cultural transmission is that it is often assumed to operate collectively, from one generation to another, rather than from one individual to another; at a supra-individual (summative) level (Boyer 1994: 265). While the process indeed takes place in a socio-ecological context that comprises multiple individuals, single individuals are always the vectors of acquisition and transmission. For Boyer, recurrence is, therefore, an abstract statistical phenomenon, the objects of which can never

enter into causal relations with material events. While we can generalize and talk about populations, we need to look at single individuals
loosely imagined as comprising these populations. Moreover, a group
of individuals with respect to knowledge acquisition and transmission have properties that are different from a group with respect to
acquisition and transmission of genes, in that individuals interact
with each other to create both transitional and end states.

With these caveats in mind, we shall examine cultural transmission under eight headings: (1) micro-process, (2) life cycles and generations, (3) forms of knowledge, (4) measurement, (5) growth and loss,
(6) interpersonal relations and contexts, (7) long-term (evolutionary)
patterns, and (8) rates of change.

Micro-processes

By 'micro-processes' we here refer to the detailed way in which
cultural information is acquired at an individual level; how culture
moves from one embodied brain to another. We refer to studies of
copying, learning and innovation, by neuroscientists, psychologists
or ethnographers, using cognitive and other theoretical frameworks.
Such approaches seek to ask whether the transmission of those mental
structures that organize ideas, actions and relationships make us any
different from other animals, beyond what we can achieve with these.

It has been suggested that there is a problem in using the very
word 'transmission', as it is too immediate or direct to refer to the
process by which cultural competence is acquired by individuals (e.g.
Lave 1988: 177; Marchand 2010a: Siv). Thus, if we examine the way
in which people acquire knowledge and skills, the process is much
more interactive and complex – even discordant – than can be conveyed by a passive conception of 'transmission', which could suggest
that this 'stuff' called culture is flowing between generations and
through time, or 'copying', which implies a 'fax' or photocopier analogy (Strauss and Quinn 1997). Recipients are not simply 'vessels to be
filled' (Reynolds 1981). The mind, like all organic learning systems, is
not a fixed generic device. Most aspects of human mental processing
are unlike the instructional principles of computer processing, depending on a principle of selection. There is no 'preformed miniature'
that is simply replicated (Boyer 1994: 278, 282). If we consider how
particular individuals learn technological processes, such as minaret
building (Marchand 2001), woodworking (Marchand 2010b), metal-
working (Keller and Keller 1996), gardening (Platten, this volume),
cheese making (West, this volume) or basket making (Puri, this
volume), cultural transmission resembles rather the development of

linguistic competence, in which representations and actions are generated, retained and communicated (McCauley and Lawson 2002: 45). We become experts not by passively absorbing knowledge, but by actively selecting it, which can take the form of several potential 'biases' (Boyd and Richerson 1985; Chudek et al. 2012). What is remarkable (and potentially deceptive) is that the consequences of most 'cultural transmission' so closely resemble what has been previously known or done, and is therefore not much reflected upon. Only when new problems arise, or when old problems present themselves in different ways, do we consciously 'innovate'. It is this degree of fidelity that must underlie any 'system' of culture that emerges.

An example that demonstrates powerfully the systemic character of transmission, even for an apparently simple social process, is that whereby a baby learns to use a spoon (Steenbergen, van der Kamp, Smitsman and Carson 1997). This is incremental, comprising gradual coordination between eye, mouth, fingers and arms. The child is motivated by the desire to connect the food on a dish with its own need to satisfy its hunger. The child already has means for connecting food to mouth, but is provided with some tools that have been specially developed by others to achieve this objective, which it is then motivated to use. But while it may also be encouraged to perform a particular sequence of actions by a parent or other person, by and large it has to work out for itself how to perform a complex chain of operations, and will generally succeed with repeated attempts and encouragement (i.e. reinforcement). Enculturation is instilling that desire, not the functional end result – having said that, humans evolved capabilities for complex copying. Multi-layered neural networks have prodigious capacities to induce complex logical relations in their input. These logical capabilities extend to much of our motor system, enabling behaviours sequenced by logical relations derived from contextual data. Behaviour and ideation may initially be connected, but skill first requires their separation and reintegration as separate components.

In the context of large datasets, of the kind sometimes examined by archaeologists and biologists (see chapters by Lycett, O'Neill and Jordan, and Shennan, this volume), these kinds of irregularities and subtleties are normalized out and the idea of 'transmission' as group-to-group flow over time becomes plausible. However complex the means and circumstances by which individuals or groups acquire and process information from others and their past and present productions, synchronous or asynchronous information transmission is required. So, rather than argue for an alternative, we are content to use the term 'cultural transmission' to refer to all levels of analysis, given that we understand its limitations.

These examples also draw our attention to the differences between field data and data gathered in laboratory settings (see also Mesoudi 2011a). Experimental studies, on the whole, tell us what can potentially happen in natural contexts, not necessarily what actually does happen. A classic example of the disjunction that can sometimes occur is found in the history of studies of chimpanzee language learning. Under controlled laboratory conditions, the potential of chimpanzees for grammatical and novel communication using signing has been impressively demonstrated, although these forms do not correspond to those used by chimpanzees in the wild (Leiber 1995; Humle and Newton-Fisher, this volume). Chimpanzees may possess similar abilities, but the need, desire and supporting social infrastructure required to use them beneficially does not appear to be in place to support them.

All this is not merely 'replication', as we might understand it when speaking of DNA (just as the relationship between DNA and a working human brain is not simple replication), but the outcome of interplay between materials and processes that reliably produce outcomes that resemble past and future productions of others (Fischer 2008). What the spoon-feeding example exemplifies is that cultural transmission is not necessarily the copying of abstract models or representations but is sometimes, at least in part, as Bourdieu (1990) insists, the 'imitation of actions'; or, we might add, emulation or stimulus enhancement. Imitation is a particular form of copying. Psychologists distinguish between imitation (copying of both the goal and all the actions that accompany the means to achieve it) and emulation (the copying of just the goal or the outcome) (Whiten et al. 2009). Copying is imitative in so far as its takes place under guidance, and improvisatory in so far as the knowledge it generates is knowledge that novices discover for themselves. Motor representations can be systematically recombined to produce physical imitation or novel articulations.

We should not, therefore, confuse mental representations with behavioural outcomes (Boyer 1994: 279). This is why Ingold (2001: fn 13, 138) prefers the notion of enskilment to that of enculturation and rejects 'classic cognitivism' in favour of a more 'emergentivist' approach (cf. Clark 1997: 53). Indeed, he offers us a forceful critique of Sperber's (1996) position that knowledge is 'mental content' in the brain waiting to be expressed, and transmission the process through which representations are discharged. Following Gibson (1979: 254) he prefers the notion of perceptual engagement through performance by 'an whole organism-person in an environment' (Ingold 2001: 135, 142), rather than of a mind inside a body. There is a sense, then, in which once particular skills have been learned it is the body that 'remembers', through constant repetition of motor routines and a kind of fixing through somatic plasticity (West, this volume). There is a similar problem in the way some psychologists and linguists use the term 'acquired' in relation to language. For Ingold (2001: 130), echoing Lock (1980), this is better understood as continually regenerating through children's developmental involvement in 'the world of speech'. All learning involves self-discovery, the retrieval of knowledge entailing 'the partial re-enactment' of the very situation(s) that led to its encoding (Barsalou et al. 2003), and for this reason every 'transmission event' is likely to modify the unit transmitted.

But accepting the cognitive and physical processes of transmission as embodied (Cohen 2010: S195), grounded in material contexts (Barsalou 2008), and irreducible to the mechanical replication of bits of biochemical information in the brain, is not the same as accepting that there are no cognitive preconditions for learning. For Sperber (1996) the problem with a *tabula rasa* is that it cannot learn. True, processing devices can themselves be learned, and this is what is happening in learning how to use tools, and in language learning – most specifically in the proposal for a 'language acquisition device' (LAD) 'furnished with specific syntactic and semantic content' (Ingold 2001: 129; see also Chomsky and Halle [1968], who argue for an innate LAD). Certainly, once the essentials of language are in place, learning and cultural transmission adopt a different form. But how do we learn the processing devices? 'Unless ... both sender and recipient possess a common set of interpretative devices' (what Tooby and Cosmides [1992: 92] call 'human metaculture') communication cannot even begin (Ingold 2001: 117). At some ontogenetic stage there has to be an interface with those genetic inputs that predispose us to learning, however much they are intertwined with the epigenetic facts of biological development. With some activities, what appears as 'cultural transmission' cannot be satisfactorily explained through notions of replication or through a generative capacity model. Rather, acquisition takes place through reinvention from first principles, building on pre-specified cognitive architecture interacting with an environment in a particular way to solve a problem. 'Cultural recurrence is not coextensive with cultural transmission' (Boyer 1994: 286).

The difficulty with this formulation, however, is that 'cognitive architectures' do not come ready-made, but themselves emerge through biological development, the properties of environmentally extended systems that cross-cut the boundaries of body and brain. Whatever is encoded in the genes is highly modified as the developmental process unfolds through physical and cultural experience. For example, any proclivity to binary opposition is reinforced through particular culturally experienced modalities (e.g. Ellen 2012: 36–38).

Ingold (2001: 122) sees the work of some evolutionary biologists as resting on a circular argument that redescribes an observed phenotype as a set of epigenetic 'rules'. Following Oyama (1989: 5), he would prefer to discard the contrast between innate cognition and acquired culture by showing how the forms and capacities of humans, like all animals, arise within processes of development. Evolutionary processes establish developmental conditions, or we might say that 'the manifold capacities of human beings ... emerge ... within fields of practice constituted by the activities of those who precede them' (Ingold 2001: 133). Thus, Ingold's approach differentiates the 'copying' he describes as part of a developmental process from the copying (imitation) attributed to memes (Dawkins 1976: 192; Blackmore 1998). However, keeping to this developmental argument, we need to ask what is being copied. Is it, for example, the behaviour of throwing, or a set of constraints that result in appropriate instantiations of throwing in different circumstances? Or are the two intertwined?

We would like to argue that what makes throwing 'cultural' is learning to copy that which cannot be directly observed, the cultural prototypes or logic for which throwing is sometimes an appropriate component for instantiation. To copy what cannot be observed requires the capacity to form by induction a logic capable of driving culturally acceptable instantiation. This is, in Ingold's terms, a developmental process, and is achievable either by inducing a logic of constraints on a simple generator, or a generative logic starting from some basic inputs. We agree with Ingold that processes are not transmitted full-fledged but as part of a developmental process, which might include 'pretend', 'play', simulated encounters, exercises, failed attempts, successful attempts and so on, which result in the ability to 'imitate' what people are usually interested in, the results of what others achieve, but not the identifiable behaviours that lead to these. That is, human imitation is teleological, and imitating outcomes is too complex to achieve without recognizing the procedural emergence of outcomes. So, whereas the processes of genetics, including the developmental aspects, are not teleological except in the most primitive sense that those interactions promoting reproduction will be transmitted and others will not; in human cultural transmission, teleology is mostly everything, and thus the ability to transmit representations of outcomes (or at least positive or negative valuations of representations) is critical.

Consider, for example, the now famous case of the transmission of the recipe for Mornay sauce. While for Sperber (1996: 61–62) the recipe includes everything you need to know to prepare the sauce in your own kitchen, and all that is necessary to replicate it is to read it, for Ingold (2001: 137) the recipe can only be replicated in the context of the readers 'prior experience of melting, stirring, of handling substances ...' and so on. The information in the recipe book is insufficient, and indeed (as we have established) there can be no form of cultural transmission that is simple replication of what has been previously known or done. Because of this there are always opportunities for minor correction loops and reflection, and innovation. This view is reinforced in the chapter by West in this volume, in his discussion of 'recipes' and the limitations of books and formal instruction in transmitting cheese-making knowledge.

But it is not only that certain things have to be known in order to acquire other things – how to hold a knife before you can cut a joint of meat – but it is by no means the case that once learned, knowledge is inevitably retained, even that which represents a considerable investment in learning. What we learn with the short-term aim of passing an examination may not survive adolescence, but even more frighteningly the young children of ethnographers who become more fluent in a local language more quickly than their parents during fieldwork may lose the language with equal rapidity if it is not 'relearned' later in life (Hansen et al. 2002; Au et al. 2008). Quite apart from individual 'forgetting' of information insufficiently deeply encoded in memory, or temporary forgetting, some cultural knowledge is age-phase dependent. The knowledge acquired by children in order to operate in the nursery or playground may be useless after adolescence, as the work of Peter and Iona Opie (1959) in documenting the acquisition of children's lore so well exemplifies. Likewise, individuals are continuously acquiring or revising cultural knowledge as they progress through life events and associated social roles (see next section).

In fact, cultural transmission cannot be limited to one kind of process, even in non-human animals (Heyes 1994). Although behaviours are the primary data available, and their reproduction is critical, what makes these cultural is their conformance to a cultural standard. It is a standard that is being 'transmitted' or enculturated. And although Ingold might refer to the development of mechanical skills or mental 'tricks' as enskilment, it is their conformance to cultural standards that serves as an evaluation measure during acquisition. Examining only the emergent behaviour does not help us with the central problem of how people acquire cultural standards and how to apply these while instantiating the behaviour or skill thus acquired. We may perform continuously but cannot partake of useful activity with others without acquiring and shaping performance around cultural standards. So, the critical skills that we need to develop for enculturation, or to receive 'transmissions', are the capacity to recognize (and accept) criticism, rejection, confusion, and inappropriate reactions (to expectations); that is a critical faculty that must underlay the successful capacity to generate or reproduce instances of cultural behaviour.

People must theorize to acquire these standards, not necessarily an individual's actual intentions, but the intentions that others must adopt to achieve cultural intelligibility. Ethnopsychological analysis about people's 'true' intentions may also be relevant, but probably not as a major part of cultural acquisition. That is, what needs to be acquired are the culturally accepted intentions and goals, standards and criteria, as these are the components available for transforming individual desires and goals into a form that others will accept and cooperate in achieving.

Life Cycles and Generations as Ontogenetic Contexts

From the micro-processes of learning we move to the temporal contexts in which learning takes place: life cycles and generations. The average human life cycle (Bogin and Smith 1996) is less than a thousand months, and sets the outer limits of opportunity for the transmission of all culturally informed behaviour. The life spans of different species of mammal are variable. Thus, while the elephant *Elephas asiaticus* has a maximum lifespan of 50–60 years and its age of first breeding is 9–10 years, the rat *Rattus rattus* has a maximum lifespan of 1–2 years and an age of first breeding of 21 days. By comparison, the sturgeon *Acipenser fulvescens* may live to be 220 years old. We might expect a strong correlation between longevity in a species and the volume of cultural behaviour transmitted. While in most species where there is evidence for cultural transmission, it operates between genetic parents and their offspring, in some it may pass from grandparents, between siblings and others who are genetically related, and in some cases where the dyads involved are not. In humans, all these interactions provide opportunities for transmission, but the volume of transmission between those who are not genetically related is sometimes much higher, and varies greatly between different human populations (Reyes-García, this volume). The extent to which individuals other than parents are involved will reflect small group size and complexity, and patterns of movement and parenting effort in relation to the maturing individual. By contrast, all core transmission is still strongly correlated with biological relatedness, although this markedly decreases as societies become more complex, larger and with divisions of labour, schools, writing and mass media. In Platten's account in this volume on the transmission of gardening knowledge in an English allotment context, the role of the mass media is ever present — contemporary ideologies of consumption encouraging new plot-holders with little gardening experience to participate, but with consequential high drop-out rates.

The window of opportunity determined by life span must, however, be further divided into phases of greater or lesser intensity of transmission. The short-term episodes during which skills and information are learned are the precondition, but the sum of transmission is not simply the aggregation of identical episodes. Learning episodes have a sequential and cumulative structure, though the trajectory is unlikely to take the same form in every case. One plausible sequence is provided by Ruddle and Chesterfield (1977: fig. 2) for learning craft skills in the Orinoco delta: (a) familiarization, (b) observation, (c) simple steps with assistance, (d) undertaking entire task complex with assistance, (e) undertaking entire task complex under supervision, (f) undertaking entire task complex as assistant to instructor, (g) individual experimentation, and (h) equal competence with instructor. We are not aware of attempts to test the validity of this sequence, but it does highlight the complexity of learning episodes within the general ontogenetic process of knowledge acquisition.

Certainly, as individuals biologically mature, the character of learning episodes alters, involving the use of more individual experience and ability to solve problems through social interaction. Learning to use a spoon at two is not the same as learning a differential equation at fifteen. Indeed, there is much learning (and therefore transmission of culture) before the acquisition of language, even before birth, which cannot of course be dependent on the role of language as a transmitter, and much of this learning involves setting up the conditions for language acquisition. Thus, we now know that the acoustical environment of the unborn child is the context in which babies learn to cry in their mother tongue (Mampe, Friederici, Christophe and Wermke 2009). Modern educational methods tend to conceptualize learning for the purpose of measurement as a series of one-off events, both in laboratories and in the real world. We can see this in the testing and marking regimes beloved of audit culture, involving so many 'learning outcomes'. But learning is not only a continuous process of accumulation, unlearning, rethinking and reinforcement, but is phase-dependent. It occurs in different ways at different stages of life, right from the moment when sentience is instantiated in the embryo through its immersion in a world of sound and movement. Both the chapter by Reyes-García and her associates on ethnobotanical knowledge, and that by Puri on basket making, suggest that different paths of transmission are relevant to different stages of the life cycle, and that paths of acquisition change with age. To generalize, and using the distinctions developed by Cavalli-Sforza and Feldman (1981), it has been suggested that early childhood is typified by higher frequency of vertical, horizontal and one-to-one transmissions, while late childhood and adolescence display a higher frequency of one-to-many and many-to-one transmissions (Hewlett and Lamb 2002; Schlegel 2011).

'The crux of the problem' therefore, as Ingold (2001: 114) reminds us, 'lies in understanding processes of ontogenetic development'. Piaget (e.g. 1960) long ago showed how the order of conceptual development is crucial to the performance of basic tasks. We cannot learn how to pour water from one container to another without mastering concepts of volume. We cannot learn needlepoint before we have mastered the intuitive physics of manipulating the needle. We, literally, cannot run before we can walk. We have to know how to use tools before we can execute the jobs that require them, except that often as not we learn how to operate a tool by repeatedly using it in a real (rather than virtual) context. The two parts of the process of learning are not completely separate. It is the idea that certain things have to be learned to acquire other things that has given rise to the idea of 'meta-culture', cultural equipment learned first in order to facilitate the learning of the rest of culture, and which we have already touched on. But precisely because these early learning skills are so important in childhood it has been suggested (Dennett 1995: 350–51) that they come with physical and 'mental filters' that often render individuals less susceptible to innovation later in life. Among the more obvious examples of this are: the establishment of a core phonological repertoire restricting later language learning (Werker and Tees 1984), sex-linked ways of body movement (Mauss 1934), basic classifying strategies (Ellen 2006), intuitive physics, intuitive numeracy, intuitive psychology, and for some, intuitive biology (Bloch 2005: 61). It is in part through the attempts to learn these behaviours that aspects of the meta-culture are acquired. We may need some understanding of volume to pour water from one container to another, but well short of mastery to begin with, and we will, through repeated attempts to pour water learn more, perhaps master, that small corner of volume. It is the conjunction of learning specialized relationships through experience, and accumulating these into an ongoing underlying representation, that is the progressive thread of learning, and the source of appearance of an ontological order. Contra Dennett, one does not need 'filters' to account for why early representation is resistant to change later in life. These fundamental relationships are so heavily leveraged to such a wide range of subsequent relationships that to change these would undermine much of the knowledge and understanding one apparently possesses. Given that all knowledge requires organization (knowledge is a net reduction of degrees of freedom), and organization requires a net expenditure of energy to maintain (degrees of freedom want to be free), the energy required for change becomes prodigious. Knowledge is its own inertia, particularly as it is leveraged, and thus appears 'fundamental'. This is, of course, one of the attractions of ethnographic documentation and analysis – to demonstrate reliably that what we consider to be fundamental relationships are in fact not, and that our life and the ideas that fuel it are apparently a house of cards. Perhaps one of the reasons underlying the obfuscation of ethnography over the past twenty years was to make it far less scary, moving the conflict from primary contact with the world of living to some murky internal existence we can well believe is screwed up.

Although socialization and enculturation are continuous processes, and patterns and learning outcomes change as we move between social roles (and indeed, at the very end, when we 'learn how to die'), there are periods in a developmental cycle when learning is more intense. Most cultural input – using the term in its most inclusive sense – is probably acquired in the first few years of life. For example, quite apart from speaking their birth language fluently, by the age of six most Qeqchi Maya children can correctly identify 80 per cent of the plant species growing in a household garden (Zarger 2002). Although new patterns of behaviour are acquired and information lost and replaced, once a particular threshold has been reached, the acquired behavioural and information repertoire has a constraining effect on change, and becomes part of the context. Life cycles and socialization ensure that we are more likely to act in predictable than unpredictable ways, and to always act conservatively in response to new stimuli.

Given the importance attached to life cycle and phase-dependency, one might wonder how life expectancy variations and other changes in the maturation process impact on the process of acquisition and transmission, and on the potential for expansion (Schlegel 2011). Relevant factors include onset of menarche, age at first reproduction, age of marriage, first age and duration of formal schooling, and other life-history variables. We assume that Pleistocene life expectancies were much shorter than those for people living in the twenty-first century, and that the average life spans of poor people living at subsistence levels in remote eastern Darfur are different from those of well-nourished urbanites living in post-industrial Kyoto (Table 0.1). Indeed, just how much variation in life expectancy we can find in a single geographical population is well exemplified by the Japanese temporal set in Table 0.1, but we also need to remember that all life-expectancy figures display wide variations in the width of the window of opportunity through which culture can be transmitted, and these will influence the effectiveness of the process. We need to ask how changes in the length of those windows for learning impact on the character and potential for transmission? Can more substantial, and more complex, cultural loads be transmitted where there are wider windows and greater overlap in life spans of transmitters and transmittees? Indeed, we might wonder what the implications of ever-increasing predictions for life expectancy hold for the process of cultural transmission. We might even engage in the kind of thought experiment suggested by the writings of J.B.S. Haldane and Olaf Stapledon, who envisage individual humanoid lives running into hundreds of years.[1]

Table 0.1 Life expectancy at birth in different human populations

Population	Life expectancy (years) at birth
Native North American pre-contact	15
Jomon Neolithic Japan	16+
Average hunter-gatherers	22
Native North American post-contact	23
Late Neolithic Japan	23
Medieval Japan	24
Average traditional agriculturalists	26
Early Modern Edo Japan 1600–1850	28
Meji Restoration Japan 1891–98	35
Post-Second World War Japan 2003	78–85

Sources: Nagaoka et al. 2006; Ward and Weiss 1976; Weiss 1981; Wells 1975; Workman et al. 1974; Wrigley and Schofield 1981.

When we coordinate serial life cycles and attempt to place them in groups of more or less contemporaneous cycles we often speak of 'generations'.[2] Cultural knowledge and practice are routinely reported as having been transmitted from one generation to the next. Here, the word 'generation' is usually understood as referring to individuals of an approximately equal relative age, ideally encapsulated in the idea of siblinghood. Members of the same generation are assumed: to associate, and through association to reinforce existing practices, or confirm innovatory ones; to receive cultural information from, and be subject to, social control of ascendant generations; and to transmit cultural information and exercise social control with respect to descendent generations. The concept is built into all human languages as a fundamental tool of social categorization, most obviously expressed in the terminologies of kinship, although the number of generations encoded varies between languages (Figure 0.1), with consequences for operationalizing selective social memory well described in the classic literature on genealogical amnesia and the suppression of time (Evans-Pritchard 1940; Geertz and Geertz 1964). Moreover, the generation has become the unit by which we measure and configure processes of cultural transmission in terms of diachronic movement, over and above the individual dyad.

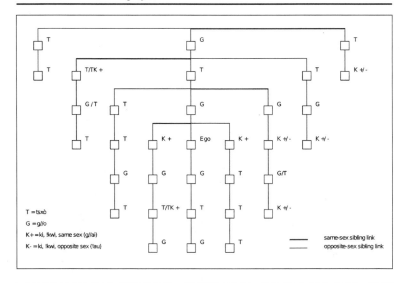

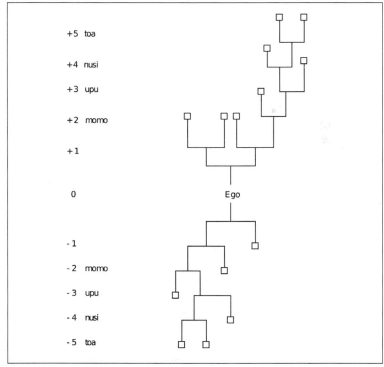

Figure 0.1. Comparison of generational kinship terms for (a) Nharo Bushmen of Botswana (Barnard 1978) and (b) Nuaulu of Eastern Indonesia (Ellen, unpublished field data).

But how we might measure a generation has never been, as far as we can see, discussed. Generation is a complex concept that emerges from the interplay between demography, kinship and social organization. From a demographic viewpoint, generational structure depends on the range of ages when females first produce live births, the period females are fertile (which is socially shaped), and on the range of age at death. On the basis of recent historical evidence for menarche, fecundity might typically begin at 15, though it is quite possible that as we recede into the past so the age of menarche and first birth comes later, consistent with what we know of contemporary socioeconomic and ecological constraints. For more distant hominids it must have been earlier, closer to the maturation cycles of other large apes. For example, chimpanzee menarche is at 7–9 years in the wild, and 11–12 years in captivity. Similarly, age of death varies widely between primate species and between different human historical and ethnographic populations (Table 0.1).

So specific parameters will be population (and culturally) dependent, but crudely we might say that a minimum human life span giving rise to effective generational transmission is 30 years, with an overlap of 15 years, this being the time available to transmit all crucial cultural behaviour assuming that core transmission is principally between parents and offspring. It might then be hypothesized that the longer the overlap the more effective the cultural transmission and the greater adaptive fitness. Where there are more grandparents and great-grandparents there are theoretically more opportunities (and perspectives) to transmit.

But generation is not simply a relationship between parent and child, but also collectively between parents and children, and in almost all societies between children and parents' parents and parents' siblings, as well as the children of parents' siblings. Further, the distribution of age differences of a group of siblings can range over 30 or more years (although 15–20 is more typical), suggesting that generation is an interlocking set of relationships rather than a uniform age-stacked concept. Indeed, variations in life expectancy require that generation, as a useful concept, not be restricted to parent-child overlap, as in many populations there is little likelihood that the parents will survive more than a few years beyond the birth of their last children, almost no likelihood that parents will survive until all their children reproduce, and there is a high rate of death during or relating to childbirth. Likewise, each child will have a different relationship with the people in the above roles, as they learn their roles, or at least change them, over time. All known human kinship terminologies use generation as a criterion for classifying some relationships. However, the breadth and structure of these relationships in a population are still tied to the average minimum generational distance between parent and child, even if some of the responsibilities for cultural transmission must be distributed because of the resulting limitations between parent and children of different birth order. Furthermore, in speculative mode, given the importance of cultural transmission in biological reproduction, the limitations in this distribution could contribute to the universality of kinship classification in human groups. While generation may extend over a considerable age range, to the extent that kinship influences social relationships and social organization the members of a common generation will share a more similar perspective within the social order than they share with the ascending or descending generation. To a lesser extent this commonality persists beyond the generation of siblings and cousins to a large number of non-kin collaterals within the same age range.

The average rate of the generational cycle influences the rate of population change, and the rate of generational turnover has important consequences for the speed and character of socio-cultural change. This is also the case for the smallest population and social group necessary for effective cultural transmission (the socio-cultural equivalent of a 'viable breeding population'), the minimum overlap of generations necessary for viable cultural transmission to take place, and the relevance of birth interval. The less that life cycles or generations overlap, the steeper the graph of transmission and the more risky the process, while the rate of cultural transmission might diminish where there is an age difference between mates or effective parents.

How Form of Knowledge Influences Transmission

How knowledge and practice are transmitted depends on their form. Ultimately, all cultural transmission relies on some kind of bodily interface, but what varies is the extent to which language is involved in the process. There are many bodily practices that are learned through self-discovery or copying, reinforced by parental actions or those of other significant persons. Much of this learning occurs with self-reflection and systematic conscious cognition, such as digging the garden in ways that are culturally specific, or tying knots. None of the knowledge required for tying a knot need be in the form of language, but occasionally this might help. In the world of practical knowledge of the environment (Ellen 1999: 104), much knowledge is, therefore, what we might call substantive, meaning that it may be quite complex and extensive but not in itself ordinarily committed to language, though it may emerge through performance. This is the case with

much folk-biological knowledge, such as that concerning plant maturation and ecology. People acquire this knowledge through a combination of long-term interaction with plants, as individuals or in social
groups; but while bound by implicit rules or scripts, the knowledge
is seldom systematically organized linguistically. By contrast, lexical
knowledge is that part encoded in language, or where the language
provides a key for accessing substantive knowledge that is not itself
lexicalized. And the transmission pathways may be different in each
case. Thus, Reyes-García's data suggest that amongst Tsimane' subjects, names of plants (lexical knowledge) is strongly correlated with
mother-daughter and father-son transmission, whereas male knowledge of skills (substantive knowledge) is only weakly associated with
the parental cohort. Similar distinctions and arguments have been
developed by others (e.g. Marchand 2003), and in this volume by
Puri, where he contrasts declarative with behavioural/performative
knowledge (both kinesthetic and managerial).

One step up from lexical knowledge is textual knowledge, in which
words are organized into sequences of utterances. To some extent we
acquire knowledge by mastering scripts that are in part encoded in
language, as when Frake (1961, 1964) famously invites us 'how to
ask for a drink' or 'how to diagnose a disease' in Subanun, a language
of Mindanao. The oral texts that compress emergent consensus and
rules may be narratives such as myths, although they may also take
on a permanent written form. Each of these forms of knowledge can be
transmitted through mimicry, copying, imprinting, but also through
language-mediated instruction (telling), and text-mediated learning,
through institutionalized teaching and learning (pedagogy, apprenticeship), and through a combination, such as informal learning in
institutional contexts (e.g. in labs).

West (this volume) shows us how standardization and bureau-
cracy, which are inevitably a consequence of a textual model of transmission, accompany new ways of transmission, while the same model
resembles closely the liturgical modality of religious transmission
developed by Whitehouse (2004) in contrast to his imagistic mode.
But transmission by example, which all of these exemplify, involves
not simply copying, but the inculcation of a set of principles and
practices that can be used to instantiate behaviour that is logically
equivalent in a given context, not materially equivalent behaviour
as copying implies. Formulaic sequences of lexical expressions are a
proper subset of these, a sub-category rather than another category.
So mimicry, copying and imprinting have a role – dealing with the
material manifestations or data that individuals require to induce
knowledge – but they are not copies of the knowledge itself. They are
simply exemplars of what the knowledge, once acquired, should be

capable of producing, and indeed, in the ongoing process of formulating knowledge, a guide to how successful acquisition has been.

But irrespective of the possible means of knowledge transmission, we must ask whether we get different patterns in different cultural domains. Are forms of bodily movement (e.g. swimming, digging or tying knots) – that as Mauss (1934; see also Shennan, this volume) demonstrated are no less culturally constituted than speaking – transmitted differently from, for example, plant names? Different skills and different kinds of knowledge take different times to acquire. Are there differences between domains constituted largely through physical objects compared with those that are more abstract and ideational, such as religion? As Whitehouse (2004: 58) has shown, there may be several modes of transmission operating simultaneously in the domain of religion, with different cognitive architectures and emotional glue. Humans absorb certain kinds of knowledge more readily than other kinds, even within the same cultural domain. Thus, explaining the transmission of cognitively costly aspects of religion may be very different from explaining transmission of language or minimally counterintuitive concepts. Much knowledge can only be transmitted in relation to the physical objects and properties to which it relates, as the objects themselves provide essential props in that transmission process: the interactive chemical properties in the different components of the betel quid, or the psychoactive character of *ayhuasca* on patterns of thought, or the physical character of the canes used by a basket maker, and of the curd used by the cheese maker. What we find is that the composition of different cultural domains as they are conventionally and emically defined depend on mixed strategies of transmission – though in urban-centred, literate and globalized society words and texts increasingly come to dominate.

Hitherto, studies of knowledge acquisition and erosion (Zent, this volume) have tended to focus on acquired or eroded elements of a single domain, for example plant knowledge, ethnomedical knowledge, or food knowledge. However, especially if we acknowledge the arbitrary or fuzzy character of domain boundaries, it is perhaps not surprising that what such an approach neglects is the relevance to transmission of simultaneous membership of several domains. In the example of ethnobotanical knowledge, erosion in one domain may accelerate erosion in another of which a particular plant is a member; or alternatively, maintenance of knowledge of the plant in the context of one domain will enable retention of knowledge in another. The more complex the domain, the more this kind of overlap is likely to be significant (Ellen 2009). At the same time, we should not forget ontogeny, for some patterns require the prior acquisition of other patterns (perhaps acquired with respect to other domains) to process and reproduce, such as advanced mathematical reasoning and ritual oratory (Mesoudi 2011b), as well as the more mundane knowledge underlying that instantiated cooperatively.

Degree of overlap in cultural domains is just one way in which we can approach issues of fragility and robustness in different kinds of transmission system. We can also see the difficulties in assuming all domains to be organized in the same way (Leaf 1972), with different kinds of selection and decision-making processes, in understandings of how craft production techniques are constituted through 'operational chains' grounded in the complex practices of local communities (Lemmonier 1992; see also Shennan in this volume). Over the longer term we can also see how different domains of knowledge are linked directly and indirectly through strong associations in patterns of diversification, as Jordan and Shennan (2005: 162–63) have shown for linguistic affiliation and pottery making in New Guinea. We have several studies of material culture in this volume (Lycett, O'Neill and Jordan, Puri, Tehrani and Collard), and these lend themselves to quantification and phylogenetic methods of analysis for very practical reasons.

Measurement

Understanding cultural transmission requires some identification of 'units', real or virtual (O'Brien et al. 2010). This is either because observers assume that the mind organizes knowledge into bits to better effect its use and replication, or because only through recognition of such units as 'character states' can it be scientifically measured. We need to compare to understand and explain patterns, and to compare we need to simplify. The terms used to describe such units are various, including memes, modules, schemes, cultural traits, cultural elements, practices, semes, 'behaviours' and culturgens (Lumsden and Wilson 1981; Hewlett and Lamb 2002), each bearing a slightly different theoretical load. In empirical contexts, these units may be words, stretches of meaningful language combining words (phrases, sentences, stories) or their instantiated material analogues (graphemes and texts) (e.g. Pocklington and Best 1997); or they may be artefacts that result from manufacturing activity, or descriptions of patterns of activity, social interaction and relationships.

The problems encountered and the ease of identifying discrete units vary between domains of cultural knowledge and practice, and whether we are dealing with material culture, language, social practices and relationships, or ideas. Even within domains the ease with which units can be identified varies. Thus, if we accept the 'twin modes of religiosity' idea explored by Whitehouse (2004: 74), the doctrinal mode with its emphasis on formal learning of identifiable components, and with its strong association with textual knowledge, is more amenable to formal measurement than the less tangible 'imagistic' mode.

This is methodologically hazardous territory (see also Bloch 2005). Some (e.g. Costopoulos 2005) have challenged the very idea that such units have any existence as entities outside the mind of the measurer; that 'memes' cannot exist in the sense of a unit of information residing in the brain (Dawkins 1982: 109) or as mental copies (phenocopies) of recurrent observable behaviour. For Daly (1982: 402), cultural innovation is Lamarckian, with transmission potentially biased, with no segregating particles or immutable models, and not necessarily replicative. That the pragmatic use of units to measure cultural composition and diversity, regardless of their memetic status, is similarly problematic is demonstrated in the long history of attempts to identify 'culture traits' in the American tradition (Lyman and O'Brien 2003). Ideas rarely copy with anything close to absolute fidelity.[3] As Atran (2001: 356–57) argues, because transformation affects ideas at a much greater rate than fidelity does, a selection bias cannot develop towards replicability. Descendant ideas cross and merge so quickly and thoroughly that there can be no identification of 'species' or 'lineages', only variably defined 'influences'. To what extent, therefore, are we simply creating 'pseudoparticulate' traits through our methodology? In the face of this critique, recent exponents of cultural phylogenetics, in their attempts to analyse changes in language or artefacts over time, have distanced themselves from memetics (e.g. Aunger 2000) on the strong conceptual grounds that units of culture are not simply replicators, and from earlier culture trait studies through the robustness of their methods (see below).

Early theorists tended to assume cultural traits to be basically mental phenomena that might have linguistic, social and material expression. Lyman and O'Brien (2003: 226) helpfully remind us that we should distinguish empirical units (the evidential 'things') from the ideational units we use to measure them. Indeed, it is possible to determine etic 'character width' in accordance with the scale and form of the analysis being conducted, defined either *intensionally*, where the character states are explicitly agreed prior to the analysis and imposed; or *extensionally*, by examining a particular set derived from selected observed features after the group has been established, as was typical for early researchers in the field of cultural trait analysis. In many respects, the boundaries of the units selected will be fairly arbitrary, because what is actually transmitted will vary from occasion to occasion, and will depend on the scale of the analysis. As Shennan and Collard (2005: 144) rhetorically ask, is every whistling of a tune, or every telling of a story, to be treated as the exemplar of a trait? If we take horse-riding skills as an example of the problem of *scale* that has historically dominated culture trait analysis, do we look at individual artefacts (bits, stirrups, bridles and so on), or at these items in relation to complexes of associated knowledge and practice? If the latter, then where do we draw the boundaries? Should we include the conditions of the manufacture of included material objects or of their use (for blacksmithing and leather-working knowledge is not identical to horse management knowledge), or should we look at the functionality of the 'system' of material objects in its entirety, or to horsemanship as an overarching set of skills and knowledge? In looking at text, is it the word that constitutes the unit or some different more inclusive or less inclusive unit, and do words and the behaviour to which they refer involve different entities (Pocklington and Best 1997, Dennett 2006: 81)? If we are looking at chimpanzee material culture, what is it that constitutes 'a behaviour' that we can measure: is it the use of the grass stalk to extract termites from a mound, or the associated knowledge and practice that leads up to that point, including the selection and making of the tool? Although these are not insurmountable problems, they are ones we constantly need to address.

While in some cases the units we identify may translate into units that senders and receivers would understand as having some discreteness (as in, say, the names of useful plants), beyond this those studying cultural transmission have devised etic units that divide up the information transmitted in ways that enable quantification, measurement and understanding, but which may not make sense to those whose culture is being analysed. This, of course, need not be a problem. In the context of studies in cultural phylogeny, the units involved commonly comprise bundles of characters that 'can be transmitted as independent units, i.e. even when other aspects of culture are not passed on' (Mace and Pagel 1994: 549). Similarly, O'Brien and Lyman (2005: 106–7) see these units as 'small elements – such as specific innovations and components of ritual practice, ... linked together in larger, potentially transmittable entities – technological systems, religion – which themselves are collected into cultures' that characterize human groups of different scales, such as kin groups, villages and ethnic groups. However, these units, and their aggregations that we describe as 'cultures', may simply be 'convenient fictions' devised in order to measure, while it is difficult to think of entire 'religions' (rather than individual rituals) or ' technological systems' (rather than individual tools) as 'transmittable entities' in any easily measurable sense.

In the same way that these kinds of difficulty were raised in relation to an earlier generation of studies of culture trait diffusion, so they are also part of the critique of cultural phylogeny approaches (e.g. Moore 1994; Terrell 1988). O'Brien and Lyman (2005: 106–7), following Boyd et al. (1997: 364), defend cultural phylogeny uses of units and scale in the face of criticism by Terrell. They recognize that there is a problem of 'cohesion' and the freedom with which components enter a set and with what frequency, but argue that the two plausible models (cultures as hierarchic systems, and cultures of assemblages of coherent traits) are not mutually exclusive. Indeed, we could argue that all forms of ethnographic or comparative analysis involve decisions about how to divide up distributions of continuously variable data, but most often such decisions are made casually or in ways that are assumed to be self-evidently true. The problem with transmission studies is that we are dealing with large formal data sets subjected to quantitative analysis, where the problems are less easy to disguise, and where measuring associations between units incorrectly established can result in spurious correlations. Vague characterization of cultural units has damaging consequences for a theory of transmission, and these have to be understood more as 'character states' showing either discrete or continuous variation, while many so-called 'discrete' character states (such as colour) are in fact continuous.

Interestingly, Lyman and O'Brien (2003: 244) suggest the notion of recipe for the unit of cultural transmission, drawing on recent work in archaeology. But they might also have drawn on the literature of medical ethnobotany, where perhaps not surprisingly the instructions for preparing particular herbal treatments in both folk and scholarly systems of medical knowledge are routinely described as 'recipes', by both practitioners and observing anthropologists. For Shore (1996: 65–66) recipes are a species of task model, along with scripts, checklists and mnemonics, 'for getting practical things done', to facilitate the memorability of complex procedures, the predictability of results and the social coordination of complex tasks. But as we have seen in Ingold's critique of Sperber's use of recipe, it is difficult to see the recipe itself as an independent unit; rather its expression depends on other assumptions. While the notion of recipe in early-twentieth-century culture trait theory works well analogically when thinking of processes of material production – making pots, for example – it is less apparent how it might work for non-material social behaviours. Although there are difficulties in forcing onto non-material ethnographic datasets what works well enough for those kinds of material datasets available to prehistoric archaeology, we may well learn something in the attempt. Consider, for example, the controversial but highly relevant debates on the transmission of religious knowledge (Lawson and McCauley 1990; Whitehouse 2004). In the case of West's industrial cheese makers, the concept of recipe works well enough since the ecology of the process has been simplified; but for the artisan cheese maker who works with not-always-predictable micro-organisms to produce a more individualized product, the concept of recipe is more problematic.

What is being questioned here, therefore, is the independence between behavioural indices and the underlying logic (or the organization) that instantiates them. Among the issues this begs are: (a) does cultural conformance require the same underlying representation or simply a logically equivalent one, and (b) if logical equivalence is all that is required, to what extent can a behaviour be transferred to a different cultural context? The assumption here is that if logical equivalence is not sufficient, any instance must have the 'same' organization and structure, and such cultural artefacts would be very brittle outside their context of formation, acquisition and instantiation. Whereas, if only logical equivalence is required (i.e. the underlying organization or logic is irrelevant as long as it produces the 'same' behaviour), then an induced logic may be applicable to, and depend on, in part or whole, other domains. The literal transmission of knowledge with high internal fidelity requires more information, and consequently more effort, than requiring only logical equivalence for knowledge productions, particularly given the capacity of observers to classify a considerable range of variation as being 'equivalent' or the 'same'. As pointed out above, a recipe may invoke the interaction of a lot of domains, each of which must be acquired. Developmentally there may be some ontogenetic issues, but once these have been undertaken, the main issues that apply to transmissibility of recipes relate to establishing logically near-equivalent domain representations, possibly the reorganization of knowledge from one configuration of domains to another, and the identification and evaluation of efficacy for missing domains from the transferee repertoire. A lot of the cross-cultural differences in material culture are in the pragmatics of how these are used, not in the material culture as such.

Growth and Loss of Cultural Knowledge and Practice

Cultural practices and knowledge are self-evidently transmitted between individuals and through time, even if the process is interactionally complex. Similarly, knowledge and experience grow or diminish in the process, although this may not emically be acknowledged. One of the reasons we seek to unitize and measure is because we wish to confirm what we intuitively know. Of course, not all knowledge is acquired from other individuals, or perhaps we should say from other individuals only. Nevertheless, its acquisition may be in every sense cultural, since learning and evaluation and storage take place within a cognitive and technical context that is itself learned. Much ethnobiological knowledge is of this kind, essentially acquired through individual experience reinforced by occasional social interaction. And not all that individuals learn for themselves is passed on. This same imperfection in the process of cultural transmission may inadvertently also cause cultural drift independent of deliberately induced changes, the effects of the properties of local ecological and social systems.

Human populations have always been subject to decimation by disease, foreign invasion and events (storms, earthquakes, volcanoes, tsunami, etc.). Much as most contain more genetic material than any small subset of the population can 'warehouse', which leads to genetic drift and founders' effects, it is likely that many cultural populations contain much more knowledge than a small set of individuals can bear. Some knowledge transmission and enactment requires considerable specialization and even populations of a critical size. If social organization and social networks are severely disrupted, persistent infrastructure destroyed, or resources disappear, it may become impossible to use or perform knowledge for one or more generations. Information relevant to this is apparent in work exemplified by Boas and Kroeber on the tiny remnants (one individual in some cases, e.g. Ishii: Kroeber and Kroeber 2003) of Amerindian populations. Similarly, Rarotonga in the Cook Islands lost about 80 per cent of its population in the early nineteenth century (Kirch and Rallu 2007: 32) which, combined with the influence of the London Missionary Society, resulted in massive change in culture to a kind of cosmopolitan creole composed largely of elements from other islands (Lyon 1995).

The starting point for understanding patterns of growth and loss is the occurrence and recognition of intracultural variability. For ethnobiological knowledge, studies of variability are now numerous (see Berlin 1992: 199–231), and have raised important issues concerning the extent of 'cultural consensus' (Romney, Weller and Batchelder 1986; Ellen 2003), and how this may impose constraints on transmission of knowledge networks deriving from structured bias and stochasticity (Casagrande 2002), knowledge exchange and flow, the information upon which subsistence decision making might be based, and strong evidence for the role of social and situational factors. Such studies have reinforced a distributional view of knowledge, but as long as knowledge remains orally articulated, or even devolved in non-linguistically coded tacit experience, it often poses obstacles to effective reproduction through the literate mode, inviting serious over-simplification, straining the limits of ordinary language as a medium of transmission, and giving rise to specialized forms of language (such as mathematical notation), or devolved in practical interactive demonstrations of which language may be the lesser part. Consider, for example, how you would explain to a child how to tie a shoelace – over the telephone.

As individuals vary in their classificatory, substantive and applied knowledge, so chance variations in small populations can have disproportionate and radical implications for transmission (Neiman 1995; Bentley et al. 2004; Eerkens and Lipo 2005). More attention has been paid in recent years to inter-individual knowledge transmission, a focus that has been accompanied by acquisition of data on the distribution of knowledge by age and generation (e.g. Stross 1973; Hunn 2002). There has been particular emphasis on studies of ethnobiological knowledge erosion, and a body of evidence (e.g. Atran and Medin 2008: 47) suggesting that substantive knowledge declines faster than lexical knowledge. This can account for the number of non-synonymous terms in circulation that cannot confidently be matched by subjects to firm folk taxonomic identifications, as with Nuaulu frogs (Ellen 1999: 104–5).

Although studies of knowledge acquisition and erosion have tended to focus on acquired or eroded elements of a single domain, as, for example, the transmission of plant knowledge, ethnomedical knowledge or food knowledge, what such an approach sometimes ignores is the relevance to transmission of simultaneous membership of several domains. Thus, erosion of plant knowledge in one domain may accelerate erosion in another of which that plant is a member; or alternatively, maintenance of knowledge of the plant in the context of one domain will enable retention of knowledge in another. The more complex the domain, the more this kind of overlap is likely to be significant (Ellen 2009).

Thus, it is not that cultural knowledge is simply transmitted, but that it can grow and diminish over time (i.e. lose and gain variants), both in terms of what individuals know and do, and in terms of aggregate population knowledge. Such losses and gains will be stimulated by several factors, such as chance, population size, selection, and rate of innovation (Neiman 1995; Eerkens and Lipo 2005). Innovation and growth in knowledge may be responses to new problems, more complex environments, and new technologies that permit the transmission of greater amounts of knowledge and practice, at the same time precipitating vast new domains of knowledge to transmit (O'Brien and Bentley 2011; Mesoudi 2011b). Loss, inversely, may be down to chance mediated by population size, or a response to the disappearance of old problems, environmental change, significant modification in social structure and organization, and demography. In the context of ethnobiological knowledge, or what is sometimes loosely described as TEK (traditional environmental knowledge), it occurs in times of ecological and economic change, in response to habitat and biodiversity loss, and to educational, market and other kinds of change (Zent, this volume). There are plenty of studies of transmission where it has failed, and plausible explanations given; but fewer studies of where knowledge and behaviour have been demonstrated to have been effectively reproduced in succeeding generations.

At the most aggregated level, the dynamics of human cultural transmission must connect to changes in human demography (Shennan 2000; Henrich 2004; Powell et al. 2009; Lycett and Norton 2010). So, population extinction will result in the extinction of a particular cultural configuration, and population decline in reduced opportunities for effective transmission (Henrich 2004; Lycett and Norton 2010). But, looking at the converse – population growth – especially over the course of long-term human history (e.g. Powell et al. 2009) we must conclude that despite local population extinction and 'the extinction of experience', the overall trend of sustained population growth and geographical expansion into virtually all global habitats, and especially exponential growth over the last five hundred years, has not only increased the sum of varying cultural practices as a correlate of population growth, but has had far-reaching feedback consequences which have led to further cultural diversity. Although we have feared the impacts of globalization and the death of geographically discrete variants since Lévi-Strauss (1955) warned us of impending 'monoculture', the objective evidence is that with larger populations we have more cultural diversity rather than less, although differently configured.

Interpersonal Relations of Transmission and their Institutional Settings

Much recent research on cultural transmission has been based on the contrast between the stereotypes of vertical transmission from parent to child, versus horizontal or 'contagious' (epidemiological) transmission between unrelated others, to which can be added oblique (from members of the parental generation other than genetic kin); and between one-to-many (e.g. teacher > class) and many-to-one (e.g. choir > listener). This has been made popular particularly through the work of Luigi Cavalli-Sforza (e.g. Cavalli-Sforza and Feldman 1981;

Hewlett and Cavalli-Sforza 1986; Ohmagari and Berkes 1997). These modelling assumptions are elegant, have been highly influential and productive (Reyes-García et al., Tehrani and Collard, O'Neill and Jordan, all this volume), but looked at from the standpoint of many socio-cultural anthropologists can seem problematic. They also differ from those of Boyd and Richerson (1985), who imply more of an analogy with genetic transmission, and who are for Shennan (1996: 293) 'more sociobiological'.

If, for example, we look at transmission processes over the short-term in a small field site of the kind common in ethnographic fieldwork, we generally find that cultural transmission is not obviously either simply vertical, horizontal or oblique. This is due to the role of ego-centred learning through rediscovery, because learning is situational and not wholly reciprocally dyadic, because it is ecologically constrained, and because of the evidence for multiple and temporal reinforcement. Core behaviours, concepts and skills may initially pass vertically, but are only instantiated through horizontal sharing, while stories will be told many times in different ways. Similarly, knowledge that passes vertically may do so (counterintuitively) from a child to an adult, as where children acquire competence in modern digital technologies quicker than their parents, and become the transmitters of practical skills (e.g. the television remote control, or texting). Learning is neither a one-off nor a uni-directional act. Moreover, although there are many cases in non-human primate social groups, and in 'traditional' small-scale human societies, of transmission between non-genetic parents and children, as societies have become more complex with specialized divisions of labour, so an increasing amount of transmission has occurred between non-kin. In such cases, identifying the vertical line of 'descent' is difficult at this level of analysis. Thus, while such assumptions have been used in knowledge erosion studies, in studies involving large datasets over a wide geographic range and timescale, and for certain kinds of transmission at particular stages in a life cycle, they do raise methodological issues that need to be addressed. For example, McElreath and Strimling (2008) have suggested that some work may have overestimated vertical and oblique (that is the role of older relations or mentors) at the expense of horizontal peer influences. In the studies included in this volume where these distinctions are central, we find, for example, that for Reyes-García, working with living subjects, oblique is more important than vertical, with no evidence for horizontal transmission, while Tehrani and Collard, working only with objects, feel sufficiently confident to distinguish vertical, oblique and horizontal, whereas O'Neill and Jordan distinguish horizontal and vertical only. This latter is what we might expect as a dataset becomes increasingly aggregated, both temporally and geographically.

We can examine the vertical/horizontal issue in various ways. To begin with it is a problem of representation, indeed often of diagramming. For Cavalli-Sforza the model derives from his experience as a biologist working on human population variation, but it might equally have been drawn from kinship studies. The basic model here is shown in Figure 0.2a, where we can see various alternative uses of the vertical/horizontal distinction. We might say that A to C and B to D are horizontal transmission, whereas A to B and C to D are vertical transmission. How then do we describe transmission from E to B or F to D? Is this vertical, or do we need to describe it as oblique? Even more difficult is to know how to describe G to B or H to D transmission. Is this horizontal because it may be acquired from individuals in the same generation and of approximately the same age, or is it vertical because ultimately the knowledge may have descended through a sibling of a parent who has in turn acquired it from their common parents? It might be thought safer, therefore, to distinguish any transmission through kin (all being vertical) from transmission from unrelated individuals; but does it then make any difference whether they are of the same age or cohort (say, of an age grade) or from an older person or cohort? In part, this is a terminological problem: whether we are referring to horizontal and vertical transmission between individuals (as the terms were originally intended) or between groups (e.g. over time versus space). This is the issue Lycett, Collard and McGrew (2009) have coped with by using the terms 'vertical intergroup transmission' and 'horizontal intergroup transmission' respectively.

Another problem linked to diagramming conventions is shown in Figure 0.2b. Both lower diagrams relate to the same genealogical relations and biological individuals. However, we know from conventional kinship notation that those on the left are the older siblings of those on the right. In the middle diagram, learned culture passing from A to B to C or D, either directly or indirectly, might be seen to be horizontal. In the lower diagram, when we lengthen the vertices to indicate relative age, the transmission might be seen as vertical, or at least oblique.

Let us take an empirical example. When a Nuaulu girl is actively learning how to make a basket (Ellen 2009) she will do so in the context of having watched other adults and girls making baskets, although the statistical likelihood is that she will have spent more time watching her mother and older sisters in her own household than both adult and immature girls from other households, to whom she is less likely to be related genetically. Her mother will begin to instruct her, and she will ask her mother how to perform certain tasks, and although these interactions are likely to be the predominant ones involved in the learning process, she will also receive instruction from aunts, grandmothers and older female siblings. She will interact with other girls of a similar age making baskets, some of whom will be from her own house and some of whom she will be only distantly related to. She will also spend a lot of time by herself, when she is learning certain procedures, not by rote instruction, but through independent problem solving based on knowledge of the end product. In other words, she will be engaged in 'reverse engineering'.

We might portray these relations as we have done in Figure 0.2, but determining which are the lines of vertical and which the lines of horizontal transmission, and whether either alone is a sufficient characterization of the process is difficult. In reality we have a network, which we can redescribe in terms of horizontality and verticality depending on what we wish to emphasize. Topologically, or in terms of graph theory, it does not matter what is 'vertical' and what

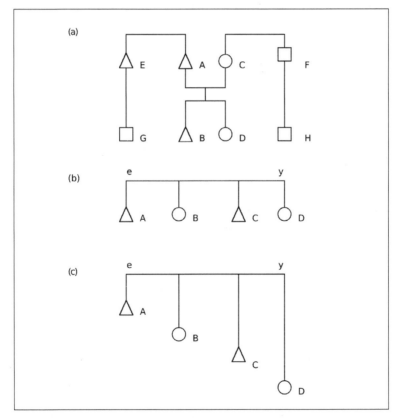

Figure 0.2. The concepts of vertical and horizontal transmission in relation to genealogical relationships.

is 'horizontal'; all that matters is the direction of flow between nodes (Figure 0.3). We might also justify the contrast between vertical and horizontal by saying that they are perfectly reasonable simplifications based on preponderant interactions of a kind that are common in scientific data processing and reasoning.

Outside the arena of kinship, we would ordinarily see transmission from teacher to child and from artisan to apprentice as vertical, but in relation to descent through kinship they might be seen as horizontal or oblique. Consider also the acquisition of cultural practices by children. Is the transmission of a rhyme between two 6 year olds to be counted as horizontal transmission, and that between a 7 year old and a 6 year old as diagonal or oblique? Perhaps diagonal transmission between individuals in the same age class but

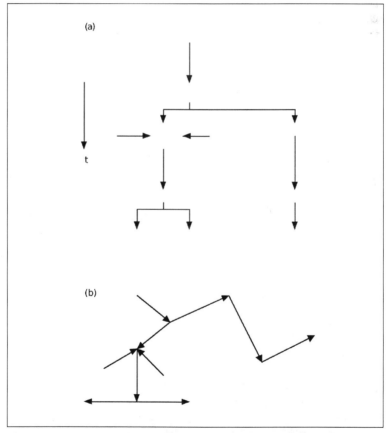

Figure 0.3. The problem of horizontality and verticality represented as a graph. (a) Paths of cultural transmission indicated in terms of conventional lines of vertical descent and horizontal transfer. (b) Identical transmission relations to those portrayed in (a) represented as an a-temporal graph.

with non-contiguous life cycles is a strong component. The Opies (1959: 7–8), in their work on the lore and language of schoolchildren, make a distinction between rhymes learned in the nursery and those learned in the playground, for while we may speculate how best to describe what is happening in the playground, in the nursery the rhymes invariably pass from parents or alloparents to very young children, who in turn may pass on those rhymes to their children or allo-children twenty years later. In Platten's example of acquiring knowledge from more experienced allotment-growers, are we to describe the transmission as horizontal or oblique?

Then there is the question of scale. If we look at lines of transmission at the interpersonal, micro-level we see a network of lines of causation and reinforcement. At a macro-level this might look like simple vertical transmission. Thus, returning to our kinship diagrams, what looks like horizontal transmission from a father's brother, looked at in another way can be represented as vertical transmission from a father. What looks like a tangled network of flows of information at one level may look like a straightforward line of transmission at another.

But interpersonal relations of learning do not exist in a social vacuum and their context may affect the content, form and rate of transmission, while processes and cycles of socio-cultural reproduction in emergent systems display properties that are more than the sum of their individual parts. We have already seen this for life cycles and generations. Individual actions are constrained by the systems in which they are situated, and at the same time provide the context for other individual actions. Thus, Platten (in this volume) shows how transmission events are set in a context of complex relations of exchange and self-discovery. As individuals grow and mature, they move through sets of social relations that change and provide different possibilities for transmission (Goody 1966), while the transmission of institutional arrangements cannot simply be modelled as the aggregation of more specific cultural components.

We can see this in relation to gender. Much core knowledge will always be gender neutral, but some is strongly gender linked, either because the opportunities are constrained by patterns of gender-biased interaction, or because specific cultural rules apply. The gender linkage may either work along descent lines, as between, say, father and son, mother and daughter, or mother's brother to sister's son, or information may pass between siblings, following birth order. Turkmen weaving skills pass from mother to daughter (Collard and Tehrani 2005), Nuaulu basket making from mother and elder female siblings to daughters and younger female siblings, Penan Benalui basket making strictly gender-linked though utilizing varied genealogical positions (Puri, this volume), and Xingu Kaibi basket making between senior and junior males in the same local kinship group (Athayde 2003); or, knowledge may be transmitted affinally, as described by Hsu (1999) for some Chinese secret medical knowledge. Alternatively, there may be gender-specific institutions constituted independent of genealogy, as in a nunnery or a madrasah, or as in Moroccan wood-carving guilds (Kaleta 2008; see also Coy 1989) or in Yemeni minaret building (Marchand 2001). If cultural information can only pass through one sex then this reduces by 50 per cent the opportunities for transmission. A similar situation applies to other divisions of labour. Specialists will by definition always be a smaller part of the whole, and therefore opportunities for transmission reduced in a population as a whole.

Patterns of descent and inheritance may influence transmission of particular kinds of knowledge or practice, irrespective of the gender of individual recipients. So, knowledge may pass through patrilines to males, or to males and females of the same patrilineage, as is the case with much Nuaulu sacred knowledge. In matrilineal societies it may be the opposite, with men acquiring knowledge through the female line, as in the case of Minangkabau elder brothers playing a crucial role in instructing the younger generation within the matrilineage. Julian Steward (1955) famously observed the association between continuity in male residence and the maintenance of ethnoecological knowledge associated with hunting among Shoshoni, while James Deetz (1968) was able to show through the combination of Chumash archaeological and ethnographic data how the movement of women associated with virilocal residence could explain variability in pottery design. Similarly, in their work on Turkmen textile design, Collard and Tehrani (2005: 128–29; also this volume) suggest that where their cladograms are inconsistent with existing ethnohistorical accounts this may be explained by textile design being inherited through the female line in an otherwise patrilineal society. Residence linked to patterns of descent may be important, with endogamy and marriage alliances determining inter-group and intra-group movement. Recipes for medicines and magic, combining both symbolic and technical elements, are often owned in whole or in part by particular descent groups, such that their transmission is skewed. Outside of kinship, other institutions have contexts and rules for cultural transmission, the effectiveness of which are enhanced through regimes of social control. Thus, Mace, Holden and Shennan (2005: 7), echoing Radcliffe-Brown, have reminded us how punishment can serve as a means of maintaining group-level codes, through maintaining social stability and ensuring a certain level of fidelity in transmission. Such non-measurable institutional phenomena are always present, and influence the conditions of transmission in significant ways (Whitehouse 2004: 293).

The transmission of esoteric symbolic knowledge may be constrained no differently from the acquisition of technical craft knowledge. Just as each craft knowledge requires specific opportunities for transmitting practical information, such that hunting skills can only be completely acquired when opportunities present themselves, so symbolic knowledge and ritual practice may be even more intermittent in providing opportunities. Certainly, how to perform a ritual can be learned in the abstract, but competence can only be acquired in practice. Many rituals occur with considerable frequency, so that opportunities to ensure fidelity of transmission are numerous, but some rituals, especially in small populations, may occur with remarkable infrequency, and participants may be faced with major problems in replicating correct performance and utterance (Ellen 2012). It is no wonder that such infrequent rituals give rise to problems, and where there is a cultural insistence on fidelity, sacred sanctions may place pressure on performers to conform. There are many ethnographic examples of prescriptive institutionally sanctioned 'conformist bias' from studies of ritual and art, and in particular of the production of art objects in the context of ritual (Forge 1967; Ellen 1990), and perhaps in its most developed form in Orthodox Christian icon painting. On the other hand, we might imagine that infrequent rituals provide precisely that opportunity in which change can occur, and there we might expect them to change more quickly than rituals or cultural events occurring more frequently, where experience and memorate knowledge is more reliable. In some cases the institutional context is quite prescriptive, requiring tight rote-learning of particular linked cultural components, as in Jewish Torah or Muslim Koran learning regimes. In other cases, the institutional constraints will be quite weak, allowing for more variation and overlap in the packages of cultural information transmitted. Sometimes, individual components can be freely transmitted between individuals, but it may also be the case that bundles of some of the same components are transmitted within specific institutional contexts. We acquire the competence to participate in rituals not only by witnessing them and hearing about what happens out of context, but also by drawing common elements and analogies from other rituals. Rituals are not transmitted as fully formed wholes, but in fragments, which only come together through social interaction on particular occasions. Cheese-making knowledge is not simply transmitted through interaction between individual producers, but also between producers and consumers.

Individual transfers are often mediated by complex contexts. Thus, Borofsky (1987) recounts how participants in a relatively reliable event, the near destruction of the atoll of Pukapuka by transgenerational storms, reformulated their strategy and practice for recovery by using a series of recollections of the few individuals who had survived a previous storm as children seventy years earlier, and had experience from serious and more frequent storms, and induction/invention from other remembered cultural domains.

Large-scale Studies of Transmission

In the early part of the twentieth century, the past as an object of study was rejected comprehensively by many anthropologists, for whom it was merely 'conjectural history', the excesses of linear cultural evolutionism and diffusionism having brought it into disrepute. But we now have methodologies and data that allow us to study the past more reliably, whether these be biological (DNA profiling), physical (various absolute and relative chronologies), archaeological, or socio-historical. While in the 1920s we did not know the past of traditional societies, we now have many plausibly accurate histories, longitudinal studies and re-studies. Moreover, diffusion, for a long time deeply unfashionable in anthropology outside of archaeology, is back in favour, especially where it draws on natural history models of contingency of the kind favoured by Gould (e.g. 1989) and Diamond (e.g. 1998), and which have built into them models of cultural selection (resulting from people making choices), co-evolution, biocultural diversity and 'the epidemiology of ideas'. Such models try to explain what happens when aggregated transmitted cultural knowledge and practice and the potential for enculturation meet ecological constraints (such as different biodiversity profiles, or constraining land masses and carrying capacities). We have become more confident in theorizing culture and sociality through time, and are consequently less likely to mistake short-term features of behaviour for long-term adaptations, and generally tend to see the social and cultural as much more dynamic.

The last twenty years have seen the growth in evolutionary approaches to the study of cultural transmission. These have displayed some diversity (as noted here by Shennan), are highly interdisciplinary (as emphasized here by Mesoudi), but all are inspired by the application of techniques and models developed in the field of theoretical biology for large spatio-temporal datasets displaying cultural variability (Cavalli-Sforza and Feldman 1981; Boyd and Richerson 1985; O'Brien and Lyman 2000). Large datasets and

long time-depth make such quantitative approaches more credible, indeed they may be the only modelling techniques we can use
(Lycett, this volume). Specifically 'phylogenetic' techniques are
a more recent development within this field (O'Brien and Lyman
2003). Several papers in this volume (e.g. Mesoudi, Lycett, O'Neill
and Jordan, Tehrani and Collard, and Shennan) explore such
themes. Tehrani and Collard, and O'Neill and Jordan, in particular,
show how, in using phylogenetic approaches to examine short-term
historical periods (hundreds rather than thousands of years), we
can see the way in which micro and macro overlap, and how specific factors, such as 'TRIMS' (transmission isolating mechanisms),
both require special explanations and confirm the utility of broad
approaches.

The process of transmission and reproduction is never perfect:
changes occur inadvertently or deliberately through selection and
adaptation. Thus, culture-bearing populations arise and diversify
from mother cultures through 'descent with modification', resulting in patterns that are tree-like (O'Brien and Lyman 2003). In such
approaches, the phylogenies identified typically describe descendent
relationships between cultural components, and computational
methods enable evolutionary hypotheses to be tested quantitatively
(e.g. O'Brien et al. 2001; Tehrani and Collard 2002; Jordan and
Shennan 2003; Lycett 2007, 2009). Cultural phylogeny models have
also looked at the patterning of adaptive features (Mace and Holden
2005). The earliest exemplars of such an approach, generating classic
tree-diagrams, are from the study of historical language relationships
(e.g. McMahon and McMahon 2003). However, such early attempts
have none of the statistical or quantitative robustness of the formal
phylogenetic methods used more recently by cultural evolutionists
mainly concerned with the study of material culture, though to some
extent with language (e.g. Pocklington and Best 1997; Levinson and
Gray 2012). Although there are huge differences, in some respects
we can see in these kinds of approach a convergence with older styles
of analysis of culture traits in the American tradition using ethnographic data, heavily influenced by culture area concepts (e.g. Driver
1970), with the much earlier evolutionary approach to material culture found in the work of Pitt-Rivers (1906), and – as Shennan points
out in his chapter – parallel developments in France, such as those of
Gabriel Tarde.

Bifurcating tree or phylogramatic models have been seen by
some as problematic when examining short-term detailed historical
and spatial evidence for cultural transmission. For example, dialect
chains suggest a situation where bifurcating components do not
completely split, and show continuing horizontal interaction over

a long period. In areas with dialect chains, or their equivalent with respect for other cultural traits, the tree has been described as having a 'rake-like' topology and weakly supported branches (Greenhill and Gray 2005: 36–37). A persistent criticism has been that human population history is less tree-like than 'rhizomatic' (Moore 1994; Terrell 1988), though others have argued that such statements are not supported by the evidence which, notwithstanding the criticism, tends to strongly support the tree model (Tehrani and Collard 2002; Collard, Shennan and Tehrani 2006; Lycett, Collard and McGrew 2009; Greenhill, Currie and Gray 2009). Trees can be arranged and interpreted in different ways, though this does not make them inherently problematic. They can be used either as a multipurpose method to show similarities and differences between units at different ranks, organized to indicate interval-scale measures of time and ancestries, or to suggest the order of appearance of certain characters – the difference between evolutionary taxonomy (with phylograms) and cladistics (with cladograms). Software designed to produce a 'tree' will always do so even where a tree model is not appropriate (Bryant, Filimon and Gray 2005), so quantitative methods must be applied to determine the strength of the tree signal.

The cultural phylogeny literature also brings us back to the issue of verticality versus horizontality in transmission. It is commonly argued that phylogenetic comparison cannot be applied to cultural change because so much arises through borrowing or hybridization of cultural traits, or from innovations – that is from phylogenesis rather than ethnogenesis. This argument begins to sound like the diffusionist critique of evolutionism, but because culture can manifestly pass horizontally between neighbours does not imply that this is all it does. 'Replicators' may be transmitted from one lineage to another, but the strength of vertical transmission in the acquisition of techniques is such that this need not 'swamp the phylogenetic signal' (Shennan 2000: 821). Indeed, if cultures are more or less reproduced over time, then vertical transmission must more or less have taken place. Similarly, if culture is continuous over space and time, it raises issues of where boundaries are drawn and of their analytic independence for comparative purposes. As Mace (2005b: 201) has indicated, this has again become an issue (though not insuperable) in studies of cultural phylogeny, arguing that phylogenetic methods are essential for resolving the problem (Mace and Pagel 1994).

Theories that are appropriate for understanding how culture is embedded in the mind or how it is innovated or transmitted between individuals, are not necessarily those most appropriate for understanding the dynamics of what happens once patterns are established and how they might change through space-time. As datasets become geographically and temporally larger so the untidy, dynamic, interactive, contingent character of cultural learning gives way to a process that can more easily be described through notions of flow and directionality, the irregularities of small datasets being statistically normalized in larger ones. Interpersonal transmission in the short-term may look very messy; over the longer term we may legitimately simplify to lines of vertical transmission: what Mesoudi (this volume) and others have referred to as micro- versus macro-evolutionary processes. As is well exemplified in this collection, and as Shennan puts it in his chapter, whereas much micro study is human-centred, macro study is attribute-centred. The issues of verticality and horizontality look different depending on degree and mode of data aggregation. It is this matter of scale that makes phylogenetic and cultural evolutionary approaches to understanding the properties of cultural change and stasis more credible, and means that we can begin to move from descriptions of short-term cultural change to models of long-term cultural evolution.

Much of the discussion in the cultural phylogenies literature arises because the existence of diversity implies that transmission is not fully exact. The default hypothesis supported by much of the evidence is that 'branching' occurs when members of a group interact less, and traditions gradually diverge through repeated splitting and growth (phylogenesis). By contrast 'blending' (ethnogenesis) is said to occur where there is continual horizontal exchange of ideas, objects and practices through a maximally connected network. Whether branching or blending is dominant is an open empirical question to be tested for particular datasets, but contrary to what is often assumed, branching may be the more prevalent process (Collard et al. 2006). Most researchers accept that this may be variable (depending on units again) and so this must be established on a case-by-case basis rather than assumed a priori. For although the 'archaeological record demonstrates long-lasting cultural traditions with recognizable coherence, there is evidence in many situations studied of extensive movement of materials and artifacts across boundaries' (Shennan and Collard 2005: 134–35). Thus, in native Californian basket making, the roles of grandmothers, mothers and daughters suggests strong vertical transmission, but there are also high levels of intermarriage and mobility that suggest a 'blurring' of these process (Jordan and Shennan 2005: 169). The same study suggests significant geographical variation, with evidence for a strong phylogenetic signal in one part of the area studied, a weaker fit in another area, and a very weak signal in yet another area (ibid., 188–89).

In this particular case, statistical analyses and correlations with local ecology were found to be consistently low, suggesting absence of environmental influence. Similarly, in some cases (immigrant cultural minorities in modern nation-states provide us with some examples) increasing interaction may lead not to greater blending in certain features relating to identity, but rather the converse, leading to more resistant cultural barriers. Thus, there are considerable problems in distinguishing independent adaptation, diffusion and descent when accounting for cultural similarities and differences.

Finally, it is no accident that studies within a cultural evolutionary framework disproportionately rely on either linguistic or artefact data, where the large datasets are relatively easy to assemble and where problems of measurement are more straightforward. Applications to people, social behaviour and abstract non-material knowledge rather than to artefacts have so far focused on small-scale societies, classrooms or laboratory situations (Chen, Cavalli-Sforza and Feldman 1982; Efferson et al. 2007; Inman et al. 2007; Rendell et al. 2011), or on secondary data (e.g. Soltis, Boyd and Richerson 1995), where the quality of data has permitted more confident quantification. In other words, our depictions of cultural complexity have tended to be constrained by the parameters of our research. Furthermore, if we maintain our position that cultural transmission relates more to an underlying logic than visible productions or behaviours, then phylogenetic studies are of specific state-specific cultural productions rather than cultural knowledge. To fully leverage phylogenetic methods we would want to understand all the possible state productions of a fragment of cultural logic, and examine the relationship between these in our datasets to provide evidence for stability or innovation in cultural transmission.

Rates of Change

It is obvious that certain cultural features change faster than others. Indeed, some elements exhibit a remarkable stability, giving the appearance of remaining unchanged for thousands of years. Consider, for example, the arrowhead, needle, fishhook and comb. Similarly, while form and decoration in pottery making can alter quickly, the motor techniques underpinning the general process of potting take much longer to both acquire and to change (Jordan and Shennan 2005). Such differential change is found in, and between, all cultural domains, but what we need to ask is whether long periods of stability in the shape of material equipment are evidence of fidelity in the transmission of cultural information and skill. An alternative explanation might be that the forms are so protean that they would anyway be constantly reinvented due to universal human patterns of problem identification and solving in relation to the constraints of sensory-motor coordination, the outcome in other words of an impulse for 'perpetual rediscovery'. It is here that phylogenetic methods can be useful, if not imperative (O'Brien and Lyman 2003; Lycett 2009). Moreover, the presence of certain items of material culture over the long-term provides strong evidence of linked persistent core motor-sensory behaviours, such as we may infer from the concept of a spoon and its use; though in such cases we cannot simply explain persistence through cultural transmission, but rather the interaction between transmitted elements, both objects and behaviours, and developmental processes of rediscovery.

Some researchers have distinguished a conservative 'core tradition' rarely affected by diffusion from other groups where there may be different rates of change between the core and the periphery, from multiple packages where everything is transmitted together (Shennan and Collard 2005: 134). The former model is eerily reminiscent of Steward's culture core, and other materialist infrastructure-superstructure models of social change. Cultural 'cores' may remain intact because they are transmitted in a conservative way, while packages are transmitted relatively independently. New cores arise mainly through population fission and divergence of daughter cultures. Isolation and integration protect the core, while peripheral elements are more subject to borrowing (Boyd et al. 1997: 365).

On a different scale, for a very different domain, the Opies (1959: 2) note the remarkable stability of children's playground rhymes over a period of several hundred years, but equally the 'miraculous' speed of innovation. 'Hark the herald angels sing, Mrs Simpson's pinched our king' appeared within weeks of the first public announcement of the constitutional crisis in November and December of 1936 (Opie and Opie 1959: 5–6). The stochastic features of the social process also influence fidelity and speed of transmission. Thus, since nursery lore is transferred via adults to children, there may be a 20 to 70 year gap between learning and teaching, while playground lore may be re-transmitted within the hour. Thus, over a period of 130 years, a rhyme such as 'Little fatty doctor, how's your wife?' may have passed through twenty successive generations (Opie and Opie 1959: 7–8). The interpersonal relationships involved in transmission, therefore, influence its speed. One-to-many transmission (as in classroom teaching or internet communication) can result in rapid change or rapid reinforcement, whereas many-to-one transmission favours cultural conservatism (Cavalli-Sforza and Feldman 1981). Looking at it differently, things that change quickly are most likely to result from individual choice, whereas things that change slowly are more likely to reflect collective choices. Moreover, with an increased rate of environmental change, there is a decrease in social learning and an increase in individual learning, and where there is a decrease in environmental change there is an increase in the value of social learning (e.g. Nettle 2009).

As we have seen, the generation as a unit of time lapse can provide insights relevant to understanding rates of change and cultural stability (Ellen 1994), for whereas the unit of a year is surprisingly arbitrary in terms of the cycles for acquiring and transmitting knowledge, the life span and its abstraction – the generation – is not. However, variation in generational width dependent on demographic and social factors also influences our measurements of cultural change and reproduction (Table 0.2). Thus, if we assume a thirty-year life span, then only 333 generations have elapsed since 10,000 BP (the neolithic revolution), and 2,000 since 60,000 BP (say, the origins of modern language and symbolic culture), while if we use a fifteen-year interval then the numbers are 667 and 4,000 respectively, and if a sixty-year interval, then 167 and 1,000 respectively. Broadly speaking, as we move from early hominins to contemporary *Homo sapiens*, so people live longer, permitting increasing overlap between two, three and in some cases four coexisting generations, depending on patterns of breeding, maturation and longevity. These kinds of overlap allow for new routes of transmission, including the skipping of entire biological generations. Technological innovations linked to culture transfer (such as writing systems and electronic communication) may have even more profound implications.

Table 0.2 Estimates of number of retrospective human generations in relation to selected chronological events, calculated for three different intervals

Event	Date	BP	Generation interval		
			15 yrs	30 yrs	60 yrs
Battle of Waterloo	AD 1815	135	12.6	6.3	3.15
Battle of Hastings	AD 1066	884	63	31	16
Birth of Christ	0	1950	134	67	33
Earliest Minoan	2,000 BC	3950	267	133	68
Earliest Mesolithic		10,000	667	333	167
Upper European Palaeolithic		60,000	4,000	2,000	1,000
Anatomically modern humans		100,000	6,667	3,333	1,667

BP = years before present (year 0 = 1950).

Conclusion

In this volume we have taken the somewhat risky decision to place our heads above the parapet, and attempt a more constructive and collaborative engagement between evolutionary biologists and socio-cultural anthropologists, in order to make sense of processes of cultural transmission. In the recent past this has been (and continues to be) a zone of considerable controversy, and blood has been spilled. Though we cannot claim this for all our contributors, the editorial team at least are convinced that the various methodologies and theoretical frameworks available are to a considerable extent complementary rather than in competition, and if we are to understand what is arguably a central theoretical issue of anthropology, we need a unified but multi-disciplinary approach. It serves little purpose to retreat into our separate intellectual comfort zones. As Shennan puts it in his chapter, 'cultural transmission needs embedding in a systemic context'.

We began this introduction with a claim that the analysis of cultural transmission occupies a central place in anthropology. Indeed, the notion of cultural transmission, as the instrument for understanding the means by which social systems reproduce themselves, must be central to any social theory and to anthropological theory in particular. This has not always been so, and a succession of 'modernist' theories during the twentieth century were preoccupied with understanding the stability of society through an examination of the functions of its institutions at a fairly abstract level (Ardener 1989). The question of stability is still central since it is this that makes possible sufficient continuity of both underpinning knowledge and practice, which itself is the paradoxical precondition for change and further complexity.

How we might best theorize the notion of transmission and develop appropriate methodologies for its study remain difficult, with many unresolved issues. Here we have tried to point to some persistent and emerging issues. This volume as a whole seeks to showcase original work which explores and synthesizes current accounts of the transmission of knowledge and practice at the level of cognitive process and local socio-ecological context, and attempts to link this with explanations for longer-term (and evolutionary) trajectories of socio-cultural change, diversification and diffusion. These chapters, together with this introduction, suggest to us some persistent and emerging questions:

(1) The first is the paradox just discussed: how might we relate the stability required to ensure effective continuity with the ability and necessity

to change? This is less of a paradox if we distinguish core stability in the apparatus of transmission (be it the motor-sensory complex for learning spoon feeding, or the cognitive apparatus for organizing categories) from the variability and potential permissiveness of everything else. Such a distinction has been criticized because of the empirical difficulties of separating metaculture from culture, cultural content from cognitive process, and systems that underlie ideation from those that underlie instantiation (Read 2002; Fischer 2004); and reifying the contrasting categories.

(2) The second relates to levels of analysis. The virtues of ethnographic approaches are not invalidated by large-scale quantitative approaches, while there is no reason to think that in analysing larger datasets we should not detect a process of 'descent with modification' or variation, drift and selection of the kind advocated in those approaches described as cultural phylogenetics and which we call evolutionary. Indeed, one is likely to inform the other. The methods for studying micro and macro are not easily interchangeable; experimental, observational and qualitative ethnographic studies involving 'thick description', must complement quantitative studies of large datasets over the longer term. Cultural evolutionary models depending on robust techniques of simplification and generalization are no more or less true, only different. Ethnographers and cultural evolutionists are often asking different questions of their (different kinds of) data.

(3) We need to avoid essentialist cognitivist assumptions about how transmission takes place, which are not always substantiated by the evidence; and should agree that at the level of the individual the process is largely one of instantiating cognitive or technical or social practices through bodily and social development.

(4) Forms of transmission vary between cultural and social domains. Evidently, carpet designs, food-getting strategies and religious ideas are not necessarily transmitted in the same way, nor do they always produce the same kind of patterns. But if there is transmission, variation and sorting of such variation, then there most certainly will be evolution in all of these, even if the pattern produced and the fundamentals of those processes differ in each case.

(5) The units we use to measure transmission must be appropriate to the scale and substantive differences in the kind of data being examined and the kind of question being posed. While there may be no theoretical difficulty in measuring continuous distributions, measuring variation in handaxes is different from measuring imagistic modes of religiosity.

(6) In making sense of transmission we need to understand that process and structure are recursive. Reproduction and change arise in systemic contexts, but those same processes give rise to the contexts in which successive processes occur. In the background, therefore, must be some kind of agency-context meta-model. This applies to both micro-level processes of innovation and interpersonal interaction, and to macro-level long-term cultural continuity and change, and to the patterns of spatial diffusion that reflect this.

In Olaf Stapledon's *First and Last Men* (1930), a work of unprecedented scale in the science fiction genre, we are invited to imagine a history of humanity from the present onwards across two billion years and eighteen distinct human species. The timescale envisaged for humanity by Stapledon might well, if it is ever played out, require different models for understanding the dynamics of cultural transmission than those reviewed here. By comparison, the time periods and data series we can realistically imagine are miniscule. Indeed, in looking at history from a Stapledonian perspective, what is remarkable is not simply the fidelity in transmitting core elements, but how rapidly in terms of geological timescales complexity has developed. The time that has elapsed since the first appearance of cities and monumental architecture, little more than five thousand years, about seventy lifetimes of seventy years, is a mere 0.002 per cent of the nearly three million years since early hominids first produced recognizable tools (Wright 2004: 16). In making sense of human cultural transmission, we must appreciate the brevity of this time-scale and the rapidity with which complexity may arise.

Acknowledgements

We thank Stephen Lycett, Sarah Johns and Patrick Mahoney for their contributions to this introduction, even though they do not necessarily agree with all of our points. David Reason has provided inimitable guidance on sources relating to Haldane and Stapledon. Earlier versions have been presented by Ellen at the Institute of Cultural and Social Anthropology in Oxford, and as the Presidential Address of the Royal Anthropological Institute delivered at the 2011 Conference of the Association of Social Anthropologists in Lampeter.

Notes

1. J.B.S. Haldane's 'Daedalus, or, Science and the Future' (a paper read to the Heretics, Cambridge, on 4 February 1923) and, deriving from it, a kind of fiction, 'The Last Judgement' (collected in Haldane 1927). From the work of Stapledon, consider a passage from Chapter XI: 'Man Remakes Himself'; Part 3, The Fifth Men, of *Last and First Men* (1930 [1963]: 222).
2. Eisenstadt (1956) understood the importance of age-stratification for ensuring reproduction of the social system, but his analysis was not phrased within the problematic of what we here call cultural transmission.
3. Similar controversies, of course, still occur in relation to the concept of gene. For Dennett (2006: 344), we cannot have a taxonomy of replicators simply because they are constantly changing and reforming.

References

Allen, N.J., H. Callan, R. Dunbar and W. James (eds). 2008. *Early Human Kinship: From Sex to Social Reproduction*. Oxford: Wiley-Blackwell.

Ardener, E. 1989. *The Voice of Prophecy and Other Essays*. Oxford: Blackwell.

Athayde, S. 2003. 'Knowledge Transmission and Change in Kaiabi (*Tupi-Guarani*) Basketwork, Southern Amazonian Region, Brazil'. Thesis submitted for M.Sc., University of Kent, Canterbury.

Atran, S. 2001. 'The Trouble with Memes: Inference Versus Imitation in Cultural Creation', *Human Nature* 12(4): 351-81.

Atran, S. and D. Medin. 2008. *The Native Mind and the Cultural Construction of Nature*. Cambridge, MA: The MIT Press.

Au, T.K., J.S. Oh, L.M. Knightly, S.-A. Jun and L.F. Romo. 2008. 'Salvaging a Childhood Language', *Journal of Memory and Language* 58: 998–1011.

Aunger, R. ed. 2000. *Darwinizing Culture: The Status of Memetics as a Science*. Oxford and New York: Oxford University Press.

Barnard, A.J. 1978. 'The Kin Terminology of the Nharo Bushmen', *Cahiers d'études africaines* 18: 607–29.

Barsalou, L.W. 2008. 'Grounded Cognition', *Annual Review of Psychology* 59: 617–45.

Barsalou, L.W., P.M. Niedenthal, A. Barbey, J. Ruppert. 2003. 'Social Embodiment', in B. Ross (ed.), *The Psychology of Learning and Motivation* 43. San Diego, CA: Academic Press, pp. 43–92.

Bentley, R.A., M.W. Hahn and S.J. Shennan. 2004. 'Random Drift and Culture Change', *Proceedings of the Royal Society B* 271: 1443–50.

Berlin, B. 1992. *Ethnobiological Classification: Principles of Categorization of Plants and Animals in Traditional Societies*. Princeton, NJ: Princeton University Press.

Blackmore, S. 1998. 'Imitation and the Definition of a Meme', *Journal of Memetics – Evolutionary Models of Information Transmission* 2. http://jom-emit.cfpm.org/1998/vol2/blackmore_s.html

Bloch, M. 2005. *Essays on Cultural Transmission*. London: Berg.

Bogin, B. and B.H. Smith. 1996. 'Evolution of the Human Life Cycle', *American Journal of Human Biology* 8(6): 703–16.

Bonner, J.T. 1980. *The Evolution of Culture in Animals*. Princeton, NJ: Princeton University Press.

Bourdieu, P. 1990. *The Logic of Practice* (trans. R. Nice). Stanford: Stanford University Press.

Borofsky, R. 1987. *Making History: Pukapukan and Anthropological Constructions of Knowledge*. Cambridge: Cambridge University Press.

Boyd, R. and P.J. Richerson. 1985. *Culture and the Evolutionary Process*. Chicago: University of Chicago Press.

Boyd, R., M.B. Mulder, W.H. Durham, and P.J. Richerson. 1997. 'Are Cultural Phylogenies Possible? ', in P. Weingart, S. D. Mitchel, P. J. Richerson, and S. Maasen (eds), *Human by Nature: Between Biology and the Social Sciences*. Mahwah, NJ: Lawrence Erlbaum Associates, pp. 355–86.

Boyer, P. 1994. *The Naturalness of Religious Ideas: A Cognitive Theory of Religion.* London: University of California Press.

Bryant, D., F. Filimon and R.D. Gray. 2005. 'Untangling our Past: Languages, Trees, Splits and Networks', in R. Mace, C. Holden and S. Shennan (eds), *The Evolution of Cultural Diversity: A Phylogenetic Approach.* London: UCL Press, pp. 67–84.

Casagrande, D.G. 2002. 'Ecology, Cognition, and Cultural Transmission of Tzeltal Maya Medicinal Plant Knowledge'. Ph.D. dissertation, University of Georgia.

Cavalli-Sforza, L.L. and M.W. Feldman. 1981. *Cultural Transmission and Evolution: A Quantitatvie Approach.* Princeton: Princeton University Press.

Chen, K.-H., L.L. Cavalli-Sforza and M.W. Feldman. 1982. 'A Study of Cultural Transmission in Taiwan', *Human Ecology* 10(3): 365–82.

Chomsky, N. and M. Halle. 1968. *The Sound Pattern of English.* New York: Harper and Row.

Chudek, M., S. Heller, S. Birch and J. Henrich. 2012. 'Prestige-biased Cultural Learning: Bystander's Differential Attention to Potential Models Influences Children's Learning', *Evolution and Human Behavior* 3: 46–56.

Clark, A. 1997. *Being There: Putting Brain, Body, and World Together Again.* Cambridge, MA: MIT Press.

Cohen, E. 2010. 'Anthropology of Knowledge', in T.J.H. Marchand (ed.), *Making Knowledge.* Special Issue of *Journal of the Royal Anthropological Institute,* pp. S193–S202.

Collard, M., S.J. Shennan and J.J. Tehrani. 2006. 'Branching, Blending, and the Evolution of Cultural Similarities and Differences among Human Populations', *Evolution and Human Behavior* 27(3): 169–84.

Collard, M. and J. Tehrani. 2005. 'Phylogenesis versus Ethnogenesis in Turkmen Cultural Evolution', in R. Mace, C. Holden and S. Shennan (eds), *The Evolution of Cultural Diversity: A Phylogenetic Approach.* London: UCL Press, pp. 109–32.

Costopoulos, A. 2005. 'Apologia of Classical Evolutionism', *Reviews in Anthropology* 34(3): 231–44.

Coy, M. (ed.). 1989. *Apprenticeship: From Theory to Method and Back Again.* Albany, NY: State University of New York.

Daly, M. 1982. 'Some Caveats about Cultural Transmission Models', *Human Ecology* 10(3): 401–8.

Dawkins, R. (1976) 1989. *The Selfish Gene.* Oxford: Oxford University Press.

———.1982. *The Extended Phenotype: The Gene as the Unit of Selection.* London: W.H. Freeman.

Deetz, J. 1968. 'The Inference of Residence and Descent Rules from Archaeological Data', in S.R. Binford and L.R. Binford (eds), *New Perspectives in Archaeology.* Chicago: Aldine, pp. 41–48.

Dennett, D.C. 1995. *Darwin's Dangerous Idea.* London: Penguin.

———.2006. *Breaking the Spell: Religion as a Natural Phenomenon.* London: Penguin.

Diamond, J.M. 1998. *Guns, Germs and Steel: A Short History of Everybody for the Last 13,000 years.* London: Vintage.

Driver, H.E. 1970. 'Statistical Studies of Continuous Geographical Distributions', in R. Naroll and R. Cohen (eds), *A Handbook of Method in Cultural Anthropology.* New York and London: Columbia University Press, pp. 620–39.

Dunbar, R.I.M. 2003. 'The Social Brain: Mind, Language, and Society in Evolutionary Perspective', *Annual Review of Anthropology* 32: 163–81.

Edelman, G.M. 1992. *Bright Air, Brilliant Fire: On the Matter of the Mind.* London: Penguin.

Eerkens, J.W. and C.P. Lipo. 2005. 'Cultural Transmission, Copying Errors, and the Generation of Variation in Material Culture and the Archaeological Record', *Journal of Anthropological Archaeology* 24: 316–34.

Efferson, C., P.J. Richerson, R. McElreath, M. Lubell, E. Edsten, T.M. Waring, B. Paciotti, and W. Baum. 2007. 'Learning, Productivity, and Noise: An Experimental Study of Cultural Transmission on the Bolivian Altiplano', *Evolution and Human Behavior* 28(1): 11–17.

Eisenstadt, S.N. 1956. *From Generation to Generation: Age Groups and Social Structure.* New York: The Free Press, London: Collier-Macmillan.

Ellen, R.F. 1990. 'Nuaulu Sacred Shields: The Reproduction of Things or the Reproduction of Images?', *Etnofoor* 3(1): 5–25.

_____.1994 'Rates of Change: Weasel Words and the Indispensable in Anthropological Analysis', in C.M. Hann (ed.), *When History Accelerates: Essays on Rapid Social Change, Complexity and Creativity.* London: Athlone, pp. 54–74.

_____.1999. 'Modes of Subsistence and Ethnobiological Knowledge: Between Extraction and Cultivation in Southeast Asia', in D.L. Medin and S. Atran (eds), *Folkbiology.* Cambridge, MA: MIT Press, pp. 91–117.

_____.2003. 'Variation and Uniformity in the Construction of Biological Knowledge across Cultures', in H. Selin (ed.), *Nature across Cultures: Views of Nature and the Environment in Non-Western Cultures.* Dordrecht: Kluwer, pp. 47–74.

_____.2006. 'Introduction: Categories, Classification and Cognitive Anthropology', in R.F. Ellen, *The Categorical Impulse: Essays on the Anthropology of Classifying Behaviour.* Oxford: Berghahn Books, pp. 1–30.

_____.2009. 'A Modular Approach to Understanding the Transmission of Technical Knowledge: Nuaulu Basket-making from Seram, Eastern Indonesia', *Journal of Material Culture* 14(2): 243–77.

_____.2010. 'Theories in Anthropology and "Anthropological Theory"', *Journal of the Royal Anthropological Institute* 16: 387–404.

_____.2012. *Nuaulu Religious Practices: The Frequency and Reproduction of Rituals in a Moluccan Society.* Leiden: KITLV Press.

Evans-Pritchard, E.E. 1940. *The Nuer: A Description of the Modes of Livelihood and Political Institutions of a Nilotic People.* Oxford: Clarendon Press.

Fischer, M.D. 2004. 'Powerful Knowledge: Applications in a Cultural Context', in A. Bicker, P. Sillitoe and J. Pottier (eds), *Development and Local Knowledge: New Approaches to Issues in Natural Resources Management, Conservation and Agriculture* [Studies in Environmental Anthropology 9]. London: Routledge, pp. 19–30.

——————.2008. 'Cultural Dynamics: Formal Descriptions of Cultural Processes', *Structure and Dynamics* 3(2). http://www.escholarship.org/uc/item/557126nz

Forge, A. 1967. 'The Abelam Artist', in M. Freedman (ed.), *Social Organization: Essays Presented to Raymond Firth*. London: Frank Cass, pp. 65–84.

Frake, C.O. 1961. 'The Diagnosis of Disease among the Subanun of Mindanao', *American Anthropologist* 63: 113–32.

——————.1964. 'How to Ask for a Drink in Subanun', *American Anthropologist* 66: 127–32.

Geertz, C. (1973) 1975. 'Thick Description: Toward an Interpretive Theory of Culture', in *The Interpretation of Cultures, Selected Essays by Clifford Geertz*. London: Hutchinson, pp. 3–30.

Geertz, H. and C. Geertz. 1964. 'Teknonymy in Bali: Parenthood, Age-grading, and Genealogical Amnesia', *Journal of the Royal Anthropological Institute* 94(2): 94–108.

Gibson, J.J. 1979. *The Ecological Approach to Visual Perception*. Boston: Houghton Mifflin.

Goody, J. (ed.). 1966. *The Developmental Cycle in Domestic Groups*. Cambridge Papers in Social Anthropology 1. Cambridge: Cambridge University Press.

Gould, S.J. 1989. *Wonderful Life: The Burgess Shale and the Nature of History*. London: Penguin.

Greenhill, S.J., T.E. Currie and R.D. Gray. 2009. 'Does Horizontal Transmission Invalidate Cultural Phylogenies?', *Proceedings of the Royal Society of London B* 276 (1665): 2299–306.

Greenhill, S.J. and R.D. Gray. 2005. 'Testing Population Dispersal Hypotheses: Pacific Settlement, Phylogenetic Trees and Austronesian Languages', in R. Mace, C. Holden and S. Shennan (eds), *The Evolution of Cultural Diversity: A Phylogenetic Approach*. London: UCL Press, pp. 31–52.

Haldane, J.B.S. 1927. *Possible Worlds and Other Essays: A Scientist Looks at the Future of Man*. London: Chatto and Windus.

Hansen, L., Y. Umeda and M. McKinney. 2002. 'Savings in the Relearning of Second Language Vocabulary: The Effects of Time and Proficiency', *Language Learning* 52(4): 653–78.

Henrich, J. 2004. 'Demography and Cultural Evolution: How Adaptive Cultural Processes can Produce Maladaptive Losses – the Tasmanian Case', *American Antiquity* 69(2): 197–214.

Hewlett, B.S. and L.L. Cavalli-Sforza. 1986. 'Cultural Transmission among Aka Pygmies', *American Anthropologist* 88(4): 922–34.

Hewlett, B.S. and M.E. Lamb. 2002. 'Integrating Evolution, Culture and Developmental Psychology: Explaining Care-giving Infant Proximity and Responsiveness in Central Africa and the USA', in

H. Keller, Y.H. Poortinga and A. Schölmerich (eds), *Between Culture and Biology: Perspectives on Ontogenetic Development*. Cambridge: Cambridge University Press, pp. 241–70.

Heyes, C.M. 1994. 'Social Learning in Animals: Categories and Mechanisms', *Biological Reviews* 69: 207–31.

Hsu, E. 1999. *The Transmission of Chinese Medicine*. Cambridge: Cambridge University Press.

Huffman, M.A. 1997. 'Current Evidence for Self-medication in Primates: A Multi-disciplinary Perspective', *Yearbook of Physical Anthropology* 40: 171–200.

Hunn, E. 2002. 'Evidence for the Precocious Acquisition of Plant Knowledge by Zapotec Children', in J.R. Stepp, F.S. Wyndham and R.K. Zarger (eds), *Ethnobiology and Biocultural Diversity: Proceedings of the Seventh International Congress of Ethnobiology*. Athens, GA: International Society of Ethnobiology, pp. 604–13.

Ingold, T. 2001. 'From the Transmission of Representations to the Education of Attention', in H. Whitehouse (ed.), *The Debated Mind: Evolutionary Psychology Versus Ethnography*. Oxford: Berg, pp. 113–53.

Inman, A.G., E.E. Howard, R.L. Beaumont and J.A. Walker. 2007. 'Cultural Transmission: Influence of Contextual Factors in Asian Immigrant Parents' Experiences', *Journal of Counselling Psychology* 54(1): 93–100.

Jordan, P. and S.J. Shennan. 2003. 'Cultural Transmission, Language and Basketry Tradition amongst the California Indians', *Journal of Anthropological Archaeology* 22: 42–74.

————. 2005. 'Cultural Transmission in Indigenous California', in R. Mace, C. Holden and S. Shennan (eds), *The Evolution of Cultural Diversity: A Phylogenetic Approach*. London: UCL Press, pp. 165–98.

Kaleta, R. 2008. 'The Cultural Significance of Thuya (*Tetraclinis articulata*): An Ethnographic Study of the Thuya Woodworking Craft and its Implications for Sustainable Management in Southern Morocco'. Thesis submitted for Ph.D. in Ethnobiology, University of Kent, Canterbury.

Keller, C.M. and J.D. Keller. 1996. *Cognition and Tool Use: The Blacksmith at Work*. Cambridge: Cambridge University Press.

Kirch, P.V and J.-L. Rallu. 2007. *The Growth and Collapse of Pacific Island Societies: Archaeological and Demographic Perspectives*. Honolulu: University of Hawaii Press.

Kroeber, K. and C. Kroeber (eds). 2003. *Ishi in Three Centuries*. Lincoln, NE: University of Nebraska Press.

Laland, K.N. and B.G. Galef (eds). 2009. *The Question of Animal Culture*. Cambridge, MA: Harvard University Press.

Lave, J. 1988. *Cognition in Practice: Mind, Mathematics and Culture in Everyday Life*. Cambridge: Cambridge University Press.

Lawson, E.T. and R.N. McCauley. 1990. *Rethinking Religion: Connecting Cognition and Culture*. Cambridge: Cambridge University Press.

Leaf, M.J. 1972. *Information and Behavior in a Sikh Village: Social Organization Reconsidered*. Berkeley: University of California Press.

Leiber, J. 1995. 'Apes, Signs, and Syntax', *American Anthropologist* 97(2): 374.

Lemmonier, P. 1992. *Elements for an Anthropology of Technology*. Anthropological Papers of the Museum of Anthropology 88. Ann Arbor, MI: University of Michigan.

Lévi-Strauss, C. 1955. *Tristes Tropiques*. Paris: Plon.

Levinson, S.C. and R.D. Gray. 2012. 'Tools from Evolutionary Biology shed New Light on the Diversification of Languages', *Trends in Cognitive Sciences* 16(3): 167–73.

Lock, A. 1980. *The Guided Reinvention of Language*. London: Academic Press.

Lumsden, C.J. and E.O. Wilson. 1981. *Genes, Mind and Culture: The Coevolutionary Process*. Cambridge, MA: Harvard University Press.

Lycett, S.J. 2007. 'Why is there a Lack of Mode 3 Levallois Technologies in East Asia? A Phylogenetic Test of the Movius–Schick Hypothesis', *Journal of Anthropological Archaeology* 26(4): 541–75.

Lycett, S.J., 2009. 'Are Victoria West Cores "Proto-Levallois"? A Phylogenetic Assessment', *Journal of Human Evolution* 56(2): 175–91.

Lycett, S.J., M. Collard and W.C. McGrew. 2009. 'Cladistic Analyses of Behavioral Variation in Wild *Pan troglodytes*: Exploring the Chimpanzee Culture Hypothesis', *Journal of Human Evolution* 57(4): 337–49.

Lycett, S.J. and C.J. Norton. 2010. 'A Demographic Model for Palaeolithic Technological Evolution: The Case of East Asia and the Movius Line', *Quaternary International* 211(1): 55–65.

Lyman, R.L. and M.J. O'Brien. 2003. 'Cultural Traits: Units of Analysis in Early Twentieth-century Anthropology', *Journal of Anthropological Research* 59(2): 225–50.

Lyon, W. 1995. *Social Context and the Limits on Symbolic Meanings* [CSAC Studies in Anthropology, 9]. Canterbury: University of Kent.

McCauley, N.R. and E.T. Lawson. 2002. *Bringing Ritual to Mind: Psychological Foundations of Cultural Forms*. Cambridge: Cambridge University Press.

McElreath, R. and P. Strimling. 2008. 'When Natural Selection Favours Imitation of Parents', *Current Anthropology* 49(2): 307–16.

McMahon, A. and R. McMahon. 2003. 'Finding Families: Quantitative Methods in Language Classification', *Transactions of the Philological Society* 101(1): 7–55.

Mace, R. 2005a. 'Introduction: A Phylogenetic Approach to the Evolution of Cultural Diversity', in R. Mace, C. Holden and S. Shennan (eds), *The Evolution of Cultural Diversity: A Phylogenetic Approach*. London: UCL Press, pp. 1–12.

————. 2005b. 'Introduction to Part II: On the Use of Phylogenetic Comparative Methods to Test Co-evolutionary Hypotheses across Cultures', in R. Mace, C. Holden and S. Shennan (eds), *The Evolution of Cultural Diversity: A Phylogenetic Approach*. London: UCL Press, pp. 199–206.

Mace, R., and C.J. Holden. 2005. 'A Phylogenetic Approach to Cultural Evolution', *Trends in Ecology and Evolution* 20(3): 116–21.

Mace, R., C. Holden and S. Shennan (eds). 2005. *The Evolution of Cultural Diversity: A Phylogenetic Approach*. London: UCL Press.

Mace, R. and M. Pagel. 1994. 'The Comparative Method in Anthropology', *Current Anthropology* 35(5): 549–64.

Mampe, B., A.D. Friederici, A. Christophe, K. Wermke. 2009. 'Newborns' Cry Melody is Shaped by their Native Language', *Current Biology* 19(23): 1994–97.

Marchand, T.H.J. 2001. *Minaret Building and Apprenticeship in Yemen*. Richmond, Surrey: Curzon Press.

_____.2003. 'A Possible Explanation for the Lack of Explanation; or, "Why the Master Builder Can't Explain What he Knows": Introducing Informational Atomism Against a "Definitional" Definition of Concepts', in J. Pottier, A. Bicker and P. Sillitoe (eds), *Negotiating Local Knowledge: Power and Identity in Development*. London: Pluto Press, pp. 30–50.

_____.2010a. 'Preface', in T.H.J. Marchand (ed.), *Making Knowledge*. Special edition of the *Journal of the Royal Anthropological Institute*, pp. Siii–Sv.

_____.2010b. 'Embodied Cognition and Communication: Studies with British Fine Woodworkers', in T.H.J. Marchand (ed.), *Making Knowledge*. Special edition of the *Journal of the Royal Anthropological Institute*, pp. S100–S120.

Mauss, M. (1934) 1973. 'Techniques of the Body' [Trans. Ben Brewster], *Economy and Society* 2(1): 70–88.

Mesoudi, A. 2011a. *Cultural Evolution: How Darwinian Evolutionary Theory can Explain Human Culture and Synthesize the Social Sciences*. Chicago: University of Chicago Press.

_____.2011b. 'Variable Cultural Acquisition Costs Constrain Cumulative Cultural Evoluton', *PLoS ONE* 6 (e18239): 1–10.

Moore, J.H. 1994. 'Putting Anthropology Back Together Again: The Ethnogenetic Critique of Cladistic Theory', *American Anthropologist* 96: 370–96.

Nagaoka, T., K. Hirata, E. Yokota and S. Matsu'ura. 2006. 'Paleodemography of a Medieval Population in Japan: Analysis of Human Skeletal Remains from the Yuigahama-minami Site', *American Journal of Physical Anthropology* 131: 1–14.

Neiman, F.D. 1995. 'Stylistic Variation in Evolutionary Perspective: Inferences from Decorative Diversity and Interassemblage Distance in Illinois Woodland Ceramic Assemblages', *American Antiquity* 60: 7–36.

Nettle, D. 2009. 'Beyond Nature versus Culture: Cultural Variation as an Evolved Characteristic', *Journal of the Royal Anthropological Institute* 15(2): 223–40.

Nishida, T. 1986. 'Local Traditions and Cultural Transmission', in B.B. Smuts, D.L. Cheney, R.M. Seyfarth, R.W. Wrangham and T.T. Strusaker (eds), *Primates Societies*. London: University of Chicago Press, pp. 462–74.

O'Brien, M.J. and R.A. Bentley. 2011. 'Stimulated Variation and Cascades: Two Processes in the Evolution of Complex Technological Systems', *Journal of Archaeological Method and Theory* 18: 309–35.

O'Brien, M.J., J. Darwent and R.L. Lyman. 2001. 'Cladistics is Useful for Reconstructing Archaeological Phylogenies: Palaeoindian Points from the Southeastern United States', *Journal of Archaeological Science* 28: 1115–36.

O'Brien, M.J. and R.L. Lyman. 2000. *Applying Evolutionary Archaeology: A Systematic Approach*. Kluwer Academic/Plenum, New York.

———. 2003. *Cladistics in Archaeology*. Salt Lake City: University of Utah Press.

———. 2005. 'Cultural Phylogenetic Hypotheses in Archaeology: Some Fundamental Issues', in R. Mace, C. Holden and S. Shennan (eds), *The Evolution of Cultural Diversity: A Phylogenetic Approach*. London: UCL Press, pp. 85–108.

O'Brien, M.J., R.L. Lyman, A. Mesoudi and T.L. VanPool. 2010. 'Cultural Traits as Units of Analysis', *Philosophical Transactions of the Royal Society B* 365: 3797–806.

Ohmagari, K. and F. Berkes. 1997. 'Transmission of Indigenous Knowledge and Bush Skills among the Western James Bay Cree Women of Subarctic Canada', *Human Ecology* 25(2): 197–222.

Opie, I.A. and P. Opie. 1959. *The Lore and Language of Schoolchildren*. Oxford: Clarendon Press.

Oyama, S. 1989. 'Ontogeny and the Central Dogma: Do We Need the Concept of Genetic Programming in Order to Have an Evolutionary Perspective?', in M. Gunnar and E. Thelen (eds.), *Systems in Development: the Minnesota Symposia on Child Psychology*, vol. 22. Hillsdale, NJ: Erlbaum, pp. 1–34.

Parkin, D. and S. Ulijaszek (eds). 2007. *Holistic Anthropology: Emergence and Convergence*. New York and Oxford: Berghahn Books.

Piaget, J. 1960. *The Child's Concept of Geometry*. London: Routledge and Kegan Paul.

Pitt-Rivers, A.H.L.F. 1906. *The Evolution of Culture and Other Essays*. Oxford: Clarendon Press.

Pocklington, R. and M.L. Best. 1997. 'Cultural Evolution and Units of Selection in Replicating Text', *Journal of Theoretical Biology* 188: 79–87.

Powell, A., S. Shennan and M.G. Thomas. 2009. 'Late Pleistocene Demography and the Appearance of Modern Human Behavior', *Science* 324: 1298–301.

Read, D. 2002. 'A Multi-trajectory, Competition Model of Emergent Complexity in Human Social Organization', *Proceedings of the National Academy of Sciences* 99 (Suppl. 3): 7251–56.

Rendell, L., R. Boyd, M. Enquist, M.W. Feldman, L. Fogarty and K.N. Laland. 2011. 'How Copying Affects the Amount, Evenness and Persistence of Cultural Knowledge: Insights from the Social Learning Strategies Tournament', *Philosophical Transactions of the Royal Society B* 366: 1118–28.

Reynolds, P.C. 1981. *On the Evolution of Human Behaviour*. Berkeley: University of California Press.

Richerson, P.J. and R. Boyd. 2005. *Not by Genes Alone: How Culture Transformed Human Evolution*. Chicago: University of Chicago Press.

Romney, A.K., S.C. Weller, W.H. Batchelder 1986. 'Culture as Consensus: A Theory of Culture and Informant Accuracy', *American Anthropologist* 88(2): 313–37.

Ruddle, K. and R. Chesterfield. 1977. *Education for Traditional Food Procurement in the Orinoco Delta* [Ibero-Americana 53]. Berkeley: University of California Press.

Schlegel, A. 2011. 'Human Development and Cultural Transmission', *Anthropologischer Anzeiger* 68(4): 457–70.

Shannon, C.E. and W. Weaver. 1949. *A Mathematical Model of Communication*. Urbana, IL: University of Illinois Press.

Shennan, S.J. 1996. 'Social Inequality and the Transmission of Cultural Traditions in Forager Societies', in J Steele and S J Shennan (eds), *The Archaeology of Human Ancestry: Power, Sex and Tradition*. London: Routledge, pp. 365–79.

——————. 2000. 'Population, Culture History, and the Dynamics of Culture Change', *Current Anthropology* 41(5): 811–35.

Shennan, S.J. and M. Collard. 2005. 'Investigating Processes of Cultural Evolution on the North Coast of New Guinea and Multivariate and Cladistic Analyses', in R. Mace, C. Holden and S. Shennan (eds), *The Evolution of Cultural Diversity: A Phylogenetic Approach*. London: UCL Press, pp. 133–64.

Shore, B. 1996. *Culture in Mind: Cognition, Culture, and the Problem of Meaning*. Oxford: Oxford University Press.

Soltis, J., R. Boyd and P.J. Richerson. 1995. 'Can Group-functional Behaviors Evolve by Cultural Group Selection? An Empirical Test', *Current Anthropology* 63: 473–94.

Sperber, D. 1996. *Explaining Culture: A Naturalistic Approach*. Oxford: Blackwell.

Stapledon, Olaf. (1930) 1963. *Last and First Men: A Story of the Near and Far Future*. Harmondsworth: Penguin.

Steenbergen, B., J. van der Kamp, A.W. Smitsman and R.G. Carson. 1997. 'Spoon Handling in Two- to Four-year-old Children', *Ecological Psychology* 9: 113–29.

Steward, J. 1955. *The Theory of Culture Change*. Urbana, IL: University of Illinois Press.

Strauss, C. and N. Quinn. 1997. *A Cognitive Theory of Cultural Meaning*. Cambridge: Cambridge University Press.

Stross, B. 1973. 'Acquisition of Botanical Terminology by Tzeltal Children', in M.S. Edmonson (ed.), *Meaning in Mayan Languages*. The Hague: Mouton, pp. 107–141.

Tehrani, J. and M. Collard. 2002. 'Investigating Cultural Evolution through Biological Phylogenetic Analyses of Turkmen Textiles', *Journal of Anthropological Archaeology* 21: 443–63.

Terrell, J.E. 1988. 'History as a Family Tree, History as a Tangled Bank', *Antiquity* 62: 642–57.

Tooby, J. and L. Cosmides. 1992. 'The Psycological Foundations of Culture', in J.H. Barkow, L. Cosmides and J. Tooby (eds), *The Adapted Mind*. London: Oxford University Press, pp. 19–136.

Ward. R. and K. Weiss (eds). 1976. *The Demographic Evolution of Human Populations*. New York: Academic Press.

Weiss, K.M. 1981. 'Evolutionary Perspectives on Human Aging', in P.T Amos and S. Harrell (eds), *Other Ways of Growing Old*. Stanford, CA: Stanford University Press, pp. 15–18.

Wells, R.V. 1975. *The Population of the British Colonies in America before 1776*. Princeton: Princeton University Press.

Werker, J.F. and R.C. Tees. 1984. 'Cross-language Speech Perception: Evidence for Perceptual Reorganization during the First Year of Life', *Infant Behavior and Development* 7: 49–63.

Whitehouse, H. 2004. *Modes of Religiosity: A Cognitive Theory of Religious Transmission*. Walnut Creek, CA: Altamira Press.

Whiten, A., J. Goodall, W.C. McGrew, T. Nishida, V. Reynolds, et al. 1999. 'Cultures in Chimpanzees', *Nature* 399: 682–85.

Whiten, A., N. McGuigan, S. Marshall-Pescini and L.M. Hopper. 2009. 'Emulation, Imitation, Over-imitation and the Scope of Culture for Child and Chimpanzee', *Philosophical Transactions of the Royal Society B* 364: 2417–28.

Workman, P.L., J.D. Niswander, K.S. Brown and W.C. Leyshon. 1974. 'Population Studies on Southwestern Indian Tribes: IV. The Zuni', *American Journal of Physical Anthropology* 41: 119–32.

Wright, R. 2004. 'Fool's Paradise: Easter Island's Unlearned Lesson'. *Times Literary Supplement*, 19 November 2004: 16. Extract from his 2004 Massey Lectures, published (2005) as *A Short History of Progress*. Toronto: House of Anansi Press.

Wrigley, E.A. and R.S. Schofield. 1981. *The Population History of England, 1540–1871*. Cambridge: Harvard University Press, pp. 243–88.

Zarger, R.K. 2002. 'Acquisition and Transmission of Subsistence Knowledge by Q'eqchi Maya in Belize', in J.R. Stepp, F.S. Wyndham and R.K. Zarger (eds), *Ethnobiology and Biocultural Diversity: Proceedings of the Seventh International Congress of Ethnobiology*. Athens, GA: International Society of Ethnobiology, pp. 593–603.

Chapter 1

WHAT ANIMALS OTHER THAN PRIMATES CAN TELL US ABOUT HUMAN CULTURAL TRANSMISSION

Kevin Laland, Alice Cowie and Tom Morgan

Introduction

To most social scientists, human culture is unique, and bears no comparison to the behavioural traditions observed in other animals. To a large extent this position is justified, since our species alone has created technologies that endlessly bring forth new innovations, allowing it to transform environments to unprecedented levels and thereby dominate the planet; not to mention humanity's extraordinary achievements in the sciences, arts, music and literature. Our success as a species is widely attributed to this capability for culture, through which we share adaptive knowledge, and fashion solutions to life's challenges (Boyd and Richerson 1985; Plotkin 1997). Yet the observation that a wide range of other animals are also capable of innovation and social learning (Heyes and Galef 1996; Laland and Galef 2009), albeit to a lesser degree, begs the question of exactly what it is that is special about the cultural capabilities of humans.

It is here that a comparative perspective can be of utility. Careful analyses of the cognitive capabilities and social behaviour of humans and other animals potentially allows researchers to characterize the truly unique aspects of human culture. This is no trivial matter, since history is littered with examples of claims along the lines of 'humans uniquely do X, or possess Y' (e.g. use tools, teach, imitate, exhibit referential communication, possess episodic memory) that have subsequently fallen by the wayside when established in another species. Such comparisons of course also isolate features that humans share with other animals, which can be equally insightful, since they pave the way to studying animals as model systems that can illuminate human behaviour. Moreover, comparisons between humans and other animals help us to reconstruct the past, and determine how, and from where, human cultural capability evolved.

Before meaningful comparisons between the 'cultures' of humans and other animals can be made, we need to specify precisely what we mean by the term culture. Once again, this is no trivial matter, since it has proven extremely difficult for social scientists to derive a satisfactory consensual definition, or to find means to operationalize culture (Kroeber and Kluckholm 1952; Durham 1991). The definition that we adopt follows Laland and Hoppitt (2003): *Cultures are those group-typical behaviour patterns shared by members of a community that rely on socially learned and transmitted information.* This broad definition is designed to encourage relevant comparative data to be collected, providing a framework with which to investigate the evolutionary roots of culture. In our view, a narrower definition, for instance, one that automatically restricted culture to humans, would not prove particularly useful, at least not to researchers interested in a comparative perspective. This is not only because the answer to the question of whether or not animals have culture would be a fait accompli; by definition, they would not. But in addition, this denotation would act as a barrier to understanding the evolutionary roots of culture. No light would be shed on how culture came into existence, nor on humans' place in nature. Premature, over-exacting distinctions potentially jeopardize our ability to see relationships between culture-like phenomena in diverse taxa.

Interestingly, when a broad definition is adopted, it transpires that some of the strongest evidence for culture in non-human animals comes not from our nearest relatives, the primates, but from a handful of distantly related and disparate animals – a few birds, whales and fish species (Laland and Hoppitt 2003). For instance, the claims of culture in chimpanzees are hotly contested (Humle and Newton-Fisher, this volume), not least because it is unclear whether the observed behavioural variation, labelled 'culture' (Whiten et al. 1999), results from differential social learning, or from differences in ecology or genetics (Laland and Janik 2006). However, we describe below experimental studies on natural populations of fish and birds that clearly demonstrate that the species concerned exhibit behavioural traditions reliant on social learning, and where population differences cannot be attributed to confounding genetic or ecological factors (Warner 1988; Slagsvold and Wiebe 2007). Likewise, arguably the best evidence for animal teaching is in meerkats (Thornton and McAuliffe 2006); for animal innovation, mental time-travel and cumulative culture, it is in birds (Clayton and Dickinson 1998; Hunt and Gray 2003; Emery and Clayton 2004; Lefebvre et al. 2004); and for vocal learning, it is in cetaceans (Rendell and Whitehead 2001). These observations become significant once we recognize the full gamut of tools offered by the comparative method.

Comparative analyses between species can allow inferences to be made about the attributes of species ancestral to humans, and allow us to understand the evolutionary history of the traits seen in modern man. In simple terms, this approach is reliant on detecting homologies that humans and closely related animals share. Naturally, the first points of comparison that spring to mind are with non-human primates, particularly the apes. Researchers are interested in our closest relatives because these species potentially exhibit homologous traits to humans, due to shared ancestry, or may perhaps exhibit precursors of unique human characteristics, such as language. Unfortunately, advocates of this approach sometimes pin too much weight on the chimpanzee–human comparison (or to a lesser extent, the other apes–human comparison) in the name of homology, reasoning that since the chimpanzee shares more genes with humans than do other species, such comparisons are likely to be especially insightful. In fact, a single comparison, such as human–chimpanzee, contributes a solitary datum to any attempt to identify reliable relationships between selective environments and adaptations. By and large, the comparative method has moved on since the 1950s, when such pairwise comparisons were pioneered by ethologists, such as Niko Tinbergen and Konrad Lorenz, to shed light on behavioural adaptations; famously, comparisons between black-headed gulls and kittiwakes suggested numerous differences, related to nest construction and chick and parental behaviour, that could be understood as adaptations to the differential risk of predation in ground- and cliff-nesting gulls (Cullen 1957; Tinbergen et al. 1962; Tinbergen 1963). At best, such comparisons serve to generate an evolutionary hypothesis: at worst, they are nothing more than a source of uninformed speculation. In the case of the gulls, further comparisons amongst closely related birds exposed to similar selection regimes were necessary to confirm the evolutionary relationships (Clutton-Brock and Harvey 1984). So it is with chimpanzee–human comparisons, which must be complemented by further comparisons in order to yield meaningful information.

Moreover, a single comparison is uninformative as to which characters are ancestral and which are derived. In principle, all of the differences between humans and chimpanzees could have evolved in the chimpanzee lineage since divergence from the common ancestor.

The assumption that all the relevant evolutionary change took place in the hominin lineage has been a constant source of error in theories of human evolution. Consider, for example, the recent work on *Ardipithecus*, which suggests that the common ancestor of humans and chimpanzees may not have been a knuckle-walker, and that researchers have been misled by a chimpanzee model (Lovejoy 2009). Researchers that fail to consider ancestral and derived traits are vulnerable to making errors. More generally, if researchers restrict themselves to a narrow comparison involving a very small number of species closely related to humans, they risk telling apparently plausible 'just-so stories' about human evolution.

Of course, just how wide a comparison across taxa is useful will depend very much on the question in hand. Comparative analyses of animal abilities suggest that some human behavioural and psychological traits have a long history. For instance, a capacity for associative learning may even have evolved in our invertebrate ancestors; an understanding of causal relationships may be common to both mammals and birds; much social behaviour, such as forming stable social bonds, developing dominance hierarchies, and an understanding of third-party social relationships, probably evolved in our pre-hominid primate ancestors; while a capacity for true imitation probably evolved in pre-hominid apes. The important point here is that the appropriate taxonomic group for comparative analysis is not inevitably restricted to primates.

In this chapter we concentrate on two further ways in which a wider taxonomic net allows light to be shed on human cultural transmission. First, animals can be used as model systems to better understand behavioural and cognitive processes shared with humans. In this case, non-primates frequently provide an opportunity for more rigorous investigation of cultural transmission as they can be more easily manipulated in an experimental setting. For instance, much of the experimental work on animal social learning carried out in our laboratory involves studies of fish and birds. That is because these animals offer practical advantages over many other vertebrates for the study of social learning. After all, the diffusion of innovations and animal traditions are group-level phenomena, and if they are to be studied reliably, researchers require not just replicate animals but replicate populations of animals. While it would be economically and practically challenging (not to mention ethically questionable) to set up large numbers of replicate populations of chimpanzees or Japanese macaques, it is extremely straightforward and cheap to set up large numbers of populations of small fish in the laboratory, and subject them to experimentation. Similarly, we have been able to set up small experimental populations of birds in which to carry out diffusion studies. These practical advantages allow for multiple conditions and good statistical power, bringing experimental rigour to any social learning investigation. Of course, such practical advantages would be worthless if birds and fish were hopeless at social learning, or never innovated, but below we provide evidence that this is not the case. On the contrary, we will describe examples of learning strategies proposed by anthropologists, psychologists and economists as rules that humans deploy that we also observe in birds and fish.

The second means of using the comparative method is to seek to identify ecological, social or life-history characters that co-vary with cognitive and behavioural traits shared by humans and animals. While the mechanisms underlying learning across species are frequently non-homologous, there are parallels at a functional level, and these are potentially informative with respect to the ecological and social factors that favour the evolution of the attribute concerned. This allows inferences to be made about the ancestral function of, and selective environment favouring, human capabilities. This method is reliant on detecting analogous processes amongst humans and distantly related animal species. Analogy is at least as powerful a comparative tool as homology (Harvey and Pagel 1991). Evolutionary hypotheses are well supported when independently derived data repeatedly suggest that a particular selection pressure consistently favours a specific character. For instance, Dunbar's (1995) observed relationship between neocortex size and group size in primates is rendered all the more compelling by the observation that convergent evolution has generated the same patterns in carnivores and ungulates (Dunbar and Bever 1998; Shultz and Dunbar 2006). Researchers who restrict themselves to homology fail to utilize a valid and powerful source of comparative data. Below we describe how comparative analyses using non-human taxa can shed light on the ecological factors that promote reliance on culture, and the capabilities that underpin it.

In summary, researchers wishing to draw inferences about human evolution based on comparisons with other species would be well advised not to focus solely on the common chimpanzee, the apes, or even the primates; nor should they pick and choose a comparator species from any single taxon. Rather, we recommend that they utilize the full power of the modern comparative method, complete with its sophisticated statistical tools (Harvey and Pagel 1991), harnessing both homology and analogy to maximal effect. In this chapter we endeavour to illustrate each of these approaches, focusing on studies of social learning and cultural transmission in animals. We suggest that non-primates can make, and indeed have made, a valid contribution using both of these approaches.

Use of Model Species

The Concept of 'Model Species'

Model organisms are species that are studied by scientists hoping to further understanding of wider biological phenomena relevant to a range of species, including humans. Of course, different model organisms are used to answer different biological questions, but most have some features in common. These include ready availability and short generation times (to enable scientists to make use of large sample sizes and experimental replication), along with being relatively easy to maintain and manipulate in a controlled experimental setting.

The use of model organisms in such fields as medicine, developmental biology and genetics is well established. For instance, the African clawed frog (*Xenopus laevis*), which produces large embryos with a high tolerance for physical and pharmacological manipulation, has proven to be a useful study species for addressing questions about vertebrate development (Jones 2005); while the single-celled yeast (*Saccharomyces cerevisiae*) is frequently used as a tool for investigating the genetic control of cellular processes (Fields and Johnston 2005).

Just as these species have thrown light on human cell functioning and embryological development, so may the study of behaviour in selected animal species (including rats, pigeons and sticklebacks) provide us with insights into cultural transmission. We can use them, for instance, to illuminate our understanding of how information flows through populations, as well as to investigate the occurrence of various 'types' of social learning, and social learning 'strategies'. Of course, if human social learning was completely different from that of other animals, any insights that model species could offer would be limited. However, as evidence suggests that this is far from the case, model species may well be of considerable use.

The Problem with Primates

When seeking to understand the evolutionary history of the processes involved in human cultural transmission – and what, if anything, makes us 'unique' – researchers can look not only at humans, but at other animals. Primates, being our closest relatives, may be the obvious choice. However, studying them – and obtaining firm evidence of their capacity for social information transfer – is often not easy. Different populations of wild chimpanzees, for example, are known to exhibit differences in their behavioural repertoires, the best-known of which is perhaps the distinct tool-using patterns seen in different groups (Whiten et al. 1999; Boesch 2003; Whiten et al. 2003). Some or all of these may be socially learnt: chimpanzees are undoubtedly capable of social learning (Whiten and Custance 1996), and experiments with captive populations have shown that, when different groups are 'seeded' with a demonstrator trained to solve a foraging task using a particular method, other members of the group acquire and maintain the same method of solving it as that of their demonstrator (Hopper et al. 2007; Whiten et al. 2007; Horner and de Waal 2009). With respect to wild chimpanzees, however, there is no irrefutable evidence that the distinct behaviour seen in groups living at different sites can be attributed to social rather than genetic or ecological factors.

Take the process of chimpanzee 'ant dipping' as an illustration. Chimpanzees at one African study site (Gombe) collect ants to eat by holding a long 'wand' (stick) in one hand and wiping a ball of ants off it with the other (the 'pull through' method), while those at another site (Taï) use a 'direct mouthing' technique, whereby a short stick held in one hand is used to catch a smaller number of ants, which are then transferred straight to the mouth. A number of researchers (Boesch and Boesch 1990; McGrew 1992; Whiten et al. 1999) contend that this difference cannot be accounted for by ecological variation between the sites, but this is debatable. On studying chimpanzees at a location (Bossou) where both forms of ant dipping are employed, Humle and Matsuzawa (2002) discovered that the technique individuals used to obtain ants was strongly influenced by the nature of their prey, which varied substantially in density and aggressiveness, and suggested that 'chimpanzees could individually be shaped by biting insects to use the strategy that resulted in the fewest bites' (Laland and Hoppitt 2003: 153). Although more recent research (Mobius et al. 2008) has claimed that differences in ant behaviour are probably not sufficient to account for the differences seen in the ant-dipping methods used by chimpanzees at Gombe and Taï, the exact extent to which social learning is responsible for the maintenance of these differences remains ambiguous.

To establish beyond doubt experimentally that a particular group-typical behaviour, such as ant dipping, is underpinned by social learning, and is not the result of genetic pre-programming or ecological influences on asocial learning processes, two manipulations are necessary. Firstly, a sample of individuals from one group must be transferred to another, preferably at a formative age. Should they adopt the form of the behaviour common to their new group, genetic causes of group behavioural differences can be discounted. Next, the populations in question must be collectively removed from their respective environments and transferred to one another's former habitats. Should they continue to exhibit group-typical behaviour that is different from that of the area's former residents, environmental influences can be rejected as being responsible for asocially shaping the actions of the group's members. Social learning will then remain as the only feasible explanation of the variation in different populations' behaviour (Laland and Hoppitt 2003).

Unfortunately, logistic and ethical considerations prevent this sort of experiment being conducted on chimpanzees (Laland and Hoppitt 2003; Whiten et al. 2007), or for that matter on most other primates; which means that if we want to find incontrovertible evidence of the existence of social information transfer resulting in group-specific behaviours in wild non-human animals ('culture' in its most basic sense), we must consider more distantly related species.

Model Species and Insights into Information Flow through Populations

One of the most elegant demonstrations to date of socially trans-mitted information determining group behaviour comes not from primates, but from fish. Using the translocation protocol described above, Helfman and Schultz (1984) were able to show that French grunts (*Haemulon flavolineatum*) – a smaller, less endangered, and much more easily moved species than chimpanzees – taken from one population and introduced to another, adopted the same schooling sites and migration routes as the already-present residents. Not only this, but control fish moved to locations from which residents had been removed, did *not* adopt the same behaviour as their former oc-cupants. Thus, Helfman and Schultz were able to conclude that infor-mation about schooling sites and migration routes must be socially transmitted between shoal-mates, rather than being environmen-tally controlled or genetically encoded. Warner (1988) carried out similar experiments on Bluehead Wrasse, again finding compelling evidence that local traditions are reliant on social learning, and per-sist for longer than the lifetime of an individual fish. Cross-fostering experiments in birds have proven equally effective. Norton-Griffiths (1967) cross-fostered oystercatcher offspring amongst groups of birds exhibiting two different foraging techniques, finding that the birds acquired their adoptive parents' behaviour. Strikingly, Slagsvold and Wiebe (2007) cross-fostered blue tits and great tits, and once again found that young birds acquired the dietary traditions of their foster parents, even though these were different species. This is a powerful illustration of the potency of cultural transmission in nature.

Experimenting on model species in a still more controlled setting – that of the laboratory – can provide illuminating details about what factors are important in the spread of social information through pop-ulations. Boogert et al. (2006, 2008) investigated the extent to which the spread of innovations in captive groups of starlings (*Sturnus vul-garis*) could be predicted by knowledge of association patterns, social rank orders, asocial learning abilities and individuals' responses to novel stimuli (neophobia). Each group was presented with six different novel foraging tasks, all containing mealworm 'rewards'. Individual tasks were presented repeatedly over one to two days, and all birds' interactions with, and solutions (defined as successful acquisition of a mealworm) to, a task were recorded. These data were then related to previously recorded measures of association, social rank, individual learning capacity and neophobia using linear models. It was found that the birds that tended to contact and solve the tasks first were those that were least hesitant to feed in the proximity of novel objects when tested in isolation, and that performed best during tests of asocial learning. They were also generally of a high competitive rank.

Boogert et al. (2008) detected a significant negative correlation between the latency of a bird contacting a task, and the length of time that elapsed before it subsequently solved the task. In other words, birds that did not begin to interact with tasks until later on in a given set of trials typically required less time to solve them than did those that approached them earlier. This was not the case in trials where the starlings were tested alone (i.e. isolated birds that took longer initially to interact with a task were no quicker at solving it once they *did* contact it, than were those that interacted with it after less of a delay). Together, these results suggested that birds that were slower to contact tasks when they were presented in a group context benefited from the opportunity to observe group-mates' task-solving demonstrations, reducing the time they themselves needed to solve the tasks once they began interacting with them (Day 2003) – an interpretation that was substantiated when network-based diffusion analyses were later applied to the data (Hoppitt et al. 2010).

Model species can also be used in the development of new experimental and analytical techniques for detecting the social transmission of information through populations. Kendal et al. (2009b) proposed the 'option-bias' method as a means of inferring the occurrence of social learning during the spread of a behaviour through a group. This method relies on the premise that, once genetic and ecological factors have been accounted for, and once alternative sources of bias (chance or asocial learning) have been ruled out on probabilistic grounds, social learning should result in greater behavioural homogeneity than would otherwise be expected. If, for instance, a task can potentially be solved in several ways, but most or all of the members of a group solve it in the same way as did the original 'innovator', this will provide strong evidence for social learning.

In one of several tests to validate the ability of the option-bias method to detect social learning, Kendal et al. (2009a) re-analysed data gathered by Coolen et al. (2003) on a species of freshwater fish, the nine-spined stickleback (*Pungitius pungitius*). This species is known to use social information, being sensitive to information conveyed by the actions of conspecifics, and even hetero-specifics (Coolen et al. 2003). In the particular experiment assessed by Kendal et al. (2009a), sticklebacks were allowed to observe demonstrator conspecifics feeding at two food patches of differing profitabilities. The number of visits they made to each patch over the ten minutes immediately after the demonstrators had been removed was recorded. Observer fish made significantly more visits to the 'richer' demonstrated patch than to the 'poor' patch, clear evidence for 'public information use'. Analysis using the option-bias method corroborated this, showing that nine-spined sticklebacks exhibited much more homogeneous patch choice behaviour than would be predicted by chance or asocial learning. In principle, these methods can also be applied to human data, and archaeologists and anthropologists are beginning to do so.

Model Species and Social Learning 'Strategies'

Sticklebacks are also proving to be a useful model species with which to investigate social learning 'strategies'. Evolutionary game theory and population genetic models predict that animals should not be indiscriminate with regards to when they copy others as opposed to relying on their own experience or asocial learning (Boyd and Richerson 1985; Rogers 1998; Giraldeau et al. 2002). Rather, they should exploit social information conditionally, according to evolved rules, or 'strategies' (Laland 2004).

Studies conducted on nine-spined sticklebacks strongly support these predictions. As described above, sticklebacks have been shown to be capable of 'public information use', extracting (and acting upon) information about the quality of food patches through observation of others' behaviour (Coolen et al. 2005). They also weight information by time, ignoring social cues if they have up-to-date and reliable knowledge of their own, but switching to exploiting public information if their personal information is outdated, unreliable, or altogether lacking (van Bergen et al. 2004; Coolen et al. 2005) – an example of a 'copy when uncertain' strategy. By relying preferentially on personal information, and utilizing social information selectively, nine-spines are able to avoid the potentially maladaptive informational cascades that could result from blindly copying the activity of others who may themselves not be behaving optimally (Giraldeau et al. 2002). Humans have also been shown to employ a similar strategy during computer-based tasks. McElreath et al. (2005) designed a task in which subjects could repeatedly plant one of two 'crops' of differing yields. Reliance on information from group-mates was found to increase when individual learning was manipulated to be relatively inaccurate, confirming use of the 'copy when uncertain' rule. Similarly, across a range of tasks, Morgan et al. (2011) found subjects were more reliant on social information when they expressed greater uncertainty in their own ability.

Another instance of humans and sticklebacks employing functionally similar (albeit, mechanistically different) social learning strategies is in the case of a 'copy when asocial learning is costly' strategy. Individual learning via direct sampling of the environment, although usually accurate, can incur significant fitness costs in the form of injury, predation, and 'missed opportunities' (loss of time or energy that could have been spent elsewhere). Boyd and Richerson's (1985) 'costly information hypothesis' proposes that animals face an evolutionary trade-off between acquiring accurate but costly 'personal' information, and less accurate but cheap 'social' information. One way in which this trade-off might be expected to manifest itself is by individuals being more inclined to exploit social information when personal information is costly. Sure enough, Coolen et al. (2003) demonstrated that nine-spined sticklebacks comply with this rule, finding that these fish prefer to shelter in vegetation (where they are presumably at less risk of predation) and base their choice of foraging patch on information gained through watching feeding conspecifics, than to sample the foraging patches for themselves before making a choice. Conversely, three-spined sticklebacks did not exhibit evidence for public information use, a finding thought to be related to their lesser vulnerability to predation (see below). In the case of humans, Morgan et al. (2011) found that individuals were more likely to copy the actions of group-mates when asocial information was manipulated to be additionally costly and when faced with a difficult (presumably time- and energy-consuming) task than when presented with an easy one, offering further evidence of the 'copy when asocial learning is costly' strategy in use.

Sticklebacks have also been found to employ one of three equally efficient strategies proposed by theoretical economist Karl Schlag (1998) as a means by which individuals (Schlag actually had humans in mind) might maximize their fitness in an environment where the success of others is unreliable and noisy. Schlag's three alternatives were 'proportional observation', 'proportional reservation', and 'proportional imitation'. In the first of these, an individual's probability of copying others in its population is related to the payoff it perceives *them* to be receiving from whatever activity they are performing; in the second, it is related to how satisfied the individual is with *its own* payoff; and in the third, an individual's propensity to copy is related to how much better other members of the population are doing *relative to it*. In experiments designed to test which, if any, of these strategies nine-spined sticklebacks employed when in a 'noisy' environment, Pike et al. (2010) found strong evidence that fish exhibited an increasing propensity to copy demonstrators as the demonstrators' payoffs rose (i.e. they adhered to the strategy of 'proportional observation'). Concerning humans, Morgan et al. (2011) found evidence for 'proportional observation' with conditional 'proportional imitation'.

Schlag's analyses (1998, 1999) reveal that this simple strategy possesses 'hill-climbing' properties. Thus the use of this rule by these fish may plausibly enable sticklebacks to exhibit cumulative increases in the efficiency with which they exploit prey. The deployment of a behavioural rule that has a possible 'ratcheting' quality has hitherto not been demonstrated in any animal other than humans, and it is interesting that the first demonstration of such a rule should come not from a fellow primate, but from a species so distantly related to us as the nine-spined stickleback.

Model Species and Different Social Learning Processes

The social transmission of information from one individual to another can occur by a number of means (for comprehensive reviews of the topic, see Whiten and Ham 1992; Heyes 1994; Zentall 1996; Hoppitt and Laland 2008). Suffice to say here that there are several known mechanisms and certain forms of 'copying' that are widely believed to be more cognitively demanding than others. 'Local enhancement' (Thorpe 1963; Hoppitt and Laland 2008), for example, occurs when a 'demonstrator's' interactions with objects at a particular location increase the probability of an 'observer' visiting or interacting with objects at that location, and is considered to be a relatively simple form of social learning. At the opposite end of the spectrum, 'production imitation' (Byrne 2002), which involves an observer seeing a demonstrator perform a novel act, sequence of acts, or combination of acts, and subsequently becoming more likely to perform that new act or sequence of acts, is generally thought to require quite complex cognition.

It is tempting to speculate that what may set human, and to some extent ape, cultural transmission apart from other animals, is our capacity for such cognitively complex, high-fidelity forms of social information transfer as imitation. Once again, however, evidence from experiments with model species reminds us that we must be cautious about making these assumptions. Some of the best available evidence of motor imitation in non-human animals has in fact been produced using birds. Akins and Zentall (1996) found strong evidence of body-movement copying by captive quail during 'two-action' tests in which birds were shown a demonstrator using either its beak or foot to depress a lever, and then allowed to interact with the lever themselves. Both pigeons (McGregor et al. 2006) and budgerigars (Dawson and Foss 1965; Heyes and Saggerson 2002) have been shown to possess similar abilities. Furthermore, there is some indication that quail are even capable of outcome-sensitive imitation, since they are less inclined to copy their demonstrators when they observe them pecking or stepping in extinction – i.e. without reward (Akins and Zentall 1998).

Summary

We advocate the use of model species in comparative studies, on three grounds. First, we have argued that the strength of homology lies in the use of multiple species, and expressed the concern that studies that limit themselves to our closest relatives may only observe a small part of the overall picture, which may be misleading. Second, we point out that model species are, by definition, amenable to experimental manipulation, and can provide rigorous and detailed information about the spread of information through populations. Finally, we have shown that studies using non-primates can yield real insights into human culture. Experimental methods and analytical techniques that are successfully developed using model organisms can later be applied to other species, including humans, in less controlled settings. The 'option-bias' method of Kendal et al. (2009b) is an example, being adopted for use in studies on human archaeological remains; while methods such as those used by Boogert et al. (2006, 2008) in their studies of captive starlings, could potentially be applied in the field to detect social transmission of behaviours in some of our close relatives, such as chimpanzees. We now go on to consider analogy, a second comparative approach that provides another investigative avenue and equally compelling results.

Non-human Animals and Functional Parallels: Insights from Non-homologous Processes

Convergent Selection for Cultural Transmission

What studies of social learning in non-primates rapidly make clear is that there is no linear, or even continuous, accumulation of cultural transmission mechanisms across species. In fact, the opposite appears to be the case, with multiple appearances of different mechanisms and often great disparity between closely related species. For example, as detailed above, although the nine-spined stickleback shows complex cultural transmission, the closely related three-spined stickleback, despite living sympatrically to the nine-spined, possesses comparatively very simple cultural transmission and appears to be incapable of public information use (Coolen et al. 2003). Such differences between closely related species may be the norm rather than the exception with regards to cultural transmission, and imply repeated bouts of convergent selection favouring cultural capabilities, and animal intelligence generally, as recently reported in primates (Reader et al. In Press).

This patchy distribution is manifest across different cultural transmission mechanisms, including those historically held to be cognitively complex, such as teaching (Hoppitt et al. 2008). Studies of animal teaching most commonly adopt the functional definition set out by Caro and Hauser (1992: 153), which states that:

> An individual actor A can be said to teach if it modifies its behaviour only in the presence of a naive observer, B, at some cost or at least without obtaining an immediate benefit for itself. A's behaviour thereby encourages or punishes B's behaviour, or provides B with experience, or sets an example for B. As a result, B acquires knowledge or learns a skill earlier in life or more rapidly or efficiently than it might otherwise do, or that it would not learn at all.

A key aspect of this definition is that it does not require the inference of any mental states in either the teacher or the pupil. Although this might seem surprising from a human perspective, where the intention to impart information is part of teaching, functional definitions are critically important to biologists as they make testable predictions due to the intense difficulty of attributing mental states to animals. It should also be noted that this definition encompasses all examples of human teaching. Perhaps more surprising, however, is that the three species in which there is currently the strongest evidence for teaching are meerkats (Thornton and McAuliffe 2006), pied babblers (Raihani and Ridley 2008) and the ant (*Temnothorax albipennis*) (Franks and Richardson 2006).

The extremely scattered distribution of cultural transmission mechanisms suggests that if we wish to piece together anything approaching a complete phylogeny we would need to perform an exhaustive investigation across a broad range of animal taxa. This endeavour would be both expensive and of debatable value. The patchy distribution instead opens up a new avenue of investigation, allowing us to consider why certain species might possess particular capabilities while others do not, and focusing not at the level of homologous mechanism but rather on analogous functionally equivalent traits.

The case of the sticklebacks provides one such opportunity, since it suggests that natural selection fashions highly specific cultural capabilities in particular species of animals, according to their ecology and life-history. The three-spined and nine-spined species live sympatrically, occupying the same areas, however there must be something different in their ecologies that leads to one species and not the other evolving the ability to use public information. During experiments on both species, Coolen et al. (2003) observed that only the nine-spined sticklebacks hid in vegetation whilst observing conspecifics. They concluded that this was to decrease the risk of predation, something that is less important for three-spined as they are protected by much larger spines and a heavily armoured torso. This is supported by evidence of predator preference for nine-spined over three-spined sticklebacks (Hoogland et al. 1957). Coolen at al. (2003) suggest that nine-spined sticklebacks evolved the ability to use public information as it avoids the risks of examining patch quality directly. The lower predation risk to three-spined sticklebacks removed this necessity and so seemingly they never required this ability. The aforementioned study implies that, while the broad capability for social learning is widespread across animals, particular species may be gifted with enhanced cultural capabilities by selection, tailored to their particular needs, in an extremely species-specific manner. Rather than expecting broad groups, such as primates, to excel at culture, we would be better placed asking which specific groups (i.e. macaques, capuchins, chimpanzees) excel. Conversely, we are likely to find that many primates (e.g. gibbons, langurs, bushbabies) are unexceptional in their cultural capabilities, and witness superior performance to these amongst non-primates.

Animal teaching provides a case in point. The seemingly bizarre taxonomic distribution of teaching has prompted discussion of what life-history traits might facilitate its evolution (Hoppitt et al. 2008). Although these examples of animal teaching are undoubtedly mechanistically dissimilar to human teaching, they are functionally equivalent and solve analogous problems. It follows that a knowledge of the selective pressures driving the evolution of teaching in animal species may shed light on the evolution of teaching in humans. Franks and Richardson (2006) examined teaching in ants, which takes the form of 'tandem-running', by which one individual teaches another the location of a food source such that it can then be harvested at a greater rate. To do this, the teaching ant slows its movement to a quarter of its typical speed and only proceeds when its following pupil catches up and taps it with their antennae. The pupil regularly runs in loops behind the teacher, identifying landmarks to aid in successful recall of the route later. Although this process impacts upon the teachers collecting efficiency, it increases the chance of others finding the food source and thereby aids the colony. Not all ant species, however, show tandem-running, others instead use the scent trails left by other individuals to locate food sources. By comparing colonies it was found that tandem-running occurs in those with smaller populations. Franks and Richardson (ibid.) argued that in these smaller groups information on food location is more likely to be lost when using just scent trails and this creates a pressure to actively pass knowledge between individuals leading to the evolution of teaching. This is confirmed by another study (Beekman et al. 2001) that found that ants were only able to use scent trails to forage effectively when their colony was over a critical size.

In the case of teaching, comparisons between dissimilar, but closely related species (as with the ants) are supplemented by studies looking for common features across the species that show teaching. From this perspective it has been argued that teaching should be viewed as a special case of cooperation (Thornton and Raihani 2008) and should therefore obey Hamilton's Rule, which states that cooperation will occur if the cost to the teacher is less than the benefit to the pupil, scaled by the relatedness between the two individuals. By this account, teaching should be more likely to appear where naïve individuals cannot easily acquire information or skills without the aid of a teacher. This is illustrated with teaching in meerkats, whereby adults educate young in the process of successfully catching and killing dangerous scorpions (Thornton and McAuliffe 2006). This is achieved by the adults catching scorpions for the young and bringing them first dead, then alive but stingless, and finally unaltered. Youngsters progress through these stages as they age, and the adults gauge the age of the young by the calls they make. Meerkats taught in this way show much better performance when catching scorpions for themselves. The danger posed by catching potentially lethal prey creates a problem of sufficient difficulty that the benefits of modifying prey to help youngsters learn outweighs the cost of the teacher having to sacrifice caught prey, even when the degree of relatedness between the two individuals is taken into account. These findings are backed up by theoretical analyses, which found that the evolution of teaching critically depends on both the degree of problem difficulty and the relatedness between individuals (Fogarty et al. 2011). The rare incidents of animal teaching appear disproportionately to occur amongst cooperative breeding species (Hoppitt et al. 2008). This may be no coincidence, since cooperative breeders frequently exhibit close relatedness amongst tutor and pupil, and multiple tutors share the burden of teaching, reducing its per capita cost. As humans too have been characterized as cooperative breeders (Hrdy 1999), conceivably this was a critical factor leading to the appearance of teaching in humans, uniquely amongst the apes.

In summary, teaching, widely assumed to require complex cognitive ability, appears in a diverse array of species not otherwise known for complex intelligence. Its otherwise conspicuous absence from our closest relatives can be explained, however, through consideration of relevant ecological and life-history factors. This suggests that such processes are not necessarily cognitive achievements, but are better viewed as solutions to particular problems faced by a subset of species. It is, in fact, the scarcity of conditions where a cost–benefit analysis favours investment in costly cultural transmission processes that dictates the rarity of the mechanism and creates the patchy distribution we observe.

Human Convergence

What does this imply for human culture? Were our ancestors merely in the right place at the right time, as it were, to face the environmental conditions necessary for the evolution of human-level culture? Furthermore, if cultural transmission can apparently be divorced from cognitive complexity, then why are humans both the most cognitively and culturally complex species on earth? We suspect that the answer to this lies in the peculiarities of human culture and cultural transmission, which is indeed distinct from that of the other animals discussed before in that it shows a high level of fidelity in information transfer (Tomasello 1994). Just as nine-spined sticklebacks were distinct from three-spined sticklebacks in that they could use cultural transmission to determine not only food location but also quality, humans are distinct from other apes in their ability to transfer information with very high fidelity across numerous generations. This is most apparent in the steady elaboration of behaviour and ideas to create improvements to existing technology – the 'ratchet effect'. This cumulative culture is typically illustrated with the progression from early stone hammering tools, through hand-held hafted hammers with metal heads, through to nineteenth-century steam hammers and twentieth-century electric hammers, though its impact is ubiquitous across human culture.

Perhaps then, if we are interested in human culture, we should focus our attention on the processes that underlie cumulative culture. It might appear that cumulative culture is as unique as human-level culture, with isolated reports of cumulative culture in wild chimpanzees (Boesch 2003) failing to be backed by experimental studies (Marshall-Pescini and Whiten 2008). However, if we broaden our scope beyond primates we again encounter species that show greater similarity to us than our nearest relatives. Evidence for cumulative culture has been suggested in cetaceans, the group comprising whales and dolphins. The appearance in humpback whales of 'lobtail' feeding, an elaboration of 'bubble-cloud' feeding that allowed greater use of a pre-existing food source, has been argued as suggestive of cumulative modification (Rendell and Whitehead 2001). However, the best evidence, outside of humans, probably comes from the corvids, a group of birds comprising crows, ravens and jays, among others. New Caledonian crows are known tool users (Hunt 1995) and use tools cut from the leaves of the *Pandanus* plant in extractive foraging. Cumulative culture has been argued in the design of these leaf tools (Hunt and Gray 2003), with three designs known across the island inhabited by the species that show continuous and overlapping ranges. The lack of an environmental correlate and the similarity in the manufacture of the three designs is highly suggestive of a single origin of leaf-tool manufacture that later elaborated and diversified through a cumulative process.

If we apply a similar logic to before, the similarities between apes and corvids should reveal insights into why these species show cultural transmission processes that allow the cumulative modification of culturally transmitted information. Although having separated over 300 million years ago and being morphologically very dissimilar, both corvids and apes show a remarkable cognitive similarity that has led some to describe corvids as 'feathered apes' (Emery 2004; Emery and Clayton 2004). As well as tool use, both groups are thought to show complex physical cognition (Seed et al. 2006; Mulcahy and Call 2006), episodic-like memory (Clayton et al. 2007) and are also capable of transitive inference, the ability to infer that if $A > B$ and $B > C$, then $A > C$ (Paz-y-miño et al. 2004), an ability which has also been found in cichlid fish (Grosenick et al. 2007). Corvids are also capable of mirror self-recognition (Gallup 1970; Prior et al. 2008) and show at least as much evidence as chimpanzees for theory of mind – the ability to understand that other individuals have goals and beliefs that are distinct from your own and may be false (Clayton et al. 2007) – although others would argue that this amounts to no evidence at all (Penn and Povinelli 2007). Thus it seems that the similarities between corvids and apes add up to a complex general intelligence of which cumulative cultural transmission, if present, is only a part. If we wish to understand why we have cumulative culture, we must also ask why we have an enhanced intellect more generally.

Unsurprisingly, the evolution of intelligence has received a great amount of attention, although it is still far from resolution. An influential theory is that of the social intelligence hypothesis, the notion that intelligence evolved in order to deal with the problems associated with group living (Humphrey 1976). This continues to receive attention today (Dunbar 2003; Bond et al. 2003). However, although there is much support, it is also clear that the social intelligence hypothesis alone cannot explain the evolution of intelligence (Holekamp 2006). Hyaenas, for example, although socially as complex as many primates, possess a much lesser intelligence, which cannot be accounted for by the social intelligence hypothesis (ibid.). Seed et al.

(2009) reasoned that as both apes and corvids show increased intelligence then shared environmental and life-history traits would provide evidence as to the driving force behind their cognitive abilities. Their review of six of the most commonly raised hypotheses found that all were applicable to corvids as well as primates. Both groups, for example, feed on spatiotemporally dispersed resources. Apes show an increased reliance on tropical plant foods, because as there are no seasons in the tropics each species fruits at a different time of year. To forage effectively apes need to keep track of both the location of plants of different species and also to know when fruit will be available from them. Similarly, many corvids cache food, burying items for later consumption. Experiments have shown that not only are corvids highly efficient at remembering the location of food caches, they also take into account the perishability of food items and so know when to return to them (Clayton and Dickinson 1998) – this provides a spatiotemporally dispersed food source, just as faced by apes. Seed et al. (2009) examined other 'physical' factors and found that omnivory, extractive foraging, complex foraging and tool use were common to both groups. They then considered 'social' factors and found that, again, both groups showed Machiavellian behavioural strategies, cooperation, coordination and complex cultural transmission. Although it may be tempting, from the perspective of this chapter, to place emphasis on the final shared factor – complex cultural transmission – this would be exceedingly premature. The common ground between the two groups adds up to a suite of complex challenges and behaviours to match them, of which cultural transmission is only one. Currently all these factors seem equally implicated in the origins of a complex intelligence capable of generating human culture.

Conclusion

It is through the two routes of homology and analogy that non-primate animals are able to increase our understanding of cultural transmission. The use of non-primate model organisms, selected for their suitability to experimentation, provides an amenable, powerful and cost-effective method to investigate cultural transmission processes. These species also allow the development of powerful statistical tools that can, and are, being used in studies of cultural transmission in other species, including humans. Furthermore, work with model organisms, even if not conducted with the specific view to answering human-related questions, is of use in broadening our general understanding of social learning processes, and in increasing our appreciation of the capabilities of animals that may be only very distantly related to us. The use of analogy in addition to homology through comparisons between species, either close relatives that show disparity, or distant relatives that show convergence, allows investigation of the different factors that drive the evolution of cultural transmission processes. The role of these studies in understanding the evolution of human cultural transmission does not rely on common mechanisms, as they represent separately derived solutions to the same problems. Whilst such comparisons suggest that many mechanisms, including teaching, need not be cognitively complex and are best considered within an evolutionary cost–benefit framework, they also reveal that human cultural transmission and cumulative culture seem tied in with an overall complex intellect. Thus, whilst work carried out with non-primates both reinforces and refines the uniqueness of human cultural transmission, it also reveals the wealth of information that non-primates offer and the necessity of their study if we are to gain a complete understanding of culture.

Acknowledgements

Research supported in part by an ERC Advanced Grant to KNL (EVOCULTURE 232823).

References

Akins, C.K. and T.R. Zentall. 1996. 'Imitative Learning in Male Japanese Quail Using the Two-action Method', *Journal of Comparative Psychology* 110: 316–20.

Akins, C.K. and T.R. Zentall. 1998. 'Imitation in Japanese Quail: The Role of Demonstrator Reinforcement', *Psychonomic Bulletin and Review* 5: 694–97.

Beekman, M., D. Sumpter and F. Ratnieks. 2001. 'Phase Transition Between Disordered and Ordered Foraging in Pharaoh's Ants', *Proceedings of the National Academy of Sciences* 98: 9703–6.

Bergen, Y. van, J. Coolen and K.N. Laland. 2004. 'Nine-spined Sticklebacks Exploit the Most Reliable Source when Public and Private Information Conflict', *Proceedings of the Royal Society of London B* 271: 957–62.

Boesch, C. 2003. 'Is Culture a Golden Barrier between Human and Chimpanzee?', *Evolutionary Anthropology* 12: 82–91.

Boesch, C. and H. Boesch. 1990. 'Tool Use and Tool Making in Wild Chimpanzees', *Folia Primatologica* 54: 86–99.

Bond, A.B., A.C. Kamil and R.P. Balda. 2003. 'Social Complexity and Transitive Inference in Corvids', *Animal Behaviour* 65: 479–87.

Boogert, N.J., S.M. Reader, W. Hoppitt and K.N. Laland. 2008. 'The Origin and Spread of Innovation in Starlings', *Animal Behaviour* 75: 1509–18.

Boogert, N.J., S.M. Reader and K.N. Laland. 2006. 'The Relation between Social Rank, Neophobia and Individual Learning in Starlings', *Animal Behaviour* 72: 1229–39.

Boyd, R. and P.J. Richerson. 1985. *Culture and the Evolutionary Process.* Chicago: University of Chicago Press.

Byrne, R.W. 2002. 'Imitation of Novel Complex Actions: What Does the Evidence from Animals Mean?', *Advances in the Study of Behavior* 31: 31–77.

Caro, T.M. and M.D. Hauser. 1992. 'Is There Teaching in Nonhuman Animals?', *The Quarterly Review of Biology* 67: 151–74.

Clayton, N.S., J.M. Dally and N.J. Emery. 2007. 'Social Cognition by Food-catching Corvids: The Western Scrub Jay as a Natural Psychologist', *Philosophical Transactions of the Royal Society of London, Series B* 362: 507–22.

Clayton, N.S. and A. Dickinson. 1998. 'Episodic-like Memory during Cache Recovery by Scrub Jays', *Nature* 395: 272–74.

Clutton-Brock, T.H. and P.H. Harvey. 1984. 'Comparative Approaches to Investigating Adaption', in J.R. Krebs and N.B. Davies (eds), *Behavioural Ecology*. Oxford: Blackwell, pp. 7–29.

Coolen, I., Y. van Bergen, R.L. Day and K.N. Laland. 2003. 'Species Difference in Adaptive Use of Public Information in Sticklebacks', *Proceedings of the Royal Society of London B* 270: 2413–19.

Coolen, I., A.J.W. Ward, P.I.B. Hart and K.N. Laland. 2005. 'Foraging Nine-spined Sticklebacks Prefer to Rely on Public Information over Simpler Social Cues', *Behavioral Ecology* 16: 865–70.

Cullen, E. 1957. 'Adaptations in the Kittiwake to Cliff-nesting', *Ibis* 99: 275–302.

Dawson, B.V. and B.M. Foss. 1965. 'Observational Learning in Budgerigars', *Animal Behaviour* 13: 470–74.

Day, R.L. 2003. 'Innovation and Social Learning in Monkeys and Fish: Empirical Findings and their Application to Reintroduction Techniques', Ph.D. thesis, University of Cambridge.

Dunbar, R.I.M. 1995. 'Neocortex Size and Group Size in Primates: A Test of the Hypothesis', *Journal of Human Evolution* 28: 287–96.

_____.2003. 'The Social Brain: Mind, Language, and Society in Evolutionary Perspective', *Annual Review of Anthropology* 32: 163–81.

Dunbar, R.I.M. and J. Bever. 1998. 'Neocortex Size Predicts Group Size in Carnivores and Some Insectivores', *Ethology* 104: 695–708.

Durham, W.H. 1991. *Co-evolution: Genes, Culture and Human Diversity.* Stanford: Stanford University Press.

Emery, N.J. 2004. 'Are Corvids "Feathered Apes"? Cognitive Evolution in Crows, Jays, Rooks and Jackdaws', in S. Watanabe (ed.) *Comparative Analysis of Minds.* Tokyo: Keio University Press, pp. 181–213.

Emery, N.J. and N.S. Clayton. 2004. 'The Mentality of Crows: Convergent Evolution of Intelligence in Corvids and Apes', *Science* 306: 1903–7.

Fields, S. and M. Johnston. 2005. 'Cell Biology: Whither Model Organism Research?', *Science* 307: 1885–86.

Franks, N.R. and T. Richardson. 2006. 'Teaching in Tandem-running Ants', *Nature* 439: 153.

Gallup, G.G. 1970. 'Chimpanzees: Self-recognition', *Science* 167: 86–87.

Giraldeau, L.A., T.J. Valone and J.J. Templeton. 2002. 'Potential Disadvantages of Using Socially Acquired Information', *Philosophical Transactions of the Royal Society of London, Series B* 357: 1559–66.

Grosenick, L., T. Clement and R. Fernald. 2007. 'Fish can Infer Social Rank by Observation Alone', *Nature* 445: 429–32.

Fogarty, L., P. Strimling, and K.N. Laland. 2011. 'The Evolution of Teaching', *Evolution* 65(10): 2760–70.

Harvey, P.H. and M.D. Pagel. 1991. *The Comparative Method in Evolutionary Biology.* Oxford: Oxford University Press.

Helfman, G.S. and E.T. Schultz. 1984. 'Social Tradition of Behavioural Traditions in a Coral Reef Fish', *Animal Behaviour* 32: 379–84.

Heyes, C.M. 1994. 'Social Learning in Animals: Categories and Mechanisms', *Biological Reviews* 69: 207–31.

Heyes, C.M. and B.G. Galef Jr. (eds). 1996. *Social Learning and the Roots of Culture.* New York: Academic Press.

Heyes, C.M. and A. Saggerson. 2002. 'Testing for Imitative and Non-imitative Social Learning in the Budgerigar Using a Two-object/Two-action Test', *Animal Behaviour* 64: 851–59.

Holekamp, K.E. 2006. 'Questioning the Social Intelligence Hypothesis', *Trends in Cognitive Sciences* 11: 65–69.

Hoogland, R., D. Morris and N. Tinbergen. 1957. 'The Spines of Sticklebacks (*Gasterosteus* and *Pygosteus*) as Means of Defence against Predators (*Pera* and *Esox*)', *Behaviour* 10: 205–37.

Hopper, L.M., A. Spiteri, S.P. Lambeth, S.J. Schapiro, V. Horner and A. Whiten. 2007. 'Experimental Studies of Traditions and Underlying Transmission Processes in Chimpanzees', *Animal Behaviour* 73: 1021–302.

Hoppitt, W., N.J. Boogert and K.N. Laland. 2010. 'Detecting Social Transmission in Networks', *Journal of Theoretical Biology* 263: 544–55.

Hoppitt, W., G. Brown, R.L. Kendal, L. Rendell, A. Thornton, M. Webster and K.N. Laland. 2008. 'Lessons from Animal Teaching', *Trends in Ecology and Evolution* 23: 486–93.

Hoppitt, W. and K.N. Laland. 2008. 'Social Processes Influencing Learning in Animals: A Review of the Evidence', *Advances in the Study of Behaviour* 38: 105–65.

Horner, V. and F.B.M. de Waal. 2009. 'Controlled Studies of Chimpanzee Cultural Transmission', *Progress in Brain Research* 178: 3–15.

Hrdy, S.B. 1999. *Mother Nature: Maternal Instincts and How They Shape the Human Species.* London: Chatto and Windus.

Humle, T. and T. Matsuzawa. 2002. 'Ant Dipping among the Chimpanzees of Bossou, Guinea, and Some Comparisons with Other Sites', *American Journal of Primatology* 58: 133–48.

Humphrey, N.K. 1976. 'The Social Function of Intellect', in P.P.G. Bateson and R.A. Hinde (eds) *Growing Points in Ethology*. Cambridge: Cambridge University Press, pp. 303–17.

Hunt, G.R. 1995. 'Manufacture and Use of Hook-tools by New Caledonian Crows', *Nature* 379: 249–51.

Hunt, G.R. and R.D. Gray. 2003. 'Diversification and Cumulative Evolution in New Caledonian Crow Tool Manufacture', *Proceedings of the Royal Society B* 270: 867–74.

Jones, E.A. 2005. 'Xenopus: A Prince among Models for Pronephric Kidney Development', *Journal of the American Society of Nephrology* 16: 313–21.

Kendal, J., L. Rendell, T.W. Pike and K.N. Laland. 2009a 'Nine-spined Sticklebacks Deploy a Hill-climbing Social Learning Strategy', *Behavioral Ecology* 20: 238–44.

Kendal, R.L., J.R. Kendal, W. Hoppitt and K.N. Laland. 2009b. 'Identifying Social Learning in Animal Populations: A New 'Option-bias' Method', *PLoS One* 4: 1–9.

Kroeber, A.L. and C. Kluckholm. 1952 'Culture: A Critical Review of the Concepts and Definitions', *Papers of the Peabody Museum of American Archaeology and Ethnology* 47: 1–223.

Laland, K.N. 2004. 'Social Learning Strategies', *Learning and Behavior* 32: 4–14.

Laland, K.N. and B.G. Galef Jr. (eds). 2009. *The Question of Animal Culture*. Cambridge, MA: Harvard University Press.

Laland, K.N. and W.J.E. Hoppitt. 2003. 'Do Animals Have Culture?', *Evolutionary Anthropology* 12: 150–59.

Laland, K.N. and V. Janik. 2006. 'The Animal Cultures Debate', *Trends in Ecology and Evolution* 21: 542–47.

Lefebvre, L., S.M. Reader and D. Sol. 2004. 'Brains, Innovations and Evolution in Birds and Primates', *Brain Behaviour and Evolution* 63: 233–46.

Lovejoy, C.O. 2009. 'Reexamining Human Origins in Light of *Ardipithecus ramidus*', *Science* 326: 74.

Marshall-Pescini, S. and A. Whiten. 2008. 'Chimpanzees (*Pan Troglodytes*) and the Question of Cumulative Culture: An Experimental Approach', *Animal Cognition* 11: 449–56.

McElreath, R., M. Lubell, P.J. Richerson, T. Waring, W. Baum and E. Edsten. 2005. 'Applying Evolutionary Models to the Laboratory Study of Social Learning', *Evolution and Human Behavior* 26: 483–508.

McGregor, A., A. Saggerson, J. Pearce and C. Heyes. 2006. 'Blind Imitation in Pigeons, *Columba livia*', *Animal Behaviour* 72: 287–96.

McGrew, W.C. 1992. *Chimpanzee Material Culture: Implications for Human Evolution*. Cambridge: Cambridge University Press.

Mobius, Y., C. Boesch, K. Koops, T. Matsuzawa and T. Humle. 2008. 'Cultural Differences in Army Ant Predation by West African Chimpanzees? A Comparative Study of Microecological Variables', *Animal Behaviour* 76: 37–45.

Morgan, T., L. Rendell, M. Ehn, W. Hoppitt and K. Laland. 2011. 'The Evolutionary Basis of Human Social Learning', *Proceedings of the Royal Society B* 279: 653–62.

Mulcahy, N.J. and J. Call. 2006. 'How Great Apes Perform on a Modified Trap-tube Test', *Animal Cognition* 9: 193–99.

Norton-Griffiths, M.N. 1967. 'Some Ecological Aspects of the Feeding Behaviour of the Oystercatcher *Haematopus ostralegus* on the Edible Mussel *Mytilus edulis*', *Ibis* 109: 412–24.

Paz-y-miño, G., A.B. Bond, A.C. Kamil and R.P. Balda. 2004. 'Pinyon Jays use Transitive Inference to Predict Social Dominance', *Nature* 430: 778–81.

Penn, D.C. and D.J. Povinelli. 2007. 'On the Lack of Evidence that Non-human Animals Possess Anything Remotely Resembling a "Theory of Mind"', *Philosophical Transactions of the Royal Society of London, Series B* 362: 731–44.

Pike, T.W., J.R. Kendal, L.E. Rendell and K.N. Laland. 2010. 'Learning by Proportional Observation in a Species of Fish', *Behavioral Ecology* 21: 570–75.

Plotkin, H. 1997. *Evolution in Mind: An Introduction to Evolutionary Psychology.* London: Allen Lane.Prior, H., A. Schwarz and O. Gunturkun. 2008. 'Mirror-induced Behavior in the Magpie (*Pica Pica*): Evidence of Self Recognition', *PloS Biology* 6: e202.

Raihani, N.J. and A.R. Ridley. 2008. 'Experimental Evidence for Teaching in Wild Pied Babblers', *Animal Behaviour* 75: 3–11.

Reader, S.M., Y. Hager and K.N. Laland. In Press. 'The Evolution of Primate General Intelligence', *Philosophical Transactions of the Royal Society of London, Series B.*

Rendell, L. and H. Whitehead. 2001. 'Culture in Whales and Dolphins', *Behavioral and Brain Sciences* 24: 309–82.

Rogers, A.R. 1998. 'Does Biology Constrain Culture?', *American Anthropologist* 90: 819–31.

Schlag, K. 1998. 'Why Imitate, and if so, How?', *Journal of Economic Theory* 78: 130–56.

————.1999. 'Which One Should I Imitate?', *Journal of Mathematical Economics* 31: 493–522.

Seed, A.M., N.J. Emery and N.S. Clayton. 2009. 'Intelligence in Corvids and Apes: A Case of Convergent Evolution?', *Ethology* 115: 401–20.

Seed, A.M., S. Tebbich, N.J. Emery and N.S. Clayton. 2006. 'Investigating Physical Cognition in Rooks (*Corvus Frugilegus*)', *Current Biology* 16: 697–701.

Shultz, S. and R.I.M. Dunbar. 2006. 'Both Social and Ecological Factors Predict Ungulate Brain Size', *Proceedings of the Royal Society B* 273: 207–15.

Slagsvold, T. and K.L. Wiebe. 2007. 'Learning the Ecological Niche', *Proceedings of the Royal Society B* 274: 19–23.

Thornton, A. and K. McAuliffe. 2006. 'Teaching in Wild Meerkats', *Science* 313: 227–29.

Thornton, A. and N.J. Raihani. 2008. 'The Evolution of Teaching', *Animal Behaviour* 75: 1823–36.

Thorpe, W. H. 1963. *Learning and Instinct in Animals* (2nd ed.). London: Methuen.

Tinbergen, N. 1963. 'On Aims and Methods in Ethology', *Zeitschrift für Tierpsychologie* 20: 410–33.

Tinbergen, N., G.J. Broekkhuysen, F. Feekes, J.C.W. Houghton, H. Kruuk and E. Szulc. 1962.   'Egg Shell Removal by the Black-headed Gull, *Larus ridibundus* L.: A Behaviour Component of Camouflage', *Behaviour* 19: 74–117.

Tomasello, M. 1994. 'The Question of Chimpanzee Culture', in R. Wrangham, W.C. McGrew, F. de Wall and P. Heltne (eds) *Chimpanzee Cultures*. Harvard: Harvard University Press, pp. 301–17.

Warner, R.R. 1988. 'Traditionality of Mating Site Preferences in a Coral Reef Fish', *Nature* 335: 719–21.

Whiten, A. and D.M. Custance. 1996. 'Studies of Imitation in Chimpanzees and Children', in B.G. Galef Jr. and C.M. Heyes (eds) *Social Learning in Animals: The Roots of Culture*. New York: Academic Press, pp. 291–318.

Whiten, A., J. Goodall, W.C. McGrew, T. Nishida, V. Reynolds, Y. Sugiyama, C.E.G. Tutin, R.W. Wrangham and C. Boesch. 1999. 'Cultures in Chimpanzees', *Nature* 399: 682–85.

Whiten, A. and R. Ham. 1992. 'On the Nature and Evolution of Imitation in the Animal Kingdom: Reappraisal of a Century of Research', *Advances in the Study of Behavior* 21: 239–83.

Whiten, A., V. Horner and S. Marshall-Pescini. 2003. 'Cultural Panthropology', *Evolutionary Anthropology* 12: 92–105.

Whiten, A., A. Spiteri, V. Horner, K.E. Bonnie, S.P. Lambeth, S.J. Schapiro and F. de Waal. 2007. 'Transmission of Multiple Traditions within and between Chimpanzee Groups', *Current Biology* 17: 1038–43.

Zentall, T.R. 1996. 'An Analysis of Imitative Learning in Animals', in C.M. Heyes and B.G. Galef Jr. (eds) *Social Learning in Animals: The Roots of Culture*. New York: Academic Press, pp. 221–34.

Chapter 2

CULTURE IN NON-HUMAN PRIMATES

DEFINITIONS AND EVIDENCE

Tatyana Humle and Nicholas E. Newton-Fisher

Definitions

The attribution of culture to non-human animals has been controversial and continues to fuel much heated debate (Galef 1992; Kendal 2008). Much of this debate hinges on how culture is defined. In 1952, Kroeber and Kluckhohn compiled a comprehensive review of how the term culture had been used in modern times up until the early 1950s. They collated 168 definitions, all implying a human prerogative, and exemplified by Tyler's classic definition of culture as 'that complex whole which includes knowledge, belief, art, morals, custom, and any other capabilities and habits acquired by man as a member of society' (Tyler 1871: 1). Kant (1786) was highly influential in originally formulating this human-centric concept of culture as that 'artifice unique to man which has permitted human beings to escape their natural animality and express their rational [and moral] humanity [... and] their freedom from the laws of nature' (Arnhart 1994: 476). The anthropological concept of culture centres on the idea that culture is learned, rather than biologically inherited, cross-generational, adaptive, and based on systems of arbitrarily assigned meanings that are shared by a society. Anthropological definitions therefore typically refer specifically to the human nature of culture centred on language, symbols, teaching and imitation (Tomasello 1999). Human-centric definitions of culture therefore leave little or no room for understanding the evolutionary origins of human culture. In their strictest sense they also reject the possibility for culture among early hominins: the australopithicines and *Homo habilis* (McGrew 1992; Lycett 2011; see also Lycett, this volume).

The supremacy of *Homo sapiens* in all domains pertaining to material and social intelligence and culture was only challenged a century after Darwin's publication of the *Descent of Man* in 1871. The diversity and complexity of bird songs fascinated and amazed Darwin; based on his extensive travels and observations, he had noted 'that an instinctive tendency to acquire an art is not peculiar to man' (p. 56). Darwin also cited Savage and Wyman (1843–44), stating 'it has often been said that no animal uses any tool; but the chimpanzee in a state of nature cracks a native fruit, somewhat like a walnut, with a stone' (Darwin 1871: 51). Nevertheless, six decades passed before another eminent scientist, the influential American cultural anthropologist Alfred L. Kroeber, would contemplate the possibility of culture in non-human animals, and apes in particular (Kroeber 1928; Kroeber and Kluckhohn 1952). The birth of Japanese primatology in the late 1940s led to the coining of terms such as 'sub-culture' and 'preculture', applied to the descriptions of potato washing among Japanese macaques (*Macaca fuscata*) of Koshima Island (Kawamura 1959: 43). A decade later, Kummer (1971: 11), a Swiss ethologist and behavioural scientist, employed – possibly for the first time – the term 'culture' in relation to non-human animals.

Besides the pioneering studies of Imanishi, Itani and Kawamura (Matsuzawa and McGrew 2008), Goodall's (1973), and McGrew and Tutin's (1978) first reports of behavioural variations among wild chimpanzees (*Pan troglodytes*) in East Africa were milestones in the study of culture in non-human animals. These studies inspired numerous publications on behavioural diversity among wild non-human primates, especially chimpanzees. Cumulatively, these observations led in the late 1990s to the emergence of 'cultural primatology' as a distinct discipline (de Waal 1999).

These studies also paved the way for more encompassing definitions of culture and for a comparative approach to the study of the roots of human culture. The broader definitions employed by many primatologists, biologists, psychologists and anthropologists range from deceptively simple ones such as culture as 'the way we do things' (McGrew 2003: 433) to more operational ones viewing culture as 'all group-typical behaviour patterns, shared by members of animal communities, that are to some degree reliant on socially learned and transmitted information' (Laland and Hoppitt 2003: 151).

Most researchers would agree that culture consists of behaviours that are (a) transmitted within groups, communities or populations via some form of social learning mechanism, (b) temporally maintained across successive generations and (c) vary in their expression or form between social groupings. The perception of culture as 'a system of socially transmitted behaviours' (van Schaik et al. 2003a: 102) stimulated a great deal of interest in the study of behavioural variation and imitative abilities among our closest living relatives – the non-human primates (hereafter, primates), especially the chimpanzee. In parallel, a number of studies revealed the prevalence of socially transmitted behavioural variants across a wide range of taxa including insects, fish, birds and cetaceans (reviewed by Fragaszy and Perry 2003; Lonsdorf and Bonnie 2010; see also Laland, this volume).

A host of experimental studies have shown cultural capacities – social learning and in some cases diffusion of a novel behaviour – in a variety of primate species, from new world monkeys (e.g. cotton-top tamarins *Saguinus oedipus*: Humle and Snowdon 2008; marmosets *Callitrix jacchus*: Voelkl and Huber 2000; capuchins *Sapajus apella*: Dindo et al. 2008) to apes, particularly chimpanzees (reviewed by Whiten et al. 2004; Hopper et al. 2007; Horner 2010; Lonsdorf and Bonnie 2010). Capuchins, and chimpanzees in particular, are capable of transmitting behaviour(s) with a relatively high degree of fidelity along a sequential chain of individuals or even – at least in chimpanzees – between groups (Horner et al. 2006; Hopper et al. 2007). Whether the propensity of chimpanzees and capuchins for culture surpasses that of other primates will likely be clarified as more data emerge from macaques and other species, such as orang-utans (*Pongo* spp.) who exhibit cultural capacities in the wild (van Schaik et al. 2003a, 2003b; Fox et al. 2004; Jaeggi et al. 2007). Such studies have clarified the mechanisms of social learning, and revealed important constraints posed by: the saliency and social relationship of the demonstrator(s) to the naïve individual(s); the possibility for co-action or joint interaction; the type of actions or degree of complexity presented by the task; the presence or absence of food in the experimental design; the duration and frequency of exposure; and the age and sex of the subjects used.

Studies in captivity have contributed markedly to our understanding of the capacity for social learning and transmission of behaviour, but unfortunately they have revealed little about the influences of the physical and social setting on behavioural diffusion and dissemination, and of behavioural interactions between knowledgeable and naïve individuals on the learning trajectory of young. They have also placed much of the emphasis in the identification of culture on the existence of social transmission of a specific, often contrived, behaviour. While this has broadened the species and behaviours that have been considered 'cultural', it arguably weakens the usefulness of comparative studies in understanding the evolutionary origins of human culture.

The attribution of differences in behavioural patterns to culture in wild primates has been critiqued for failing to consider more parsimonious explanations (Galef 1992; Tomasello 1999; Ingold 2001; Laland and Janik 2006; Laland, Cowie and Morgan, this volume). The critics maintain that none of the reported putative cultural variants among wild primates can irrefutably be attributed to social learning rather than genetic or environmental factors. It is the case that translocation experiments of a kind necessary to refute categorically environmental and genetic influences in explaining observed variations in behaviour (e.g. Helfman and Schultz 1984; see Laland, Cowie and Morgan, this volume) are typically not feasible for field primatologists, in part for ethical reasons. The extended life-histories of primates, especially among great apes, also pose considerable logistical difficulties that constrain our ability to infer culture and to investigate patterns of transmission and maintenance of behavioural patterns across generations. Nevertheless, field studies have provided evidence of social transmission, and as we argue below, are critical to a comparative understanding of culture.

In this context it is important to recognize and distinguish between a 'tradition', which we define for our immediate purposes as a socially transmitted behaviour that varies in its form between groups, and a 'culture'. If the term 'culture' is to avoid becoming redundant through synonymy with the presence of social learning, and if it is to be a concept usefully applied to both human and non-human animals, it must refer to more than a single tradition. The use in humans, across particular definitions, provides a collective description of the behavioural variation between groups: behaviours that are shared among group members, persistent across generations, not merely being transmitted socially. Moreover, culture in humans typically refers to a collection of socially transmitted behavioural variants – an array of shared, persistent traditions – that span a number of domains. Social learning may be a key mechanism by which behavioural variants are spread, and how traditions are created and maintained, but it is the presence of this cross-domain array of shared, persistent traditions that defines culture. To return to McGrew's (2003) definition, culture is 'the way we do *things*'.

Cultural Primatology: Insights from the Field

Identifying Cultures

Investigation of culture in primates has focused on the process of social transmission using experiments with captive animals, and on the identification of putative cultural variants within and between wild-living populations. This identification process, based on the detection of geographic variations in behaviour, is referred to variously as the ethnographic method (Wrangham et al. 1994), group comparison (Fragaszy and Perry 2003) or the method of elimination (van Schaik et al. 2003a). A behaviour is classed as a possible cultural variant if it occurs sufficiently frequently in one or more populations or social groups to be consistent with social transmission, and yet is absent in one or more other groups of the same species where environmental explanations for such absence can be rejected (cf. Whiten et al. 1999, 2001).

The production of comprehensive group- or community-specific ethograms often requires decades of field presence. The collection of exhaustive lists of behavioural variants depends, on the one hand, on research effort across seasons and years, and the number of observers *in situ*, and on the other hand, on the frequency of occurrence of behaviours, observation conditions or, for tool use, the reliability with which we can infer behaviour based on artefacts. For instance, it took more than three decades of research to produce a comprehensive list of tool-use behaviours among the chimpanzees of Bossou (Figure 2.1).

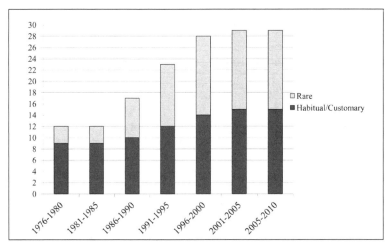

Figure 2.1. Cumulative number of observed rare, habitual and customary tool-use behaviours recorded among the chimpanzees (*Pan troglodytes verus*) of Bossou, Guinea, West Africa. For definitions of 'rare', 'habitual' and 'customary' see Whiten et al. 1999.

As many as six customary tool-use behaviours were initially unnoticed as a consequence of seasonal biases in research effort and poor levels of habituation during the first decade and a half of research (Matsuzawa et al. 2011).

Nevertheless, systematic and detailed fieldwork has enabled us to appreciate better the impressive within-species variability in behaviour across a range of domains. The classic examples of sweet-potato washing and wheat sluicing among the Japanese macaques of Koshima (summarized in Hirata et al. 2001) or the stone-handling patterns of Japanese macaques (Leca et al. 2007) suggest further that primates can build on earlier achievements and socially transmit those novel behaviours to other group members. Do these examples demonstrate the 'ratchet effect' at work, an effect proposed as a distinguishing characteristic of human culture (Tomasello 1999)? The 'ratchet effect' in material culture implies cumulative modifications and incremental improvements thus resulting in increasingly elaborate technologies. Indirect, but perhaps compelling, evidence for cumulative cultural evolution in wild chimpanzees comes from the enormous variability in tool-use techniques, such as for termite fishing and ant dipping.

Ant dipping is one of the most widespread uses of sticks as tools among wild chimpanzees. The targeted army ants (*Dorylus* sp.) are ubiquitous across Africa, and while several wild chimpanzee communities exhibit this behaviour, some such as the Sonso community in Budongo do not. Across the communities who do target these ants there is further variation, for example in the length of the wands used, and in the context in which the behaviour is displayed (dipping for ants at their nest versus when in a column or hunting). Perhaps unsurprisingly, chimpanzees use longer tools when targeting ants at their nests (when they are more aggressive) or targeting inherently more aggressive species (Humle and Matsuzawa 2001; Schoning et al. 2008). Tool length, in turn, is a likely influence on the technique used to remove ants from the tool: *direct mouthing* of shorter tools through the mouth/lips, or *pulling-through* of longer tools through the closed fingers of one hand and then bringing the ants to the mouth (Humle and Matsuzawa 2002). Moebius et al. (2008) showed that, despite the influence of prey ecology on the variation in tools employed, neither prey behaviour, characteristics, availability or density could account for all variation in ant dipping behaviour between the chimpanzees of Bossou and those of the Taï forest, Côte d'Ivoire. They conclude that these differences must therefore be cultural. This set of studies highlights the intricate inter-relationship between ecology and culture (Humle 2010).

Furthermore, while chimpanzees typically use a single tool, a dipping probe, to harvest army ants, chimpanzees in the Goualougo Triangle, Republic of Congo, use a 'tool-set' – the serial use of more than one type of tool to achieve a goal (Brewer and McGrew 1990) – in army ant predation (Sanz et al. 2010). This tool-set combines a puncturing tool and 'dipping' probe, and differs from other types of tool combinations used by these chimpanzees to prey upon termites or gather honey (Sanz and Morgan 2007, 2009; Sanz et al. 2010). The use of a tool-set is thought to improve harvesting efficiency and prey exploitation over longer periods of time. In the case of army ant predation, the use of a tool-set minimizes the risk of eliciting the colony's premature migration and desertion from the nest (Sanz et al. 2010).

Systematic collation of behavioural differences across long- to medium-term field studies has generated profiles for social groups that represent arrays of putative cultural behaviour in a number of primate species. Socially learned traditions have been proposed in relation to food processing techniques, tool uses and social conventions in wild capuchin monkeys (*Cebus* and *Sapajus* spp.: Panger et al. 2002; Perry et al. 2003; Ottoni and Izar 2008; Mannu and Ottoni 2009) and in stone-handling patterns in Japanese macaques (*Macaca fuscata*) (Leca et al. 2007). Researchers have so far recognized at least thirty-nine candidates for cultural variants in chimpanzees (Whiten et al. 1999), fourteen in bonobos (*Pan paniscus*) (Hohmann and Fruth 2003) and twenty-four in orang-utans (van Schaik et al. 2003a). Recorded numbers of putative cultural variants are likely to increase as more groups, communities and populations are studied, and as researchers pay more careful attention to subtle behavioural details.

The putative cultural variants in great apes range across a wide spectrum of behavioural domains, including foraging, tool use, communication, defence, self-maintenance, and social customs. These great ape species therefore demonstrate arrays of behavioural variants, each variant a good candidate for transmission by social learning. Even if rigorous demonstration of social learning for each of those variants is lacking, positing the existence of culture as an explanation for these behavioural variants remains a sensible working hypothesis. Without it, why should we look for evidence of social transmission, and how would we know which behaviours were good candidates for such an investigation? Without it, we would fail to appreciate the depth of behavioural diversity prevalent among social groups – to our ignorance and, given the precarious conservation status of these species, to their detriment.

Identifying Social Transmission in the Field

Primates are long-lived with extended inter-birth intervals, ranging in the great apes from a mean of 5.6 years in chimpanzees to 7.7 years in orang-utans (*Pongo* sp.) in their natural habitat (Wich et al. 2009). They also have long periods of maturation and development during which young acquire and perfect skills and behaviours, which are often, but not always, essential to their survival and key to managing life in a group. For example, Bossou chimpanzees typically do not demonstrate first success in combining anvil and hammer stones to crack oil-palm nuts (*Elaeis guineensis*) before the age of 3.5 to 5 years (Inoue-Nakamura and Matsuzawa 1997), and take another 3 to 5 years to attain an adult level of proficiency (Biro et al. 2006).

It may take years, therefore, to amass the necessary longitudinal and cross-sectional data necessary to gain some understanding of the developmental trajectory of young individuals, and the degree to which behaviours are socially transmitted. It took 163 days, spread across four years, for Lonsdorf (2006) to gather the necessary data to evaluate maternal contribution to the acquisition of termite fishing behaviour among chimpanzees (*P. t. schweinfurthii*) of the Gombe National Park in Tanzania. Similarly, Humle et al. (2009) required data across eight years to explore social learning influences on the acquisition of ant dipping among the chimpanzees of Bossou.

The Humle et al. (2009) study provided good evidence for social learning. She found that mothers were the prime models for their offspring during the first five years of their life. Since infants whose mothers are keen ant dippers have the opportunity to observe ant dipping earlier, they acquired the ant dipping behaviour sooner than those whose mothers dipped less frequently, and were also more efficient in this behaviour that others of the same age. Across infants, as performance improved, time spent observing ant dipping being performed decreased.

Perry (2009) conducted a seven-year-long study to investigate social influence on the acquisition of food processing techniques of *Luehea candida* fruits among wild white-faced capuchins (*Cebus capucinus*). The two techniques recorded to extract the seeds were equally efficient. Female infants, as with the chimpanzees in Lonsdorf's (2006) study, were more likely than male infants to match their mother's technique. Overall, individual capuchins typically settled on the technique they most frequently observed.

Jaeggi et al. (2010) accumulated nearly two thousand observation hours to explore social learning of diet and foraging skills among immature wild Bornean orang-utans (*Pongo pygmaeus wurmbii*). The diets of immature orang-utans were essentially identical to their mothers', even though mothers differed in their diets. Direct teaching

was never recorded, but immature orang-utans selective observation of their mothers performing extractive foraging tasks guided
their practice and acquisition of these complex skills. These data
nicely complement records of 'traditional' dietary differences among
Bornean orang-utan populations (Bastian et al. 2010).

However painstaking the research process, and despite the absence of control conditions, such studies provide convincing evidence
for the role of social learning in the diffusion (within the social unit)
and maintenance of group-typical behaviours among wild primates.
The real bonus of this approach lies in its social and ecological contextual validity. It presents enormous potential in helping us to elucidate
influential factors which may either hinder or promote diffusion of
cultural variants, including the role of ecological and social opportunity, and also to address potential patterns of sex differences in learning trajectories.

Field-based Experiments

In this approach, exemplified by the work of Matsuzawa and colleagues, researchers stimulate the occurrence of tool-use behaviours
in a locale within the natural range of the wild population or group
under study. This setting is equivalent to an outdoor 'laboratory'
where tools, food availability, distribution and type can readily be
manipulated, and observational conditions are maximized (e.g.
chimpanzees: Matsuzawa 1994; bearded capuchins *Sapajus libidinosus*: Fragaszy et al. 2010). At Bossou, reliable, consistent longitudinal
data on chimpanzee tool use has been gathered over the course of
several weeks per year since 1988 for oil-palm nut cracking, and since
2000 for water drinking with leaves (Inoue-Nakamura & Matsuzawa
1997; Tonooka 2001; Biro et al. 2003, 2006; Sousa et al. 2009).

These experiments have yielded insights into the acquisition of
nut cracking (Inoue-Nakamura and Matsuzawa 1997) and water
drinking (Sousa et al. 2009). Young chimpanzees acquire the skill of
using leaves for drinking water at around the age of 1.5 years. Infants
initially rely on leftover tools for drinking, and only begin to manufacture their own leaf tools at 3.5 years of age (Sousa et al. 2009).
Stone-tool use appears more complex, and is acquired during a
critical period spanning the ages of 3.5 to 5 years. During this period,
young chimpanzees repeatedly observe the behaviour of able nut
crackers from close range and practice the behaviour on their own
(Figure 2.2), a process termed 'education by master-apprenticeship'
(Matsuzawa et al. 2001). Evidence of active demonstration and assistance in canalizing an immature's acquisition of these skills was not
found in the Bossou chimpanzees, but Boesch (1991) reported numerous examples from the Taï forest of chimpanzee mothers facilitating

Figure 2.2. 'Education by master-apprenticeship' during the acquisition of nut cracking amongst chimpanzees at Bossou: (a) a juvenile female chimpanzee, *Joya*, sits beside her mother, *Jire*, who is cracking oil palm nuts with a mobile hammer and anvil stone; (b) *Joya* approaches and closely observes her mother's behaviour; (c) *Joya* grabs a hammer-anvil stone set and practices nut cracking. Although she is able to successfully combine anvil and hammer stones and the nut, *Joya* has a hard time efficiently manipulating the hammer stone to strike the nut. She will continue to repeatedly observe her mother or other proficient nut-crackers within the community until she perfects the skills on her own. (Photos by Boniface Zogbila, KUPRI/IREB)

the acquisition of nut-cracking skills by their offspring, including two examples of active teaching.

Propagation of socially learnt behaviours *between groups* of primates remains poorly understood and logistically daunting to demonstrate. Field experiments have been used as an indirect approach to investigating social transmission of putative cultural variants between neighbouring chimpanzee communities. These studies indicate that dissemination of socially learned behaviours across wild chimpanzee communities does not follow a simplistic pattern of chain transmission yielding cultural zones (Biro et al. 2003; Koops et al. 2008; Gruber et al. 2009).

Cracking of oil-palm nuts with hammer stones is customary among the Bossou chimpanzees. However, it is almost certainly absent from the chimpanzee community of the Seringbara area, 6 km from Bossou, despite the presence of oil palms (Humle and Matsuzawa 2001, 2004). Koops et al. (2008) provided Seringbara chimpanzees with oil-palm nuts and suitable anvil and hammer stones across several locations that they were known to frequent. Motion-triggered cameras showed that none of the chimpanzees who encountered the nuts and stones attempted to perform nut cracking. This suggests that the lack of nut cracking in the Seringbara chimpanzee community is fundamentally due to a lack of cultural knowledge, rather than a lack of ecological opportunity (cf. McGrew et al. 1997; Humle and Matsuzawa 2004).

Nuts of *Panda oleosa* are hard to crack, but chimpanzees in the Taï forest crack them with the aid of heavy wooden or stone hammers (Boesch and Boesch 1983). This nut species does not naturally occur in the range of the Bossou chimpanzees. When Biro et al. (2003) presented Bossou chimpanzees with *Panda* nuts in the outdoor laboratory, no member of the community transferred their nut-cracking skills from oil-palm nuts to the unfamiliar *Panda* nuts. Consequently, Bossou chimpanzees failed to innovate *Panda* nut cracking (Biro et al. 2003).

The Bossou chimpanzees were also provided with *Coula edulis* nuts, a second species absent from their home range. These nuts are cracked and consumed at Taï (Boesch and Boesch 1983), as well as on the Ivorian side of the Nimba Mountains only 14 km from Bossou (Humle and Matsuzawa 2001). A clear conservatism was obvious in the chimpanzees' response. With the exception of juveniles (4–7 year olds), most members of the community initially sniffed the nuts but otherwise ignored them and continued to crack the familiar oil-palm nuts.

One exception was an adult female, Yo, who spontaneously started cracking the *Coula* nuts. Yo was recorded as an adult member of the

Bossou community when observations began in 1976. Her spontaneous cracking of *Coula* nuts was therefore either an innovation in response to the ecological opportunity created by the experiment, or evidence that she had once been a member of a community in which *Coula* nuts were cracked and consumed, memory of a behaviour not used in twenty-four years. In support of the idea that Yo transferred in from another *Coula*-nut-cracking community, she was never observed to pestle pound, despite feeding on the petiole of palm fronds: pestle pounding is complex and unique tool-using behaviour common among adult members of the Bossou community (Yamakoshi and Sugiyama 1995).

Whether an innovation or distant memory, the juveniles paid close attention to Yo's behaviour and soon began cracking the novel *Coula* nuts on their own. This behaviour eventually spread among both juvenile and adult members of the community, providing good evidence of social transmission of a novel behaviour. The conservatism of the adults and the observation that juveniles use one another, or older individuals, as models, have implications for the selection of captive subjects for experimental investigations of social transmission.

The natural conservatism of adult chimpanzees is further demonstrated in the results of recent field experiments conducted in East Africa. Gruber et al. (2009) presented two habituated communities of wild chimpanzees in Uganda – Kanyawara in Kibale and Sonso in Budongo – with drilled horizontal logs loaded with honey to stimulate honey-feeding behaviour, and used motion-triggered cameras to record the chimpanzees' response. The Sonso chimpanzees, who do not typically use stick tools but will use leaf sponging to gather water, solved this task by using leaves and/or their fingers to obtain the honey, whereas the Kanyawara community, who customarily use sticks to gather honey, employed sticks to obtain the honey contained within the log.

The Necessity of Field Studies

In a field setting, with the absence of control conditions, gathering the empirical data necessary to demonstrate social learning of cultural variants is not easy, in contrast to experiments conducted in captivity. Despite this, field studies provide the only meaningful way of establishing the array of behavioural traditions that constitute the cultures of groups living under natural social and ecological conditions, and are the best means of probing the environmental, social and development influences on behavioural transmission and variation. Studies of captive animals might establish the cultural capabilities of a species, but only field studies of wild individuals can document their cultures.

Chances for witnessing individual migration events between groups or communities and potential dissemination of putative cultural variants based on an a priori comprehensive knowledge of both the individual's and the host group or community's behavioural repertoire are few. One of the rare published examples was the introduction of a novel social grooming variant, a form of hand-clasp grooming, into the M-group of chimpanzees at Mahale, Tanzania, with the immigration of a female chimpanzee from the K-group (Nakamura and Uehara 2004). This female also adopted types of hand-clasp allogrooming displayed by members of her new community (Figure 2.3). Her immigration increased heterogeneity in this social custom in the M-group. Although cultural transmission is predicted to yield homogeneity in behaviour, this example and others across different behavioural domains suggest that chimpanzees tend to maintain idiosyncratic behavioural preferences once acquired and suited to their purposes (e.g. ant-dipping techniques among Bossou chimpanzees: Humle et al. 2009). The habituation and study of neighbouring groups and communities is gradually creating more opportunities for recording migration events that are key to understanding social diffusion and dissemination of novel behavioural variants in primates.

Field researchers are only now beginning to appreciate the possibility for cumulative cultural evolution in primates other than humans, with successive generations building on earlier achievements. Research on stone-tool use in both chimpanzees and capuchins is also starting to provide key insights into the interpretation of early hominin lithic technology (Haslam et al. 2009).

Field studies focused on understanding patterns of transmission of socially learned behaviours in wild primates are also yielding key data useful to experimental researchers working with primates in captive settings. Our current understanding of what is going on in the wild should help to develop or refine experimental paradigms and focus research onto a wider range of behavioural domains, including communication and social customs (e.g. Watson and Caldwell 2009).

Novel Approaches

Primate Archaeology

Archaeological methods have recently been applied to the study of primate material culture, focusing on the lithic technology used to crack nuts (Haslam et al. 2009). Mercader et al. (2002) provided descriptions of recent buried remains of unintentionally fractured stone and organic residues resulting from the nut-cracking activities of modern chimpanzees in the Taï forest. This study highlighted the

Figure 2.3. Examples of allogrooming in chimpanzees. (a) Typical form of wrist-to-wrist hand-clasp grooming, a social custom observed among Mahale chimpanzees in Tanzania (photograph by Michio Nakamura); (b) Budongo chimpanzees of the Sonso community never perform hand-clasp grooming but will groom simultaneously without this structure (photograph by Nicholas Newton-Fisher).

potential in applying archaeological methods to the study of material culture among non-human extant primates and in identifying the type of material assemblages that could characterize ancient nut-cracking sites of chimpanzees (e.g. Carvalho et al. 2008, 2009). Chimpanzees and humans share several important elementary technological attributes, including the transport of stones to cracking sites, the optimal combination of locally available raw materials, size, shape and weight criteria to efficiently crack a given species of nut, and the accumulation and concentration of stones, flake and shell remains resulting from percussive activities at specific sites within the landscape. Excavated sites can be dated by standard archaeometric techniques, such as radiocarbon dating. Chimpanzee sites excavated thus far have ranged from hundreds (Mercader et al. 2002) to thousands (Mercader et al. 2007) of years old.

No sites of wild capuchins have yet been excavated in this manner. However, emerging data indicate that capuchin monkeys use hard level surfaces, including large embedded stones or wooden logs, as anvils, and mobile stones as hammers to crack open palm nuts, and transport hammer stones as well as nuts to anvil sites (Visalberghi et al. 2007). Wild capuchins thus provide an additional point of reference for interpreting hominin stone assemblages. Stone handling during play, and stone throwing in Japanese macaques, also represent group-specific behavioural traditions, which are shedding some important insights into the evolution of stone technology in hominids (Leca et al. 2007).

Cladistic Analysis

Cladistic analysis techniques traditionally applied to evolutionary biology have proved useful in explaining diversity in human material culture (Collard 2010; Lycett 2010). Lycett et al. (2007, 2010) have recently applied this phylogenetic analytical method to the accumulated database of cultural arrays across chimpanzee communities to help to refute the hypothesis that genetic differences underlie reported behavioural differences among chimpanzee communities. Some researchers are now using these results and methods to ask specific questions, such as what is the correlation between group size and the number of putative cultural traits across chimpanzee communities. Lind and Lindenfors (2010) have suggested that it correlates with the number of females within communities, but not with the number of males. Their result agrees with observational studies and our knowledge of wild chimpanzees: maternal (vertical) transmission and female emigration are indispensable in promoting behavioural diffusion and dissemination in chimpanzees.

The gradual accumulation of datasets or studies of the ontogeny of behavioural acquisition, group demographics and social dynamics, feeding ecology and so on, are providing increased opportunities for meta-analytical studies and refinements to models of cultural transmission. The next step is to feed in the empirical data and generate new testable hypotheses.

The Future of Cultural Primatology

Cultural primatology is still in its infancy. Future field studies – both observational and experimental – together with experiments using captive subjects, are likely to yield many more insights into the cultural propensities of primates, how these and non-primate cultures differ from those of humans, and how social dynamics, ecology and demographics shape culture and the diffusion and dissemination of socially learned behaviours. This will increasingly be the case as additional data are collected and more refined analyses and meta-analyses conducted. A major challenge is also our surprisingly limited understanding of cultural transmission processes in humans, but anthropologists and psychologists are rapidly filling this knowledge gap (e.g. Caldwell and Millen 2009, 2010). New statistical methods are also being developed and tested which should help us to identify more readily the spread of behavioural innovations through social transmission (Hoppitt et al. 2010). It is also essential that experimental (comparative) psychologists ask questions and frame experiments using growing insights from field-based studies. Similarly, primatologists in general need to be more attentive to models and hypotheses generated beyond the field of primatology, and should seek to gather the necessary empirical data with which to test the predictions of such models (e.g. Laland and Kendal 2003).

References

Arnhart, L. 1994. 'The Darwinian Biology of Aristotle's Political Animals', *American Journal of Political Science* 38(2): 464–85.

Bastian, M.L., N. Zweifel, E.R. Vogel, S.A. Wich and C.P. van Schaik. 2010. 'Diet Traditions in Wild Orangutans', *American Journal of Physical Anthropology* 143(2): 175–87.

Biro, D., N. Inoue-Nakamura, R. Tonooka, G. Yamakoshi, C. Sousa and T. Matsuzawa. 2003. 'Cultural Innovation and Transmission of Tool-use in Wild Chimpanzees: Evidence from Field Experiements, *Animal Cognition* 6: 213–23.

Biro, D., C. Sousa and T. Matsuzawa. 2006. 'Ontogeny and Cultural Propagation of Tool Use by Wild Chimpanzees at Bossou, Guinea: Case Studies in Nut Cracking and Leaf Folding', in T. Matsuzawa, M. Tomonaga and M. Tanaka (eds), *Cognitive Development in Chimpanzees*. New York: Springer, pp. 476–508.

Boesch, C. 1991. 'Teaching among Wild Chimpanzees', *Animal Behaviour* 41: 530–32.

Boesch, C. and H. Boesch. 1983. 'Optimisation of Nut Cracking with Natural Hammers by Wild Chimpanzees', *Behaviour* 83(3–4): 265–86.

Brewer, S.M. and W.C. McGrew. 1990. 'Chimpanzee Use of a Tool-set to Get Honey', *Folia Primatologica* 54: 100–4.

Caldwell, C.A., and A.E. Millen. 2009. 'Social Learning Mechanisms and Cumulative Cultural Evolution: Is Imitation Necessary?', *Psychological Science* 20(12): 1478–83.

Caldwell, C.A. and A.E. Millen. 2010. 'Human Cumulative Culture in the Laboratory: Effects of (Micro) Population Size', *Learning and Behavior* 38(3): 310–18.

Carvalho, S., D. Biro, W.C. McGrew and T. Matsuzawa. 2009. 'Tool-composite Reuse in Wild Chimpanzees (*Pan troglodytes*): Archaeologically Invisible Steps in the Technological Evolution of Early Hominins?, *Animal Cognition* 12: S103–14.

Carvalho, S., E. Cunha, C. Sousa and T. Matsuzawa. 2008. 'Chaines Operatoires and Resource-exploitation Strategies in Chimpanzee (*Pan troglodytes*) Nut Cracking', *Journal of Human Evolution* 55(1): 148–63.

Collard, M. 2010. 'Integrating Anthropological Genetics with Cultural Anthropology and Archaeology: New Opportunities', *Journal of Anthropological Science* 88: 239–42.

Darwin, C. 1871. *The Descent of Man and Selection in Relation to Sex*. London: John Murray.

Dindo, M., B. Thierry and A. Whiten. 2008. 'Social Diffusion of Novel Foraging Methods in Brown Capuchin Monkeys (*Cebus apella*)', *Proceedings of the Royal Society B-Biological Sciences* 275(1631): 187–93.

Fox, E.A., C.P. van Schaik, A. Sitompul and D.N. Wright. 2004. 'Intra- and Interpopulational Differences in Orangutan (*Pongo pygmaeus*) Activity and Diet: Implications for the Invention of Tool Use', *American Journal of Physical Anthropology* 125(2): 162–74.

Fragaszy, D.M., R. Greenberg, E. Visalberghi, E.B. Ottoni, P. Izar and Q. Liu. 2010. 'How Wild Bearded Capuchin Monkeys Select Stones and Nuts to Minimize the Number of Strikes per Nut Cracked', *Animal Behaviour* 80(2): 205–14.

Fragaszy, D.M. and S.E. Perry. 2003. *The Biology of Traditions: Models and Evidence*. Cambridge University Press.

Galef, B.G. 1992. 'The Question of Animal Culture', *Human Nature* 3: 157–78.

Goodall, J. 1973. 'Cultural Elements in a Chimpanzee Community', in E.W. Menzel (ed.), *Precultural Primate Behaviour*. Basel: Karger. pp. 195–249.

Gruber, T., M.N. Muller, P. Strimling, R. Wrangham and K. Zuberbuhler. 2009. 'Wild Chimpanzees Rely on Cultural Knowledge to Solve an Experimental Honey Acquisition Task', *Current Biology* 19(21): 1806–10.

Haslam, M., A. Hernandez-Aguilar, V. Ling, S. Carvalho, I. de la Torre, A. DeStefano, A. Du, B. Hardy, J. Harris, L. Marchant et al. 2009. 'Primate Archaeology', *Nature* 460: 339–44.

Helfman, G.S. and E.T. Schultz. 1984. 'Social Tradition of Behavioural Traditions in a Coral Reef Fish', *Animal Behaviour* 32: 379–84.

Hirata, S., K. Watanabe, M. Kawai and T. Matsuzawa. 2001. '"Sweet-potato Washing" revisited', in T. Matsuzawa (ed.), *Primate Origins of Human Cognition and Behavior.* Tokyo: Springer-Verlag, pp. 487–508.

Hohmann, G. and B. Fruth. 2003. 'Culture in Bonobos? Between-species and Within-species Variation in Behavior', *Current Anthropology* 44: 563–71.

Hopper, L.M., A. Spiteri, S.P. Lambeth, S.J. Schapiro, V. Horner and A. Whiten. 2007. 'Experimental Studies of Traditions and Underlying Transmission Processes in Chimpanzees', *Animal Behaviour* 73: 1021–32.

Hoppitt, W., N.J. Boogert, and K.N. Laland. 2010. 'Detecting Social Transmission in Networks', *Journal of Theoretical Biology* 263(4): 544–55.

Horner, V. 2010. 'The Cultural Mind of Chimpanzees: How Social Tolerance can Shape the Transmission of Culture', in E.V. Lonsdorf, S.R. Ross and T. Matsuzawa (eds), *The Mind of the Chimpanzee.* Chicago and London: University of Chicago Press, pp. 101–15.

Horner, V., A. Whiten, E. Flynn and F.B.M. de Waal. 2006. 'Faithful Replication of Foraging Techniques along Cultural Transmission Chains by Chimpanzees and Children', *Proceedings of the National Academy of Sciences of the United States of America* 103(37): 13878–83.

Humle, T. 2010. 'How are Army Ants Shedding New Light on Culture in Chimpanzees', in E.V. Lonsdorf, S.R. Ross and T. Matsuzawa (eds), *The Mind of Chimpanzees.* Chicago and London: University of Chicago Press, pp. 116–25.

Humle, T. and T. Matsuzawa. 2001. 'Behavioural Diversity among the Wild Chimpanzee Populations of Bossou and Neighbouring Areas, Guinea and Cote d'Ivoire, West Africa', *Folia Primatologica* 72: 57–68.

———. 2002. 'Ant Dipping among the Chimpanzees of Bossou, Guinea, and Comparisons with Other Sites', *American Journal of Primatology* 58: 133–48.

———. 2004. 'Oil Palm Use by Adjacent Communities of Chimpanzees at Bossou and Nimba Mountains, West Africa', *International Journal of Primatology* 25: 551–81.

Humle, T. and C.T. Snowdon. 2008. 'Socially Biased Learning in the Acquisition of a Complex Foraging Task in Juvenile Cottontop Tamarins (*Saguinus oedipus*)', *Animal Behavaviour* 75: 267–77.

Humle, T., C.T. Snowdon and T. Matsuzawa. 2009. 'Social Influences on Ant-dipping Acquisition in the Wild Chimpanzees (*Pan troglodytes verus*) of Bossou, Guinea, West Africa', *Animal Cognition* 12: S37–S48.

Ingold, T. 2001. 'The Use and Abuse of Ethnography', *Behavioral and Brain Science* 24: 337.

Inoue-Nakamura, N. and T. Matsuzawa. 1997. 'Development of Stone Tool Use by Wild Chimpanzees (*Pan troglodytes*)', *Journal of Comparative Psychology* 111: 159–73.

Jaeggi, A.V., L.P. Dunkel, M.A. van Noordwijk, S.A. Wich, A.A.L. Sura and C.P. van Schaik. 2010. 'Social Learning of Diet and Foraging Skills by Wild Immature Bornean Orangutans: Implications for Culture, *American Journal of Primatology* 72: 62–71.

Jaeggi, A.V., L. Dunkel and C.P. van Schaik. 2007. 'The Role of Social Learning in the Acquisition of Foraging Skills in Wild Bornean Orang-utans (*Pongo pygmaeus*)', *American Journal of Physical Anthropology* Suppl. 44: 135.

Kant, I. 1786. 'Mutmasslicher Anfang der Menschengeschichte', *Berlinische Monatschrift* 176: 1–27.

Kawamura, S. 1959. 'The Process of Sub-cultural Propagation among Japanese Macaques, *Primates* 2: 43–60.

Kendal, R.L. 2008. 'Animal "Culture Wars"', *The Psychologist* 21: 312–15.

Koops, K., W.C. McGrew and T. Matsuzawa. 2008. *Nut-cracking and the Chimpanzees of the Nimba Mountains, Guinea, West Africa: An Experimental Approach to the Study of Ape Technology*, International Primatological Society. Edinburgh: Primate Eye-PSGB, Abst #395.

Kroeber, A.L. 1928. 'Sub-human Culture Beginnings', *Quaterly Review of Biology* 3: 325–42.

Kroeber, A.L. and C. Kluckhohn. 1952. 'Culture: A Critical Review of Concepts and Definitions', *Papers of the Peabody Museum of American Archaeology and Ethnology* 47: 1–223.

Kummer, H. 1971. *Primate Societies: Group Techniques of Ecological Adaptation*. Chicago: Aldine.

Laland, K.N. and W. Hoppitt. 2003. 'Do Animals have Culture?', *Evolutionary Anthropology* 12: 150–59.

Laland, K.N. and V.M. Janik. 2006. 'The Animal Cultures Debate', *Trends In Ecology and Evolution* 21: 542–47.

Laland, K.N. and J.R. Kendal. 2003. 'What the Models say about Animal Social Learning', in D.M. Fragaszy and S. Perry (eds), *The Biology of Traditions: Models and Evidence*. Cambridge: Cambridge University Press, pp. 33–55.

Leca, J.B., N. Gunst and M.A. Huffman. 2007. 'Japanese Macaque Cultures: Inter- and Intra-troop Behavioural Variability of Stone Handling Patterns across 10 Troops', *Behaviour* 144: 251–81.

Lind, J. and P. Lindenfors. 2010. 'The Number of Cultural Traits Is Correlated with Female Group Size but Not with Male Group Size in Chimpanzee Communities', *PLoS One* 5: e9241.

Lonsdorf, E.V. 2006. 'What is the Role of Mothers in the Acquisition of Termite-fishing Behaviors in Wild Chimpanzees (*Pan troglodytes schweinfurthii*)?', *Animal Cognition* 9(1): 36–46.

Lonsdorf, E.V. and K.E. Bonnie. 2010. 'Opportunities and Constraints when Studying Social Learning: Developmental Approaches and Social Factors'. *Learning and Behavior* 38(3): 195–205.

Lycett, S.J. 2010. 'The Importance of History in Definitions of Culture: Implications from Phylogenetic Approaches to the Study of Social Learning in Chimpanzees', *Learning and Behavior* 38(3): 252–64.

———.2011. '"Most Beautiful and Most Wonderful": Those Endless Stone Tool Forms', *Journal of Evolutionary Psychology* 9(2): 143–71.

Lycett, S.J., M. Collard and W.C. McGrew. 2007. 'Phylogenetic Analyses of Behavior Support Existence of Culture among Wild Chimpanzees', *Proceedings of the National Academy of Sciences of the United States of America* 104(45): 17588–92.

———.2010. 'Are Behavioral Differences among Wild Chimpanzee Communities Genetic or Cultural? An Assessment Using Tool-use Data and Phylogenetic Methods', *American Journal of Physical Anthropology* 142(3): 461–67.

Mannu, M. and E.B. Ottoni. 2009. 'The Enhanced Tool-kit of Two Groups of Wild Bearded Capuchin Monkeys in the Caatinga: Tool Making, Associative Use and Secondary Tools', *American Journal of Primatology* 71(3): 242–51.

Matsuzawa, T. 1994. 'Field Experiments on Use of Stone Tools by Chimpanzees in the Wild', in R.W. Wrangham, W.C. McGrew, F.B.M. de Waal and P.G. Heltne (eds), *Chimpanzee Cultures*. Cambridge: Harvard University Press, pp. 351–70.

Matsuzawa, T., D. Biro, T. Humle, N. Inoue-Nakamura, R. Tonooka, G. Yamakoshi and T. Matsuzawa. 2001. 'Emergence of Culture in Wild Chimpanzees: Education by Master-apprenticeship', in T. Matsuzawa (ed.), *Primate Origins of Human Cognition and Behavior.* Tokyo: Springer-Verlag, pp. 557–74.

Matsuzawa, T., T. Humle and Y. Sugiyama (eds). 2011. *The Chimpanzees of Bossou and Nimba.* Tokyo: Springer-Verlag.

Matsuzawa, T. and W.C. McGrew. 2008. 'Kinji Imanishi and 60 years of Japanese Primatology', *Current Biology* 18(14): R587–R591.

McGrew, W.C. 1992. *Chimpanzee Material Culture: Implications for Human Evolution.* Cambridge: Cambridge University Press.

———.2003. 'Ten Dispatches from the Chimpanzee Culture Wars', in F.B.M. de Waal and P.L. Tyack (eds), *Animal Social Complexity Intelligence, Culture and Individualized Societies.* Cambridge: Havard University Press, pp. 419–39.

McGrew, W.C., R.M. Ham, L.J.T. White, C.E.G. Tutin and M. Fernandez. 1997. 'Why Don't Chimpanzees in Gabon Crack Nuts? *International Journal of Primatology* 18: 353–74.

McGrew, W.C. and C.E.G. Tutin. 1978. 'Evidence for a Social Custom in Wild Chimpanzees?', *Man* 13(2): 234–51.

Mercader, J., H. Barton, J. Gillespie, J. Harris, S. Kuhn, R. Tyler and C. Boesch. 2007. '4,300-year-old Chimpanzee Sites and the Origins of Percussive Stone Technology', *Proceedings of the National Academy of Sciences of the United States of America* 104(9): 3043–48.

Mercader, J., M. Panger and C. Boesch. 2002. 'Excavation of a Chimpanzee Stone Tool Site in the African Rainforest', *Science* 296: 1452–55.

Mobius, Y., C. Boesch, K. Koops, T. Matsuzawa and T. Humle. 2008. 'Cultural Differences in Army Ant Predation by West African Chimpanzees? A Comparative Study of Microecological Variables', *Animal Behaviour* 76: 37–45.

Nakamura M. and S. Uehara. 2004. 'Proximate Factors of Two Types of Grooming-hand-clasp in Mahale Chimpanzees: Implication for Chimpanzee Social Custom', *Current Anthropology* 45(1):108–14.

Ottoni, E.B. and P. Izar. 2008. 'Capuchin Monkey Tool Use: Overview and Implications', *Evolutionary Anthropology* 17(4): 171–78.

Panger, M.A., S. Perry, L. Rose, J. Gros-Louis, E. Vogel, K.C. Mackinnon and M. Baker. 2002. Cross-site Differences in Foraging Behavior of White-faced Capuchins (*Cebus capucinus*), *American Journal of Physical Anthropology* 119(1): 52–66.

Perry, S. 2009. 'Conformism in the Food Processing Techniques of White-faced Capuchin Monkeys (*Cebus capucinus*)', *Animal Cognition* 12(5): 705–16.

Perry, S., M. Baker, L. Fedigan, J. Gros-Louis, K. Jack, K.C. MacKinnon, J.H. Manson, M. Panger, K. Pyle and L. Rose. 2003. 'Social Conventions in Wild White-faced Capuchin Monkeys – Evidence for Traditions in a Neotropical Primate', *Current Anthropology* 44(2): 241–68.

Sanz, C.M. and D.B. Morgan. 2007. 'Chimpanzee Tool Technology in the Goualougo Triangle, Republic of Congo', *Journal of Human Evolution* 52(4): 420–33.

———. 2009. 'Flexible and Persistent Tool-using Strategies in Honey-gathering by Wild Chimpanzees', *International Journal of Primatology* 30(3): 411–27.

Sanz, C.M., C. Schoning and D.B. Morgan. 2010. 'Chimpanzees Prey on Army Ants with Specialized Tool Set', *American Journal of Primatology* 72(1): 17–24.

Schaik, C.P. van, M. Ancrenaz, G. Borgen, B. Galdikas, C.D. Knott, I. Singleton, A. Suzuki, S.S. Utami and M. Merrill. 2003a. 'Orangutan Cultures and the Evolution of Material Culture', *Science* 299(5603): 102–5.

Schaik, C.P. van, E.A. Fox, and L.T. Fechtman. 2003b. 'Individual Variation in the Rate of Use of Tree-hole Tools among Wild Orangutans: ImSchoning, C., T. Humle, Y. Mobius and W.C. McGrew. 2008. 'The Nature of Culture: Technological Variation in Chimpanzee Predation on Army Ants Revisited', *Journal of Human Evolution* 55(1): 48–59.

Sousa, C., D. Biro and T. Matsuzawa. 2009. 'Leaf-tool Use for Drinking Water by Wild Chimpanzees (*Pan troglodytes*): Acquisition Patterns and Handedness', *Animal Cognition* 12: S115–S125.

Tomasello, M. 1999. *The Cultural Origins of Human Cognition*. Cambridge, MA: Harvard University Press.

Tonooka, R. 2001. 'Leaf-folding Behavior for Drinking Water by Wild Chimpanzees (*Pan troglodytes verus*) at Bossou, Guinea', *Animal Cognition* 4: 325–34.

Tyler, E.B. 1871. *Primitive Culture*. London: Murray.

Visalberghi, E., D. Fragaszy, E. Ottoni, P. Izar, M.G. de Oliveira and F.R.D. Andrade. 2007. 'Characteristics of Hammer Stones and Anvils Used by Wild Bearded Capuchin Monkeys (*Cebus libidinosus*) to Crack Open Palm Nuts, *American Journal of Physical Anthropology* 132(3): 426–44.

Voelkl, B. and L. Huber. 2000. 'True Imitation in Marmosets', *Animal Behaviour* 60: 195–202.

Waal, F.B.M. de. 1999. 'Cultural Primatology Comes of Age', *Nature* 399: 635–36.

Watson, C.F.I. and C.A. Caldwell. 2009. 'Understanding Behavioral Traditions in Primates: Are Current Experimental Approaches too Focused on Food?', *International Journal of Primatology* 30(1): 143–67.

Whiten, A., J. Goodall, W.C. McGrew, T. Nishida, V. Reynolds, Y. Sugiyama, C.E. Tutin, R.W. Wrangham and C. Boesch. 1999. 'Cultures in Chimpanzees', *Nature* 399(6737): 682–85.

————.2001. 'Charting Cultural Variation in Chimpanzees', *Behaviour* 138: 1481–516.

Whiten, A., V. Horner, C.A. Litchfield and S. Marshall-Pescini. 2004. 'How do Apes Ape?', *Learning Behavaviour* 32(1): 36–52.

Wich, S.A., S.S. Utami Atmoko, T. Mitra Setia and C.P. van Schaik (eds). 2009. *Orangutans: Geographic Variation in Behavioral Ecology and Conservation*. Oxford: Oxford University Press.

Wrangham, R.W., F.B.M. de Waal and W.C. McGrew. 1994. 'The Challenge of Behavioral Diversity', in R.W. Wrangham, W.C. McGrew, F.B.M. de Waal, P.G. Heltne and L.A. Marquardt (eds), *Chimpanzee Cultures*. Cambridge: Harvard University Press, pp. 1–18.

Yamakoshi, G. and Y. Sugiyama. 1995. 'Pestle-pounding Behavior of Wild Chimpanzees at Bossou, Guinea: A Newly Observed Tool-using Behavior', *Primates* 36(4): 489–500.

Chapter 3

CULTURAL TRANSMISSION THEORY AND FOSSIL HOMININ BEHAVIOUR

A DISCUSSION OF EPISTEMOLOGICAL AND METHODOLOGICAL STRENGTHS

Stephen J. Lycett

Introduction

We have in the study of fossil hominin behaviour a most difficult but worthy subject. It involves the study of individuals long since dead, many of whom did not even belong to our own species. Hence, while palaeoanthropology shares many aims with other areas of archaeology and anthropology more generally, it has the added complications of extreme time depth, paucity of preserved evidence, and the possibility of evolving cognitive and biomechanical abilities in hominin populations over time. Here, it is argued that cultural transmission theory provides a rigorous and productive framework in approaching the issue of fossil hominin behaviour, both epistemologically and methodologically. Principally, cultural transmission theory enables the framing of explicit hypotheses, and facilitates their testability via the use of analytical methods adopted and adapted from biology. Use of cultural transmission theory allows not only issues of particular relevance to palaeoanthropology to be addressed, but may also help to integrate human evolutionary research with wider anthropological concerns.

A Dead Record?

> Material culture patterns are in the first place material behaviour pat-
> terns – patterns of socially acquired actions and activities condensed in
> solid form.
>
>   – D.L. Clarke, *Analytical Archaeology*

Palaeontology is the study of artefactual products (i.e. fossils) of
biological processes that cannot be observed directly, only by proxy.
Likewise, archaeology is the study of artefactual products of behavioural processes that cannot be observed directly, only by proxy
(Binford 1983). When this task extends to people of our own species
that lived perhaps several hundred or several thousand years ago, it
presents a severe challenge to intellectual and scientific pursuit. When
the challenge is to understand the behaviour of individuals who lived
hundreds of thousands or even several million years ago, and who did
not necessarily belong to our species, the challenge multiplies in terms
of tractability.

Cultural transmission – as the chapters in this volume testify –
appears something of a rare unifying theme in anthropology (see
also Mesoudi et al. 2006). Regardless of broad differences of interest,
geographic, chronological or epistemological focus, cultural transmission it seems, is an important issue for anyone broadly concerned
with 'anthropological' questions. The social learning and transmission of knowledge, skills, beliefs, ideas, habits and customs appears
essential to the human experience, thus providing a common theme
of interest to those who study humanity, regardless of (intra)disciplin-
ary ilk. Equally, however, we should not turn this into an anthropo-
centric pursuit (see Laland et al. and Humle and Newton-Fisher, this
volume). The social transmission of information (broadly defined) is
not the exclusive purview of our own species, our own genus (*Homo*),
or even just our own order (Primates). This, however, is not to deny
that humans might socially transmit unique forms of information
in ways that other animals do not. What it does provoke, is recognition that when anthropologists are engaging in the study of social
(or 'cultural') transmission, they are engaging in a topic that has
ramifications beyond the confines of the immediate community they
happen to be studying. Such study has the potential to be important
to the study of humanity in a much broader sense; one that takes into
account the social transmission capacities of other species and situ-
ates current knowledge of human cultural transmission alongside
them in a comparative framework. Indeed, even to make claims that
human cultural transmission is 'special', 'unique', or 'evolutionarily
derived' demands that anthropologists consider fully the extent and

character of cultural transmission in species other than our own, including our closest extinct relatives that we know only through fossil remains and, if we are lucky, the material artefacts they left behind – most frequently in the form of flaked stone tools and the debris that resulted from their manufacture.

Even assuming that such an ecumenical view is accepted, we are still, however, left with an intellectual dilemma: how can we study social transmission in species other than our own, who lived millennia ago and are known only through a fragmentary record of material remains? Resolution to such dilemma, I will argue, requires extension of a framework sometimes currently applied to the behaviour of *Homo sapiens*, which applies quantitative methods and principles derived from biology and which were originally designed to study genetic transmission and the patterns that it produces. The utility of such a framework for studying cultural transmission and the material patterns it creates was recognized by some perhaps as early as the 1960s (Clarke 1968), and saw an expansion of its theoretical and methodological toolkit in the 1970s and 1980s (Cavalli-Sforza and Feldman 1981; Boyd and Richerson 1985). More recently, further theoretical and methodological expansion has been fostered by an ever-growing number of scholars working across the disciplinary boundaries of anthropology, archaeology and psychology (e.g. Neiman 1995; Bettinger and Eerkens 1999; O'Brien and Lyman 2000, 2003; Shennan 2000, 2001; Collard and Shennan 2000; Tehrani and Collard 2002, 2009; Jordan and Shennan 2003; Bentley et al. 2004; Mesoudi et al. 2004; Eerkens and Lipo 2005; Collard et al. 2006; Greenhill et al. 2009; Lipo et al. 2006; Buchanan and Collard 2007; Mesoudi and O'Brien 2008; Hamilton and Buchanan 2009; Lycett 2009a, 2011; Mesoudi 2011). This approach advocates that patterns in material remains (along with other cultural phenomena) are, at least in part, brought about by social transmission factors, and that such patterns are amenable to numerical and statistical analyses. This, in turn, facilitates a robustness to be brought to bear on a topic that can otherwise all too easily be subject to wild speculation and seductive narrative. Note that this does not directly mean that such speculations are 'incorrect', nor that the framework I am advocating will strictly bring about the 'correct' answers on all occasions. Rather, what this approach does is lay knowledge claims in an explicit framework where assumptions (both theoretical and methodological) are laid bare, and the answers provided can thus be tested, prodded and poked as new data and refined methods of inquiry become available. Importantly, if the answers provided by this framework are 'wrong', they can be shown to be so at a later date, and the reasons as to why the new answers are 'better' can be made clear.

The Cultural Transmission Capacities of the Last Common Ancestor of all Hominins

To place cultural transmission centrally in pursuing the behaviour of extinct species may seem to some like putting the cart before the horse. However, thanks to a vast growth in knowledge over the last forty years about the abilities of our closest living primate relatives to socially transmit habits and behaviours, we are in a position to build – on the grounds of phylogenetic parsimony – strong inferences regarding the minimal social transmission capacities of the last common ancestor of the human–chimpanzee clade. Such studies have been conducted both with captive and free-living chimpanzee populations (*Pan paniscus* and *Pan troglodytes*) and allow us to build a strong baseline model of social transmission capacities for all hominins. Some of these studies are reviewed in the present volume by Humle and Newton-Fisher (for additional recent reviews, see e.g. McGrew 2004; Horner and de Waal 2009; Whiten et al. 2009; Biro et al. 2010; Lycett 2010a; Whiten 2010). I do not intend here to review, in full, information that is readily available elsewhere; however, I do wish to draw attention to a few salient points and to draw out their implications for a baseline model of social transmission capabilities for hominins.

The first point to make concerning social transmission in the genus *Pan* is that in the case of material culture usage in the wild (of which tool-use in feeding behaviours is a prominent category), social learning appears crucial to the propagation and sustainment of behavioural patterns that are widespread, both within a given community and across time, such that they might genuinely be referred to as 'traditions' (see e.g. Biro et al. 2006; Londsdorf 2006; Humle et al. 2009). Indeed, the absence of certain behavioural patterns in certain communities may in part be related to disruption of pathways of social transmission and/or demographic parameters, rather than necessarily factors relating to environment or opportunity (Henrich 2004; Wrangham 2006; Lind and Lindenfors 2010; Lycett and Norton 2010). Phylogenetic analyses of chimpanzee behavioural data have additionally shown that such behavioural variation is inconsistent with a genetic explanation for such patterning (Lycett et al. 2007, 2009, 2010, 2011). However, recent theoretical and experimental work has shown that rather simple means of social learning, such as stimulus enhancement, can lead to the establishment of stable traditions (Franz and Matthews 2010; Matthews et al. 2010). Hence, although social transmission mechanisms need not *necessarily* be complex, the opportunity for social learning in regard to chimpanzee material culture behaviour patterns appears crucial. The recent work of Humle et al. (2009) on ant dipping in the chimpanzee (*P. t. verus*) community at Bossou (Guinea) exemplifies this. At this site, juveniles (≤ 5 years of age) whose mothers spent a higher percentage of time ant dipping (thus presenting greater opportunity for learning) started to perform this particular tool behaviour sooner and demonstrated greater proficiency compared with juveniles whose mothers spent less time ant dipping.

As crucial as studies in the wild are for understanding the social learning capacities of the genus *Pan*, practical and ethical considerations always place some constraints on the types of data that might be gained (see Humle and Newton-Fisher, this volume, for discussion). It is here that studies conducted on captive individuals can be used to complement and augment the data that is being accumulated in the wild (Whiten 2009). In regard to establishing baseline capacities for fossil hominins, these studies are especially valuable since individuals can be encouraged to engage in behaviours (such as breaking stones to make cutting tools) that they may not otherwise exhibit in the wild. Some of the most sophisticated experiments carried out to date have involved introducing novel tool-use behaviours into captive groups of *P. troglodytes* and tracking the diffusion of these behaviours across the group. Such experiments have shown not only the successful diffusion of these behaviours in different groups, but also a marked tendency towards within-group fidelity of technique in instances where alternative techniques may be used to gain the food reward from the same apparatus, thus reinforcing the role of social contact in their diffusion (Whiten et al. 2005). In other experiments, 'transmission chains' have been established whereby an individual is shown how to remove a food reward from a box using either a 'lift-the-door' or 'slide-the-door' technique (Horner et al. 2006). Transmission chains using both of these alternative techniques have demonstrated fidelity of technique in chains of up to six individuals. As Horner et al. (ibid.: 13881) point out, given that female chimpanzees in the wild give birth to their first offspring at around 13–14 years of age, six such transmission events in the wild across generations could represent over eighty years of cultural continuity, thus giving insight into the mechanisms underlying behavioural patterns observed in the wild.In a particularly ambitious experimental setting, a bonobo chimpanzee (*P. paniscus*) has even demonstrated a capacity to learn how to knock ('knap') sharp flakes from cores of stone using a hammerstone, after observing a human demonstrator perform this behaviour (Toth et al. 1993; Schick et al. 1999). Although it took the individual bonobo (Kanzi) used in these trials several weeks of practice to detach stone flakes successfully, he was by the end of the first day hitting two stones together, presumably encouraged by the fact that he had also been shown how to use the resultant sharp flakes to cut through a cord, which allowed him access to a box containing a food reward (Toth et al. 1993: 84). Other bonobos that have observed Kanzi make and use stone tools, also now appear to show an interest in this behaviour and have begun making tools of their own (Whiten et al. 2009: 427). While Kanzi's knapping skills fall short of the levels of skill exhibited in the earliest observed archaeological instances of stone knapping seen in Africa from around 2.6 million years ago (Toth et al. 2006), these experiments establish that the ability to engage in some rather sophisticated instances of tool manufacture and use, having observed modelled examples of such behaviour, is within the capacities of the genus *Pan*.

The combined results of these numerous studies, from both the wild and captivity, demonstrate several points. Firstly, the last common ancestor of both chimpanzees and humans would have been capable of social transmission both within communities and across genera-tions. Secondly, given that both human and chimpanzee groups use socially acquired information as part of their subsistence behaviours, it is probable that hominins also did this from a period extending back to the last common ancestor of both lineages, even if much of this remains archaeologically invisible (for example, because it involved simple manipulation of organic matter that does not preserve). Finally, the experiments with Kanzi demonstrate that an ability to observe others in a social context and learn some of the most basic techniques of stone tool manufacture that are associated with the ini-tial emergence of stone cutting tools in the stratigraphic record were already present in the common ancestor of the hominini–panini clade (Whiten et al. 2009). Thus, when material culture within the hominin lineage did eventually 'appear' around 2.6 million years ago in the form of stone-cutting flakes, stone cores and cut-marked bones (e.g. Semaw et al. 2003; Domínguez-Rodrigo et al. 2005), social transmission will have formed an important component in the manifestation of these archaeologically visible patterns – even if only (*minimally*) in the form of directing attention towards the various required behavioural components (stimulus-enhancement) through repeated demonstration within a feeding context.

The Study of Cultural Transmission in Stone Artefacts:
A Theoretical and Quantitative Framework

When a skill such as the manufacture of stone tools is learned in a social context, at least some particular means of doing the required actions can potentially be copied and replicated as individuals learn via the observation of others. Patten (2005: 54–55) has introduced the term 'process controls' to describe the particular techniques that stone workers use to ensure that desired outcomes are achieved by the flaking process. Such process controls might include holding the stone core at particular angles, or bracing it against the leg in a particular manner and at a particular point. Other process controls might involve careful and deliberate preparation of the core prior to it being struck (such as through the removal of tiny chips or through rough grinding at the point of percussion), such that certain flaking aims are achieved with greater predictability of certain outcomes. In other words, particular traditions of manufacture may develop which are contingent upon a multitude of potentially rather subtle differences between the details of stone tool manufacture deployed by different communities of tool makers.

We currently know very little about the points at which various process controls were employed by hominins in given circumstances. It might be surmised that the very earliest stone tools that emerged in East Africa 2.6 million years ago (referred to generally as 'Oldowan' or 'Mode 1') lacked such controls entirely. However, detailed comparative analysis of some of these earliest stone artefacts alongside examples produced by Kanzi the bonobo chimpanzee, suggest that even the very earliest hominin stone knappers had achieved a level of skill that exceeds that exhibited by Kanzi (Toth et al. 2006). This conclusion is reinforced by additional studies of Oldowan material that evince an ability to reduce stone systematically and with a skill that ensured productivity in terms of repeated successful instances of flaking (Delagnes and Roche 2005). Such evidence cautions against any hasty supposition that socially transmitted process controls were entirely absent from communities of the earliest hominin stone-tool makers. By 1.6 million years ago, new forms of artefact had begun to emerge in East Africa, which certainly take considerable skill and many months of extended practice to be replicated by modern knappers (Edwards 2001). These artefacts, known as 'Acheulean handaxes', consist of relatively large (generally ≥ 10 cm in length) pieces of stone from which flakes have been removed on two sides resulting in an elongated 'bifacial' tool that has a cutting edge extending around much of its boundary (Schick and Toth 1993). Manufacture of such products implies the use of particular techniques and skills that in the case of ethnographically recorded instances of stone tool manufacture are facilitated, transmitted and reinforced through extended periods of social interaction with more experienced individuals (Stout 2005; Weedman 2010).

Equally, it should be emphasized that it is not merely the deliberate use of process controls that will lead to specific traditions of manufacture. Social transmission is not perfect: ask anyone who has ever attempted to teach something formally to others, even using rather sophisticated social transmission methods such as deliberate combinations of verbal and visual stimuli. Thus imperfect copying is likely to introduce variations into socially transmitted material culture patterns (Eerkens and Lipo 2005). Again, the work examining social transmission in captive chimpanzee populations demonstrates that corruptions to socially learned behaviours can and do occur when even relatively simple mechanisms of social learning are at work (Whiten 2010). Hence, even unintended features (i.e. 'errors') or arbitrary conventions, when copied and replicated by others, even unconsciously, will manifest themselves in the form of different 'lineages' of socially transmitted patterns (O'Brien and Lyman 2000: 17), or what otherwise would be referred to as distinct 'traditions' of manufacture.

One of the first archaeologists to attempt to formulate some of these insights into a quantitative programme for the study of items such as knapped stone artefacts was David Clarke (1968). Figure 3.1 (A and B) shows modified versions of diagrams that Clarke (1968: 160, 182) used to illustrate these principles. These diagrams are highly schematic, summarizing a rather more complicated series of processes and outcomes than might appear at first sight and, as such, require close examination. In Figure 3.1A, which Clarke (1968: 182) titled 'How pattern gets into the system', the knapper possesses a set of concepts, ideas, craft skills, and knowledge that are employed in the manufacture of stone artefacts (*Concepta*). The artefacts are used in a set of roles or activities thus engaging with environment and social context (*Designata*). The relationship between *Designata* and *Concepta* may be reciprocal. When learning a craft skill, the manufacturer is – via a process of social interaction – influenced by others (*Percepta*), who in turn are ultimately influenced by the cumulative *Designata* and *Concepta* of previous generations. The artefacts thus produced vary within and between themselves in terms of a series of attributes (i.e. features, characteristics or traits which can be described, counted and/or measured), and these individual attributes will vary in different sets of artefacts through time. Clarke (1968: 649) was keen to emphasize that within such a scheme there are inter-relationships between artefacts (via inter-relationships between *Designata*, *Percepta* and *Concepta*), inter-relationships between people (via *Percepta* and *Concepta*) and inter-relationships between artefacts at the time of manufacture and physical environment (via *Designata*). In principle, inter-relationships between artefacts at the time of manufacture and their environment (either physical or social) could, therefore, not only involve intended roles (i.e. functions), but also interactions between

Concepta and the raw media of manufacture (i.e. stone raw materials and the various tools that might be engaged in manufacture). Within what will inevitably be a dynamic socially mediated context, variations in the attributes of artefacts will reflect these inter-relationships, such that 'the artefact population has continuity in its trajectory and yet is continuously shifting its attribute format and dispersion' (Clarke 1968: 181).

Figure 3.1B schematically illustrates Clarke's notion of an artefact population comprising several quantitative attributes that vary in terms of their statistical properties (i.e. mean, range, mode, standard deviation). As noted earlier, Clarke (1968: 170) emphasized that there will be 'time changes in the distribution or dispersion of the artefact population in terms of each attribute'. Figure 3.2 is similar to diagrams used by Clarke (see e.g. 1968: 169–71) and illustrates how a single attribute in three different populations will shift and diverge through time in terms of their statistical properties, such that each population will come to exhibit a quite distinct (albeit with overlap) statistical pattern. In the case of Figure 3.2, the changing distribution pattern of the attribute in 'Population 1' illustrates that, what were earlier relatively rare forms of the attribute, are at the later point in time much more common in that population and display a narrower

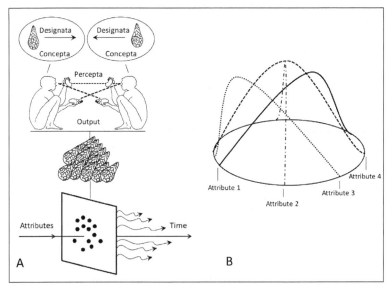

Figure 3.1. David Clarke's (1968) model of 'how pattern gets in the system'. Social transmission between people contributes to the structure of attributes of artefacts. In a socially dynamic context, individual attributes of artefact populations will vary through time (a). A single 'population' of artefacts will express a range of statistical variations in its attributes (b). (Heavily modified from Clarke 1968: 160, 182).

range. Such a change in distribution would be consistent with the idea that the rarer variants of this attribute had been preferentially selected – for example, either through aesthetic preference or because they were functionally superior in the context that the makers of 'Population 1' happened to be applying these artefacts. However, it must also be remembered that stochastic processes or 'drift' can produce shifts in the distribution patterns of single attributes, so a clearer assessment of the precise mechanism underlying this shift in dispersion pattern would require further analysis. 'Population 2' exhibits a more stable distribution of attribute variation through time, either suggesting that stabilizing selection is operating in this particular

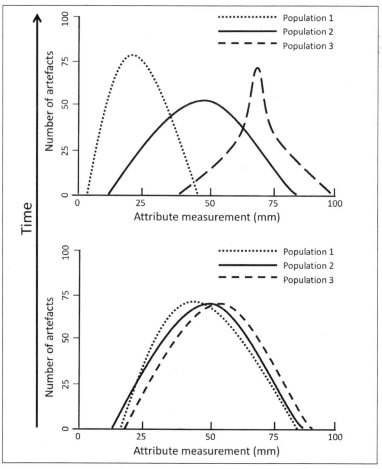

Figure 3.2. Single attributes will vary through time in their range, mode and standard deviations. Such statistical shifts will be mediated through factors such as drift (i.e. chance factors and copying errors) and selection (both natural and cultural, and both functional and aesthetic).

instance and/or that the social or environmental context in which the artefact was operating had not shifted. In the case of 'Population 3', relatively rarer variants of the attribute again seem to be represented in greater numbers than at the earlier point in time. Again, drift or selection might be at work in this case.

We can extend these ideas back to the case of populations of artefacts comprising multiple attributes, which although closely related, show quite distinct patterns of attribute variation when examined within a multivariate framework (Figure 3.3). Although Clarke (1968) never used the phrase (nor even, somewhat surprisingly, cited Darwin), many today would recognize the framework being advocated by Clarke as an application of Darwin's (1859) idea of 'descent with modification' that was formulated in order to describe how biological change through time was similarly brought about through the combined effects of heredity, variation, and the sorting of variation with passing generations (see e.g. O'Brien and Lyman 2000; Shennan 2000, 2004a; Lycett and Chauhan 2010). In this sense, Clarke's ideas were an early attempt to apply the principles of a 'population genetic' framework and phylogenetic considerations to cultural data (Lycett 2010b). Indeed, as O'Brien (2010: 314–17) points out, Clarke (1968: 134) was well aware that his framework implied the creation of phylogenetic patterns through time. This is

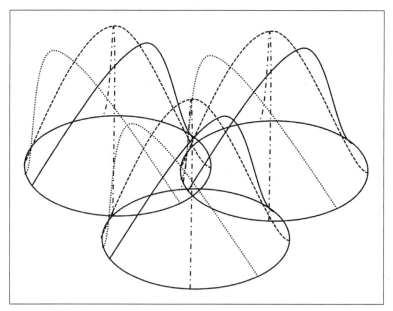

Figure 3.3. Related populations of artefacts will tend to overlap in the statistical distributions of individual attributes, emphasizing the need for multivariate analyses of population variation.

well expressed by Clarke (ibid.) in the phrase '[t]he population entity has a "heredity" – an antecedent trajectory'.

Extending Clarke's ideas still further, we could therefore, illustrate populations of artefacts with varying degrees of relatedness (i.e. varying degrees of phylogenetic proximity) that are manifest in the multivariate distribution patterns of the attributes that these artefactual populations possess (Figure 3.4). O'Brien (2010: 316) notes, however, that Clarke himself repeated the mistake that other archaeologists had made previously when he suggested that collective similarity alone might provide insight into degrees of relatedness between populations of artefacts. Clarke (1968: 513) was influenced in his thinking on this by the 'numerical taxonomy' school of phylogenetic estimation to which biology was largely enthralled at the time, but which was eventually supplanted by the 'cladistic' school of thinking (Gee 2000; O'Brien and Lyman 2003). In contrast to the notion of 'overall similarity' to estimate phylogeny, cladistics combines the principle of parsimony (i.e. a minimization of necessary assumptions) with the recognition of uniquely shared characters (or what are termed 'shared-derived' characters), and privileges these over total similarity when determining how closely related taxa are (Lyman and O'Brien

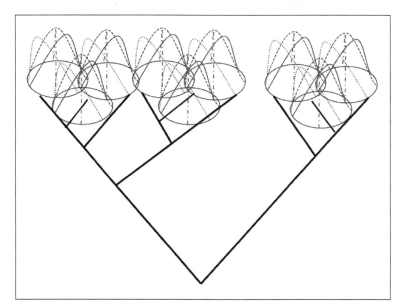

Figure 3.4. A phylogeny of related artefact populations, expressing overlap in the variation of some characters. Such phylogenies are the inevitable result of the combined effects of cultural transmission, variation in the expression of attributes (either deliberate or accidental), and the differential sorting of patterns of variation in different populations through time (either through drift or cultural and/or natural selection).

2003). Cladistic methods within the context of stone tools were mentioned by Foley (1987), but in that particular application artefacts were expressly treated as direct equivalents of the hominin biological phenotype and a concept of social transmission was not applied as the means of understanding the nature of phylogenetic relationships between various artefacts. Hence, a more thorough correction of this oversight by Clarke (and others), did not occur in archaeology until Michael O'Brien and Lee Lyman (O'Brien et al. 2001; O'Brien and Lyman 2003) produced the first formal applications of cladistics to artefacts and combined this with explicit concepts of 'descent with modification' mediated by social transmission.

As several commentators have noted (e.g. Shennan 1989, 2004a; O'Brien and Lyman 2000; O'Brien 2010), many of the insights provided by Clarke (1968) were overlooked for a considerable time. This was perhaps due to the combined effects of Clarke's untimely death (Isaac 1977; Hammond 1979) and the complexity of many the concepts he was attempting to outline (Chapman 1979; Lycett and Chauhan 2010; O'Brien 2010). In the succeeding decades, however, either influenced by Clarke or (perhaps more commonly) via independent convergence of thought, many aspects of this general framework have been elaborated, both theoretically and – perhaps more importantly – methodologically, especially via empirical case studies (e.g. Cavalli-Sforza and Feldman 1981; Boyd and Richerson 1985; Neiman 1995; Bettinger and Eerkens 1999; O'Brien and Lyman 2000, 2003; Shennan 2000, 2001; Shennan, and Wilkinson 2001; Collard and Shennan 2000; Tehrani and Collard 2002, 2009; Jordan and Shennan 2003; Bentley et al. 2004; Mesoudi et al. 2004; Eerkens and Lipo 2005; Collard et al. 2006; Greenhill et al. 2009; Lipo et al. 2006; Buchanan and Collard 2007; Lycett 2008, 2009a, 2009b; Mesoudi and O'Brien 2008; Hamilton and Buchanan 2009).

Despite these developments, resistance to the 'evolutionary' or 'biological' connotations of this work sometimes provokes harsh reaction, most frequently as a result of misunderstandings about the nature of biological evolution and/or the manner in which 'descent with modification' is being applied to cultural entities (see e.g. Ingold 2007 and the subsequent response by Mesoudi et al. 2007). The word 'evolution' might have a tendency to conjure false images of 'biological determinism' (thus denying concepts of social 'agency' in cultural process), or be taken to imply that misplaced concepts of ladder-like 'progress' are being invoked. The foregoing discussion should demonstrate just how misplaced such negative reactions are to the application of evolutionary principles (i.e. the concept of descent with modification) and/or the application of methods derived from biology that might assist in this endeavour. Indeed, as Shennan (2004b) has pointed out, given that this approach places social interaction and social process at the heart of the matter, concepts such as 'selection' and 'drift' (and the methods to study them empirically) perhaps allow concepts such as 'agency' to be situated within a framework of empirical study with a firmer basis. 'Selection' can take place via a variety of different processes, including artificial or 'cultural' selection due to preference that is motivated by concerns far removed from the survival and fecundity factors involved in the case of natural selection. In this sense, the application of evolutionary principles (and the quantitative methods to study evolutionary processes) through concepts of social transmission, is actually a 'bottom up' approach to cultural change rather than a 'top down' approach as the phrase 'evolution' may sometimes be mistakenly be interpreted by some social scientists.

Stone Artefacts and Cultural Transmission in Fossil Hominins: Example Case Studies

Within the last ten years, the framework described above has been applied to studies of stone artefacts made in deep antiquity, prior to the onset of our current geological epoch some ten thousand years ago (i.e. prior to the onset of the Holocene). This project obviously relies on the premise that at least some of the patterns of variation seen in the attributes of stone artefacts reflect patterns of socially transmitted behaviour. As Clarke (1968: 135) put it, 'the artefact is the focussed result, directively correlating a whole set of actions, sequences of actions, or behaviour ... [t]he very manufacture of the artefact directively correlates sets of actions and their resultant attributes'. The view that variation in attributes reflects (in any clear way) socially transmitted actions or sequences of actions could, however, be challenged in the case of stone artefacts. For instance, it has long been thought that a significant, if not primary, source of variation between populations of such artefacts is variation in the physical properties of the stone raw materials used (Goodman 1944). Sources of stone that are suitable for the manufacture of tools must possess specific properties of hardness, brittleness, elasticity and homogeneity (Whittaker 1994), but as a natural material, stone sources will inevitably vary to some degree in terms of these properties. If such raw material variations are on all occasions the dominant source of variation in the attributes of stone artefacts, then addressing the issue of social transmission becomes problematic.

In one recent case study, Costa (2010) tackled this issue directly, looking at the shapes of handaxes made from both bone and stone at the site of Castel di Guido (Italy), which dates to around three hundred thousand years ago. Costa applied a geometric morphometric analysis to the handaxes that enabled shape variations in their outline form to be emphasized over simply size disparities between artefacts. As Costa (ibid.: 26, 36–37) notes, given the differential fracturing properties of bone and stone, raw material influences might reasonably be expected to be high in this instance, if not dominant. As such, these factors might be expected to countermand culturally transmitted shape preferences and/or any culturally transmitted actions and techniques of manufacture that manifest themselves in common shape properties. Using this quantitative and statistical framework, Costa showed that a null hypothesis of 'no difference' between the outline shapes of the bone and stone bifaces from this site could not be rejected. In other words, despite the sophisticated methods of shape quantification employed, the shapes of the handaxes made from bone were statistically indistinguishable from those made of stone. Costa suggests that these results can 'be interpreted as support for the argument that in some cases the plan shape of Acheulean bifaces is influenced more by anthropogenic (i.e. cultural) forces than natural ones'.

In another informative study on this issue, Clarkson (2010) examined remnant cores resulting from the manufacture of various tools from five sites located in South Africa. Collectively, the cores in these assemblages are considered to belong to a techno-complex known as the 'Howiesons Poort', and date to around sixty to sixty-five thousand years (ibid.: 44). Clarkson quantified a series of attributes for these cores, describing their angles, convexities and numerous features that describe aspects of the flake scars left by the knapper. Thereafter, he applied a statistical classification technique called Discriminant Function Analysis (DFA) to these variables. DFA allows it to be ascertained how reliably (in percentage terms) the assembled quantitative variables enable assignment of individual artefacts to their correct pre-defined group based on some independent parameter (e.g. locality). Clarkson (ibid.: 52) found that cores could be assigned to their correct group based on their geographic region in 72.8 per cent of cases, whereas cores were correctly classified on the basis of their raw material in only 46 per cent of cases. As Clarkson (ibid.: 53) correctly observes, while this does not necessarily rule out a role for raw material in producing variability between artefacts, it does appear to provide clear evidence that raw material is 'subservient to other causes of variation in creating differences between regions'. More specifically, he goes on to note that this patterning points to the existence of 'ancient cultural lineages in place in these regions' (ibid.: 56).

Also using the multivariate method of DFA, Lycett and Gowlett (2008) examined patterns of variation in Acheulean handaxes from ten sites located in Africa, the Near East, India and Europe. Using a dataset comprised of sixty handaxe attributes, they found that handaxes could be assigned to their correct locality in over 70 per cent of cases – much higher than the 10 per cent level that would be dictated by chance alone. Their analyses also found regional patterns of variation, with African handaxes and non-African handaxes showing the greatest disparity, but also indicating regional patterns of variation within the non-African populations. As with Clarkson's (2010) analysis, such regional patterns of variation did not appear to be based on raw material factors, but are consistent with locally distinct networks of social transmission. However, Lycett and Gowlett (2008) also stressed that high levels of overlap between sites and patterns of variation were evident from their analyses – individual handaxes can be, and indeed were, misclassified – suggesting overlap in some of the handaxe attributes from different regions. Such patterns of overlap would suggest that variation in handaxe assemblages is similar to that schematically indicated in Figure 3.3, with different populations showing distinct statistical patterns when examined multivariately, but with levels of overlap in specific attributes.

Lycett and Gowlett (2008: 307–9) also noted that such patterns of variation could potentially indicate something about the nature of Acheulean social transmission networks. For instance, they noted that previous workers had suggested that social learning of stone-knapping techniques in these early stages of prehistory might resemble the manner in which juvenile chimpanzees learn activities such as tool-assisted termite fishing or nut cracking from their mother in a manner of 'one-to-one' transmission. However, Lycett and Gowlett noted that theoretical models of social transmission (Cavalli-Sforza and Feldman 1981) predict that highly discrete patterns of variation are expected in such learning systems, since idiosyncrasies will closely match genetic lineages in these circumstances. This, these workers suggested, was inconsistent with the levels of overlap they were seeing between different handaxe assemblages and some of their attributes. As Lycett and Gowlett note (2008: 307–8), such patterns of variation are more consistent with a 'many-to-one' pattern of learning, whereby an individual learns not just from one individual (e.g. their mother), but is influenced by a number of different individuals. Many-to-one learning of this type results in low rates of cultural change across time and space and, as such, is more consistent with the Acheulean patterns of variation observed. A many-to-one pattern of social learning for handaxe manufacture, which presents challenges even for contemporary knappers (e.g. Edwards 2001), might also suggest there were some similarities to ethnographically recorded instances of stone tool manufacture involving somewhat similar stone artefacts, where long-term 'apprenticeships' of learning involving several members of the social group have been observed (e.g. Stout 2005). We should, of course, take care not to impose the ethnographic present indiscriminately onto the past. Such examples of stone manufacture are understandably rare in the contemporary world, ensuring that our sample of ethnographic data points is sparse, to say nothing of being biologically incongruent and anachronistic. Nevertheless, to suggest that the cultural transmission of handaxe manufacture in Acheulean hominins was *more like* that seen in ethnographic instances of many-to-one learning than one-to-one learning, does not exceed the bounds of currently available evidence.

Studies such as those of Clarkson (2010) and others should inspire us to look more earnestly for the factors that might actually be driving the divergence of various individual traits in Palaeolithic artefacts (e.g. as in Figure 3.2). Drawing explicitly on terminology and principles taken from the field of quantitative genetic studies, Vaughan (2001) looked at the issue of variation in Acheulean handaxe assemblages and considered how the factors of drift and selection of different attributes might be reflected in sets of these artefacts. Using published illustrations of handaxes, Vaughan measured variation in examples from Europe, Africa and western Asia. The analyses he undertook were based on the premise that functionally related areas of outline form would be subject to greater selection, and in turn, exhibit relatively less variation. Vaughan (ibid.: 160) found that attributes associated with the width of the handaxe were always less variable compared with other areas (e.g. the tip or base of the handaxe) regardless of the locality or date of the assemblages concerned. In other words, Vaughan proposed that functionally related selection operated on variation in attributes associated with width, while other aspects of handaxe form (e.g. variations in tip-shape across time and space) were subject to chance factors and thus mediated by cultural drift. Vaughan embedded his use of the term 'selection' in classic biological terms, suggesting that factors associated with handaxe width might actually have increased the biological 'fitness' of the artefact makers. Others have since pointed out that evidence of selection in attributes such as these does not necessarily imply fitness-related selection alone (i.e. natural selection), but could actually be directed by 'cultural selection' for aesthetic or arbitrary factors (e.g. Lycett 2008, 2010b). Nevertheless, such caveats reiterate just how much theoretical progress has been made within a relatively short time period, even when using methodologies derived directly from population genetic theory.

Biological phylogenetic methods (i.e. 'tree building' methods) designed to recover genealogical relationships of evolving lineages, have also now been applied to artefacts from the Lower and Middle Palaeolithic. Application of these methods requires procedures to measure variation in the overlap and dispersion of different traits in the various study assemblages, thus incorporating the theoretical framework schematically illustrated in Figure 3.4 (Lycett 2007, 2009a, 2009b). Such methods have helped to distinguish instances of technological convergence in Palaeolithic artefacts that look superficially similar and indeed, as a result, were sometimes thought to represent cases of direct technological antecedence (Lycett 2009a, 2011). Such analyses are important in reiterating the point that convergence is an expected outcome of descent with modification in both biological and cultural entities (Mesoudi et al. 2004). Phylogenetic methods have also enabled the testing of hypotheses regarding hominin dispersals (Lycett 2009b), which in combination with population genetic methods (Lycett and von Cramon-Taubadel 2008) have provided evidence that patterns of variation in handaxe assemblages are – at least in part – mediated by population dispersal(s) from Africa.

Gene-culture Co-evolution in the Study of Stone Artefacts and Hominin Fossils?

> Cultural transmission is a primary determinant of behaviour, and there is little doubt that it is one of the most effective means of evolutionary inheritance that nature could ever develop. (O'Brien 2010: 317)

Cultural attributes are either successfully or unsuccessfully transmitted during acts of social enculturation, interaction and engagement with the wider world (both social and ecological) and thus either proliferate or are winnowed from the sociocultural repositories of communities through time (cf. Ohmagari and Berkes 1997). As a direct consequence of this, one aspect of cultural transmission that cannot be ignored is the fact that as various cultural attributes either flourish or decline in frequency and/or expression, they also potentially change the selective parameters within which biological patterns of reproduction and transmission occur. As such, the relationship between cultural and genetic patterns of variation and reproduction can sometimes be reciprocal, under a framework that has been termed 'gene-culture co-evolution' or 'dual inheritance' (e.g. Cavalli-Sforza and Feldman 1981; Boyd and Richerson 1985; Durham 1991). The classic example of this occurring during the last few thousand years of human history is the increase in the cultural practice of drinking milk from cattle, itself mediated by the cultural practices that surround pastoralism and dairying (Durham 1991:

226–85). In a variety of situations across the world, the ability of human adults to digest lactose (milk sugar) – which has a direct genetic basis – is much higher in communities with long histories of animal dairying than in regions without cultural practices of dairying and/or where there is a cultural practice for processing milk (e.g. into cheese) rather than drinking fresh milk. As such, current evidence suggests that cultural practices (i.e. dairying) have had a direct influence on the evolution of specific gene frequencies (Holden and Mace 1997). It is important not to understate the reciprocal aspect of this gene-culture co-evolutionary process: that is, as dairying became more common through time, adult milk drinkers became more common, thus encouraging the further proliferation of dairying, and so on. This reiterates that even where investigators of cultural transmission wish to juxtapose biological considerations alongside the sociocultural dimension (and examine correlations between the two), a deterministic ('genes = behaviour') attitude is not a prerequisite.

The issue of gene-culture co-evolution is arguably growing as a research agenda (Richerson and Boyd 2005; Laland et al. 2010). Given the evidence that cultural transmission has been a component of hominin behaviour since the inception of our lineage, interactions between biological and cultural evolution in hominins should be an important topic of focus (Kuhn 2004). Indeed, in a similar manner to the way in which cultural evolution might provide a common focus of endeavour within the social sciences (Mesoudi et al. 2006), it has recently been proposed that the study of cultural evolution may potentially act as a synthesizing force for what can sometimes be surprisingly disparate elements of human evolutionary study, such as physical anthropology and Palaeolithic archaeology, and their relationship to other aspects of cultural and evolutionary study (Lycett 2011). However, as with all scientific endeavours, such a project requires empirical case studies more than it does warm words.

One potential example of gene-culture co-evolution – which has drawn attention since the days of Darwin (e.g. Engels 1876) – is the idea that because our hands are no longer directly involved in locomotion (as they are in our closest quadrupedal ape relatives), the evolution of our hands might have been influenced by cultural behaviours such as tool-use and artefact manufacture. As Washburn (1959: 24) stated some time ago, '[t]he hand was freed by the assumption of bipedal locomotion. Then new selection pressures coming with the use of tools changed the ape hand into the human hand'. Broadly supporting this scenario is evidence from comparative anatomy showing that the human hand and wrist possess unique features that allow gripping and manipulatory behaviours which are different from those of other living apes (Marzke and Marzke 2000). Such features include relatively short fingers and a strong thumb, which due to a well-developed muscle in our forearms (the flexor pollicis longus), ensures that we can 'pinch' items between our thumb and tips and sides of our fingers with much greater force than other apes. However, given that our closest chimpanzee relatives also use tools, we know that for the 'tool use hypothesis' of human hand evolution to be correct, it must have been *specific* categories of tool usage and manufacture that played the key role rather than 'tool use' as a broad and indiscriminate category.

Unsurprisingly, the most frequently invoked evolutionary cause of human hand evolution is the pressures associated with stone tool use and manufacture (reviewed in Tocheri et al. 2008). The association of even the very earliest examples of stone tools alongside evidence of meat eating (for example in the form of cut-marked and smashed bones) has further fuelled such suggestions. Incorporated alongside this is a recognition that 'more complex foraging behaviour' in our ancestors – of which use of stone cutting tools to process animal remains would form a pre-eminent example – must have played a role in other aspects of human anatomy such as our relatively large brains combined with our relatively small digestive tracts (Aiello and Wheeler 1995: 207). A majority of studies examining this topic have focused on the manufacture of stone flakes through percussion (e.g. Marzke et al. 1998). Such studies have found evidence that the unique aspects of human hand anatomy are heavily recruited during stone flake manufacture, consistent with the evolutionary hypothesis. Far fewer studies, however, have focused on the issue of whether a cultural tradition of using simple stone flakes for cutting might alone have exerted selective forces on hand anatomy.

Given that we currently know little about the emergence of stone tool use and manufacture, at least in terms of whether use of naturally occurring sharp edges preceded the first deliberate instances of stone flaking (Panger et al. 2002), it might be particularly important to determine if the use of simple cutting tools alone may have exerted evolutionary pressures on hominin hands. To this end, Alastair Key and I recently investigated experimentally whether variations in the handsizes of individuals – a variable known to be correlated with specific human gripping capacities – translated into statistically significant effects in the efficiency of simple cutting tools when applied to a replicable cutting task (Key and Lycett 2011). This version of the 'tool use hypothesis' for hand evolution is particularly relevant since efficiency in the actual act of cutting, and thus achieving the goal of the cutting behaviour with greatest ease, is the most immediate factor that natural selection could potentially operate upon. We tested

whether hand variation translated into differences of cutting efficiency, using sixty volunteer participants. Half of these participants
used replicated stone flakes similar in form to those known from the
Oldowan, while the other half used small unhafted steel blades. The
handsize of each participant was first measured and they were then
asked to cut through a 10 mm-diameter piece of natural-fibre rope.
Cutting efficiency for this task was measured both by the length of
time it took to completely sever the rope, as well as by counting the
number of cutting strokes that this act required. Our experiments
found that both measures of cutting efficiency were related to participant handsize to a statistically significant extent. Importantly,
no statistical effect was found for differences between the two tool
categories employed in the experiments, nor between variations in
the form of individual stone flakes and cutting efficiency. These latter
results suggest that, all else being equal, the most dominant effect on
efficiency in these experiments was exerted by the physical attributes
of the participant concerned. As such, these results support the hypothesis that factors relating directly to efficiency during the actual
use of simple cutting tools, even in the absence of flaking behaviours,
would have exerted evolutionary pressures upon hand anatomy in
the earliest stone-tool-using hominins. Moreover, the importance of
better understanding the process of social transmission and cultural
evolution within the hominin lineage in order to further understand
the prevalence and character of gene-culture co-evolution during
our evolution is reiterated.

Conclusion: Cultural Transmission – An Integrative Analytical Framework for the Human Evolutionary Sciences *and* Anthropological Endeavour?

Cultural transmission theory provides a quantitative framework for
studying patterns of variation in artefacts made by fossil hominins
many millennia ago. As can be seen from the foregoing, this quantitative framework facilitates statistical analysis and the specific framing
and testing of hypotheses against formal theoretical models (see also
Lycett and Chauhan 2010). It enables patterns of artefact variation
to be assessed in order to help determine the extent of other potential
influences on artefactual variation (such as raw material), and determine which is having a relatively dominant effect. Moreover, 'cultural transmission' is a multi-faceted phenomenon that can occur via
different pathways, be subject to various different pressures, and thus
ultimately result in a variety of different patterns. This ensures that
the study of 'cultural transmission' is not a univariate pursuit, but

gives potential insight into a variety of key issues, many of which can be seen as matters of classic 'anthropological' concern – who is interacting with whom and what is the character and outcome of that interaction. It is partly for these reasons that some have suggested that the study of cultural transmission (especially via dedicated analysis of patterns of cultural inheritance, patterns of cultural variation and how these shift and relate through time) might provide a means of synthesizing various strands of research within the social sciences (e.g. Mesoudi et al. 2006).

As this volume aptly illustrates, the study of cultural transmission in fossil hominins sits phylogenetically (i.e. in terms of relative relatedness) between other lineages of social transmission – those of modern humans and those of primates and other animals. This means that the study of cultural transmission in any one of these lineages (including that of fossil hominins) leads to a possibility that individual lines of study could, and arguably should, speak to one another. Given some recent exchanges (e.g. Ingold 2007 vs. Mesoudi et al. 2007), the biggest stumbling block to such integration will most likely be a divide between those who see advantages (both practical and epistemological) in couching their studies in overtly biological terminology and draw heavily on the quantitative principles and methodologies so successfully exploited by that discipline, and those who fiercely resist such endeavours.

For those who study cultural transmission in fossil hominins, there will perhaps be little choice as to which way to proceed in regard to such debates. With a requirement to understand the principles of biological variation, inheritance and variant sorting through time (i.e. the key fundamental factors in Darwinian evolution) over the inevitably deep time-frames of such study, they will understandably find it convenient to couch both cultural and biological evolution in common terminology. This is especially so when common methodological techniques of analysis are being applied, even if – as should be readily apparent from the foregoing – the study of cultural evolution in Darwinian terms does not necessitate a slavish desire to find *exact* parallels in both cases. Cultural and biological modes of descent with modification can, and do, have different mechanisms of effecting the inheritance, variation and sorting of the properties concerned in each case, as well as similarities (e.g. Eerkens and Lipo 2005; Mesoudi 2007; Lycett 2008, 2010b). However, by necessity, the study of cultural transmission in hominins – unlike the study of cultural transmission in living humans or other animals for their own sake – has a vast time depth with which to contend. Over the course of such evolutionary time-scales, genetic and physiological changes occurred on a scale unlike that encountered when examining extant species. The study of each of the different branches of cultural evolution (humans, primates and other taxa) can potentially provide insights and questions for the study of hominin cultural evolution – and vice versa. Equally, through the study of factors such a gene-culture co-evolution, there is greater potential for integration between various aspects of the evolutionary sciences (Lycett 2011). As a result, the study of hominin cultural evolution not only provides a key integrative component between various workers who study cultural transmission in living species, but also – through the types of methodology discussed here –provides a means of placing the evolution of human biology and human culture in a common terminological and analytical framework.

Acknowledgements

I am grateful to Roy Ellen, Sarah Johns, Kerstin Schillinger and Noreen von Cramon-Taubadel for their helpful comments on an earlier draft of this chapter.

References

Aiello, L.C. and P. Wheeler. 1995. 'The Expensive Tissue Hypothesis: The Brain and the Digestive System in Human and Primate Evolution', *Current Anthropology* 36(2): 199–221.

Bentley, R.A., M.W. Hahn and S. Shennan. 2004. 'Random Drift and Culture Change', *Proceedings of the Royal Society of London B* 271: 1443–50.

Bettinger, R.L. and J. Eerkens. 1999. 'Point Typologies, Cultural Transmission, and the Spread of Bow-and-arrow Technology in the Prehistoric Great Basin', *American Antiquity* 64(2): 231–42.

Binford, L.R. 1983. *In Pursuit of the Past*. London: Thames and Hudson.

Biro, B., S. Carvalho and T. Matsuzawa. 2010. 'Tools, Traditions, and Technologies: Interdisciplinary Approaches to Chimpanzee Nutcracking', in E.V. Lonsdorf, S.R. Ross and T. Matsuzawa (eds), *The Mind of the Chimpanzee: Ecological and Experimental Perspectives*. Chicago: Chicago University Press, pp. 141–55.

Biro, D., C. Sousa and T. Matsuzawa. 2006. 'Ontogeny and Cultural Propagation of Tool Use by Wild Chimpanzees at Bossou, Guinea: Case Studies in Nut Cracking and Leaf Folding', in T. Matsuzawa, M. Tomonaga and M. Tanaka (eds), *Cognitive Development in Chimpanzees*. New York: Springer, pp. 476–508.

Boyd, R. and P.J. Richerson. 1985. *Culture and the Evolutionary Process*. Chicago: University of Chicago Press.

Buchanan, B. and M. Collard. 2007. 'Investigating the Peopling of North America through Cladistic Analyses of Early Paleoindian Projectile Points', *Journal of Anthropological Archaeology* 26(3): 366–93.

Cavalli-Sforza, L.L. and M.W. Feldman. 1981. *Cultural Transmission and Evolution: A Quantitative Approach.* Princeton, NJ: Princeton University Press.

Chapman, R. 1979. '"Analytical Archaeology" and After', in N. Hammond, G.L. Isaac, R. Chapman, A.G. Sherratt and S.J. Shennan (eds), *Analytical Archaeologist: Collected Papers of David L. Clarke.* London: Academic Press, pp. 109–43.

Clarke, D.L. 1968. *Analytical Archaeology.* London: Methuen.

Clarkson, C. 2010. 'Regional Diversity within the Core Technology of the Howiesons Poort Techno-complex', in S.J. Lycett and P.R. Chauhan (eds), *New Perspectives on Old Stones: Analytical Approaches to Paleolithic Technologies.* New York: Springer, pp. 43–59.

Collard, M. and S. Shennan. 2000. 'Processes of Cultural Change in Prehistory: A Case Study from the European Neolithic', in C. Renfrew and K. Boyle (eds), *Archaeogenetics: DNA and the Population Prehistory of Europe.* Cambridge: McDonald Institute for Archaeological Research, pp. 89–97.

Collard, M., S.J. Shennan and J.J. Tehrani. 2006. 'Branching, Blending, and the Evolution of Cultural Similarities and Differences among Human Populations', *Evolution and Human Behavior* 27(3): 169–84.

Costa, A.G. 2010. 'A Geometric Morphometric Assessment of Plan Shape in Bone and Stone Acheulean Bifaces from the Middle Pleistocene Site of Castel di Guido, Latium, Italy', in S.J. Lycett and P.R. Chauhan (eds), *New Perspectives on Old Stones: Analytical Approaches to Palaeolithic Technologies.* New York: Springer, pp. 23–41.

Darwin, C. 1859. *On the Origin of Species by Means of Natural Selection.* London: John Murray.

Delagnes, A. and H. Roche. 2005. 'Late Pliocene Hominid Knapping Skills: The Case of Lokalalei 2C, West Turkana, Kenya', *Journal of Human Evolution* 48: 435–72.

Domínguez-Rodrigo, M., T.R. Pickering, S. Semaw and M.J. Rogers. 2005. 'Cutmarked Bones from Pliocene Archaeological Sites in Gona, Afar, Ethiopia: Implications for the Function of the World's Oldest Stone Tools', *Journal of Human Evolution* 48: 109–21.

Durham, W.H. 1991. *Coevolution: Genes, Culture and Human Diversity.* Stanford, CA: Stanford University Press.

Edwards, S.W. 2001. 'A Modern Knapper's Assessment of the Technical Skills of the Late Acheulean Biface Workers at Kalambo Falls', in J.D. Clark (ed.), *Kalambo Falls Prehistoric Site: Volume III.* Cambridge: Cambridge University Press, pp. 605–11.

Eerkens, J.W. and C.P. Lipo. 2005. 'Cultural Transmission, Copying Errors, and the Generation of Variation in Material Culture and the Archaeological Record', *Journal of Anthropological Archaeology,* 24: 316–34.

Engels, F. (1876) 1934. 'The Part Played by Labour in the Transition from Ape to Man', *Dialectics of Nature.* Moscow: Progress Publishers.

Foley, R.A. 1987. 'Hominid Species and Stone Tool Assemblages: How Are They Related?', *Antiquity* 61: 380–92.

Franz, M. and L.J. Matthews. 2010. 'Social Enhancement can Create Adaptive, Arbitrary and Maladaptive Cultural Traditions', *Proceedings of the Royal Society B* 277: 3363–72.

Gee, H. 2000. *Deep Time: Cladistics, the Revolution in Evolution*. London: Fourth Estate.

Goodman, M.E. 1944. 'The Physical Properties of Stone Tool Materials', *American Antiquity* 9(4): 415–33.

Greenhill, S.J., T.E. Currie and R.D. Gray. 2009. 'Does Horizontal Transmission Invalidate Cultural Phylogenies?', *Proceedings of the Royal Society of London B* 276 (1665): 2299–306.

Hamilton, M.J. and B. Buchanan. 2009. 'The Accumulation of Stochastic Copying Errors Causes Drift in Culturally Transmitted Technologies: Quantifying Clovis Evolutionary Dynamics', *Journal of Anthropological Archaeology* 28: 55–69.

Hammond, N. 1979. 'David Clarke: A Biographical Sketch', in N. Hammond, G.L. Isaac, R. Chapman, A.G. Sherratt and S.J. Shennan (eds), *Analytical Archaeologist: Collected Papers of David L. Clarke*. London: Academic Press, pp. 1–10.

Henrich, J. 2004. 'Demography and Cultural Evolution: How Adaptive Cultural Processes can Produce Maladaptive Losses: The Tasmanian Case', *American Antiquity* 69(2): 197–214.

Holden, C. and R. Mace. 1997. 'Phylogenetic Analysis of the Evolution of Lactose Digestion in Adults', *Human Biology* 69(5): 605–28.

Horner, V. and F.B.M. de Waal. 2009. 'Controlled Studies of Chimpanzee Cultural Transmission', *Progress in Brain Research* 178: 3–15.

Horner, V., A. Whiten, E. Flynn and F.B.M. de Waal. 2006. 'Faithful Replication of Foraging Techniques along Cultural Transmission Chains by Chimpanzees and Children', *Proceedings of the National Academy of Sciences USA* 103(37): 13878–83.

Humle, T., C.T. Snowdon and T. Matsuzawa. 2009. 'Social Influences on Ant-dipping Acquisition in the Wild Chimpanzees (*Pan troglodytes verus*) of Bossou, Guinea, West Africa', *Animal Cognition* 12(S1): 37–48.

Ingold, T. 2007. 'The Trouble with "Evolutionary Biology"', *Anthropology Today* 23(2): 13–17.

Isaac, G.L. 1977. 'David Leonard Clarke 1937–1976: Obituary', *American Anthropologist* 79(3): 642–44.

Jordan, P. and S. Shennan. 2003. 'Cultural Transmission, Language, and Basketry Traditions amongst the California Indians', *Journal of Anthropological Archaeology* 22: 42–74.

Key, A.J.M. and S.J. Lycett. 2011. 'Technology Based Evolution? A Biometric Test of the Effects of Handsize versus Tool Form on Efficiency in an Experimental Cutting Task', *Journal of Archaeological Science* 38(7): 1663–70.

Kuhn, S.L. 2004. 'Evolutionary Perspectives on Technology and Technological Change', *World Archaeology* 36(4): 561–70.

Laland, K., J. Odling-Smee and S. Myles. 2010. 'How Culture Shaped the Human Genome: Bringing Genetics and the Human Sciences Together', *Nature Reviews Genetics* 11: 137–48.

Lind, J. and P. Lindenfors. 2010. 'The Number of Cultural Traits is Correlated with Female Group Size but not with Male Group Size in Chimpanzee Communities', *PLoS ONE* 5 (e9241): 1–3.

Lipo, C.P., M.J. O'Brien, M. Collard and S. Shennan. 2006. 'Cultural Phylogenies and Explanation: Why Historical Methods Matter', in C.P. Lipo, M.J. O'Brien, M. Collard and S. Shennan (eds), *Mapping Our Ancestors: Phylogenetic Approaches in Anthropology and Prehistory*. New Brunswick, NJ: Aldine Transaction, pp. 3–16.

Lonsdorf, E.V. 2006. 'What is the Role of Mothers in the Acquisition of Termite-fishing Behaviors in Wild Chimpanzees (*Pan troglodytes schweinfurthii*)?', *Animal Cognition* 9: 36–46.

Lycett, S.J. 2007. 'Why is there a Lack of Mode 3 Levallois Technologies in East Asia? A Phylogenetic Test of the Movius-Schick Hypothesis', *Journal of Anthropological Archaeology* 26(4): 541–75.

————.2008. 'Acheulean Variation and Selection: Does Handaxe Symmetry fit Neutral Expectations?', *Journal of Archaeological Science* 35(9): 2640–48.

————.2009a. 'Are Victoria West Cores "proto-Levallois"? A Phylogenetic Assessment', *Journal of Human Evolution* 56(2): 175–91.

————.2009b. 'Understanding Ancient Hominin Dispersals Using Artefactual Data: A Phylogeographic Analysis of Acheulean Handaxes', *PLoS ONE* 4 (10/e7404): 1–6.

————.2010a. 'The Importance of History in Definitions of "Culture": Implications from Phylogenetic Approaches to the Study of Social Learning in Chimpanzees', *Learning and Behavior* 38(3): 252–64.

————.2010b. 'Cultural Transmission, Genetic Models and Palaeolithic Variability: Integrative Analytical Approaches', in S.J. Lycett and P.R. Chauhan (eds), *New Perspectives on Old Stones: Analytical Approaches to Palaeolithic Technologies*. New York: Springer, pp. 207–34.

————.2011. '"Most Beautiful and Most Wonderful": Those Endless Stone Tool Forms', *Journal of Evolutionary Psychology* 9(2): 143–71.

Lycett, S.J. and P.R. Chauhan. 2010. 'Analytical Approaches to Palaeolithic Technologies: An Introduction', in S.J. Lycett and P.R. Chauhan (eds), *New Perspectives on Old Stones: Analytical Approaches to Palaeolithic Technologies*. New York: Springer, pp. 1–22.

Lycett, S.J., M. Collard, and W.C. McGrew. 2007. 'Phylogenetic Analyses of Behavior Support Existence of Culture among Wild Chimpanzees', *Proceedings of the National Academy of Sciences USA* 104(45): 17588–92.

————.2009. 'Cladistic Analyses of Behavioral Variation in Wild *Pan troglodytes*: Exploring the Chimpanzee Culture Hypothesis', *Journal of Human Evolution* 57(4): 337–49.

————.2010. 'Are Behavioral Differences among Wild Chimpanzee Communities Genetic or Cultural? An Assessment using Tool-use Data and Phylogenetic Methods', *American Journal of Physical Anthropology* 142(3): 461–67.

————.2011. 'Correlations between Genetic and Behavioural Dissimilarities in Wild Chimpanzees (*Pan troglodytes*) do not Undermine the Case for Culture', *Proceedings of the Royal Society B* 278: 2091–93.

Lycett, S.J. and N. von Cramon-Taubadel. 2008. 'Acheulean Variability and Hominin Dispersals: A Model-bound Approach', *Journal of Archaeological Science* 35(3): 553–62.

Lycett, S.J. and J.A.J. Gowlett. 2008. 'On Questions Surrounding the Acheulean "Tradition"', *World Archaeology* 40(3): 295–315.

Lycett, S.J. and C.J. Norton. 2010. 'A Demographic Model for Palaeolithic Technological Evolution: The Case of East Asia and the Movius Line', *Quaternary International* 211(1): 55–65.

McGrew, W.C. 2004. *The Cultured Chimpanzee: Reflections on Cultural Primatology*. Cambridge: Cambridge University Press.

Marzke, M.W. and R.F. Marzke. 2000. 'Evolution of the Human Hand: Approaches to Acquiring, Analysing and Interpreting the Evidence', *Journal of Anatomy* 197: 121–40.

Marzke, M.W., N. Toth, K. Schick, S. Reece, B. Steinberg, K. Hunt, R.L. Linscheid and K.-N. An. 1998. 'EMG Study of Hand Muscle Recruitment during Hard Hammer Percussion Manufacture of Oldowan Tools', *American Journal of Physical Anthropology* 105: 315–32.

Matthews, L.J., A. Paukner and S.J. Suomi. 2010. 'Can Traditions Emerge from the Interaction of Stimulus Enhancement and Reinforcement Learning? An Experimental Model', *American Anthropologist* 112(2): 257–69.

Mesoudi, A. 2007. 'Biological and Cultural Evolution: Similar but Different', *Biological Theory* 2(2): 119–23.

————.2011. *Cultural Evolution: How Darwinian Evolutionary Theory Can Explain Human Culture And Synthesize the Social Sciences*. Chicago, IL: University of Chicago Press.

Mesoudi, A. and M.J. O'Brien. 2008. 'The Cultural Transmission of Great Basin Projectile Point Technology I: An Experimental Simulation', *American Antiquity* 73(1): 3–28.

Mesoudi, A., A. Whiten and K.N. Laland. 2004. 'Is Human Cultural Evolution Darwinian? Evidence Reviewed from the Perspective of *The Origin of Species*', *Evolution* 58(1): 1–11.

————.2006. 'Towards a Unified Science of Cultural Evolution', *Behavioral and Brain Sciences* 29: 329–83.

————.2007. 'Science, Evolution and Cultural Anthropology', *Anthropology Today* 22: 18.

Neiman, F.D. 1995. 'Stylistic Variation in Evolutionary Perspective: Inferences from Decorative Diversity and Interassemblage distance in Illinois Woodland Ceramic Assemblages', *American Antiquity* 60(1): 7–36.

O'Brien, M.J. 2010. 'The Future of Palaeolithic Studies: A View from the New World', in S.J. Lycett and P.R. Chauhan (eds), *New Perspectives on Old Stones: Analytical Approaches to Palaeolithic Technologies*. New York: Springer, pp. 311–34.

O'Brien, M.J., J. Darwent and R.L. Lyman. 2001. 'Cladistics is Useful for Reconstructing Archaeological Phylogenies: Palaeoindian Points from the Southeastern United States', *Journal of Archaeological Science* 28: 1115–36.

O'Brien, M.J. and R.L. Lyman. 2000. *Applying Evolutionary Archaeology: A Systematic Approach*. New York: Kluwer Academic/Plenum.

_____.2003. *Cladistics and Archaeology*. Salt Lake City: University of Utah Press.

Ohmagari, K. and F. Berkes. 1997. 'Transmission of Indigenous Knowledge and Bush Skills among the Western James Bay Cree Women of Subarctic Canada', *Human Ecology* 25(2): 197–222.

Panger, M.A., A.S. Brooks, B. Richmond and B.Wood. 2002. 'Older than the Oldowan? Rethinking the Emergence of Hominin Tool Use', *Evolutionary Anthropology* 11: 235–45.

Patten, B. 2005. *Peoples of the Flute: A Study in Anthropolithic Forensics*. Denver, CO: Stone Dagger Publications.

Richerson, P.J. and R. Boyd. 2005. *Not by Genes Alone: How Culture Transformed Human Evolution*. Chicago: University of Chicago Press.

Schick, K.D. and N. Toth. 1993. *Making Silent Stones Speak: Human Evolution and the Dawn of Human Technology*. London: Weidenfeld and Nicolson.

Schick, K.D., N. Toth and G. Garufi. 1999. 'Continuing Investigations into the Stone Tool-making and Tool-using Capabilities of a Bonobo (*Pan paniscus*)', *Journal of Archaeological Science* 26: 821–32.

Semaw, S., M.J. Rogers, J. Quade, P.R. Renne, R.F. Butler, M. Dominguez-Rodrigo, D. Stout, W.S. Hart, T. Pickering and S.W. Simpson. 2003. '2.6-Million-year-old Stone Tools and Associated Bones from OGS-6 and OGS-7, Gona, Afar, Ethiopia', *Journal of Human Evolution* 45: 169–77.

Shennan, S. 1989. 'Archaeology as Archaeology or as Anthropology? Clarke's *Analytical Archaeology* and the Binfords' *New Perspectives in Archaeology* 21 Years On', *Antiquity* 63: 831–35.

_____.2000. 'Population, Culture History, and the Dynamics of Culture Change', *Current Anthropology* 41(5): 811–35.

_____.2001. 'Demography and Cultural Innovation: A Model and its Implications for the Emergence of Modern Human Culture', *Cambridge Archaeological Journal* 11(1): 5–16.

_____.2004a. 'Analytical Archaeology', in J. Bintliff (ed.), *A Companion to Archaeology*. Oxford: Blackwell, pp. 3–20.

_____.2004b. 'An Evolutionary Perspective on Agency in Archaeology', in A. Gardner (ed.), *Agency Uncovered*. London: UCL Press, pp. 19–32.

Shennan, S. and J.R. Wilkinson. 2001. 'Ceramic Style Change and Neutral Evolution: A Case Study from Neolithic Europe', *American Antiquity* 66(4): 577–93.

Stout, D. 2005. 'The Social and Cultural Context of Stone Knapping Skill Acquisition', in V. Roux and B. Bril (eds), *Stone Knapping: The Necessary Conditions for a Uniquely Hominin Behaviour*. Cambridge: McDonald Institute for Archaeological Research, pp. 331–40.

Tehrani, J. and M. Collard. 2002. 'Investigating Cultural Evolution through Biological Phylogenetic Analyses of Turkmen Textiles', *Journal of Anthropological Archaeology* 21: 443–63.

_____.2009. 'On the Relationship between Inter-individual Cultural Transmission and Inter-group Cultural Diversity: A Case Study of Weaving in Iranian Tribal Populations', *Evolution and Human Behavior* 30(4): 286–300.

Tocheri, M.W., C.M. Orr, M.C. Jacofsky and M.W. Marzke. 2008. 'The Evolutionary History of the Hominin Hand since the Last Common Ancestor of *Pan* and *Homo*', *Journal of Anatomy* 212: 544–62.

Toth, N., K.D. Schick, E.S. Savage-Rumbaugh, R.A. Sevcik and D.M. Rumbaugh. 1993. 'Pan the Tool-maker: Investigations into the Stone Tool-making and Tool-using Capabilities of a Bonobo (*Pan paniscus*)', *Journal of Archaeological Science* 20: 81–91.

Toth, N., K. Schick and S. Semaw. 2006. 'A Comparative Study of the Stone Tool-making Skills of *Pan*, *Australopithecus*, and *Homo sapiens*', in N. Toth and K. Schick (eds), *The Oldowan: Case Studies into the Earliest Stone Age*. Gosport, IN: Stone Age Institute Press, pp. 155–222.

Vaughan, C.D. 2001. 'A Million Years of Style and Function: Regional and Temporal Variation in Acheulean Handaxes', in T.D. Hurt and G.F.M. Rakita (eds), *Style and Function: Conceptual Issues in Evolutionary Archaeology*. Westport, CT: Bergin and Garvey, pp. 141–63.

Washburn, S.L. 1959. 'Speculations on the Interrelations of the History of Tools and Biological Evolution', in J.N. Spuhler (ed.), *The Evolution of Man's Capacity for Culture*. Detroit, MI: Wayne State University Press, pp. 21–31.

Weedman, A.K. 2010. 'Feminine Knowledge and Skill Reconsidered: Women and Flaked Stone Tools', *American Anthropologist* 112(2): 228–43.

Whiten, A. 2009. 'The Identification and Differentiation of Culture in Chimpanzees and Other Animals: From Natural History to Diffusion Experiments', in K.N. Laland and B.G. Galef (eds), *The Question of Animal Culture*. Cambridge, MA: Harvard University Press, pp. 99–124.

_____.2010. 'A Coming of Age for Cultural Panthropology', in E.V. Lonsdorf, S.R. Ross and T. Matsuzawa (eds), *The Mind of the Chimpanzee: Ecological and Experimental Perspectives*. Chicago: Chicago University Press, pp. 87–100.

Whiten, A., V. Horner and F.B.M. de Waal. 2005. 'Conformity to Cultural Norms of Tool Use in Chimpanzees', *Nature* 437: 737–40.

Whiten, A., K. Schick and N. Toth. 2009. 'The Evolution and Cultural Transmission of Percussive Technology: Integrating Evidence from Palaeoanthropology and Primatology', *Journal of Human Evolution* 57(4): 420–35.

Whittaker, J.C. 1994. *Flintknapping: Making and Understanding Stone Tools*. Austin, TX: University of Texas Press.

Wrangham, R.W. 2006. 'Chimpanzees: The Culture Zone Concept Becomes Untidy', *Current Biology* 16(16): 634–35.

Chapter 4

STUDYING CULTURAL TRANSMISSION WITHIN AN INTERDISCIPLINARY CULTURAL EVOLUTIONARY FRAMEWORK

Alex Mesoudi

Introduction

Cultural transmission is the process by which knowledge, beliefs, skills, practices, norms, values and other forms of non-genetic information are passed from individual to individual via social learning mechanisms such as imitation and teaching. This surely places cultural transmission at the heart of pretty much every social science discipline, not just anthropology but also psychology, sociology, linguistics, history, political science and economics. Yet cultural transmission is surprisingly under-appreciated in many of these disciplines. Often, cultural influences on human behaviour are ignored or downplayed in favour of explanations in terms of individual responses to non-social stimuli, with no explicit consideration of social influence. Within anthropology, for example, cultural ecologists (Steward 1955), cultural materialists (M. Harris 1989) and human behavioural ecologists (Winterhalder and Smith 2000) all tend to explain human behaviour in terms of individual adaptation to local environmental conditions rather than as the result of cultural transmission. Similarly, cognitive psychologists typically study how single individuals understand and learn about the world largely independently from other people, while economists of the 'rational choice theory' school assume that people individually calculate the costs and benefits of different behaviours with little cultural influence (see Gintis 2007). Other disciplines stress the role of genetic rather than cultural inheritance, such as some evolutionary psychologists' assertion that much variation in human behaviour is generated by evoked genetic responses to different environmental conditions ('evoked culture') rather than resulting from cultural transmission (Tooby and Cosmides 1992; Gangestad, Haselton and Buss 2006). None of these popular and reputable approaches to the study of human behaviour place much importance on cultural transmission.

In certain respects this unwillingness to explain human behaviour in cultural terms is understandable given the often vague and unscientific way in which cultural transmission is conceptualized in the social sciences, including social anthropology. It is often assumed that people somehow absorb the cultural beliefs, values, norms and such like of the previous generation by some mysterious, almost magical process of 'enculturation', 'acculturation' or 'socialization'. It is, for example, argued that 'acculturation occurs through a process of constant immersion of each person in a sea of cultural phenomena, smells, tastes, postures, the appearance of buildings, the rise and fall of spoken utterances' (Fracchia and Lewontin 1999: 73) or 'what each generation contributes to the next are ... the specific circumstances under which successors, growing up in a social world, can develop their own embodied skills and dispositions, and their powers of awareness and response' (Ingold 2000: 237–38). Such vague statements are far from conducive to the generation of specific, testable, refutable hypotheses (how does one quantify and attempt to measure the consequences of a 'sea of postures', for example?), and it is little wonder that psychologists and economists reject cultural explanations for human behaviour on these very grounds (see for example Tooby and Cosmides 1992: 41; Guiso, Sapienza and Zingales 2006: 23). There is little attempt in the social sciences to explain the population-level, intergenerational persistence of ideas and beliefs in terms of specific and measurable individual-level processes – who is copying what idea or belief from whom, and when. In large part this stems from the move within the social sciences towards social constructionist, interpretivist and hermeneutic stances, and the associated anti-reductionist unwillingness to explain cultural and social phenomena in terms of lower-level causes (see Slingerland 2008).

Yet this is not to say that there is no robust scientific evidence for the influence of cultural transmission on human behaviour. On the contrary, there is a growing body of rigorous and fully scientific cross-cultural research showing substantial cultural influence on various aspects of human behaviour, albeit often coming from experimental psychology and economics rather than anthropology (Heine and Norenzayan 2006; Henrich, Heine and Norenzayan 2010). Significant cross-cultural variation has been demonstrated in levels of aggression (Cohen et al. 1996), vulnerability to perceptual illusions (Segall, Campbell and Herskovits 1963), categorization of, and memory for, objects (Nisbett et al. 2001), self identity (Heine et al. 1999) and cooperation in economic games (Henrich et al. 2005), amongst other fundamental psychological and behavioural phenomena. This variation cannot be explained by individual adaptation, given that it seldom corresponds to local ecological conditions (Hewlett, De Silvestri and Guglielmino 2002), and cannot be explained in terms of genetic differences given evidence that immigrants adopt the norms of the local society in just one or two generations, too fast for genetic adaptation to have occurred (Heine and Norenzayan 2006). In sum, there is robust evidence that numerous aspects of human behaviour and cognition are significantly shaped by cultural transmission.

Cultural Evolution

The foregoing discussion presents a problem: there is increasingly robust evidence that culturally transmitted information significantly shapes various aspects of human behaviour, yet most social scientists either ignore cultural transmission entirely or conceptualize it in vague, non-scientific terms that preclude the generation and testing of refutable hypotheses. I suggest that an approach that can address these problems is that of 'cultural evolution' (Cavalli-Sforza and Feldman 1981; Boyd and Richerson 1985; Henrich and McElreath 2003; Mesoudi 2011; Mesoudi, Whiten and Laland 2006). This approach views cultural change (i.e. changes in culturally transmitted beliefs, norms, values, etc.) as a Darwinian evolutionary process that acts in parallel to genetic/biological evolution. Before outlining the advantages of this approach, it is useful to specify exactly what is (and is not) meant by 'Darwinian evolutionary process'.

Darwin explained the diversity and complexity observed in the natural world in terms of just three simple principles (Lewontin 1970): (1) *variation*: individuals within a population vary in their characteristics; (2) *differential fitness*: due to limited resources, not all individuals are equally likely to survive and reproduce, and their likelihood of reproduction is determined at least in part by their characteristics; and (3) *inheritance*: offspring resemble their parents in their characteristics more than a randomly selected individual. Given these three empirically demonstrable principles, over time those characteristics that increase an individual's chances of survival and reproduction increase in frequency in the population, ultimately combining with other beneficial traits to form complex adaptations such as eyes and wings, and causing different populations to diverge to generate the diversity of species we see today.

The theory of cultural evolution rests on the premise that cultural change exhibits these same Darwinian principles of variation, differential fitness and inheritance (Mesoudi, Whiten and Laland 2004). First, cultural traits, such as words, technological innovations, beliefs and attitudes, vary across individuals within a population. Second, not all traits are equally likely to persist or get passed on to other individuals – some ideas are more memorable than others, some practices more effective, some customs more socially acceptable. Third, traits are inherited from individual to individual via cultural transmission mechanisms such as imitation and teaching. Over time, those cultural traits that are better at being transmitted (the more memorable, more effective, more socially acceptable, etc.) increase in frequency in the population, ultimately combining with other beneficial traits to form complex cultural adaptations such as telescopes and aeroplanes, and causing different societies to diverge to generate the cultural diversity we see in the ethnographic and historical record.

Importantly, a Darwinian theory of cultural evolution makes no further claims about the mechanisms by which these basic principles operate, regarding how variation is generated, how it is transmitted and what causes differential fitness between variants. For example, we now know that biological inheritance is particulate, that is to say it involves the transmission of discrete packages of information, genes, in an all-or-nothing fashion. Yet this is not a necessary requirement of Darwinian evolution. Indeed, Darwin himself knew nothing of genes, and believed (incorrectly, for the biological case) that continuous, non-discrete biological traits blended when transmitted. In many cases there is good evidence that the mechanisms underlying biological and cultural change are quite different. Particularity of variation is a good example of this: whereas genetic inheritance is particulate, cultural transmission in many cases appears to be non-particulate. These differences are explicitly incorporated into cultural evolution models, as is discussed below.

It is also important to note that cultural evolutionary theory is not simply an extension of sociobiology, evolutionary psychology or other disciplines seeking to explain human behaviour primarily in terms of genetic evolution, as is sometimes claimed – for example, Ingold's grouping of the cultural evolutionary approach taken by Mesoudi et al. (2006) with 'neo-Darwinian "evolutionary biology" ... evolutionary psychology and memetics' (Ingold 2007: 14). Although some theoretical analyses of gene-culture co-evolution seek to explain the origin of cultural transmission dynamics in terms of genetic evolution (e.g. Boyd and Richerson 1989), many other analyses focus solely on the cultural transmission dynamics themselves. Indeed, theoretical analyses suggest that the very reason why cultural transmission is genetically adaptive is because it allows genes to forego direct control over behaviour, and permits organisms to acquire adaptive behaviour culturally instead of genetically, given that cultural learning can better respond to rapid environmental change than genetic evolution (Boyd and Richerson 1995; Aoki, Wakano and Feldman 2005). Moreover, because of this uncoupling of genetic and cultural evolution, the latter can often lead to the spread of genetically maladaptive cultural traits (Boyd and Richerson 1985). Cultural evolution is therefore explicitly *not* genetically reductionist (Plotkin 1995).

The Advantages of Analysing Cultural Transmission as an Evolutionary Process

That both biological and cultural change exhibit the same basic principles is not simply an academic curiosity of interest to philosophers of science. Viewing cultural change as a Darwinian process means that culture can be analysed using similar evolutionary methods to those used by biologists to understand biological/genetic change, suitably modified to incorporate the differences between biological and cultural change. In many cases these evolutionary methods result in significantly improved understanding of cultural phenomena than traditional, non-evolutionary social science methods. Perhaps the most important conceptual tool is what Mayr (1982) has called 'population thinking'. In the biological case this is where population-level 'macroevolutionary' change, such as speciation and adaptation, is explained in terms of individual-level 'microevolutionary' processes, such as different forms of selection (e.g. directional, stabilizing, sexual), genetic drift, mutation, recombination, migration and so on. In the early part of the twentieth century, population geneticists such as Fisher, Haldane and Wright constructed formal mathematical models that explicitly linked microevolutionary processes to specific macroevolutionary patterns. In a typical model of this kind, a hypothetical population of individuals is specified, with these individuals varying in their genetic traits. The modeller then specifies a set of quantifiable microevolutionary processes, such as selection or drift, that act to change the genetic variation in the population over successive time periods. Mathematical techniques are used to determine the long-term, population-level dynamics of different microevolutionary processes, such as whether a particular process increases or decreases genetic variation over time. Back in the 1920s and 1930s, these formal analyses resolved outstanding problems or misunderstandings that had hitherto hindered progress in biology. One such was Fisher's (1930) mathematical demonstration that the existence of discrete traits that are transmitted in an all-or-nothing fashion (i.e. genes), as had been demonstrated earlier by experimental geneticists such as Gregor Mendel, was nevertheless consistent with continuous phenotypic variation (e.g. in height or fur colour) because these phenotypic traits were determined by multiple discrete genes rather than a single gene. In other words, the model linked microevolutionary processes discovered experimentally in the lab (particulate non-blending inheritance) to macroevolutionary phenomena observed in the world by naturalists (continuous variation in a trait in the population as a whole).

In the 1980s, Cavalli-Sforza and Feldman (1981) and Boyd and Richerson (1985) used similar mathematical modelling techniques to analyse cultural evolution. These models typically specify a population of individuals, with each individual varying in their cultural traits, and specifies quantifiable cultural selection and cultural transmission processes that act to change that variation over successive periods of time. Mathematical techniques or computer simulations are used to determine the long-term, population-level dynamics, such as whether a particular trait will go to fixation or coexist with other traits at equilibrium, or the diffusion dynamics of different transmission processes. As in biology, these models have two key benefits: (1) they force the researcher to specify in precise and quantitative terms exactly how a particular cultural transmission process acts to change the frequency of some cultural trait over time, in contrast to the vague notion of 'acculturation' or 'socialization' encountered above, and (2) they allow the researcher to explore the long-term, population-level consequences of different cultural transmission processes with a precision that is simply not possible with purely verbal, informal reasoning.

Importantly, Cavalli-Sforza and Feldman (1981) and Boyd and Richerson (1985) recognized in these models that the details of cultural microevolution may be very different to those of biological microevolution. In many cases they drew on existing research in social psychology, social anthropology, sociology and sociolinguistics when constructing their modified models. First, whereas biologists have established that genetic inheritance is of high fidelity and involves the all-or-nothing transmission of discrete units of inheritance (i.e. genes), Cavalli-Sforza and Feldman (1981) and Boyd and Richerson (1985) instead modelled cultural transmission as potentially being of much lower fidelity. This is consistent with experimental findings from social psychology that cultural transmission is a process of low-fidelity transformation rather than high-fidelity replication (Bartlett

1932), and in some cases involves the blending of continuously vary-ing cultural traits rather than discrete gene-like units, as observed by sociolinguists for dialect change (Lehmann 1992). Second, whereas biologists model genetic inheritance as strictly non-Lamarckian, with acquired characteristics never directly inherited by offspring, Boyd and Richerson (1985) modelled the Lamarckian-like cultural process of 'guided variation', where people systematically transform cultural-ly acquired representations towards a pre-existing favoured form, and then transmit this modified form to another person. Third, whereas genetic inheritance is largely parent-to-offspring, or 'vertical', in ver-tebrate species (although horizontal gene transfer is common in plants and bacteria), Cavalli-Sforza and Feldman (1981) modelled not only vertical cultural transmission (from parents) but also oblique (from unrelated members of the parental generation) and horizontal (from unrelated members of the same generation) cultural transmission, consistent with evidence that much human cultural transmission is non-vertical (J. Harris 1995). Moreover, oblique and horizontal trans-mission was modelled as either one-to-one, representing direct face-to-face instruction, or one-to-many, as in teaching or the mass media (Cavalli-Sforza and Feldman 1981). Fourth, Boyd and Richerson (1985) modelled three types of cultural transmission: (1) content-bi-ased cultural transmission, where certain traits are intrinsically more attractive or memorable than others for psychological reasons, as has been proposed by cognitive anthropologists (Sperber and Hirschfeld 2004); (2) conformist and anti-conformist cultural transmission, where people preferentially adopt the most or least common trait in the population as has been observed by social psychologists (Jacobs and Campbell 1961; Moscovici, Lage and Naffrechoux 1969); and (3) prestige-biased cultural transmission, where people preferentially adopt the traits exhibited by particularly successful or prestigious individuals, consistent with research in social psychology (Bandura, Ross and Ross 1963), socio-linguistics (Labov 1972) and sociology (Rogers 1995). Finally, Cavalli-Sforza and Feldman (1981) modelled the cultural analogue of genetic drift, where cultural traits are copied entirely at random with no intrinsic differences between traits, and of migration, where people move across social group boundaries and take their traits with them.

Just as population geneticists determined the population-level con-sequences of biological microevolutionary processes, Cavalli-Sforza and Feldman (1981) and Boyd and Richerson (1985) modelled the population-level macroevolutionary consequences of these cultural microevolutionary processes. In other words, Darwinian population thinking and formal mathematical models that treat cultural change as a Darwinian evolutionary process allow links to be made between the micro- and the macro-levels in the social/behavioural sciences – the former studied by experimental psychologists and economists in the lab or ethnographers in the field concerned with the details of who learns what from whom, and the latter studied by ethnologists, archaeologists, sociologists, historians and historical linguists concerned with long-term cultural change or between-society cultural variation. This micro–macro divide has been a perennial problem in the social sciences, and previous attempts to bridge the gap (e.g. Schwartz and Mead 1961) have been informal and consequently ultimately unfruitful. The formal evolutionary models of Cavalli-Sforza and Feldman (1981) and Boyd and Richerson (1985) allow the micro–macro divide to be bridged more effectively and potentially to synthesize these various macro and micro branches of the social sciences (Mesoudi, Whiten and Laland 2006; Mesoudi 2007, 2011).

Case Study: Prehistoric Projectile Point Evolution in the Great Basin

To illustrate the value of decomposing population-level macroevolutionary patterns of cultural variation down into underlying microevolutionary cultural transmission biases, I will discuss a case study involving projectile points – stone artefacts such as arrowheads and dart tips. The points in question are from the Great Basin region of the south-western United States and date to around AD 300–600. Archaeologists Bettinger and Eerkens (1999) documented systematic differences in the variation in the points found across two sites in this region. Points found at a site in present-day central Nevada were found to exhibit little variation in their attributes, such as length, width, thickness and shape, such that only a few combinations of attribute values occurred. For example, points that were corner-notched (i.e. had hook-like notches in their base that prevented them from coming loose when embedded in flesh) were almost always thin and light: in other words, the two attributes shape and thickness were linked. In contrast, points from another site in eastern California featured no systematic linkage between attributes; points that were corner-notched were no more likely to be thick than thin, for example. This generated far more within-site diversity in California than in Nevada.

Having ruled out potential explanations for these differences in point variation across the two sites in terms of raw material or prey, Bettinger and Eerkens (1999) turned to an explanation in terms of the aforementioned cultural transmission biases. Specifically, they argued that point designs in California originally spread via guided variation, where people acquire a design from another person but then modify that design according to their own idiosyncratic individual learning styles. This latter individual learning would have eliminated any links between attributes, as different people modified different attributes separately. In the Nevadan site, on the other hand, Bettinger and Eerkens proposed that point designs were copied via prestige-biased (or more generally 'indirect') cultural transmission, where people acquire a design from a single successful or prestigious individual with no further modification of that design (Boyd and Richerson 1985). If everyone in a group is copying the same successful model, then soon everyone will have the same point design and attributes will be linked in the way documented in Nevada. In sum, Bettinger and Eerkens had explained population-level cultural variation (linked vs. unlinked point attributes) in terms of individual-level cultural transmission biases (prestige bias vs. guided variation).

Michael O'Brien and I have extended Bettinger and Eerkens' (1999) work by simulating their proposed cultural transmission scenario both experimentally in the psychology lab and theoretically using agent-based simulations (Mesoudi and O'Brien 2008a, 2008b). The value of theoretical simulations is that they allow us to check formally Bettinger and Eerkens' intuitions regarding the population-level consequences of their proposed transmission biases in this specific case, while the value of experimental simulations is that they can tell us whether people can and do engage in these proposed transmission biases. Barring the invention of a time machine, neither of these is possible with purely archaeological/historical methods.

In the lab experiments (Mesoudi and O'Brien 2008a), participants were faced with the task of designing a 'virtual arrowhead' via a computer programme by entering values for its attributes (length, width, thickness, shape and colour). They could then test their design by going on a series of 'virtual hunts' during which they got feedback on its effectiveness in the form of calories obtained. Participants were placed in groups of five or six, and different phases simulated the different transmission biases proposed by Bettinger and Eerkens (1999). An initial 'prestige bias' phase allowed the participants to copy the arrowhead design of one of a group of previous players of the game, having been given information about the previous players' success. The vast majority of participants during this phase did indeed choose to copy the most successful hunter, confirming previous social psychological findings that people prefer to copy prestigious or successful individuals. A subsequent 'guided variation' phase comprised a series of hunts during which there was no opportunity to copy other group members, relying instead solely on individual trial-and-error learning. As Bettinger and Eerkens had predicted, arrowhead designs during the prestige bias phase featured significantly lower attribute variation than arrowhead designs following the guided variation phase, supporting their proposed transmission scenario.

However, the experiments (Mesoudi 2008; Mesoudi and O'Brien 2008a) and theoretical models (Mesoudi and O'Brien 2008b) revealed an important limitation on Bettinger and Eerkens' (1999) hypothesized scenario. In designing our experiments we were forced to specify fitness functions for the virtual arrowheads – that is to say, mathematical expressions that translate attribute dimensions into calorific payoffs. One possibility is a simple linear, unimodal set of functions such that there is a single optimal arrowhead design that gives the highest payoff, with payoffs declining steadily the further the design gets from this optimum. Agent-based simulations (Mesoudi and O'Brien 2008b) revealed a problem with this assumption, in that during the 'guided variation' phase each isolated individual learner eventually converged on the same single optimal arrowhead design through individual trial-and-error learning. This resulted in low cultural variation in the guided variation phase, exactly the same end result as in the prestige bias phase, and counter to Bettinger and Eerkens' proposed scenario. Instead, we assumed in the experiments multimodal fitness functions. To borrow a biological concept introduced by Wright (1932), we can envisage arrowhead fitness as a landscape where the height of the landscape represents fitness and each coordinate in the landscape represents a different combination of attributes (length, width, thickness, etc.). The unimodal functions generate a single peak in this landscape with all points leading uphill to the single optimum. Multimodal functions, on the other hand, feature several peaks of different heights representing several locally optimal designs of different fitness. Assuming this multimodal adaptive landscape meant that variation was not eliminated during the guided variation phase, because individual learners became stuck on different locally optimal peaks. Any deviation from their chosen peak reduced their payoff, even though there may have been, unbeknownst to them, a higher peak (a better arrowhead design) elsewhere in the design space. Prestige bias still eliminated variation in multimodal landscapes because each member of the group copied the most successful group member, namely the one who had found the highest peak in the landscape, such that every group member converged on this same peak. In sum, Bettinger and Eerkens' hypothesis only works if one is willing to assume a multimodal adaptive landscape underlying projectile point evolution.

But is this assumption valid? Experimental studies conducted by Cheshier and Kelly (2006) suggest that it may be. They fired replica arrowheads into animal carcasses and measured their durability and penetrative power, finding tradeoffs between different demand characteristics. For example, long and thin arrowheads were easier to aim and more likely to penetrate the animal's skin, but created smaller wounds that would have been less likely to kill the animal. Wide and thick arrowheads, on the other hand, were more difficult to aim and fire, but when they did hit the target they created larger wounds that would have been more likely to kill the animal. This suggests the existence of at least two peaks: a 'long, thin, penetrative' peak and a 'wide, thick, wounding' peak. Further experimental and ethnographic studies might quantitatively determine the exact shape of the adaptive landscape underlying arrowhead fitness, informed by the aforementioned simulations.

In sum, this series of studies illustrates the value of (1) explaining population-level patterns such as between-site differences in artefact diversity in terms of precisely specified individual-level cultural transmission processes, and (2) using a range of methods – archaeological, experimental and theoretical modelling – to explore the validity and applicability of these individual-level explanations. The traditional fractionated state of the social sciences has frequently hindered such interdisciplinary exchange of findings, methods and concepts. However, the micro–macro bridge facilitated by Darwinian population thinking encourages such links. Both lab experiments and computer simulations, for example, have the advantage over archaeological/historical methods of allowing us to directly observe people copying one another according to known transmission biases, to obtain complete and uninterrupted data records, and to manipulate variables (e.g. fitness functions) in order to explore the limits of the proposed explanation. Of course, what we gain in control and manipulation when conducting simulations is offset by what we lose in external validity: the people participating in experiments (typically undergraduates) are very different from the prehistoric hunters who would have made the original points, and the computer-based task employed in the lab is hugely simplified compared to the real-life task of hunting and manufacturing points. But by constantly cross-checking experimental and theoretical results with archaeological findings, and vice versa, as illustrated above, hopefully these strengths and weaknesses will complement one another.

Other Micro–Macro Links

In addition to the case study discussed above, several other studies have linked the aforementioned microevolutionary processes to real-world data regarding specific cultural phenomena (Mesoudi 2007). For example, Henrich (2001) has shown theoretically that content-biased cultural transmission, where people preferentially copy 'more-effective' traits exhibited by other people, causes novel beneficial traits to diffuse through populations in a distinct S-shaped fashion, where uptake is slow at first, then rapid, then slow again. In contrast, guided variation, where people independently modify acquired traits according to individual trial-and-error learning, generates r-shaped diffusion curves which do not exhibit the initial slow uptake. Given that sociologists have observed S-shaped diffusion curves for the vast majority of real-life cases of technological diffusion (Rogers 1995), Henrich (2001) suggests that content-biased transmission is more important in real-life technological cultural change than guided variation, in contrast to the assumptions of many economists and sociologists who emphasize individual learning over cultural transmission.

In another example, cultural drift – the copying of cultural traits entirely at random with no selection or transmission biases – has been shown theoretically to generate a distinct 'power-law' distribution of cultural traits, where a small number of traits are extremely popular and a large number of traits are very rare (Bentley, Hahn and Shennan 2004), in contrast to non-random cultural transmission biases such as conformity and anti-conformity which do not generate power laws (Mesoudi and Lycett 2009). The power-law distribution characterizes several real-life cultural datasets such as first names, dog breeds, patent and scientific article citations, and prehistoric pottery decorations, suggesting that each of these phenomena are governed by a drift-like random copying bias (Bentley, Hahn and Shennan 2004).

Other cultural evolution researchers have begun to use the ethnographic method to test for the presence and form of microevolutionary processes in small-scale societies. Tehrani and Collard (2009), for example, used the ethnographic method to address a long-standing issue in anthropology over whether cultural macroevolution is branching or blending. Kroeber (1948) famously argued that whereas biological macroevolution is a branching, tree-like process, because when two species diverge they stay separated, cultural macroevolution features the frequent transmission of customs, practices, words and beliefs across societal boundaries such that it better resembles a reticulated bush than a bifurcating tree. This purported difference has subsequently been used to argue against the application of phylogenetic methods to reconstruct cultural macroevolution (e.g. Moore 1994), which were originally designed by biologists to deal with branching biological datasets (although see Collard, Shennan and Tehrani 2006). Tehrani and Collard (2009) argued that this criticism actually rests on untested assumptions concerning the extent of vertical vs. horizontal transmission across social group boundaries at the microevolutionary level. Their ethnographic study of Iranian weavers found that women typically learned weaving techniques exclusively from their mothers, indicating vertical cultural transmission, and learned weaving patterns typically from other members of the community, indicating horizontal transmission. However, even in the latter case the weaving patterns were seldom learned from women from other social groups due to norms restricting the movement of women. So even with substantial horizontal cultural transmission at the individual level, a tree-like branching pattern of textile pattern macroevolution was maintained because of impermeable social group boundaries. Again, this study shows how knowledge of cultural microevolutionary cultural transmission biases can inform our understanding of cultural macroevolution.

Conclusions

Studying cultural transmission within a Darwinian evolutionary framework has several methodological advantages. Darwinian population thinking encourages researchers to think about the long-term, population-level consequences of different cultural transmission processes. Formal evolutionary methods borrowed from population genetics force researchers to quantify in precise terms exactly how cultural transmission acts to change cultural variation in a population, and to provide tools that can be used to determine the long-term, population-level cultural dynamics generated by different transmission processes with a precision not possible with purely verbal, informal notions of transmission. Finally, in bridging the micro–macro divide in this way, new interdisciplinary avenues open up as the transmission processes studied in the lab by psychologists and experimental economists are used to explain patterns and trends documented in the archaeological and ethnographic record by anthropologists, sociologists and historians. The consequent exchange of theories, concepts and methods across what are, traditionally, impermeable disciplinary boundaries promise to stimulate a similar 'evolutionary synthesis' to that which occurred in evolutionary biology in the 1930s and 1940s in response to similar formal evolutionary methods that bridged biological micro- and macro-evolution (Mesoudi 2007, 2011). Given the subsequent success of evolutionary biologists in explaining biological diversity and complexity, it is hoped that similar success will attend the study of cultural change in the coming years.

An evolutionary framework also points to potential areas in which research efforts might be most profitably directed. The biggest post-synthesis advance in biology was Watson and Crick's discovery of the structure of DNA, constituting a molecular basis for genetic inheritance. The equivalent underlying basis of cultural transmission would concern how information is represented in the brain, and how that information is transmitted from one brain to another at the neural level. Yet neuroscientists currently have little understanding of such processes. Initial findings related to 'mirror neurons', neurons that respond both to oneself performing an action and observing another person performing that same action (Rizzolatti and Craighero 2004), provide a preliminary glimpse of a potential neural mechanism for imitation (Rizzolatti et al. 2002), although this is just a very basic starting point and applies to manual skills such as tool use rather than cognitive representations such as beliefs and values.

At the other end of the spectrum, there is a need to explain the existence of large-scale cooperative cultural institutions such as business firms and nation-states. Some cultural evolution researchers have explained these institutions as products of a process of cultural group selection (Henrich 2004; Cordes et al. 2008; Boyd and Richerson 2009), whereby cultural transmission processes such as conformity generate cohesive social groups that then compete with one another, with more cooperative groups selected over less cooperative groups. This macroevolutionary process of cultural group selection may then generate novel selection pressures at the microevolutionary level, such as the spread of group-beneficial cultural practices and beliefs, in an instance of macroevolution shaping microevolution rather than vice versa as is commonly considered. Yet the precise cultural transmission processes that permit the formation of stable large-scale institutions have yet to be identified. Although the challenges of explaining cultural phenomena at multiple levels, from neurons to institutions, all within a single explanatory framework, may seem insurmountable, the beginnings of such a project can be detected in the interdisciplinary research that is currently being facilitated by the synthetic cultural evolutionary framework outlined here.

References

Aoki, K., J.Y. Wakano and M.W. Feldman. 2005. 'The Emergence of Social Learning in a Temporally Changing Environment: A Theoretical Model', *Current Anthropology* 46: 334–40.

Bandura, A., D. Ross and S.A. Ross. 1963. 'A Comparative Test of the Status Envy, Social Power, and Secondary Reinforcement Theories of Identificatory Learning', *Journal of Abnormal and Social Psychology* 67: 527–34.

Bartlett, F.C. 1932. *Remembering*. Oxford: Macmillan.

Bentley, R.A., M.W. Hahn and S.J. Shennan. 2004. 'Random Drift and Culture Change', *Proceedings of the Royal Society B* 271: 1443–50.

Bettinger, R.L. and J. Eerkens. 1999. 'Point Typologies, Cultural Transmission, and the Spread of Bow-and-arrow Technology in the Prehistoric Great Basin', *American Antiquity* 64: 231–42.

Boyd, R. and P.J. Richerson. 1985. *Culture and the Evolutionary Process*. Chicago, IL: University of Chicago Press.

_____.1989. 'Social Learning as an Adaptation', *Lectures on Mathematics in the Life Sciences* 20: 1–26.

_____.1995. 'Why Does Culture Increase Human Adaptability?', *Ethology and Sociobiology* 16: 125–43.

_____.2009. 'Culture and the Evolution of Human Cooperation', *Philosophical Transactions of the Royal Society B* 364: 3281.

Cavalli-Sforza, L.L. and M.W. Feldman. 1981. *Cultural Transmission and Evolution*. Princeton: Princeton University Press.

Cheshier, J. and R.L. Kelly. 2006. 'Projectile Point Shape and Durability: The Effect of Thickness:Length', *American Antiquity* 71: 353–63.

Cohen, D., R.E. Nisbett, B.F. Bowdle and N. Schwarz. 1996. 'Insult, Aggression, and the Southern Culture of Honor: An Experimental Ethnography', *Journal of Personality and Social Psychology* 70: 945–60.

Collard, M., S. Shennan and J.J. Tehrani. 2006. 'Branching, Blending, and the Evolution of Cultural Similarities and Differences among Human Populations', *Evolution and Human Behavior* 27: 169–84.

Cordes, C., P.J. Richerson, R. McElreath and P. Strimling. 2008. 'A Naturalistic Approach to the Theory of the Firm: The Role of Cooperation and Cultural Evolution', *Journal of Economic Behavior and Organization* 68: 125–39.

Fisher, R.A. 1930. *The Genetical Theory of Natural Selection*. Oxford: Clarendon Press.

Fracchia, J. and R.C. Lewontin. 1999. 'Does Culture Evolve?', *History and Theory* 38: 52–78.

Gangestad, S.W., M.G. Haselton and D.M. Buss. 2006. 'Evolutionary Foundations of Cultural Variation: Evoked Culture and Mate Preferences', *Psychological Inquiry* 17: 75–95.

Gintis, H. 2007. 'A Framework for the Unification of the Behavioral Sciences', *Behavioral and Brain Sciences* 30: 1–61.

Guiso, L., P. Sapienza and L. Zingales. 2006. 'Does Culture Affect Economic Outcomes?', *The Journal of Economic Perspectives* 20: 23–48.

Harris, J.R. 1995. 'Where Is the Child's Environment? A Group Socialization Theory of Development', *Psychological Review* 102: 458–89.

Harris, M. 1989. *Cows, Pigs, Wars and Witches: The Riddles of Culture*. New York: Vintage.

Heine, S.J., D.R. Lehman, H.R. Markus and S. Kitayama. 1999. 'Is There a Universal Need for Positive Self-Regard?', *Psychological Review* 106: 766–94.

Heine, S.J. and A. Norenzayan. 2006. 'Toward a Psychological Science for a Cultural Species', *Perspectives on Psychological Science* 1: 251–69.

Henrich, J. 2001. 'Cultural Transmission and the Diffusion of Innovations', *American Anthropologist* 103: 992–1013.

_____.2004. 'Cultural Group Selection, Coevolutionary Processes and Large-scale Cooperation', *Journal of Economic Behavior and Organization* 53: 3–35.

Heine, S.J., R. Boyd, S. Bowles, C. Camerer, E. Fehr, H. Gintis et al. 2005. '"Economic Man" in Cross-cultural Perspective: Behavioral Experiments in 15 Small-scale Societies', *Behavioral and Brain Sciences* 28: 795–855.

Heine, S.J., S.J. Heine and A. Norenzayan. 2010. 'The Weirdest People in the World?', *Behavioral and Brain Sciences* 33: 61–135.

Heine, S.J. and R. McElreath. 2003. 'The Evolution of Cultural Evolution', *Evolutionary Anthropology* 12: 123–35.

Hewlett, B., A. De Silvestri and C.R. Guglielmino. 2002. 'Semes and Genes in Africa', *Current Anthropology* 43: 313–21.

Ingold, T. 2000. 'Evolving Skills', in H. Rose and S. Rose (eds), *Alas, Poor Darwin: Arguments against Evolutionary Psychology*. London: Jonathan Cape, pp. 225–46.

_____.2007. 'The Trouble with "Evolutionary Biology"', *Anthropology Today* 23: 3–7.

Jacobs, R.C. and D.T. Campbell. 1961. 'The Perpetuation of an Arbitrary Tradition through Several Generations of a Laboratory Microculture', *Journal of Abnormal and Social Psychology* 62: 649–58.

Kroeber, A.L. 1948. *Anthropology*. New York: Harcourt, Brace and Co.

Labov, W. 1972. *Sociolinguistic Patterns*. Philadelphia, PA: University of Pennsylvania Press.

Lehmann, W.P. 1992. *Historical Linguistics: An Introduction*. London: Routledge.

Lewontin, R.C. 1970. 'The Units of Selection', *Annual Review of Ecology and Systematics* 1: 1–18.

Mayr, E. 1982. *The Growth of Biological Thought*. Cambridge, MA: Harvard University Press.

Mesoudi, A. 2007. 'A Darwinian Theory of Cultural Evolution can Promote an Evolutionary Synthesis for the Social Sciences', *Biological Theory* 2: 263–75.

_____.2008. 'An Experimental Simulation of the "Copy-Successful-Individuals" Cultural Learning Strategy: Adaptive Landscapes, Producer–Scrounger Dynamics and Informational Access Costs', *Evolution and Human Behavior* 29: 350–63.

_____.2011. *Cultural Evolution: How Darwinian Evolutionary Theory can Explain Human Culture and Synthesize the Social Sciences*. Chicago, IL: University of Chicago Press.

Mesoudi, A. and S.J. Lycett. 2009. 'Random Copying, Frequency-dependent Copying and Culture Change', *Evolution and Human Behavior* 30: 41–48.

Mesoudi, A. and M.J. O'Brien. 2008a. 'The Cultural Transmission of Great Basin Projectile Point Technology I: An Experimental Simulation', *American Antiquity* 73: 3–28.

_____.2008b. 'The Cultural Transmission of Great Basin Projectile Point Technology II: An Agent-based Computer Simulation', *American Antiquity* 73: 627–44.

Mesoudi, A., A. Whiten and K.N. Laland. 2004. 'Is Human Cultural Evolution Darwinian? Evidence Reviewed from the Perspective of *The Origin of Species*', *Evolution* 58: 1–11.

_____.2006. 'Towards a Unified Science of Cultural Evolution', *Behavioral and Brain Sciences* 29: 329–83.

Moore, J.H. 1994. 'Putting Anthropology Back Together Again: The Ethnogenetic Critique of Cladistic Theory', *American Anthropologist* 96: 925–48.

Moscovici, S., E. Lage and M. Naffrechoux. 1969. 'Influence of a Consistent Minority on the Responses of a Majority in a Color Perception Task', *Sociometry* 32: 365–80.

Nisbett, R.E., K. Peng, I. Choi and A. Norenzayan. 2001. 'Culture and Systems of Thought: Holistic versus Analytic Cognition', *Psychological Review* 108: 291–310.

Plotkin, H. 1995. *Darwin Machines and the Nature of Knowledge*. London: Penguin.

Rizzolatti, G. and L. Craighero. 2004. 'The Mirror-Neuron System', *Annual Review of Neuroscience* 27: 169–92.

Rizzolatti, G., L. Fadiga, L. Fogassi and V. Gallese. 2002. 'From Mirror Neurons to Imitation: Facts and Speculations', in A.N. Melzhoff and W. Prinz (eds), *The Imitative Mind: Development, Evolution and Brain Bases*. Cambridge: Cambridge University Press, pp. 247–66.

Rogers, E. 1995. *The Diffusion of Innovations*. New York: Free Press.

Schwartz, T. and M. Mead. 1961. 'Micro- and Macro-cultural Models for Cultural Evolution', *Anthropological Linguistics* 3: 1–7.

Segall, M.H., D.T. Campbell and M.J. Herskovits. 1963. 'Cultural Differences in the Perception of Geometric Illusions', *Science* 139: 769.

Slingerland, E. 2008. *What Science Offers the Humanities*. Cambridge: Cambridge University Press.

Sperber, D. and L.A. Hirschfeld. 2004. 'The Cognitive Foundations of Cultural Stability and Diversity', *Trends in Cognitive Sciences* 8: 40–46.

Steward, J. 1955. *Theory of Culture Change*. Illinois: University of Illinois Press.

Tehrani, J.J. and M. Collard. 2009. 'On the Relationship between Interindividual Cultural Transmission and Population-level Cultural Diversity: A Case Study of Weaving in Iranian Tribal Populations', *Evolution and Human Behavior* 30: 286–300.

Tooby, J. and L. Cosmides. 1992. 'The Psychological Foundations of Culture', in J.H. Barkow, L. Cosmides and J. Tooby (eds), *The Adapted Mind*. London: Oxford University Press, pp. 19–136.

Winterhalder, B. and E.A. Smith. 2000. 'Analyzing Adaptive Strategies: Human Behavioral Ecology at Twenty-Five', *Evolutionary Anthropology* 9: 51–72.

Wright, S. 1932. 'The Roles of Mutation, Inbreeding, Crossbreeding and Selection in Evolution', *Proceedings of the Sixth International Congress of Genetics* 1: 356–66.

Chapter 5

DO TRANSMISSION ISOLATING MECHANISMS (TRIMS) INFLUENCE CULTURAL EVOLUTION?

EVIDENCE FROM PATTERNS OF TEXTILE DIVERSITY WITHIN AND BETWEEN IRANIAN TRIBAL GROUPS

Jamshid J. Tehrani and Mark Collard

Introduction

There are important differences in the ways that genes and cultural traits can be transmitted among human individuals. Whereas genes can only be transmitted 'vertically' from parents to children, cultural practices and ideas can be acquired from a variety of sources (Cavalli-Sforza and Feldman 1981; Boyd and Richerson 1985). While the ethnographic record demonstrates that many craft skills, subsistence techniques and other important cultural behaviours are vertically transmitted (e.g. Hewlett and Cavalli-Sforza 1986; Ohmagari and Berkes 1997; Shennan and Steele 1999; Greenfield et al. 2000; Lozada et al. 2006), it also shows that learners often acquire specialized knowledge from unrelated members of the older generation such as teachers and master craftsmen ('oblique transmission') (e.g. Hewlett and Cavalli-Sforza 1986; Ohmagari and Berkes 1997; Aunger 2000; Henrich and Gil-White 2001; Reyes-Garcia et al. 2009; Tehrani and Collard 2009a). In addition, individuals can copy traits from unrelated members of their own generation ('horizontal transmission').

In view of these differences, many anthropologists have assumed that patterns of cultural evolution are bound to be far more complex and intertwined than patterns of genetic evolution (Boas 1940; Kroeber 1948; Terrell 1988; Moore 1994). Recently, however, this assumption has been challenged by a number of researchers (e.g. Durham 1990, 1992; Mace et al. 2005; Collard et al. 2006; Tehrani and Collard 2009a). One of the most influential of these critiques was developed by William Durham (1990, 1992). Durham argued that whereas cultural transmission within groups is facilitated by common language, intermarriage and shared social norms, transmission between groups is often constrained by ecological boundaries, language barriers, endogamy, rivalry/warfare, in-group conformity and xenophobic attitudes. He termed these factors 'Transmission Isolating Mechanisms' (TRIMS), analogous to the reproductive isolating mechanisms that prevent gene flow between species. Contrary to the classical view in social anthropology, Durham proposed that the prevalence of TRIMS in the ethnographic record indicates that societies usually inherit the bulk of their cultural traits from their ancestors through branching processes of descent with modification (phylogenesis). Thus, despite the differences in genetic and cultural transmission between individuals, the processes involved in generating between-group cultural similarities and differences are, according to this view, fundamentally similar to the processes that give rise to biodiversity.

Durham's hypothesis is consistent with a number of recent empirical studies suggesting that phylogenesis has played an important role in generating cultural and linguistic diversity among populations (e.g. Mace et al. 2005; Collard et al. 2006; Lipo et al. 2006). Only one of these studies, however, directly examined the role played by TRIMS in generating these patterns. The study in question was one we carried out some years ago on the evolution of textile designs among a group of Turkmen tribes in north-eastern Iran, Turkmenistan and Afghanistan (Tehrani and Collard 2002). We examined weavings produced during two periods of Turkmen history. The first period was prior to the military conquest of the Turkmen by Imperial Russian forces in the 1880s, during which time the Turkmen practised a nomadic-pastoralist lifestyle. The second period was after the Russian colonization, which led to the forced settlement of the Turkmen and the increasing commercialization of craft production. Cladistic analyses of rug designs suggested that phylogenesis dominated the evolution of Turkmen rug traditions in both periods. These results were consistent with ethnohistorical data, which indicated that cultural transmission among the tribes is likely to have been inhibited by two important

TRIMS, namely endogamy and endemic warfare. At the same time, we found evidence that the rate of borrowing increased when these constraints were weakened following the Russian conquest, after which the tribes were forcibly pacified and gradually became politically and economically integrated into the new regime.

While the results of our Turkmen study supported the proposal that TRIMS play a major role in cultural phylogenesis, the hypothesis makes other important predictions that have yet to be studied empirically. One of these is that patterns of cultural diversity between groups should exhibit greater phylogenetic structure than patterns within groups. Here, we present a study that was specifically designed to test this prediction.

The study focused on woven textiles produced by tribal populations in western Iran. Textile weaving is the dominant craft activity in these communities and is carried out exclusively by females. Ethnographic evidence suggests that there are likely to be powerful TRIMS that constrain the transmission of weaving knowledge between tribes (Tehrani and Collard 2002, 2009a, 2009b). First, the tribes, or *Il*, are organized into territorially distinct political/ethnic groupings, and were until recently frequently in conflict with each other and the Iranian state (e.g. Barth 1961; Garthwaite 1983; Beck 1986). Secondly, intermarriage between the tribes was prevented by norms of tribe endogamy. This is likely to be particularly relevant to the transmission of weaving, because core craft skills are transmitted vertically from mother to daughter. Given that girls are almost always born into their mothers' natal tribes, this means that new weaving techniques from other groups are rarely introduced into the tribe (Tehrani and Collard 2009a). Endogamous marriage is also likely to influence the degree of transmission of designs. Unlike techniques, designs are frequently learned through oblique and horizontal transmission among women in the same community (Tehrani and Collard 2009a). The main way in which weavers come into contact with women belonging to other communities is when they get married and move to their husband's village. Since they marry into villages belonging to the same tribe, this would not be expected to lead to the transmission of patterns between tribal groups.

While social organization and marriage practices are likely to have operated as TRIMS on between-group craft transmission, we hypothesize that they probably encouraged the circulation of weaving traits within tribes. Members of the same tribe (*Il*) recognized a common leader, the *il khan*, who had the power to raise taxes and recruit armies from the patrilineal clans (*tayfeh*) that constituted the tribe. Disputes between the clans over migration routes, pasture or water resources would either be resolved by the leaders of the groups involved (*kadkhodas*), who were directly responsible for these issues, or when necessary mediated by higher-level authorities (such as the *il khan* or his deputies, the *il beg*). This quasi-legal system helped to maintain the unity of the tribe and ensure harmony among its constituent parts. Consequently, whereas we expect cultural transmission between tribes to have been inhibited by the hostile character of their relationships, the cooperative institutions that existed within tribes would have facilitated exchanges between clans. Similarly, while endogamous marriage would be expected to prevent the transfer of weaving traits between tribes, it would not inhibit the flow of traits among clans. Although individuals often express a preference for marriage between patrilineal relatives, marriages between members of different patrilines are far from uncommon. For example, Digard (2002: 22) estimates that marriages between patrilineal relatives accounts for only 18–43 per cent of all marriages. In the field, JJT encountered many cases where women married into another patriline.

In sum, Iranian weaving traditions provide an ideal context in which to test Durham's TRIMS hypothesis. Based on the ethnographic data outlined above, we predict that patterns of craft diversity between tribes will exhibit greater phylogenetic structure than patterns of craft diversity between clans belonging to the same tribe.

Materials and Methods

Data on between-group patterns of textile diversity comprised designs associated with communities belonging to four tribes in southwestern Iran: the Bakhtiari, Qashqai, Papi and Boyer Ahmad (Figure 5.1). The weavings of the Bakhtiari, Qashqai and Boyer Ahmad were sampled during a survey of craft production in the Zagros Mountains conducted by JJT over the course of three visits to the area between May 2001 and June 2003. The weavings of the Papi were studied through a catalogue of the extensive collections of Papi material culture held at the Copenhagen Museum of Ethnography published by Mortensen and Nicolaisen (1993). A total of eighty designs were recorded on rugs, woven bags and blankets, and packing bands produced by these groups (Figure 5.2). The presence/absence of each design in each tribe was recorded in a matrix.

Data on within-group patterns of textile diversity was drawn from rug designs associated with five communities belonging to the Bakhtiari tribe. Each community comprised between one and three villages belonging to the same patrilineal clan. The communities were situated in the districts of Chehelgerd, the Chahar Mahal valley,

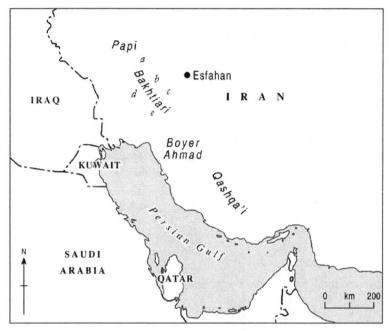

Figure 5.1. Map showing the approximate locations of the Iranian tribal territories (italics) and Bakhtiari clans included in the study (a = Aligudarz, b = Chahar Mahal, c = Boldaji, d = Chehelgerd, e = Bazoft).

Figure 5.2. Examples of Iranian tribal textile ornaments (above) and border patterns (below).

Bazoft, Boldaji and Aligudarz. The weavings of these communities were sampled during two field trips to the region, in April–July 2002 and May 2003. A total of fifty carpet ornaments were identified and recorded for each tribe on a presence/absence basis.

Both datasets were analysed using the cladistic method of phylogenetic reconstruction. Cladistics has been widely used in a variety of culture study areas: biological (e.g. Kitching et al. 1998; Page and Holmes 1998; Schuh 2000), linguistic (Gray and Jordan 2000; Holden 2002; Rexová et al. 2003; Ben Hamed et al. 2005), philological (Eagleton and Spencer 2006) and material (e.g. Robinson and O'Hara 1996; Robson-Brown 1996; O'Brien et al. 2001; Tehrani and Collard 2002, 2009a, 2009b; Jordan and Shennan 2003, 2009; O'Brien and Lyman 2003; Shennan and Collard 2005; Collard et al. 2006; Buchanan and Collard 2007, 2008; Lycett 2007, 2009a, 2009b; Lycett et al. 2007; Cochrane 2008). Based on a model of evolution in which new taxa arise from the bifurcation of existing ones and subsequently undergo modification, cladistics defines relationships among taxa in terms of relative recency of common ancestry. Two taxa are deemed to be more closely related to one another than either is to a third taxon if they share a common ancestor that is not also shared by the third taxon. Exclusive common ancestry is indicated by 'synapomorphies'. Synapomorphies are similarities among taxa that are both the result of shared ancestry and derived relative to the ancestral state for the taxa under study. Synapomorphies are distinguished from 'symplesiomorphies', 'autapomorphies' and 'homoplasies'. Symplesiomorphies are character states that are inherited from the last common ancestor shared by all the taxa under study, and have not evolved subsequently. Autapomorphies are character states that are derived relative to the ancestral state for the study group, but only occur in a single taxon. Symplesiomorphies and autapomorphies are not useful for phylogenetic reconstruction because they do not allow subgroups of taxa to be delineated. Homoplasies are derived character states that are shared by more than one taxon in a study group as a result of processes other than descent from a common ancestor, such as convergence, parallelism, or horizontal transmission across lineages.

In its simplest form, cladistic analysis proceeds via four steps. First, a character state data matrix is generated. This shows the states of the characters exhibited by each taxon. Next, the direction of evolutionary change among the states of each character is established. Several methods have been developed to facilitate this, the currently favoured being outgroup analysis (Arnold 1981; Maddison et al. 1984). Outgroup analysis entails examining a close relative of the study group. When a character occurs in two states among the study group, but only one of the states is found in the outgroup, the principle of parsimony is invoked and the state found only in the study group is deemed to be evolutionarily novel with respect to the outgroup state. Having determined the probable direction of change for the character states, the next step in a cladistic analysis is to construct a branching diagram of relationships for each character. This is done by joining the two most derived taxa by two intersecting lines, and then successively connecting each of the other taxa according to how derived they are, or how many synapomorphies they contain. Each group of taxa defined by a set of intersecting lines corresponds to a clade, and the diagram is referred to as a cladogram. The final step in a cladistic analysis is to compile an ensemble cladogram from the character cladograms. Ideally, the distribution of the character states among the taxa will be such that all the character cladograms imply relationships among the taxa that are congruent with one another. Normally, however, a number of the character cladograms will suggest relationships that are incompatible. This problem is overcome by generating an ensemble cladogram that is consistent with the largest number of characters and therefore requires the smallest number of homoplasies to account for the distribution of character states among the taxa (Figure 5.3). This approach is based on the principle of parsimony, the methodological injunction that states that explanations should never be made more complicated than is necessary (Sober 1988).

To test the prediction that patterns of diversity at the tribe level should be significantly more tree-like than patterns of diversity at the clan level, we carried out two analyses. In the first we used the Permutation Tail Probability (PTP) test (Archie 1989). PTP was originally proposed as a method of determining whether or not a given dataset contains a statistically significant phylogenetic signal (Archie 1989; Faith and Cranston 1991). However, following criticism (e.g. Carpenter 1992), it is now considered to be a heuristic device rather than a statistical test (Kitching et al. 1998). In the PTP test, a taxonomic dataset is randomly reshuffled multiple times without replacement, and the length of the most parsimonious cladogram is computed after each permutation. Thereafter, the length of the most parsimonious cladogram obtained from the un-permuted data is compared to the distribution of lengths of the most parsimonious cladograms yielded by the permutations. If the original cladogram is shorter than 95 per cent or more of the cladograms derived from the permutations, then the dataset is considered to contain a phylogenetic signal. Before carrying out the PTP tests, we added scores for an outgroup to each dataset. The outgroup we employed were the weavings of the Shahsevan. Previous analyses suggest that the Shahsevan weavings belong to a

	Character 1	Character 2	Character 3	Character 4	Character 5	Character 6
TAXON A	1	1	0	0	0	1
TAXON B	1	1	1	1	0	1
TAXON C	1	1	1	1	1	0
TAXON X	0	0	0	0	0	0

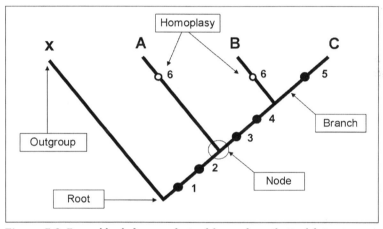

Figure 5.3. Ensemble cladogram derived from a hypothetical dataset.

distinct but closely related tradition of the Qashqai, Bakhtiari, Boyer Ahmad and Papi assemblages (Tehrani and Collard 2009a, 2009b). The PTP tests were carried out in PAUP* 4.0 (Swofford 1998) with ten thousand permutations of each dataset. Our test prediction was that the between-group dataset would pass the PTP test while the within-group dataset would fail it.

In the second analysis, we identified the most parsimonious tree for each dataset and then compared the trees' 'retention indices'. The Retention Index (RI) is a measure of the number of homoplastic changes a cladogram requires that are independent of its length (Farris 1989a, 1989b). The RI of a single character is calculated by subtracting the number of character state changes required by the focal cladogram (s) from the maximum possible amount of change required by a cladogram in which all the taxa are equally closely related (g). This figure is then divided by the result of subtracting the minimum amount of change required by any conceivable cladogram (m) from g. The RI of two or more characters is computed as $(G - S) / (G - M)$, where G, S, and M are the sums of the g, s and m values for the

individual characters. A maximum RI of 1 indicates that the cladogram requires no homoplastic change, and the level of homoplasy
increases as the index approaches 0. The RI is a particularly useful
goodness-of-fit measure because, unlike some other measures (e.g.
the Consistency Index), it is not affected by number of taxa or number
of characters, and can therefore be used to compare phylogenetic signals in different datasets and character sets. As in the PTP tests, the
Shashevan were added to both datasets as an outgroup. This analysis was also carried out with the aid of PAUP* 4.0 (Swofford 1998).
The test prediction in this analysis was that the RI of the inter-tribal
cladogram would be higher than the RI of the intra-tribal cladogram
due to a higher rate of borrowing in the latter dataset.

Results

As predicted, the PTP test found a significant phylogenetic signal
in the inter-tribal data ($p < 0.01$), but not in the inter-clan data ($p
= 0.53$). Thus, the PTP test-based analysis supported the TRIMS
hypothesis.

The cladistic analyses returned a single most parsimonious
cladogram for each dataset (Figures 5.4 and 5.5). The inter-tribal
cladogram suggests that the Papi, Boyer Ahmad and Bakhtiari
share an exclusive common ancestor that is not shared with the
Qashqai. This is consistent with the fact that these three tribes
belong to the same ethno-linguistic group, the Lors (e.g. Amanolahi
1988), whereas the Qashqai are Turkic (e.g. Oberling 1974). The
cladogram also suggests that the Bakhtiari and Papi form a clade
that excludes the Boyer Ahmad. At present there are no other lines
of evidence with which to compare this finding. Similarly, there are
currently no data to validate the phylogenetic relationships among
different Bakhtiari clans suggested by the intra-tribal cladogram.
The RI of the between-group cladogram was 0.70, which is high
compared to the RIs returned by empirical and simulated datasets
(Collard et al. 2006; Nunn et al. 2010). At 0.38, the RI of the within-
group cladogram was much lower. Thus, like the PTP test-based
analysis, the RI test supports the TRIMS hypothesis.

Discussion

The results of the PTP and RI analyses support the TRIMS hypothesis, which predicts that patterns of cultural diversity between groups
should exhibit greater phylogenetic structure than patterns within

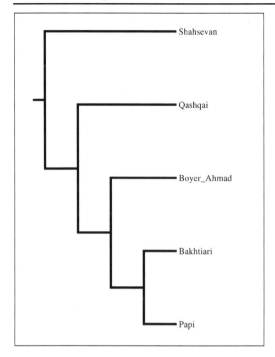

Figure 5.4. Iranian inter-tribe textile cladogram.

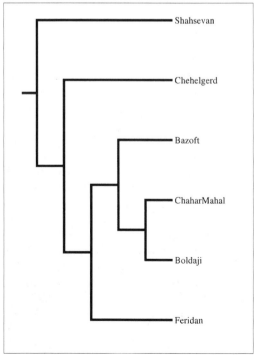

Figure 5.5. Iranian inter-clan textile cladogram.

groups. There are, however, two potential criticisms that could be levelled at this interpretation of our results. First, some research- ers have claimed that because cladistic algorithms are designed to maximize the fit between a dataset and the tree model, a high RI, such as that obtained from the inter-tribal textile data, cannot be assumed to reflect phylogenesis (e.g. Borgerhoff Mulder et al. 2006; McElreath 2009). It has been suggested that it is possible to obtain high RI values from datasets that have actually been structured by horizontal processes, or even from random data (McElreath 2009). However, tests of these assertions have shown them to be invalid. For example, we have recently compared the RI value of the most parsimonious tree derived from an Iranian textile dataset to the RI values of the most parsimonious trees derived from one thousand datasets that were generated by randomizing the character states (Tehrani and Collard 2009a). The highest RI obtained from the randomized datasets (0.35) was just over half the value of the RI returned by the original dataset (0.59). This indicates that cla- distic analyses of random data are unlikely to produce trees with high RIs. Another study by Nunn et al. (2010) examined the RIs returned by cladistic analyses of datasets that were artificially gen- erated under varying rates of vertical and horizontal transmission between groups. They concluded that phylogenesis can be reliably inferred when the RI is roughly equal to, or higher than, 0.6. Given that the RI of the inter-tribal textile tree (0.7) comfortably exceeds this value, we can confidently assume that between-group patterns evolved through branching descent with modification.

The second potential criticism of our conclusions is that differences in the phylogenetic signals recovered from different cultural datas- ets may reflect amounts of evolutionary change rather than rates of vertical versus horizontal transmission between taxa (e.g. Nunn et al. 2010). Thus, a dataset may have less phylogenetic structure than another because of the accumulation of convergences, reversals in character state changes, and so on, rather than because of borrow- ings. However, since the last common ancestor of the Bakhtiari clans is almost certainly of much more recent origin than the last common ancestor of the tribes, we would expect the characters in the inter- tribal dataset to have evolved much more than the characters in the inter-clan dataset. Therefore, the difference in the phylogenetic signal recovered from each dataset is much more likely to be due to rates of borrowing between clans being higher than rates of borrowing between tribes.

The findings of the study reported here are compatible with our interpretation of the results of previous analyses of textile evo- lution in this region. We found that between-group patterns of diversity among Turkmen tribes (Tehrani and Collard 2002) and Iranian tribes (Tehrani and Collard 2009a, 2009b) evolved mainly through phylogenesis, which we attributed to the operation of TRIMS like tribe endogamy, language barriers, restrictions on women travelling and hostile relations among groups. By confirming the importance of these mechanisms, this study provides new evidence to support Durham's hypothesis that TRIMS produce cultural patterns similar to those that result from speciation. The corollary of this point is that when cultural datasets contain a strong phylogenetic signal, it is reasonable to infer that TRIMS are likely to have been present. Archaeological phylogenies of stone tools (e.g. O'Brien and Lyman 2003; Buchanan and Collard 2007, 2008; Lycett 2007, 2009a, 2009b), pottery assemblages (Collard and Shennan 2000; Cochrane 2008) and other artefacts might therefore provide important information for mapping the boundaries between populations and assessing their fluidity/robustness.

Likewise, when phylogenetic signals in cultural datasets are weak, this may indicate the relative absence of barriers to transmission among populations. This is supported by evidence from a study of cultural evolution in Californian Indians carried out by Jordan and Shennan (2003, 2009). These authors used cladistics, phylogenetic network analysis, correspondence analysis and Mantel tests to study the evolution of these groups' basketry traditions. They found that basket assemblages were influenced more by borrowing and blending among neighbouring groups than inheritance from ancestral populations. This is consistent with ethnohistorical data that suggested that members of these societies traded and intermarried with one another extensively. Hence, as far as the TRIMS hypothesis is concerned, Jordan and Shennan's case study can be seen as an exception that proves the rule.

Of course, the specific character and strength of TRIMS will vary from case to case, and it remains to be seen how important those that have been identified here – such as endogamy – are in other times and places. More importantly, even when powerful TRIMS do exist, they are never completely impermeable. For instance, although endogamy and social distinctions between the Iranian tribes have been effective in containing textile traits, they have provided little resistance to the spread of other behaviours, such as cigarette smoking, tea drinking and Western medicine. Rather than identifying TRIMS with Reproductive Isolating Mechanisms in biological species, it may be more productive to think of them as a specific parameter in the diffusion of innovations that concerns the differential in the cost of learning a trait from a member of the same social group versus the cost of learning it from a member of a different social group. This would allow traits that are highly useful (e.g. antibiotics) or easy to acquire (e.g. smoking) to spread among populations more easily than traits that are arbitrary or difficult to learn (e.g. textile patterns). While such a model would require a reformulation of Durham's original conception of TRIMS, it is one that, in our view, would better capture the evolutionary dynamics of cultural diversification.

Acknowledgements

This chapter was made possible by the support of Research Councils UK, the Arts and Humanities Research Council, the Economic and Social Research Council, the British Columbia Knowledge Development Fund, the Canada Research Chairs Program, the Canada Foundation for Innovation, Simon Fraser University, the Social Sciences and Humanities Research Council, University College London, the Royal Anthropological Institute and the Wenner-Gren Foundation.

References

Amanolahi, S. 1988. *Tribes of Iran. Volume 1 – The Tribes of Luristan, Bakhtiari, Kuh Gilu and Mamasani*. New Haven: Human Relations Area Files.

Archie, J.W. 1989. 'A Randomization Test for Phylogenetic Information in Systematic Data', *Systematic Zoology* 38: 219–52.

Arnold, E.N. 1981. 'Estimating Phylogenies at Lower Taxonomic Levels', *Zeitschrift fur Zoologische Systematik und Evolutionsforschung* 19: 1–35.

Aunger, R. 2000. 'The Life History of Culture Learning in a Face-to-Face Society', *Ethos* 28: 1–38.

Barth, F. 1961. *Nomads of South Persia*. Oslo: Oslo University Press.

Beck, L. 1986. *The Qashqa'i of Iran*. New Haven: Yale University Press.

Ben Hamed, M., P. Darlu and N. Vallée. 2005. 'On Cladistic Reconstruction of Linguistic Trees through Vowel Data', *Journal of Quantitative Linguistics* 12: 79–109.

Boas, F. 1940. *Race, Language and Culture*. Chicago: Chicago University Press.

Borgerhoff Mulder, M., C. Nunn and M. Towner. 2006. 'Cultural Macroevolution and the Transmission of Traits', *Evolutionary Anthropology* 15: 52–64.

Boyd, R. and P. Richerson. 1985. *Culture and the Evolutionary Process*. Chicago: University of Chicago Press.

Buchanan, B. and M. Collard. 2007. 'Investigating the Peopling of North America through Cladistic Analyses of Early Paleoindian Projectile Points', *Journal of Anthropological Archaeology* 26: 366–93.

————.2008. 'Phenetics, Cladistics and the Search for the Alaskan Ancestors of the Paleoindians: A Reassessment of the Relationships among the Clovis, Nenana and Denali Archaeological Complexes', *Journal of Archaeological Science* 35: 1683–94.

Carpenter, J.M. 1992. 'Random Cladistics', *Cladistics* 8: 147–53.

Cavalli-Sforza, L.L. and M. Feldman. 1981. *Cultural Transmission and Evolution: A Quantitative Approach*. Princeton, NJ: Princeton University Press.

Cochrane, E.E. 2008. 'Migration and Cultural Transmission: Investigating Human Movement as an Explanation for Fijian Ceramic Change', in M.J. O'Brien (ed.), *Cultural Transmission in Archaeology: Issues and Case Studies*. Washington, DC: Society for American Archaeology, pp. 132–45.

Collard, M. and S.J. Shennan. 2000. 'Ethnogenesis versus Phylogenesis in Prehistoric Culture Change: A Case-study Using European Neolithic Pottery and Biological Phylogenetic Techniques', in C. Renfrew and K. Boyle (eds), *Archaeogenetics: DNA and the Population Prehistory of Europe*. Cambridge: McDonald Institute for Archaeological Research, pp. 89–97.

Collard, M., S.J. Shennan and J.J. Tehrani. 2006. 'Branching, Blending and the Evolution of Cultural Similarities and Differences among Human Populations', *Evolution and Human Behavior* 27: 169–84.

Digard, J-P. 2002. 'The Bakhtiari', in J. Thompson and R. Tapper (eds), *The Nomadic Peoples of Iran*. London: Thames and Hudson, pp 48–90.

Durham, W.H. 1990. 'Advances in Evolutionary Culture Theory', *Annual Review of Anthropology* 19: 187–210.

————.1992. 'Applications of Evolutionary Culture Theory', *Annual Review of Anthropology* 21: 331–55.

Eagleton, C. and M. Spencer. 2006. 'Copying and Conflation in Geoffrey Chaucer's Treatise on the Astrolabe: A Stemmatic Analysis Using Phylogenetic Software', *Studies in History and Philosophy of Science Part A* 37: 237–68.

Faith, D.P. and P.S. Cranston. 1991. 'Could a Cladogram this Short have Arisen by Chance Alone? On Permutation Tests for Cladistic Structure', *Cladistics* 7: 1–28.

Farris, J.S. 1989a. 'The Retention Index and Homoplasy Excess', *Systematic Zoology* 38: 406–7.

————.1989b. 'The Retention Index and the Rescaled Consistency Index', *Cladistics* 5: 417–19.

Garthwaite, G.R. 1983. *Khans and Shahs: A Documentary Analysis of the Bakhtiyari in Iran*. Cambridge: Cambridge University Press.

Gray, R. and F. Jordan. 2000. 'Language Trees Support the Express-train Sequence of Austronesian Expansion', *Nature* 405: 1052–55.

Greenfield, P.M., A.E. Maynard and C.P. Childs. 2000. 'History, Culture, Learning, and Development', *Cross-Cultural Research* 34: 351–74.

Henrich, J. and F. Gil-White. 2001. 'The Evolution of Prestige: Freely Conferred Status as a Mechanism for Enhancing the Benefits of Cultural Transmission', *Evolution and Human Behavior* 22: 165–96.

Hewlett, B.S. and L.L. Cavalli-Sforza. 1986. 'Cultural Transmission among Aka Pygmies', *American Anthropolgist* 88: 922–34.

Holden, C. 2002. 'Bantu Language Trees Reflect the Spread of Farming across Sub-Saharan Africa: A Maximum Parsimony Analysis', *Proceedings of the Royal Society of London, Series B-Biological Sciences* 269: 793–99.

Jordan, P. and S.J. Shennan. 2003. 'Cultural Transmission, Language, and Basketry
Traditions amongst the Californian Indians', *Journal of Anthropological Archaeology* 22: 42–74.

————.2009. 'Diversity in Hunter-Gatherer Technological Traditions: Mapping Trajectories of Cultural "Descent with Modification" in Northeast California', *Journal of Anthropological Archaeology* 28: 342–65.

Kitching, I.J., P.L. Forey, C.J. Humphries and D. Williams. 1998. *Cladistics: The Theory and Practice of Parsimony Analysis*. Oxford: Oxford University Press.

Kroeber, A.L. 1948. *Anthropology: Race, Language, Culture, Psychology and Prehistory*. New York: Brace.

Lipo, C., M. O'Brien, M. Collard and S.J. Shennan (eds). 2006. *Mapping our Ancestors: Phylogenetic Approaches in Anthropology and Prehistory*. New Brunswick: Aldine Transaction.

Lozada, M, A. Ladio and M. Weingandt. 2006. 'Cultural Transmission of Ethnobotanical Knowledge in a Rural Community of Northwestern Patagonia, Argentina', *Economic Botany* 60: 374–85.

Lycett, S.J. 2007. 'Why is there a Lack of Mode 3 Levallois Technologies in East Asia? A Phylogenetic Test of the Movius-Schick Hypothesis', *Journal of Anthropological Archaeology* 26: 541–75.

————.2009a. 'Are Victoria West Cores "Proto-Levallois"? A Phylogenetic Assessment', *Journal of Human Evolution* 56: 175–91.

————.2009b. 'Understanding Ancient Hominin Dispersals using Artefactual Data: A Phylogeographic Analysis of Acheulean Handaxes', *PLoS ONE* 4 (10)/e7404: 1–6.

Lycett, S.J., M. Collard and W.C. McGrew. 2007. 'Phylogenetic Analyses of Behavior Support Existence of Culture among Wild Chimpanzees', *Proceedings of the National Academy of Sciences* 104: 17588–92.

McElreath, R. 2009. 'Linking the Micro and Macro in Cultural Evolution (Review of Shennan, Pattern and Process in Cultural Evolution)', *Trends in Evolution and Ecology* 24: 588–89.

Mace, R., C. Holden and S. Shennan. 2005. *The Evolution of Cultural Diversity: A Phylogenetic Approach*. London: University College London Press.

Maddison, W.P., M.J. Donoghue and D.R. Maddison. 1984. 'Outgroup Analysis and Parsimony', *Systematic Zoology* 33: 83–103.

Moore, J.H. 1994. 'Putting Anthropology Back Together Again: The Ethnogenetic Critique of Cladistic Theory. *American Anthropologist* 96: 370–96.

Mortensen, I.D. and I. Nicolaisen. 1993. *Nomads of Luristan: History, Material Culture and Pastoralism in Western Iran*. London: Thames and Hudson.

Nunn, C., C. Arnold, L. Matthews and M. Borgerhoff Mulder. 2010. 'Simulating Trait Evolution for Cross-cultural Comparison', *Philosophical Transactions of the Royal Society B* 365(1559): 3807–19.

O'Brien, M.J., J. Darwent and R.L. Lyman. 2001. 'Cladistics is Useful for Reconstructing Archaeological Phylogenies: Paleoindian Points from the Southeastern United States', *Journal of Archaeological Science* 28: 1115–36.

O'Brien, M.J. and R.L. Lyman. 2003. *Cladistics and Archaeology*. Salt Lake City: University of Utah Press.

Oberling, P. 1974. *The Qashqa'i Nomads of Fars*. The Hague: Mouton.

Ohmagari, K. and F. Berkes. 1997. 'Transmission of Indigenous Knowledge and Bush Skills among the Western James Bay Cree Women of Subarctic Canada', *Human Ecology* 25: 197–222.

Page, R.D.M. and E.C. Holmes. 1998 *Molecular Evolution: A Phylogenetic Approach*. Oxford: Blackwell.

Rexová, K., D. Frynta and J. Zrzavy. 2003 'Cladistic Analysis of Languages: Indo-European Classification Based on Lexicostatistical Data', *Cladistics* 19: 120–27.

Reyes-García, V.J. et al. 2009. 'Cultural Transmission of Ethnobotanical Knowledge and Skills: An Empirical Analysis from an Amerindian Society', *Evolution and Human Behavior* 30(4): 274–85.

Robinson, P.M.W. and R.J. O'Hara. 1996. 'Cladistic Analysis of an Old Norse Manuscript Tradition', *Research in Humanities Computing* 4: 115–37.

Robson-Brown, K.A. 1996. 'Systematics and Integrated Methods for the Modelling of the Pre-modern Human Mind', in P. Mellars and K. Gibson (eds), *Modelling the Early Human Mind*. Cambridge: McDonald Institute for Archaeological Research, pp. 103–17.

Schuh, R.T. 2000. *Biological Systematics: Principles and Applications*. Ithaca, NY: Cornell University Press.

Shennan, S.J. and M. Collard. 2005. 'Investigating Processes of Cultural Evolution on the North Coast of New Guinea with Multivariate and Cladistic Analyses', in R. Mace, C. Holden and S.J. Shennan (eds), *The Evolution of Cultural Diversity: A Phylogenetic Approach*. London: University College London Press, pp. 133–64.

Shennan, S.J. and J. Steele. 1999. 'Cultural Learning in Hominids: A Behavioural Ecological Approach', in H.O. Box and K.R. Gibson (eds), *Mammalian Social Learning: Comparative and Ecological Perspectives*. Cambridge: Cambridge University Press, pp. 367–88.

Sober, E. 1988. *Reconstructing the Past: Parsimony, Evolution, and Inference*. Cambridge, MA: MIT Press.

Swofford, D.L. 1998. *PAUP* 4. Phylogenetic Analysis Using Parsimony (*and Other Methods)*. Version 4. Sunderland, MA: Sinauer.

Tehrani, J.J. and M. Collard. 2002. 'Investigating Cultural Evolution through Biological Phylogenetic Analyses of Turkmen Textiles', *Journal of Anthropological Archaeology* 21: 443–63.

————.2009a. 'On the Relationship between Inter-individual Cultural Transmission and Population-level Cultural Diversity: A Case Study of Weaving in Iranian Tribal Populations', *Evolution and Human Behavior* 30(4): 286–300.

————.2009b. 'The Evolution of Cultural Diversity in the Tribes of Iran', in S. Shennan (ed.), *Pattern and Process in Cultural Evolution*. Berkeley: University of California Press, pp. 99–111.

Terrell, J.E. 1988. 'History as a Family Tree, History as a Tangled Bank', *Antiquity* 62, 642–57.

Chapter 6

CO-EVOLUTION BETWEEN BENTWOOD BOX TRADITIONS AND LANGUAGES ON THE PACIFIC NORTHWEST COAST

Sean O'Neill

Introduction

If culture is largely a system of inheritance, then it is reasonable to attempt to understand long-term patterns and processes of cultural transmission through the paradigm of neo-Darwinian evolution (Durham 1976; Dunnell 1978). In the past two decades especially, efforts in this direction have borne explanatory fruit. The innovative importation of methods of analysis from evolutionary biology and population genetics into anthropology (Mace and Pagel 1994) and archaeology (Neiman 1995; O'Brien and Lyman 2003) have aided us in gaining a more detailed understanding of 'what happened in history', helping us to answer old questions, and frame some new ones. This chapter continues in this empirical tradition. We apply phylogenetic systematics (cladistics) to a sample of bentwood (kerfed) boxes collected from the Pacific Northwest coast of North America during the ethnographic era, in order to trace possible geographically defined patterns of 'descent with modification' on the central Pacific Northwest coast. The distinctive bentwood boxes usually have four walls made from a single piece of wood that has been scored, steamed and bent. I compare this with a language tree to help us to understand if there were any co-evolutionary relationships between this complex material culture tradition and language. I started with a new database of 142 traits on nine bentwood box specimens, each from different settlements or settlement catchment areas down the coast. With both traditions, I have been interested in tracing transmission mechanisms following a phylogenetic, tree-like pattern, with branching patterns of descent suggesting heritable continuity in box-making traditions, versus evidence for the mixing and hybridization of box-making traits between groups.

I aimed to answer the following questions:

- Is it possible to create a robust new database on box-making traditions, one that is amenable to quantitative analysis?

- Using phylogenetic methods on the ethnographic dataset, is there evidence for tree-like (branching) patterns of diversification in box-making traditions, or are the patterns more reticulate?

- Furthermore, can I trace any co-evolutionary relationships between box-making traditions and a language tree for the coast?

New Life for Old Ethnographic Collections

Most of the material culture that we study from north-west coast peoples during the ethnographic era was collected over only a few generations, between roughly 1870 and 1930. As we cross-pollinate new quantitative methods and approaches to understanding cultural transmission, and are able to use robust data from an ethnographically reconstructed present to track evolutionary relationships into a deeper past – in some cases, millennia – we argue here that we will continue to benefit from the work of the ethnographic collectors from a century ago. No matter how 'primitive' their methods were, 'it is not uncommon for even old collecting techniques to have been systematic to one degree or another' (Brown 1981: 65), and 'these neglected offspring of so many past anthropological expeditions, can ... be studied in ways unimagined at the time of their acquisition' (Cantwell and Rothschild 1981: 581). If one adds to this rich body of evidence knowledge gleaned from reverse engineering and experimental archaeology – as conducted by Hilary Stewart (1984) in the case of reconstructing the bentwood boxes from the coast, and a whole generation of new practitioners since then – then there is scope for further original contributions to historical knowledge of coast peoples.

Phylogenetic Systematics

In order to make sense of their finds, archaeologists have been exploring and using various systems of classification, especially in the preceding century. These can be arrived at through explicit methods (Dunnell 1971), but all too often they have been based on implicit approaches – on intuitive seriation and 'common sense' taxonomics which merely echo scientific procedures for categorization. O'Brien and Lyman (2003) have pointed out that many archaeologists are still working implicitly within a Linnaean taxonomic system, constructing seriation studies based on morphological similarity or dissimilarity, with the most important distinctions made by way of nominal (named) categories, which may or may not then be turned over to quantification. They have suggested that it could be more productive to look further at ways to understand historical change and continuity by thinking in terms of evolutionary *processes*, rather than just simply observed patterns. Archaeologists are primarily interested in tracking history in a diachronic way. Therefore, models that have been developed to understand ancestral and derived trait states as a way to analyse canalized trends are well suited to archaeology. Cladistics represents a rigorous approach to tracking developments, especially in prehistory, where written records are not available.

Hennig (1966) called for a more rigorous approach to understanding evolutionary relationships by way of phylogenetic systematics (or what is often referred to as 'cladistics'). These discard any classificatory distinction that does not aid phylogenetic analysis, and give us reliable branching patterns of evolutionary development. They track the direction of the derived traits over time (called 'polarity'), in a process that would reconstruct the actual historical/evolutionary relationships between existing taxa. The findings are expressed in tree-like structures, which bring classificatory systems beyond the realm of intuition and otherwise arbitrary assignation. Within the past two decades, phylogenetic methods have been used in studies of cultural diversification. They have helped us to (a) classify relationships between traditions, (b) analyse cultural resemblances, and therefore (c) make wider and more accurate inferences about culture history.

From the very beginning of data collecting for analysis, the method is both quantitative in its approach, and concerned with hypothesizing evolutionary relationships over time as the ultimate goal. Taxa are grouped together based on shared derived traits; in a tree all share some earlier traits, but closer to 'the tips' of the tree small groupings exhibit more recently shared traits. From these patterns of heritable continuity, 'descent with modification' can be deduced – an accurate rendering of a chain of successive trait derivations. It is these shared derived derivations held in common that establish the evolutionary closeness of specimens. There has been much debate about the appropriateness of importing cladistics from evolutionary biology into cultural studies (Terrell 1988; Bamforth 2002; arguments reviewed in O'Brien 2008). Opponents of the method depict cultural phenomena as both diverging and converging in a pattern that has been compared to an 'entangled bank', as opposed to a neat and clean tree. A former ancestral trait can be lost and then be picked up again from elsewhere, or rediscovered later as a new environmental adaptation. These processes cause reticulation, a kind of blurring effect caused by the mixing of traits between populations. In the synchronic direct observation of any culture, these forces will be observed to a greater or lesser extent; therefore tree-like patterns may not always be appropriate at that scale of magnitude. However, phylogenetic modelling can reconstruct histories of material culture traditions as evidenced by the traits – through the clearer identification of patterns and processes of descent with modification. It could be argued that most archaeologists to a certain extent think along phylogenetic lines already, however implicitly. Most are concerned with patterns of cultural transmission (though not all are interested in making the patterns clear or in apprehending the mechanisms that determine them). Cladistics merely makes these inferred processes more explicit (and reliable) by way of quantified statistical methods.

Biologists use phylogenetic analysis to reconstruct genealogies of organisms, based on the principle that evolutionary relationships between species can be represented by a branching tree diagram (Hennig 1966). The presence or absence of traits are identified across a range of taxa, with descent relationships reconstructed by determining which similarities are derived from shared common ancestry (homologies), as opposed to those which are brought about by other processes, such as borrowing and hybridization (homoplasies; Hennig 1966). Homologies signal branching evolutionary relationships; homoplasies indicate convergences, which tend to blur branching signals. Both patterns can be measured statistically. Anthropologists are interested in both, as either pattern can predominate in a given culture-historical setting. Analyses of cultural data generating a phylogenetic tree model point to homology, indicating descent with modification; polytomies (bush-like patterns) suggest homoplasy, indicating ethnogenesis, descent by association (O'Brien and Lyman 2003). Phylogenetic analysis can be carried out with a number of software packages. For the bentwood boxes dataset, PAUP* 4.0b10 was used with the following settings: optimality criterion as parsimony; starting trees obtained via stepwise addition and the branch swapping algorithm set as a tree-bisection-reconnection.

The results were interpreted using the outgroup method (Forey et al. 1992), with the Salish-speaking Bella Coola as the outgroup, on the basis of their being a language isolate in the region, whereas all of the other communities are aligned with the coast's larger language families (Thompson and Kinkade 1990). A further statistical method measures the reliability of the phylogenetic signal (as computer algorithms will construct trees from random data). The 'Retention Index' (R.I.) calculates the amount of homoplasy as a fraction of the maximum possible homoplasy (0 to 1.0; Forey et al. 1992: 75). R.I. results can be compared across cases. Collard et al. (2006) were able to compare the relative strength of branching signals from twenty-one cases which analysed either biological or cultural datasets, and were able to show that 0.6 indicates a strong phylogenetic signal (with cultural data this means the predominance of 'phylogenesis' over ethnogenesis). Finally, bootstrap analysis, a random sampling programme, calculates percentage levels of support for each branch in a tree (Forey et al. 1992: 76); a level of support of over fifty per cent should be interpreted as a measure of the accuracy of a tree structure.

Database 1:
Investigating the Bentwood Boxes in New Ways

The peoples inhabiting the coast at the time of first contact in the seventeenth century were amongst the most socially complex hunter-fisher-gatherer groups ever encountered by Europeans, with great intra-regional language diversity, a highly stratified rank society preoccupied ceremonially with prestige and status, sophisticated fishing technologies and provision for long-term food storage (Matson and Coupland 1995). Another remarkable characteristic was that, despite there being little horticultural activity, these groups were sedentary for a large part of the year in winter villages with monumental architecture. The so-called Developed Northwest Coast Pattern (ibid.) had evolved over millennia, marked by innovative cultural adaptations to a number of environmental changes. Firstly, rising sea levels caused salmon and other anadromous fish stocks to proliferate in the rivers about five thousand years ago. Secondly, processes of food preservation and storage in sealed containers developed, starting approximately four thousand years ago. Thirdly, the rectangular-plan, multi-family 'big houses' appear in the archaeological record three thousand years ago, coinciding with a proliferation of red cedar (*Thuja plicata*) in the region (Carlson and Dalla Bona 1996).

We have access to hundreds of surviving specimens of the kerfed, airtight storage containers from the ethnographic era, well cared for in both large museums and smaller private collections. Usually, studies in this tradition cover a limited set of boxes, and do not cover the region as a whole.

There has been relatively little done to study variations between the containers in a systematic way, beyond qualitative iconographic and decorative (and often aestheticized and mytho-interpretive) studies of their two-dimensional painted graphic design – but see Holm's classic codification of the graphic arts of the coast (1965), Stewart's concise reconstruction (1984) of 'recipes for action' involved in the construction of the boxes, based on ethnographies and experimental archaeology, and McLennan and Duffek's (2000) attempts to recover a new archive of the painted graphics on bentwood containers along with architectural appurtenances and edifices. None of the published studies take comparative statistical approaches, and furthermore no systemic, isochrestic rule-based approach for understanding the grammar of the art has been undertaken. Holm's treatise on the elements of the art (1965) presents what could be deemed a visual 'vocabulary', but not a syntax describing *how* and explaining *why* these elements are put together in the specific ways that they are. Despite a general historical bias for collecting boxes from the more northerly groups, it became apparent that for this study there would be an opportunity to prepare a rigorous new database which could be analysed with quantitative methods in order to identify derived traits which would help us to track patterns and processes of descent with modification in this tradition.

The containers performed central social and utilitarian functions for the peoples of the coast, both in terms of economic and symbolic power. The vital importance of the boxes to sustenance and survival was inculcated in small children by various games they played (Ford 1941: 65), and the abundant archaeological presence of containers in some places such as Ozette (Friedman 1975) also underlines the essential function of this form of social storage over millennia, coinciding archaeologically with the rise of a complex, stratified hunter-fisher-forager society. Ethnographically, the boxes were central to the gifting process in the Developed Northwest Coast Pattern (best manifested in the potlatch); but on a daily basis also, hundreds of boxes – large and small – could be stored in each big house, as there were as many as three hundred per household at Ozette (Friedman 1975; Samuels 1991). Kwakwaka'wakw Chief Charley Nowell discussed the many boxes stored in his house in Fort Rupert, near the northern tip of Vancouver Island, in the 1870s:

> All of these boxes were piled up on top of each other at the side of our house [against an interior wall] – the biggest ones on the bottom and so on up. Each fire had its own boxes piled up on the side of the community house. When we have our meals in the wintertime, we open these boxes and take out what we want. In the summertime, we mostly eat the fresh things and keep filling the boxes up for the next winter. (Ford 1941: 53)

The boxes were essential equipment for household moving operations during the annual round, as well as for trading, hunting and foraging expeditions. Covered containers were also taken out to sea for carrying fishing tackle, food and fresh water. Some of the boxes functioned as sacred 'arks', keeping closely guarded and rarely seen shamanic paraphernalia within. They could function as secular storehouses of wealth, securing treasures such as the highly revered coppers distributed within the coast-wide copper complex. Most containers had more mundane roles, being so humdrum that they were used as something to sit on in canoes or out in front of houses in the warmer weather.

The more elaborately decorated/carved chests and square boxes are perhaps the most complex and systematized examples of the conventions of the famous Pacific Northwest coast art, with its emphasis on lively interplay between positive and negative shapes, zoomorphic forms and sophisticated woodworking skills. A study of the fine detail of their construction yields definite canalized traditions, based on cultural choices transmitted from one generation to the next.

Usually all four sides of the box were made from a single smoothed plank, steam-bent at three corners and bound at the fourth open ('rabbeted') end. Two or more men worked simultaneously on steam bending each box (Boas 1909); and they were usually created in the winter season during hunting-fishing downtime (Oberg 1973: 75). A working assumption here is that the more ephemeral nature of the boxes and their greater quantities (in comparison with, say, the years-long construction processes of the big houses) would have enabled more innovative, less conservative approaches to construction and visual representation. Indeed, no two known boxes are identical. However, Codere points to certain traits that remained constant, and there was a propensity to 'repeat success' in a form of mass production of artefacts:

> Although Kwakiutl manufacturing did not make use of machines and jigs and scales in fractions of an inch or metre it must be emphasized that the orderly and precise procedures resulted in a high degree of standardization in the end products ... it was as though in manufacturing as well as in food production there was no point at which further

expenditure of effort in more of the same items was felt to be superfluous. (Codere 1950: 19)

This suggests that there could have been strong local traditions of canalized, repeated traits. It is also noteworthy that there is no similar bentwood technology for storage containers from anywhere else in the world. Therefore, there is a case to be made here for a closed, intraregional transmission of the traditions, in a clearly demarcated context, without exogenous/ethnogenetic influences from similar technical complexes outside the region. Despite the potential for tracing local traditions, a key problem for scholars has been the strong conventionalization of the visual arts traditions on the coast, which have created a kind of distributional 'blur', rendering the disentangling and tracking of prehistoric patterns of cultural transmission difficult (Holm 1965: 22–23; Ames 1996: 122). This has led to a situation where, as Ames (1996: 125) puts it, 'the history of regional variants is little understood'.

This situation can perhaps be remedied partially by application of quantitative methods from evolutionary biology to test hypotheses, using appropriate datasets. A key point is that we might be able to 'chip away' at the problem of tracing variation by the association of visual design patterns with other traits that coincide with them, beyond a few simple 'rules of thumb' – for instance, through examination of small details of the construction of the boxes themselves that have co-evolved with the images, but which have eluded careful study and multivariate comparison up until now. Therefore, it was resolved to attempt to disentangle the patterns through (a) a new approach to recording trait states of a sample of boxes, not systematized or published before, with a special emphasis on construction micro-decisions – the 'narcissism of small details' – and then (b) bringing phylogenetic methods to bear that could tell us whether these details appear in 'canalized', socially transmitted forms, co-evolving together through descent with modification.

Before a new database could be constructed, classes of boxes were considered. The containers come in many forms and performed widely varying functions (Figure 6.1).

Initially, I distinguished three useful classes of bentwood boxes, each with two or more specific functions:

Chests

These varied in size, and can be defined as having a length greater than their height (Stewart 1984: 84). Often the most elaborately carved and decorated containers were used as gifting/exchange items. Unlike the big house frames and the totem poles of the more

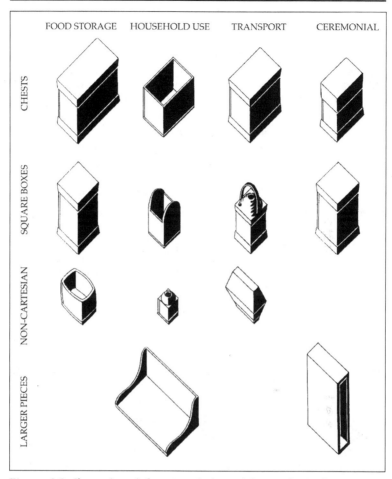

Figure 6.1. Classes (rows), functions (columns) for Pacific Northwest coast containers.

northerly groups in the study area, these elaborate boxes did not necessarily stay in one place over time and were not intended to mark the legitimacy of the specific privileges and prerogatives of a family. They were made to be exchangeable.

The special shamanic chests were, as a rule, smaller and had a telescoping design with telescopic bentwood sides attached to both the base and the cover of the box (see archetypal form at upper-right-hand corner of Figure 6.1). A very wide range of decoration and carved form was often involved, with projecting carved representational figures-in-the-round rising above the usual shallow bas-relief surface, a wider palette for painted decoration, and often mounted opercula and abalone shell.

Square Boxes

Square boxes (Figure 6.1) played a key role in the preparation, storage and gifting of food. Defined as having a height greater than their width, covered with a lid or uncovered, decorated elaborately or not at all, square boxes served many day-to-day functions. Watertight, they could be used for boiling water (although watertight cedar root baskets could also be used for this purpose), for the cooking of food through many different processes, as a bucket for carrying water, and as a receptacle for collecting urine, among many other uses. Many of the square boxes were left undecorated, or were simply carved with fluting on all sides to create a pleasing aesthetic effect (and for easier, less-slippery handling perhaps). As one moves south in the region, there is a tendency for decoration and carving of the boxes to reduce – where the salmon stocks begin to diminish so did the need for storage of fish – and distribution of the boxes drops at a commensurate rate (south of the Columbia River they disappear almost entirely, and basketry gains in importance as the primary vessel of use).

Irregularly Shaped Vernacular Boxes

These were largely for more specialized, everyday use, and some functional forms were probably less likely to be gifted or traded. Further north, some of the boxes had highly specialized designs. In order to fulfil specialist functions, some of these boxes become so modified in form away from cubic, Cartesian characteristics that they must be classed in further sub-categories (third row, Figure 6.1).

A new database would afford us the flexibility of inputting new traits (Dunnell 1971) throughout the long process of learning about the boxes, and minimize any biases I might have had involving the weighting of certain diagnostic traits. But while on site with collections, an attempt was also made to identify new diagnostic traits deemed to be *significata*, that is to say, characters that clearly reveal variation between units. The nine boxes used in this study were chosen from a sample of fifty-nine specimens selected from a survey of boxes from the British Museum, American Museum of Natural History, Cambridge University Museum of Archaeology and Anthropology, University of British Columbia Museum of Anthropology, and the Field Museum in Chicago was assembled as a consideration set for a pilot project for the recording of the presence or absence of an ultimate list of 142 traits for statistical comparison. The majority of the boxes were studied at first hand; in some cases gaps in the regional continuum were filled with data from published sources if these were complete. Beforehand, in the selection process, the descriptive work on construction details by Boas (1909) and Stewart (1984) and on codified design elements of two-dimensional art by Holm (1965) were consulted, but also Inverarity (1950) Smithsonian Institution (1974), Hawthorn (1979), Holm (1981), Bridgewater and Bridgewater (1991) and McLennan and Duffek (2000) provided invaluable preparation for assembling the initial list of traits. These traits were carefully considered and chosen as likely to be diagnostic in reading variation, with an emphasis on revealing possible canalized *cultural choices* made by the craftsmen.

In order to describe sought-after traits accurately, especially concerning the complex forms of kerfing structures and techniques of sewing and pegging the rabbeted ends and bottoms of the boxes, all normally covered boxes in the collection had to be carefully opened with the assistance of a museum curator. Wall planes and corners were carefully observed, usually with a magnifying glass. During this process, a number of potential new diagnostic traits became apparent, in addition to traits chosen from authoritative sources mentioned above. A number of new kerf designs – the particular form of the carved tracks along which the skilful bending would take place (Figure 6.2) – that had not been previously published were observed and recorded, as well as a much wider typology of painted cross-hatching (albeit displayed on a minority of the specimens). All of these were coded for, and became a part of, the database. If these traits were encountered anew in the middle of the process, a new row of presence/absence data could be added in the paradigmatic matrix, with all previous specimens simply tagged with '0' ('not present') for the anomalous trait.

All available box categories were included in the sample indiscriminately, as the traits that were deemed to be diagnostic were potentially present in all three basic classes of box, and we were interested in tracking the movement of clustered traits themselves, independent of the specific intended function of the box. In the absence of ethnographic detail on the matter, we could not presume a craft specialization system that precluded a master (with his own favoured preferences) from working on a chest, a square box, or a bowl – all within the same season of work. Also, during data collection it became apparent that known provenance would be problematic. For example, of the fifty-nine boxes originally observed, less than 40 per cent of all observed specimens at the American Museum of Natural History (AMNH) could be attributed to a specific settlement, while another 20 per cent of attributions only mention overall tribe – for example, 'Haida' (but not settlement). This left 40 per cent of the specimens fully unprovenanced (although some educated guesses based on qualitative observations were plausible, no actual determinations were made unless documentary proof could be found via accession numbers in the museum archives). Compounding this problem, many of the most meticulous and conscientious ethnographers collecting at around the turn of the twentieth century (such as Emmons, among the Tlingit) noted that boxes they collected from certain settlements were known to have been carved or recently arrived from elsewhere, often far from the settlement, and often by craftspeople from a different ethnolinguistic group. These complex provenances were occasionally tracked by circumspect collectors (for example, in Emmons's meticulous notes on his finds), but usually they were not. The hard reality is that gifting networks may have created an impenetrable 'blurring' of the distribution of actual production centres for the boxes.

Table 6.1 shows the final list of traits recorded as present or absent for the consideration set of fifty-nine boxes. These include data on basic box construction, techniques of painting and carving, and details of iconography.

Table 6.1 The 142 bentwood box traits accounted for in new database

Construction	Basic form	1	Long box
		2	Made to have removable lid
		3	Fixed top
		4	Hole in fixed top
		5	(2) holes in fixed top
		6	Trapezoidal box
		7	Base dug out
		8	Lid dug out inside
		9	L-shaped lid
	Box base	10	Morticed
		11	Platform
		12	Completely flat base
		13	L-shaped base
	Walls	14	Telescoping walls
		15	One single board bent for walls
		16	Two boards bent for walls
		17	Four separate boards for walls
		18	Walls cut down
		19	Wall width/depth not equal
		20	Walls cut convex on one axis
		21	Walls cut convex on two axes
		22	Top of box curved/open
		23	Handle across open top
	Kerfs	24	Slotted V
		25	Half V
		26	Slotted square
		27	Square
		28	Slotted/slanted

		29	Slanted
		30	U-shape
		31	Slotted-U
		32	Half-U
		33	Ziggurat
	Sewing	34	Horizontal
		35	Vertical
		36	Diagonal
		37	Base sewn on
	Pegging	38	Horizontal
		39	Horizontal/perpendicular to one wall
		40	V-pattern pegging series
		41	Base pegged on
	Sewing & Pegging	42	Together
	Thread	43	Spruce Root
		44	Gut/thread
	Changing function	45	Former bowl
Paint media	Painting	46	Solid black
		47	Solid red
		48	Black formline dominant
		49	Red formline dominant
		50	Black secondary
		51	Red secondary
		52	Rusty red ochre
		53	Primary red (China)
		54	Blue-green
		55	Blue
		56	Green
		57	White
		58	Bare wood as colour
		59	Band of space (horror vacui)
	Painted hatching	60	Diagonal
		61	Parallel lines
		62	Parallel-broken evenly
		63	Dashed hatching
		64	Cross-hatching
		65	Radial hatching
		66	Radial crossed
		67	Very thick cross hatching
Carving	Carving	68	Shallow relief
		69	Bas relief
		70	In-the-round projections
		71	Ramp cuts
		72	Concave cuts
		73	Incised shapes

Table 6.1 continued

		74	Incised contours (independent of shapes)
		75	Square cuts
		76	Smooth finish
		77	Crude finish
		78	Carved cross-hatching
		79	Single carved horizontal channel
		80	Double carved hor. chan./parallel
		81	Horizontal fluting
		82	Vertical fluting
	Special enhance	83	4-opercula groupings
		84	6-opercula groupings
		85	8-opercula groupings
		86	More than 8-opercula in a single grouping
		87	Abalone
		88	Extra binding
		89	Human hair
Iconography	**Depiction**	90	Configurative
		91	Expansive
		92	Distributive
		93	Extremely abstract (a la 'final exam')
	Representation	94	Zoomorphic
		95	Anthropomorphic
	Extremities	96	Human hands
		97	Feet
		98	Claws
		99	Tail
		100	Wings
	Ovoids	101	Concave on bottom
		102	Flat on bottom
		103	Upside down
		104	Salmon-trout's-head design
		105	Non-concentric pattern
	U-Forms	106	Primary U
		107	Secondary/Tertiary U
		108	Eye U
		109	Split U
		110	Angular U
		111	Outlined U
	Tertiary shapes	112	S-Shape
		113	L-Shape
		114	Eyebrow (round)
		115	Eyebrow (angled)

		116	Eyebrow (pointed)
		117	Eyebrow (hump-backed)
		118	Double-eye
		119	Circle-shaped eyes/joints
	Joins	120	V-join
		121	A-join
		122	Beek-join
	Transitional devices	123	Smile shape
		124	Circle
		125	3-point star
		126	3-point star with added 'smile'
	Symmetrical configuration	127	Nose-to-nose
		128	Head front
		129	Torso front
		130	Back-centred
		131	Split anatomy
		132	Abrupt, geometrically divided spaces
	Planar configuration	133	Front/back
		134	Side/side
		135	Wrap-around
		136	Corner-centric
	Face ratio	137	Face 1/3
		138	Face 1/2
		139	Face 2/3
		140	Face cover entire plane
		141	Mouth full width
		142	No ovoid joints in lower left and right

Full background detail on each trait state is provided in O'Neill (2011). Here, a few examples of discovered, quantifiable variation between traits will suffice to underpin the efficacy of the database. As mentioned, unexpected variation in the kerfs themselves was found (Figure 6.2). The 'rabbeted end' was bound either by sewing or pegging (or sometimes both). These techniques required great precision, and when observable (most of the work was sunken into the structure of the sides and often concealed with deer tallow and paint) provided a great range of variation (also Figure 6.3).

I noticed that often the same weave was used regardless of whether the container was a chest, a square box or some other form of a more specialist kind, confirming that the personal and cultural preferences

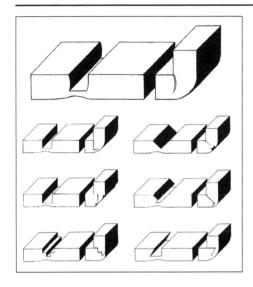

Figure 6.2. Some kerf cuts from the Pacific Northwest with their diagnostic states.

of the craftsperson could be consistent across many different types of pieces made.

Specific trait states relating to decoration were carefully recorded, separately from carving. The stages of the working process meant that decorative painting (if present) would always precede carved decoration (if present). This is because the former functioned to frame the latter in all cases where they appear together on a box (Holm 1965, 1981; Smithsonian Institution 1974). However, often a box would be painted and not carved, and vice versa. Usually, a more vernacular box would have neither (e.g. most of the Kwakiutlan specimens relevant to this study were not decorated with paint or relief carving at all).

The new binary database was then prepared for phylogenetic analysis, results from which will be reported below.

Database 2:
A Language Tree for the Coast

Amongst linguists, the precise genetic relationships of the languages on the coast are always in question. At present it is difficult to attempt to associate them through the systematic comparison of lexical, morphological or syntactical structures for the scope and purposes of this study (though this would not be an impossible project to undertake in the future). It has been speculated that up to three major language groups may have crossed Beringia at different times in prehistory, each forming their own distinctive pattern of descent

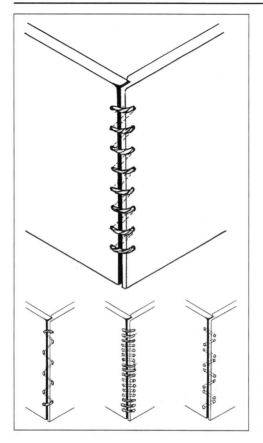

Figure 6.3. A sample of sewing and/or pegging techniques observed in Pacific Northwest coast specimens.

with modification in the Americas. These ancestral languages probably cannot be traced in a neat, tree-like phylogenetic pattern rooted with a Beringian entry point. It has been hypothesized that the three major waves of *phyla* (the earliest being Amerind, the first and most pervasive wave through the Americas, then Na-Dene and most recently Aleut-Eskimo) had converged into close proximity with each other on the coast, having emanated from radically different temporal and spatial sources in Asia (Greenberg et al. 1986). In this conception, arguably Athapascan, Eyak, Tlingit and Haida are in the Na-Dene family, while Wakashan and Salish languages derive from the earlier Amerind family. If this is correct, then any possible genetic relationships between linguistic *phyla* on the coast could go considerably further back in time than the generally accepted *terminus post quem* of approximately thirteen thousand years for the peopling of the Americas; the search for a common linguistic ancestor could go back as far as fifty thousand years, or more – and these would need to be triangulated in Asia, not North America.

For our purposes, the qualitatively reconstructed tree for languages employed by Jordan and O'Neill (2010), based on the seventeen ethnolinguistic groups covered in detail in the 'Cultural Elements Distributions XXVI' (CED) (Drucker 1950) will suffice (Figure 6.4).

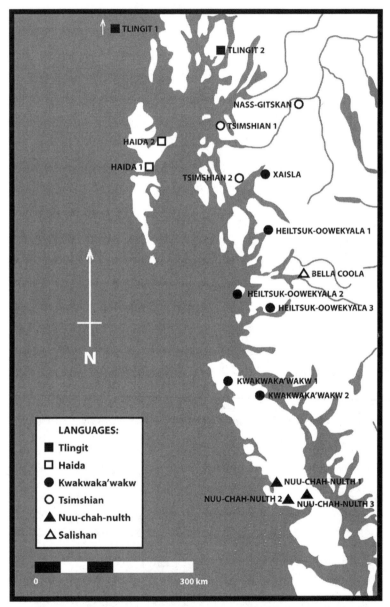

Figure 6.4. Map pinpointing the seventeen Pacific Northwest villages in Drucker 1950 (after Jordan and O'Neill 2010).

Here genetic language distance is reasonably inferred by attaching fractional values to each binary relationship between: language spoken in the same village, related dialects, languages, linguistic families and phyla/families (these are all nominal categorical designations compiled from Thompson and Kincade 1988: 34–35). From this new dataset it was possible to hand-build a language tree employing MACCLADE 4.05 software (Maddison and Maddison 2000), in preparation for comparison with other datasets. This reconstructs the hypothesized ancestral relationships reflecting best current consensus among linguists working in the region. A tree can be rooted with the presence of an 'outgroup', or the taxon hypothesized to be the most evolutionarily distant from the other taxa. The Bella Coola group was used as the outgroup for this language tree, as it was a Salish language isolate in the region. In this way, we have been able to bring a descriptive tree into the form of a phylogenetic one, for comparison with others.

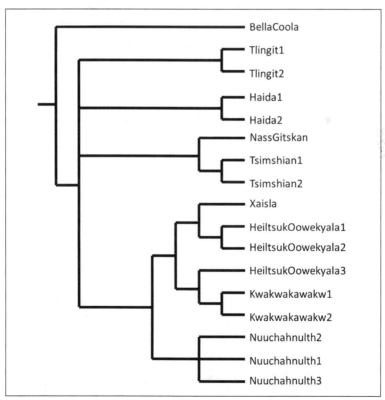

Figure 6.5. Hand-built phenetic language tree for the seventeen Pacific Northwest ethnolinguistic groups in Drucker 1950 (after Jordan and O'Neill 2010).

Databases Pared Down for Comparison

With these two databases, I wanted to understand if there were any possible co-evolutionary relationships between the movement of bentwood box traditions, and languages. A single box specimen was chosen from either the settlement covered by the language database, or the territory within the catchment area of that settlement, as opposed to any others (this was done by drawing Thiessen polygons between the seventeen pinpointed settlements in the CEDs used for language analysis – O'Neill 2011). In cross-referencing between the available box sample and the pinpointed location of languages, there was a match in nine of the seventeen settlements covered by the CEDs: there was a box of stated provenance in only nine of them. These nine became the choice set for co-evolutionary analysis: the nine languages which corresponded with one of the nine samples. A new truncated language tree was deduced with only the nine chosen groups, using the same criteria of relationships as above (Figure 6.6).

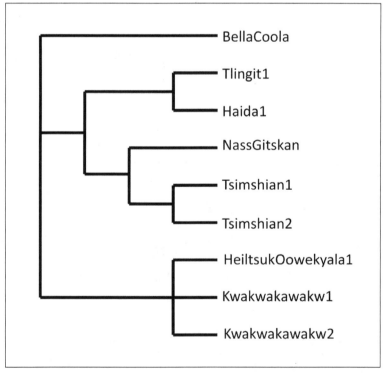

Figure 6.6. Truncated language tree corresponding with available Pacific Northwest box taxa.

Phylogenetic Analysis of the Box Sample for Comparison with Languages

In the past decade, a number of studies tracing the phylogenetic relationships between material culture specimens of other cultures have been carried out successfully. These studies have infiltrated archaeology (O'Brien et al. 2001; O'Brien and Lyman 2003; Buchanan and Collard 2008; Cochrane 2008; Lycett this volume) and anthropology (Jordan and Shennan 2003; Jordan and Mace 2006; VanPool et al. 2008; Jordan and O'Neill 2010), and have had interesting implications for political as well as ethnological history (Tehrani and Collard 2002). The following is work we have done in this vein with the new bentwood box data described above.

A heuristic analysis in PAUP 4.01b was conducted, again with the Bella Coola specimen used as the outgroup; for direct comparison, the same outgroup must be used for the tree on languages, with the Bella Coola as the outgroup. The test returned two trees that were similar in topography, and which showed all phylogenetic relationships, save for the three Kwakiultan groups in the south, which were shown to be in a polytomous relationship between them (bush-like and not branch-like – Figure 6.7). A number of statistical 'goodness-of-fit' tests for these trees were carried out. Firstly, a consensus tree was built by bootstrapping at 50 per cent majority rule consensus tree (*mrct*) – this process strictly reconciles homoplasy in the tree, and tells us how likely it is that different branches of the topography are accurate. The branches of the tree that were returned were all well supported. Secondly, the consensus trees carried a consistency index (CI) of .717; this gives us a measure of the amount of homoplasy in a cladogram; the more the fraction approaches 1.0, the less homoplasy is indicated. Finally, a retention index (RI) of .644 tells us that there are many more homologies in the tree (character states that are evolutionarily linked) than there are homoplasies (characters not linked). This is solid confirmation of the robustness of this tree, as Collard et al. (2006) have shown that an RI above .6 is as significant as findings in evolutionary biology/evolutionary genetics.

It was striking that the topography of this tree under bootstrapping was identical to the hypothesized language tree for the nine groups in the choice set – identical in every way (compare Figure 6.6 and 6.7). It is important to remember that these two trees were created by wholly different means – the language tree was first inferred and sketched by hand, based on known language distances, and the tree for the bentwood boxes was deduced by different software employing algorithms based on optimum parsimony,

hypothesizing evolutionary relationships by comparing the presence or absence of 142 traits of nine different box specimens from
nine different locations down the coast.

Discussion

Traceable co-evolutionary relationships between the development of
material culture traditions and languages are not always apparent.
Jordan and Mace (2006) found there was no close co-evolutionary fit
between all of the known architectural traditions and languages on
the coast; however, Jordan and O'Neill (2010) found that there was
indeed a co-evolutionary relationship that could be understood between the construction of the monumental residential houses alone,
and language. Normally, it is impossible to estimate accurately the co-
evolutionary relationships between even very similar trees without
mapping them onto each other statistically. There are several ways
to track the comparative, co-evolutionary relationships between
phylogenies of social culture such as language, social structure,
political complexity and customs, and other cultural lineages such

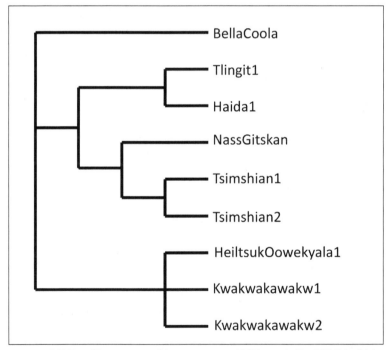

Figure 6.7. Final bootstrapped language tree (50% *mrct*) CI: .717, RI: .644
(100 replications).

as material culture traditions (Mace and Pagel 1994; Tehrani and Collard 2002; Jordan and Shennan 2003; Jordan and Mace 2006; Jordan and O'Neill 2010; Currie et al. 2010). A suite of different statistical tools gives us a range of ways to do this, but contingent upon specific types of questions and modes of data, some procedures will be more appropriate than others. Some approaches use the original data to make comparisons; others work with comparisons between already-built phylogenetic trees. One way to compare trees, a triplets test conducted in Component 2.0 (see Jordan and O'Neill 2010), compares the number of identical branching triplet relationships between taxa across different trees. However, if the trees are identical in their branching patterns, then the NEXUS-format syntax representing them would also be identical, precluding the need to test for closeness of fit.

The fact that the two trees are identical in their branching pattern suggests that there is indeed a co-evolutionary relationship between the bentwood box traditions and language.

Conclusions

To return to the three questions that this chapter set out to answer, the above work indicated that it may indeed be useful to revisit ethnographic material culture collections generally, and to research what they can tell us happened in prehistory in different parts of the world. More specifically, phylogenetic methods could be of value in advancing scholarship on the bentwood boxes of the coast and perhaps other traditions here and elsewhere, where complex variations in traits – and the way they cluster – are inherent in a tradition. We had a clear phylogenetic signal with the boxes, which suggests a strong pattern of heritable continuity in box-making traditions, a finding which perhaps begins to remedy the problem of attempting to understand local traditions better, in the face of distributional blur as discussed by Ames (1996). Finally, I found evidence of a co-evolutionary relationship between language and the bentwood box traditions, which was not predicted. In future, data on boxes representing more of the ethnolinguistic groups on the coast could be added and tested against a larger language tree.

Acknowledgements

I would like to thank the UK's Arts and Humanities Research Council (AHRC) for my Ph.D. studentship (RC/APN111956). Special thanks go to Curator Laila Williamson at the American Museum of Natural History in New York, who generously gave up three full weeks of her time during 2009 and 2010 – trapped in the museum stores with me – and patiently educating me about the history and lore of the bentwood boxes.

References

Ames, K.M. 1996. 'Archaeology, Style and the Theory of Coevolution', in H.D.G. Maschner (ed.), *Darwinian Archaeologies*. London: Plenum Press, pp. 109–31.

Bamforth, D.B. 2002. 'Evidence and Metaphor in Evolutionary Archaeology', *American Antiquity* 67: 435–52.

Boas, F. 1909. 'The Kwakiutl of Vancouver Island', *Publications of the Jesup North Pacific Expedition* 5: 301–522.

Bridgewater, A. and G. Bridgewater. 1991. *Carving Totem Poles and Masks*. New York: Sterling Publishers.

Brown, J.A. 1981. 'The Potential of Systematic Collections for Archaeological Research', in A. Cantwell, J.B. Griffin, N.A. Rothschild (eds), *The Research Potential of Anthropological Museum Collections*. New York: The New York Academy of Sciences, Vol. 376, p. 65.

Buchanan, B. and M. Collard. 2008. 'Testing Models of Early Paleoindian Colonization and Adaptation using Cladistics', in M.J. O'Brien (ed.), *Cultural Transmission and Archaeology: Issues and Case Studies*. Washington, DC: SAA Press, pp. 59–76.

Cantwell, A. and B. Rothschild. 1981. 'The Future of the Past', in A. Cantwell, J.B. Griffin, N.A. Rothschild (eds), *The Research Potential of Anthropological Museum Collections*. New York: The New York Academy of Sciences, Vol. 376, pp. 579–84.

Carlson, R.L. and L. Dalla Bona (eds). 1996. *Early Human Occupation in British Columbia*. Vancouver: UBC Press.

Cochrane, E. 2008. 'Migration and Cultural Transmission: Investigating Human Movement as an Explanation for Fijian Ceramic Change', in M.J. O'Brien (ed.), *Cultural Transmission and Archaeology: Issues and Case Studies*. Washington DC: SAA Press, pp. 132–45.

Codere, H. 1950. *Fighting with Property: A Study of Kwakiutl Potlatching and Warfare 1792–1930*. London: University of Washington Press.

Collard, M., S.J. Shennan and J.J. Tehrani. 2006. 'Branching, Blending and the Evolution of Cultural Similarities and Differences among Human Populations', *Evolution and Human Behaviour* 27(3): 169–84.

Currie, T.E., S.J. Greenhill, R.D. Gray, T. Hasegawa and R. Mace. 2010. 'Rise and Fall of Political Complexity in Island South-East Asia and the Pacific', *Nature* 467: 801–4. (doi:10.1038/nature09461)

Drucker, P. 1950. 'Cultural Element Distributions XXVI, Northwest Coast', *Anthropological Records* 9, 157–294.

Dunnell, R.C. 1971. *Systematics in Prehistory*. New York: The Free Press.

————.1978. 'Style and Function: A Fundamental Dichotomy', *American Antiquity* 43: 192–202.

Durham, W.H. 1976. The adaptive significance of cultural behaviour. *Human Ecology* 4, 89–121.

Ford, C.S. (ed.). 1941. *Smoke from their Fires: The Life of a Kwakiutl Chief.* New Haven, CT: Yale University Press.

Forey, F.L., C.J. Humphries, I.L. Kitching, R.W. Scotland, D.J. Siebert, and D.M. Williams. 1992. *Cladistics. A Practical Course in Systematics.* Oxford: Clarendon Press.

Friedman, J. 1975. 'The Prehistoric Uses of Wood at the Ozette Archaeological Site'. Unpublished Ph.D. dissertation. Pullman, WA: Washington State University, Department of Anthropology.

Greenberg, J.H., C.G. Turner II and S.L. Zegura. 1986. 'The Settlement of the Americas: A Comparison of the Linguistic, Dental, and Genetic Evidence', *Current Anthropology* 27(5): 477–97.

Hawthorn, A. 1979. *Kwakiutl Art.* London: University of Washington Press.

Hennig, W. 1966. *Phylogenetic Systematics.* Urbana: University of Illinois Press.

Holm, B. 1965. *Northwest Coast Indian Art: An Analysis of Form.* Seattle: University of Washington Press.

————.1981. 'Will the Real Charles Edenshaw Please Stand Up? A Problem of Attribution in Northwest Coast Indian Art', in D.N. Abbott (ed.), *The World is as Sharp as a Knife: An Anthology in Honour of Wilson Duff.* British Columbia: British Columbia Provincial Museum.

Inverarity, R.B. 1950. *Art of the Northwest Coast Indians.* Berkeley: University of California Press.

Jordan, P.D. and R. Mace. 2006. 'Tracking Culture-historical Lineages: Can "Descent with Modification" be Linked to "Association by Descent"?', in C. Lipo et al. (eds), *Mapping Our Ancestors: Phylogenetic Approaches in Anthropology and Prehistory.* London: AldineTransaction.

Jordan, P.D. and S. O'Neill. 2010. 'Untangling Cultural Inheritance: Language Diversity and Long-house Architecture on the Pacific Northwest Coast', in J. Steele, E. Cochrane, P. Jordan (eds), 'Cultural and Linguistic Diversity: Evolutionary Approaches', *Philosophical Transactions of the Royal Society B* 365: 3875–88. (doi:10.1098/rstb.2010.0092)

Jordan, P.D. and S.J. Shennan. 2003. 'Cultural Transmission, Language, and Basketry Traditions amongst the California Indians', *Anthropological Archaeology* 22: 42–74.

Mace, R. and M. Pagel. 1994. 'The Comparative Method in Anthropology', *Current Anthropology* 35: 549–64.

McLennan, B. and K. Duffek. 2000. *The Transforming Image: Painted Arts of Northwest Coast First Nations.* Vancouver: UBC Press.

Maddison, D.R. and W.P. Maddison. 2000. *MacClade 4: Analysis of Phylogeny and Character Evolution.* Sunderland, MA: Sinauer.

Matson, R.G. and G. Coupland. 1995. *The Prehistory of the Northwest Coast.* London: Academic Press.

Neiman, F.D. 1995. 'Stylistic Variation in Evolutionary Perspective: Inferences from Decorative Diversity and Interassemblage Distance in Illinois Woodland Ceramic Assemblages', *American Antiquity* 60: 7–36.

Oberg, K. 1973. *The Social Economy of the Tlingit Indians*. Seattle: University of Washington Press.

O'Brien, M.J. (ed.). 2008. *Cultural Transmission and Archaeology: Issues and Case Studies*. Washington, DC: SAA Press.

O'Brien, M.J., J. Darwent, R.L. Lyman. 2001. 'Cladistics is Useful for Reconstructing Archaeological Phylogenies: Paleoindian Points from the Southeastern United States', *Journal of Archaeological Science* 28: 1115–36.

O'Brien, M.J. and R.L. Lyman. 2003. *Cladistics and Archaeology*. Salt Lake City: The University of Utah Press.

O'Neill, S. 2011. 'An Investigation of Patterns and Processes of Cultural Transmission on the Pacific Northwest Coast of North America'. Unpublished Ph.D. dissertation. Aberdeen: University of Aberdeen.

Samuels, S.R. 1991. *Ozette Archaeological Project Research Reports. Volume 1. House Structure and Floor Midden*. WSU Department of Anthropology, Reports of Investigations 63, National Parks Service, Pacific Northwest Regional Office.

Smithsonian Institution. 1974. *Boxes and Bowls: Decorated Containers by Nineteenth-century Haida, Tlingit, Bella Bella, and Tsimshian Indian Artists*. Washington, DC: Smithsonian Institution Press.

Stewart, H. 1984. *Cedar, Tree of Life to the Northwest Coast Indians*. Vancouver: Douglas and McIntyre.

Swofford, D.L. 1998. *PAUP*: Phylogenetic Analysis Using Parsimony (*and Other Methods)* (version 4.0b10). Sunderland, MA: Sinauer.

Tehrani, J. and M. Collard. 2002. 'Investigating Cultural Evolution through Biological Phylogenetic Analyses of Turkmen Textiles', *Journal of Anthropological Archaeology* 21: 443–63.

Terrell, J.E. 1988. 'History as a Family Tree, History as an Entangled Bank: Constructing Images and Interpretations of Prehistory in the South Pacific', *Antiquity* 62: 642–57.

Thompson, L.C. and D. Kinkade. 1990. 'Language', in W. Suttles (ed.), *Handbook of North American Indians/Volume 7/Northwest Coast*. Washington, DC: Smithsonian Institution.

VanPool, T., C.T. Palmer and C.S. VanPool. 2008. 'Horned Serpents, Tradition, and the Tapestry of Culture', in M.J. O'Brien (ed.), *Cultural Transmission and Archaeology: Issues and Case Studies*. Washington, DC: SAA Press, pp. 77–90.

Chapter 7

THE TRANSMISSION OF ETHNOBOTANICAL KNOWLEDGE AND SKILLS AMONG TSIMANE' IN THE BOLIVIAN AMAZON

Victoria Reyes-García, James Broesch
and TAPS Bolivian Study Team

Introduction

Cultural transmission refers to the process of social reproduction in which the technology, knowledge, behaviour, language and beliefs of a human population are communicated and acquired (Cavalli-Sforza and Feldman 1981; Hewlett and Cavalli-Sforza 1986). Researchers have hypothesized that, unlike biological traits, largely transmitted by a vertical path through genes, cultural traits can be transmitted through at least three distinct – but not mutually exclusive – paths: (1) from parent to child (vertical transmission), (2) between any two individuals of the same generation (horizontal transmission), and (3) from non-parental individuals of the parental generation to members of the filial generation (oblique transmission) (Cavalli-Sforza and Feldman 1981).

The modelling of cultural transmission is of great importance for understanding the maintenance, erosion and spread of cultural traits and innovations. Quantitative data on the mechanisms of transmission of cultural traits could be useful in predicting within-group variability, stability of cultural traits over time and space, and the evolution of culture (Cavalli-Sforza and Feldman 1981; Boyd and Richerson 1985; Richerson and Boyd 2005). For example, as Cavalli-Sforza and

Feldman (1981) discuss, vertical transmission is highly conservative, may maintain individual variation, and is associated with slower rates of diffusion in a population when compared with horizontal or oblique transmission. Innovations would spread slowly in a society where transmission of knowledge takes place mainly through vertical transmission. By contrast, horizontal transmission is hypothesized to result in faster diffusion of new cultural traits if contact with transmitters is frequent. Horizontal and oblique transmission – involving many transmitters to one receiver – tend to generate the highest uniformity within a social group, while allowing for generational cultural change. Since these pathways are not mutually exclusive, the interaction between them and their relative role in the transmission of a trait is also important. For example, if vertical transmission is relatively weak, coupling it with oblique transmission might prevent traits being eliminated from a population more than if it was coupled with horizontal transmission. However, the opposite is true if vertical transmission is strong (Cavalli-Sforza and Feldman 1981: 351).

Recent modelling work has shown that different pathways of transmission are favoured under different conditions. When the environment is stable, selection is strong, or the transmission refers to cultural traits affecting fertility, then vertical transmission would be favoured over oblique transmission. However, when environments are variable, selection is relatively weak, or it refers to cultural traits affecting survival to adulthood, then oblique transmission is favoured over vertical transmission (McElreath and Strimling 2008). Because cultural transmission can occur through different mechanisms that are likely to be relatively more or less important depending on the context, and because the mechanisms through which cultural transmission occurs affect the stability of cultural traits over time and space, it is important to assess the relative weight of each mechanism.

Here we estimate the relative weight of vertical, horizontal and oblique transmission of an important technology in a small-scale society: ethnobotanical competence, defined as both ethnobotanical knowledge and skills. To do this, we estimate the association between a person's ethnobotanical competence and the ethnobotanical competence of that person's (a) same-sex parent (vertical transmission), (b) age-peers (horizontal transmission), and (c) individuals from the parental cohort other than the parents (oblique transmission). We focus on ethnobotanical competence because researchers have hypothesized that ethnobotanical knowledge and skills confer many benefits to people in small-scale societies (Johns 1996; McDade et al. 2007; Reyes-García et al. 2008b). For the empirical analysis, we draw upon a unique body of primary data collected from adults (≥16 years of age) in thirteen villages of a gatherer-horticulturalist society in the Bolivian Amazon (Tsimane'). Data include individual-level information on ethnobotanical knowledge and skills for a sample of adults related by both kinship (parents and their offspring) and spatial and temporal proximity (birth date and village of residency during childhood). For the analysis, we use same-sex parent knowledge, and not average parental knowledge, because the division of labour among the Tsimane' follows sex lines.

The Transmission of Folk Biological Knowledge

We start by reviewing the literature on the transmission of folk biological knowledge, focusing on the acquisition of folk biological knowledge in indigenous and rural societies, and on the empirical evidence for the horizontal, vertical and oblique transmission of folk biological knowledge.

Learning

The literature on how people learn the everyday skills and tasks that shape their interactions with the environment has reached three main conclusions: (1) cultural learning occurs through a temporal sequence that runs from childhood to adulthood, (2) people learn from others, but knowledge acquisition is faster if people can practise their theoretical knowledge, and (3) people need direct contact with nature to accumulate folk biological knowledge.

First, a body of research suggests that people learn most about folk biology during childhood. Children in subsistence societies master great quantities of empirical knowledge about their natural environment and subsistence-related skills before twelve years of age (Stross 1973; Zarger 2002). Simple skills, such as the ability to identify and prepare medicinal plants, are mastered before adolescence. For instance, primary school children in rural and indigenous societies have been shown to self-medicate with local herbs (Sternberg et al. 2001; Geissler et al. 2002). By the time children reach adolescence, their ability to name plants and describe their uses peaks, and it seems to remain largely unchanged for the rest of their lives (Stross 1973; Hunn 2002; Zarger and Stepp 2004). However, complex skills, such as hunting or craft production, may require years of experience to be perfected and mastery may not be reached until adulthood (Gurven et al. 2006).

Second, learning in small-scale societies is typically experimental and unlikely to occur in schools or school-like settings (Atran and Sperber 1991). Qualitative studies of children's acquisition of folk biological knowledge suggest that children acquire most of their folk biological knowledge through hands-on-experience, play, and direct observations (Zarger 2002), rather than through organized and verbal instruction. Furthermore, parents and other elders do not see their duty towards children as primarily one of instruction, although interactions with parents, siblings, and other adults matter in the transmission of folk biological knowledge (Ruddle and Chesterfield 1977; Zarger 2002). Research also suggests that children must practise tasks to learn folk biological knowledge (Ohmagari and Berkes 1997; Chipeniuk 1998). For example, Ruddle and Chesterfield (1977) examined the traditional system of knowledge transmission on Guara Island, in the Orinoco Delta of Venezuela. They concluded that learning occurs through repeated practice over time, rather than through simple observation of adults' performance.

Third, research suggests that contact with nature is of pivotal importance for the acquisition of folk biological knowledge (Nabhan and St. Antoine 1993; Chipeniuk 1995; Zent 1999; Wolff et al. 1999; Atran et al. 2004). For example, in a cross-cultural study, Ross and colleagues (2003) administered the same task to groups of rural and urban children from the United States. They found that urban children performed worse than even the youngest rural children due to their impoverished experience of the natural world. Recent theoretical work has also pointed out that learners engage in 'critical social learning' first, and then switch to individual learning and experimentation when social learning does not reach their expected performance threshold (Enquist et al. 2007; Enquist and Ghirlanda 2007).

Paths for the Transmission of Folk Biological Knowledge

Genetic and cultural factors are likely to affect the acquisition of cultural knowledge. Genetic inheritance might not be involved in terms of the specific cultural content of knowledge acquired (i.e. there are no genes for knowing that plant X does Y), but genes might underlie learning capacity, or speed of learning, which would influence the acquisition of cultural knowledge. However, since our goal here is to estimate the relative weight of paths for cultural transmission, and not to compare the relative role of genetic and cultural factors, in this section we focus on quantitative research related to the cultural – not genetic – transmission paths.

Vertical transmission: Some researchers have stated that folk biological knowledge is mainly transmitted from one generation to the next by parents to offspring (Lancy 1999; Hewlett et al. 2002). The intuition that folk biological knowledge is transmitted directly from parents can be theoretically explained (Cronk 1991; McElreath and Strimling 2008) and finds support in several empirical studies (Hewlett and Cavalli-Sforza 1986; Ohmagari and Berkes 1997; Lozada et al. 2006). For example, in a study of a rural population in Argentina, Lozada et al. (2006) analysed the transmission of knowledge of medicinal and edible plants. They concluded that family members (especially mothers) were the most important source for the acquisition of knowledge, followed by experienced non-familial traditional healers.

The results of another study in the transmission of cultural traits suggest that vertical transmission might not be preferential, but contextual to the type of knowledge being transmitted. In a study in the transmission of cultural traits and skills among Aka in the tropical forest of Africa, Hewlett and Cavalli-Sforza (1986) found that parents were singled out as the transmitters of 81 per cent of the studied skills, followed by 'watching others' (10 per cent), and grandparents (4 per cent). However, data suggest that vertical transmission was dominant only for highly shared knowledge, and that new knowledge was mostly diffused through horizontal and oblique paths.

Oblique transmission: Some anthropologists, sociologists and developmental psychologists have argued that parent-child transmission might not be the dominant mode of transmission during cultural learning (Henrich and Gil-White 2001), at least when a person's total lifespan is considered (Aunger 2000). Vertical transmission is based on two models, whereas oblique and horizontal transmissions are based on larger samples, and larger samples might provide more accurate (less biased) information (Henrich and Boyd 1998). Oblique transmission can take the form of (a) one-to-many, when one person (e.g. a teacher) transmits information to many people of a younger generation, or (b) many-to-one, when the person learns from adults other than the parents (Cavalli-Sforza and Feldman 1981).

Quantitative studies of oblique transmission of ethnobotanical knowledge are scarce, and focus on the transmission of knowledge from one-to-many. For example, Lozada and colleagues (2006) found that experienced traditional healers outside the family are important in the transmission of ethnobotanical knowledge, while Hewlett and Cavalli-Sforza (1986) found that non-parental older family members contributed only 1.4 per cent to the transmission of bush skills among the Aka in the tropical forest of Africa.

Horizontal transmission: Several authors have argued that there are also social and evolutionary reasons to expect intra-generational transmission of some types of cultural knowledge (Boyd and Richerson 1985; Harris 1999). Observational studies suggest that, in some domains, children learn a considerable amount from age-peers (Lancy 1999; Zarger 2002). For example, children regularly teach each other tasks and skills during the course of their daily play (Lancy 1999). Zarger (2002) showed that siblings pass along extensive information to one another about plants, including where to find them, their uses, and how to harvest or cultivate them. Research also suggests that, later in life, young adults turn to age-peers rather than to parents for information. In non-stable environments, age-peers are the individuals most likely to have tracked changes and should provide the best information to update the information previously acquired from parents (Cavalli-Sforza and Feldman 1981; Aunger 2000). Furthermore, asking age-peers is less socially risky than asking parents because, at certain ages, parents might reproach offspring for their inability in certain skills.

The importance of age-peers in the transmission of cultural knowledge has only been sparsely tested in relation to ethnobotanical competence, but dovetails with studies in developmental psychology and in cultural anthropology. Studies in developmental psychology stress the importance of age-peers in the acquisition of knowledge and socialization, even in school (Vygostky 1978; Shaeffer 1996). Cultural anthropologists have conducted time allocation studies with children to show that children spend large portions of time with siblings and age-peers (Whiting and Whiting 1975; Weisner and Gallimore 1977). Time spent together gives children the opportunity to share knowledge. Time spent together also allows for staggered learning, in which children learn from someone who knows just a little more than them but is not necessarily an expert. It might be easier to learn from these individuals than it would be to learn from an adult because adults might be less accessible, might move quickly over things, and might be less willing to deal with the naïve learner.

In sum, previous empirical research has outlined the importance of the vertical path in the transmission of folk biological knowledge. Theoretical models and empirical evidence from fields other than anthropology suggest that the importance of vertical transmission may be overstated (Aunger 2000), and that neither vertical nor oblique transmission should be expected to dominate across all domains (McElreath and Strimling 2008).

Tsimane': Social Organization and Acquisition of Ethnobotanical Competence

The Tsimane' number approximately eight thousand people and live in the rainforests and savannahs at the foothills of the Andes, mostly in the Department of Beni, Bolivia. Relatively isolated until the mid-twentieth century, they started to engage in more frequent and prolonged contact with Westerners after the arrival of Protestant missionaries in the late 1940s and early 1950s (Daillant 2003; Huanca 2008). Like many native Amazonians, the Tsimane' practise a mix of slash-and-burn farming, hunting, fishing, and plant gathering (Vadez et al. 2004).

Ethnographic observations suggest that, as in other gatherer-horticulturalist societies, cultural knowledge is transmitted orally and through informal means among the Tsimane'. The Tsimane' have been exposed to schooling since the 1950s, but despite nearly five decades of exposure to schools, Tsimane' adults have little formal schooling (Reyes-García et al. 2010). Given the limited levels of literacy among the Tsimane', it is accurate to say that cultural transmission requires personal interaction, either through oral communication or imitation of observed behaviours.

In previous publications we have provided ethnographic details on the Tsimane', including descriptions of Tsimane' ethnobotanical knowledge (Reyes-García et al. 2006; Huanca 2008). Here we focus on describing Tsimane' social organization and the learning process for the acquisition of ethnobotanical competences. We focus on social organization because it might be central to understanding the potential paths for the transmission of cultural traits.

Tsimane' Social Organization

Until recently, the Tsimane' were a highly autarkic and egalitarian society (Ellis 1996). Polygynous in the past, most Tsimane' presently practise monogamy and live in nuclear households run jointly by an adult female and an adult male. Each household contains an average of 6.25 people (SD=2.85) including 2.66 adults (SD=1.10) and 3.59 children (SD=2.31), defined as people under the age of 16. Although nowadays most Tsimane' households are nuclear, households related by kin are usually organized in village clusters and situated at a short distance one from another. The villages included in this study contain an average of 24 nuclear households (SD=10.88).

The Tsimane' kinship system is Dravidian and provides the main framework for social organization (Daillant 2003). The Tsimane' practise cross-cousin marriage, meaning that a man weds the daughter of his mother's brother or of his father's sister. This preferential system of marriage generates a dense network of relations and multiple alliances (ibid.), Tsimane' using the term *chatidye* (relative) to refer to and address any other Tsimane'. Social visits within a village occur on a daily basis and visits to family and friends in other villages are also frequent, sometimes lasting several weeks or even months. Ethnographers have stressed the importance of visiting for the transmission of cultural knowledge among the Tsimane' (Ellis 1996).

The Learning Process

In previous research (Reyes-García et al. 2007) we found that, like other indigenous groups, the Tsimane' acquire most of their ethnobotanical knowledge during childhood. The increase of ethnobotanical knowledge is slow after adolescence and more important for the acquisition of skills than for the acquisition of theoretical knowledge. From ethnographic work, we also know that Tsimane' learning is based on observation and direct experience. Children are free to play, explore and interact with the natural world with little or no restriction or supervision. Children above five years of age usually spend a good portion of each day solely in the company of brothers, sisters, cousins and friends carrying out daily activities, such as household chores, babysitting, playing, bathing, or looking for snack foods. As in other subsistence societies (Lancy 1999; Zarger 2002), Tsimane' play and work activities are frequently intertwined. For example, boys organize and go on fishing expeditions by themselves. Girls are expected to perform household tasks and accompany mothers and older siblings to agricultural fields where they often play with, and take care of, younger siblings.

The early acquisition of ethnobotanical competence is important for Tsimane' youngsters. The skills of young unmarried Tsimane' boys and girls are typically evaluated by their potential in-laws as well as by their own parents, who worry about their children's ability to meet their expected duties in their future homes. The Tsimane' stress the need to acquire competence in sex-specific tasks before marriage, and many of these tasks require a certain degree of folk biological knowledge. For example, a boy needs to go on a hunting expedition alone and hunt with his bow and arrow before being able to form a new household. Similarly, girls must know how to prepare fermented beverages, farm and weave. Excelling in subsistence-related activities (some of them highly dependent on ethnobotanical competence) is a source of social status for the Tsimane' (Reyes-García et al. 2008a).

Estimation Strategy

In this chapter we estimate the relative weight of parents, age-peers and the parental cohort in the transmission of ethnobotanical competence. Because the statistical analysis of the transmission of cultural knowledge is highly problematic, with no straightforward or completely agreed body of methods, our estimations suffer from several biases that we discuss in the following paragraphs. By acknowledging assumptions and potential biases in our estimations, we hope to progress the quantitative empirical analysis of knowledge transmission more generally.

Our empirical estimations assess the association between (1) two outcome variables (ethnobotanical knowledge and ethnobotanical skills), and (2) ethnobotanical knowledge and skills of (a) a same-sex parent, (b) age-peers, and (c) the parental cohort. We assume that an association between own and same-sex parent's ethnobotanical competence implies vertical transmission of cultural knowledge, that an association between own and age-peer's ethnobotanical competence implies horizontal transmission of knowledge, and that an association between own and parental cohort's ethnobotanical competence implies oblique transmission of knowledge. However, any conclusion as to the paths for the transmission of knowledge from these estimates is based on four strong assumptions.

First, we assume that all the information analysed has been transmitted through social learning – that is to say, we disregard the possibility that any correlation between knowledge of two individuals is due to one or both of them having acquired their knowledge through individual rather than social learning. Second, to imply transmission of knowledge from the associations in our model, we need to assume endogenous effects, or that individual ethnobotanical competence varies with group ethnobotanical competence. But because our data suffer from what is known as 'reflection problem' (Manski 1993), so individual ethnobotanical competence could also co-vary with the distribution of background characteristics of the group (i.e. contextual effects), or just be associated with a group ethnobotanical competence because both – the individual and the group – operate in a similar environment (i.e. correlated effects). Third, to imply transmission of knowledge from the associations in our model, we also need to assume that causality runs from the explanatory to the outcome variable. This is a strong assumption given that children can actually transmit knowledge to parents (Harris 1999). Last, we assume that a contemporaneous association illustrates past transmission of knowledge.

Potential biases in our estimations relate to three factors: random measurement error, omitted variables, and redundant predictors. First, we might have measurement error in our proxy measures of ethnobotanical competence. For example, the test for skills is based on self-reports, where we ask informants to recall whether they have ever crafted an item from a plant. So, our measure of ethnobotanical skills might suffer from random measurement error if, for example, some informants have better memory than others. Second, our estimations might be biased by the role of omitted variables. The underlying assumption of the econometric model is that a person acquires cultural knowledge through vertical, horizontal or oblique transmission only. However, there might be other paths for the transmission of cultural knowledge. For example, genetic inheritance might be confounded with vertical transmission of knowledge. Failure to control for other variables that might influence transmission of knowledge will bias our estimations in an unknown magnitude and direction. Third, our estimates could suffer from having redundant predictors, which raises questions about the assumption of independence of predictors (Manski 2007). For example, parental ethnobotanical competence might not be independent with respect to parental cohort ethnobotanical competence. As we explain below, parental cohort competence is calculated as the average of a group. For each observation the number of values averaged changes according to the age of the person, and the identity of the parents. However, this variation might not be enough to ensure independence of the two predictors.

Keeping these assumptions and caveats in mind, we use the following expression to model the association between ethnobotanical competence (Y) and covariates:

[1] $OK_{ijv} = \alpha + \beta PK_{ijv} + \gamma SK_{ijv} + \theta CK_{ijv} + \phi D_{ijv} + \phi' V_v + \varepsilon_{ijv}$

The term OK_{ijv} refers to a person's ethnobotanical knowledge, where i is the participant, j the household, and v the village. We use ethnobotanical knowledge for ease of exposition, but the expression also applies to ethnobotanical skills. We differentiate between ethnobotanical knowledge and ethnobotanical skills because the two dimensions of ethnobotanical competence might be transmitted through different paths. PK_{ijv} captures the ethnobotanical competence of the same-sex parent. SK_{ijv} captures the average ethnobotanical competence of the subject's age-peers (excluding the subject's own competence). The measure of same age-peers might include some, but not all and not only, of the subject's siblings. CK_{ijv} captures the average ethnobotanical competence of the parental cohort. D_{ijv} is a vector of variables that captures the demographic attributes of the participant (e.g. age, sex, school attainment). V_v is a vector of dummy variables to control for the subject's village of residency, and ε_{ijv} is a random error term with standard properties.

By including the ethnobotanical competence of parents, age-peers and parental cohort in the same equation, we can compare the coefficients and significance of the three variables. If transmission of ethnobotanical competence occurs mainly from parents to offspring, then the knowledge of parents and offspring should be highly correlated, and the coefficient β should be positive and larger than γ and θ. If the three paths of transmission have a similar weight, then the three coefficients, γ, β, and θ, should be positive, statistically significant and of similar magnitude.

To estimate the parameters, we used ordinary-least square regressions with robust standard errors. We ran regressions with clustering of individuals by households (at the time of the interview) because individuals are nested in households and because individuals from a household are more likely to be similar in their ethnobotanical competence than individuals from different households. We include a full set of dummies for village of residency to control for village-level attributes that are of pivotal importance in explaining the pathways for the transmission of ethnobotanical knowledge and skills. For example, it is possible that the transmission of ethnobotanical knowledge and skills in a village is affected by its given ecological context, or by the presence of a charismatic or knowledgeable person who lives (or lived) in the village and from whom all the people learned. By including village dummies we can partially control for these unmeasured phenomena.

Methods

Data collection was conducted through the auspices of the Tsimane' Amazonian Panel Study (http://www.tsimane.org) and it took place during June–September 2005. Four experienced interviewers and translators, who had been working with the Tsimane' Amazonian Panel Study since 1999, undertook the survey. The study protocol was approved by Northwestern University and Brandeis University Review Boards for research involving human subjects. The Tsimane' Grand Council approved the study, and individual consent was obtained before enrolment.

Sample

We collected data from nearly all households (n=252) in thirteen Tsimane' villages straddling the Maniqui River. The villages surveyed differed in their proximity to the market town of San Borja (population approximately 19,000) (mean=25.96 km; SD=16.70). Our initial sample included every person over sixteen years of age (or younger if they headed a household) willing to participate (n=642). During interviews, we asked informants to provide their father's and mother's name and village of residency. We interviewed parents who were part of the studied villages, but did not attempt to find parents who resided in villages outside our sample. From the 642 adults who answered the survey, only 270 (123 men and 147 women) from 163 households had the same-sex parent in the sample.

Measuring Ethnobotanical Knowledge

To measure ethnobotanical knowledge we mentioned to informants the Tsimane' names of 15 plants selected at random from a list of 92, developed in an earlier study (Reyes-García et al. 2006). We asked participants whether they knew or recognized the name of the plant, and recorded positive answers as one and negative answers as zero. Responses show a high inter-correlation (Cronbach's alpha=0.78) so we used them to construct an individual summary measure of ethnobotanical knowledge by adding the answers to the 15 questions. We transformed knowledge scores to natural logarithms to ease the reading of the coefficients from regression analysis.

Own Ethnobotanical Skills

To measure ethnobotanical skills, we asked subjects whether they had ever used 12 plants for specific purposes (e.g. 'Have you ever used *coyo*j [*Zantedeschia sp.*] for medicine?'). None of the questions was purposefully false. If participants reported having used the plant, we coded the answer as one; otherwise, we coded the answer as zero. Responses were inter-correlated (Cronbach's alpha=0.75), so we used them to construct a summary measure of ethnobotanical skills by adding the answers to the 12 questions. Twenty-two people (14 women and 8 men) or 8 per cent of the sample had scores of zeros in the test of ethnobotanical skills, so we added 1 to subject's scores before transforming data to logarithms.

Same-Sex Parent Ethnobotanical Competence

We used the same test to measure subject's and parent's ethnobotanical knowledge and skills. Using pair-wise Pearson correlations, we found that father–son's ethnobotanical knowledge scores were correlated ($r=0.225$, $p=0.003$) whereas ethnobotanical skills were not ($r=0.03$, $p=0.6$). Mother–daugther's ethnobotanical knowledge ($r=0.505$, $p<0.001$) and skills ($r=0.443$, $p<0.001$) scores were positively correlated.

Correlations of scores do not indicate actual match in responses. Two people with the same score might have answered correctly a totally different set of questions. To measure actual match in ethnobotanical knowledge and skill between a subject and his/her same-sex parent, we generated two new variables. We compared parent's and offspring's responses to each of the questions in our tests, and added one point to the new variable each time both – parent and offspring – had a correct answer in the test. The pair-wise Pearson correlation coefficient between the variable that measures parent–offspring matches in the ethnobotanical knowledge and the ethnobotanical skills tests was relatively high and statistically significant ($r=0.553$, $p<0.0001$). To avoid collinearity between outcome (own knowledge) and explanations (number of positive matches between parent–offspring in the knowledge test), in regression analyses we use the variable that measures positive matches in ethnobotanical skills as an explanatory variable in the model with ethnobotanical knowledge as outcome, and vice versa.

Age-Peers' Ethnobotanical Competence

We asked informants to report their birth date, or estimated age in years, and their village of residency during childhood, and used this to group subjects into cohorts. For each individual in the sample, we generated a group of age-peers, defined as people who spent childhood in the same village as the subject, and who were born within 4 years of the subject's year of birth. The composition of age-peer cohorts changed for each individual in the sample. We did not calculate actual matches between an individual and his/her cohort, but simply used as an explanatory variable the average knowledge of the cohort, excluding the individual's knowledge. We followed the same procedure to calculate age-peers' ethnobotanical skills.

Parental Cohort Ethnobotanical Competence

To define parental cohort, we first estimated the average difference in age between subjects and their parents: between a woman and her mother it was 31.5 years (SD=12.5), and between a man and his father was 35.4 years (SD=12.4). We defined parental cohort as someone who was born between 20 and 40 years before the subject and who lived in the village where the subject spent his/her childhood. As with age-peers cohorts, to calculate parental cohort ethnobotanical knowledge, we averaged the measured ethnobotanical knowledge scores of informants in each group, excluding the ethnobotanical knowledge of the subject's parents. We followed a similar procedure to calculate parental cohort ethnobotanical skills.

Controls

Controls for the regression analysis include age, schooling, and a full set of dummies for village of residency.

Results

Table 7.1 contains a definition and summary statistics of the variables used in the regression analysis. Table 7.2 contains the regression results for ethnobotanical knowledge (part A) and ethnobotanical skills (part B). In column [a] we include only men (n=123), in column [b] only women (n=147), and in column [c] the full sample (n=270).

Table 7.1 Definition and descriptive statistics of variables used in Tsimane' regression analysis (n=270)

Variable	Definition	Mean	Stand dev
I. Outcome variable			
Ethnobotanical knowledge	Score in test of plant knowledge; subjects were asked if they knew names of 15 wild and semi-domesticated plants. In regression entered in natural logarithms.	11.61	2.78
Ethnobotanical skills	Reported use of 12 wild and semi-domesticated plants. In regression entered in natural logarithms.	4.39	2.68
II. Explanatory variables			
Same-sex parent ethnobotanical knowledge	Number of matches in responses to the ethnobotanical knowledge test between a person and his/her same-sex parent.	3.13	2.15
Age-peers ethnobotanical knowledge	Average ethnobotanical knowledge score of people who were born within 4 years of the subject's year of birth and who lived in the same village during childhood (excluding subject's knowledge).	12.15	2.04
Parental cohort ethnobotanical knowledge	Average ethnobotanical knowledge score of people who were born between 20 and 40 years before the subject and who lived in the subject's village of childhood, excluding parental knowledge.	13.08	1.61
Same-sex parent ethnobotanical skills	Number of matches in responses to the ethnobotanical skill test between a person and his/her same-sex parent.	4.39	2.68
Age-peers ethnobotanical skills	Average ethnobotanical skills score of people who were born within 4 years of the subject's year of birth and who lived in the same village during childhood (excluding subject's knowledge).	4.59	1.42
Parental cohort ethnobotanical skills	Average ethnobotanical knowledge score of people who were born between 20 and 40 years before the subject and who lived in the subject's village of childhood, excluding parental knowledge.	6.04	1.57
III. Control			
Male	Sex of the subject, Male=1	0.44	0.49
Age	Age in years	27.31	11.15
Schooling	Maximum school grade achieved by subject	2.62	2.10

Table 7.2 Regression results: transmission paths for ethnobotanical knowledge and skills, Tsimane' adults

Dependent Variables							
Ethnobotanical knowledge (log)				B. Ethnobotanical Skills (log)			
	[a]	[b]	[c]		[a]	[b]	[c]
	Male	Female	Pool		Male	Female	Pool
Explanatory variables							
Same-sex parent skills (log)	.025**	.023**	.022***	Same-sex parent knowledge (log)	−.010	.073***	.038**
Age-peers knowledge (log)	−.314	.235	−.074	Age-peers skills (log)	−.186	−.121	−.198
Parental cohort knowledge (log)	.618***	.372*	.373**	Parental cohort skills (log)	.460*	−.160	−.008
Control variables							
Male	^	^	.078***		^	^	.146**
Schooling	−.009	−.021	−.015*		−.054***	−.051	−.055***
Age	.008***	−.004**	.006**		.013**	.003	.009**
Constant	1.154	.653	1.44***		1.083	1.514	1.442**
R^2	0.58	0.55	0.54		0.38	0.40	0.33
N	123	147	270		123	147	269

Note: ***, ** and * significant at ≤1%, ≤5%, and ≤10%. Regressions are ordinary-least squares. Robust standard errors used when probability of exceeding 2 value in Breusch-Pagan test <5%. ^ = variable intentionally left out. Regressions contain a full set of dummy variables for village of residency (not shown). For definition of variables, see Table 7.1.

Ethnobotanical Knowledge

The analysis of the possible transmission of ethnobotanical knowledge among men (column [a]) suggests that a man's ethnobotanical knowledge is associated with his father's ethnobotanical skills and with the knowledge of the parental cohort, but not with the knowledge of his age-peers. A 1 per cent increase in the measure of father's skill is associated with a 0.02 per cent increase in the ethnobotanical knowledge of the man (p=0.04), and a 1 per cent increase in the ethnobotanical knowledge of the parental cohort is associated with a 0.62 per cent increase in the ethnobotanical knowledge of the man (p=0.008).

The analysis of the paths for the possible transmission of ethnobotanical knowledge among women (column [b]) suggests a similar pattern. A woman's ethnobotanical knowledge bears a positive and statistically significant association with the measure of her mother's skills and a low association with the ethnobotanical knowledge of her parental cohort. As for men's ethnobotanical knowledge, woman's ethnobotanical knowledge is not associated with the ethnobotanical knowledge of her age-peers. A 1 per cent increase in the measure of mother's ethnobotanical skills is associated with a 0.023 per cent increase in the ethnobotanical knowledge of the woman (p=0.01). A 1 per cent increase in the average ethnobotanical knowledge of a woman's parental cohort is associated with a 0.37 per cent increase in the ethnobotanical knowledge of the woman (p=0.10).

In column [c], we present results from the pooled sample. We found that the strongest association in real terms was between an individual's ethnobotanical knowledge and the knowledge of the individual's parental cohort. Doubling the average knowledge of the person's parental cohort would be associated with a 37 per cent increase in the person's ethnobotanical knowledge (p=0.01), whereas doubling the number of matches with the same-sex parent's in the skills test would be only associated with a 2 per cent increase in the person's knowledge (p<0.0001).

Ethnobotanical Skills

Results for the transmission of ethnobotanical skills differ from results for the transmission of ethnobotanical knowledge. We found that a man's ethnobotanical skills were weakly associated with the average skills of the parental cohort, but not associated with his father's knowledge or with the skills of his age-peers. A 1 per cent increase in the average skills of the parental cohort would be associated with a 0.46 per cent increase in a man's ethnobotanical skills (p=0.09). A woman's ethnobotanical skills were associated with her mother's knowledge. A 1 per cent increase in the number of matches between a woman and her mother would be associated with a 0.07 per cent increase in the woman's knowledge (p=0.003).

Results from the transmission of ethnobotanical skills with the pool sample (Table 7.2, Section B, column [c]) suggest a low association between the skills of an individual and the ethnobotanical knowledge of the person's same-sex parent. A 1 per cent increase in the number of matches between a person and the same-sex parent in the ethnobotanical knowledge test would be associated with a 0.038 per cent increase in the person's knowledge (p=0.01).

In sum, we generally found that (a) the ethnobotanical competence of the same-sex parent is generally associated with a person's ethnobotanical competence, (b) parental cohort knowledge is associated with a person's ethnobotanical knowledge (the association is stronger for men than for women), and (c) age-peers ethnobotanical competence is not associated in a statistically significant way with own ethnobotanical competence.

Discussion

We organize the discussion around findings from the three paths to explain the transmission of ethnobotanical knowledge and skills analysed. First, we found that our proxies for same-sex parental ethnobotanical competence are consistently associated with own ethnobotanical competence with one exception: a father's ethnobotanical knowledge is not associated with his son's skills. The finding of the association between own and parental knowledge meshes with previous empirical findings on the transmission of ethnobotanical knowledge, thus corroborating the hypothesis that parents play an important role in the transmission of cultural knowledge (Hewlett and Cavalli-Sforza 1986; Ohmagari and Berkes 1997; Lozada et al., 2006). However, our findings suggest that the effect of the association is small in real terms. Doubling same-sex parental ethnobotanical competence (an unlikely event) would only result in a 2 per cent increase of offspring ethnobotanical knowledge and a 3 per cent increase of offspring ethnobotanical skills.

Second, we find that knowledge of the parental cohort is generally associated with the subject's ethnobotanical knowledge, but for the women in the sample, only the skills of the parental cohort are associated with own skills. The magnitude of the association for parental cohort ethnobotanical knowledge is larger than the magnitude of the association for same-sex parental ethnobotanical knowledge, suggesting that the real weight of the oblique transmission path is larger than the real weight of the vertical path, at least for ethnobotanical knowledge. A possible explanation for the finding lies in Tsimane' social organization. As explained above, Tsimane' social organization provides ample opportunities to interact with same and older age kin, and friends from a young age. Those interactions facilitate the exchange of information across age groups outside the dyad parent–offspring, thus facilitating oblique transmission of knowledge.

Another potential explanation for the increased magnitude of oblique pathways compared to vertical pathways may be the changing social context that the Tsimane' are currently experiencing. Theoretical modelling suggests that non-stable environments favour reliance on oblique rather than vertical transmission (McElreath and

Strimling 2008). For example, with increasing exposure to market economy and products, ethnobotanical competence might need to be used in new situations or in interaction with new products. The learner might select from a wider subset of the population models (like non-parental adults) that have been effective at navigating these cultural shifts.

Third, we find that age-peers ethnobotanical competence is not associated in a statistically significant way with own ethnobotanical competence. Several authors have argued that there are social and evolutionary reasons to expect intra-generational transmission of cultural knowledge (Boyd and Richerson 1985; Harris 1999; Lancy 1999; Zarger 2002). We did not find evidence of horizontal transmission of ethnobotanical knowledge in our sample.

Our data also suggest that there might be differences in the transmission of ethnobotanical competences among men and women, the differences being stronger for the transmission of ethnobotanical skills than for ethnobotanical knowledge. Why would the paths for the transmission of ethnobotanical knowledge and ethnobotanical skills among Tsimane' men and women differ? And why would ethnobotanical knowledge and skills be transmitted through different paths? Differences in the paths for the transmission of ethnobotanical knowledge and skills among Tsimane' men and women might reflect differences in time allocation and sexual division of labour. For example, from a young age, Tsimane' girls are expected to perform household tasks and accompany mothers and other relatives to agricultural fields. Such close interaction could facilitate the transmission of ethnobotanical knowledge and skills from the older to the younger generation. In contrast, Tsimane' men are reluctant to take young children to the forest with them because of the dangers, and because children might make noise, thus spoiling hunting opportunities. This could result in boys having fewer opportunities to interact with, and learn directly from, their fathers. Thus, it is possible that Tsimane' boys' learning from parents is of a more indirect nature than Tsimane' girls' learning from mothers. Because boys' learning from parents is more indirect, it could be superseded more easily by parental cohort knowledge.

Why would ethnobotanical knowledge and skills be transmitted through different paths? A possible explanation might be related to the different characteristics of ethnobotanical knowledge and skills. Research shows that ethnobotanical knowledge, such as names or traits used for recognition, is easier to acquire than ethnobotanical skills, and is mainly acquired during childhood. Knowledge relies on cumulative memory, and individuals can learn quickly and effectively through relatively few interactions; therefore, individuals can acquire ethnobotanical knowledge from many sources. Learning skills might require higher investment by the learner. Acquiring skills is more costly in time and requires a number of direct observations and repetition within a particular ecological context. Individuals might be more conservative in selecting models for the transmission of skills, and place more weight on information acquired from older informants or from informants with more expertise than their peers.

We conclude by discussing the potential implications of our findings for understanding Tsimane' cultural change. Given that oblique transmission involving many transmitters to one receiver tends to generate the highest uniformity within a social group, while allowing for generational cultural change, if, as our data suggest, Tsimane' favour the oblique path for the transmission of cultural knowledge, then one would expect uniform cultural changes in Tsimane' society. In the study presented here, we analyse associations between members of an adult population, under the assumption that a present association would reflect past transmission of knowledge – but if ethnobotanical knowledge and skills are acquired across the life span, then different paths of transmission might play a different role through time. Further empirical research on the transmission of cultural knowledge should address the longitudinal dimension of knowledge acquisition. Further research should follow children into adulthood in order to provide a better understanding of how knowledge and behaviours are first acquired and latter changed as individuals age and are exposed to other sources of information.

Acknowledgments

The contents of this chapter first appeared in V. Reyes-García, J. Broesch, L. Calvet-Mir, N. Fuentes-Pelaez, T.W. McDade, S. Parsa, S. Tanner, T Huanca, W.R. Leonard and M.R. Martínez-Rodríguez. 2009. 'Cultural Transmission of Ethnobotanical Knowledge and Skills: An Empirical Analysis from an Amerindian Society', *Evolution and Human Behavior* 30(4): 274–85. The material has been reproduced with the permission of the journal. Research was funded by grants from the Cultural Anthropology and Physical Anthropology Programs, National Science Foundation (BCS-0134225, BCS-0200767, BCS-0322380). We thank M. Aguilar, J. Cari, S. Cari, E. Conde, D. Pache, J. Pache, P. Pache, M. Roca and E. Tayo for help in collecting data and for logistical support. Thanks also go to the Tsimane' and the Gran Consejo Tsimane' for their continuous support, and to ICRISAT-Patancheru for providing office facilities to Reyes-García. We thank Amélia Frazâo-Moreira, Ricardo Godoy, Ori Heffetz, Colleen M. O'Brien, and the UC Davis Human Behavioral Ecology team for bibliographic leads and comments on previous versions of the article. A preliminary version of the article was presented in the *I Jornada de Antropología y Ecología*

(Barcelona, 27 September 2007). We thank participants for their useful comments.

References

Atran, S., D. Medin and N. Ross. 2004. 'Evolution and Devolution of Knowledge: A Tale of Two Biologies', *Journal of the Royal Anthropological Institute* 10: 395–420.

Atran, S. and D. Sperber. 1991. 'Learning without Teaching: Its Place in Culture', in L.T. Landsmann (ed.), *Culture, Schooling, and Psychological Development*. Norwood, NJ: Ablex Publishing Corporation, pp. 39–55.

Aunger, R. 2000. 'The Life History of Culture Learning in a Face-to-face Society', *Ethos* 28: 1–38.

Boyd, R. and P. Richerson. 1985. *Culture and the Evolutionary Process*. Chicago: University of Chicago Press.

Cavalli-Sforza, L.L. and M. Feldman. 1981. *Cultural Transmission and Evolution: A Quantitative Approach*. Princeton: Princeton University Press.

Chipeniuk, R. 1995. 'Childhood Foraging as a Means of Acquiring Competent Human Cognition about Biodiversity', *Environment and Behavior* 27: 490–512.

———. 1998. 'Childhood Foraging as Regional Culture: Some Implications for Conservation Policy', *Environmental Conservation* 25: 198–207.

Cronk, L. 1991. 'Human Behavioral Ecology', *Annual Review of Anthropology* 20: 25–53.

Daillant, I. 2003. *Sens Dessus Dessous. Organization sociale et spatiale des Chimane d'Amazonie boliviane*. Nanterre: Societe d'ethnologie.

Ellis, R. 1996. 'A Taste for Movement: An Exploration of the Social Ethics of the Tsimane' of Lowland Bolivia', Ph.D. thesis. St Andrews, Scotland: University of St Andrews.

Enquist, M., K. Eriksson and S. Ghirlanda. 2007. 'Critical Social Learning: A Solution to Rogers' Paradox of Non-adaptive Culture', *American Anthropologist* 109: 727–34.

Enquist, M. and S. Ghirlanda. 2007. 'Evolution of Imitation does not Explain the Origin of Human Cumulative Culture', *Journal of Theoretical Biology* 246: 129–35.

Geissler, P., S.A. Harris, R. Prince, A. Olsen, R.A. Odhiambo, H. Oketch-Rabah, P.A. Madiega, A. Andersen and P. Molgaard. 2002. 'Medicinal Plants used by Luo Mothers and Children in Bondo District, Kenya', *Journal of Ethnopharmacology* 83: 39–54.

Gurven, M., H. Kaplan and M. Gutierrez. 2006. 'How Long does it Take to Become a Proficient Hunter? Implications for the Evolution of Delayed Growth', *Journal of Human Evolution* 51: 454–70.

Harris, J. 1999. *The Nurture Assumption: Why Children Turn Out The Way They Do*. London: Bloomsbury.

Henrich, J. and R. Boyd. 1998. 'The Evolution of Conformist Transmission and the Emergence of Between-Group Differences', *Evolution and Human Behavior* 19: 215–41.

Henrich, J. and F. Gil-White. 2001. 'The Evolution of Prestige: Freely Conferred Deference as a Mechanism for Enhancing the Benefits of Cultural Transmission', *Evolution and Human Behavior* 22: 165–96.

Hewlett, B.S. and L.L. Cavalli-Sforza. 1986. 'Cultural Transmission among Aka Pygmies', *American Anthropologist* 88: 922–34.

Hewlett, B.S., A. De Silvestri and C. Guglielmino. 2002. 'Semes and Genes in Africa', *Current Anthropology* 43: 313–21.

Huanca, T. 2008. *Tsimane' Oral Tradition, Landscape, and Identity in Tropical Forest.* La Paz: Imprenta Wagui.

Hunn, E.S. 2002. 'Evidence for the Precocious Acquisition of Plant Knowledge by Zapotec Children', in J.R. Stepp, F.S. Wyndham and R. Zarger (eds), *Ethnobiology and Biocultural Diversity.* Athens, GA: International Society of Ethnobiology, pp. 604–13.

Johns, T. 1996. *The Origins of Human Diet and Medicine: Chemical Ecology.* Tucson: University of Arizona Press.

Lancy, D. 1999. 'Playing on the Mother-ground: Cultural Routines for Children's Development', in Anonymous, *Culture and Human Development.* New York: Guilford Press.

Lozada, M., A.H. Ladio and M. Weigandt. 2006. 'Cultural Transmission of Ethnobotanical Knowledge in a Rural Community of Northwestern Patagonia, Argentina', *Economic Botany* 60: 374–85.

McDade, T., V. Reyes-García, W. Leonard, S. Tanner and T. Huanca. 2007. 'Maternal Ethnobotanical Knowledge is Associated with Multiple Measures of Child Health in the Bolivian Amazon', *Proceedings of the National Academy of Sciences of the United States of America* 104: 6134–39.

McElreath, R. and P. Strimling. 2008. 'When Natural Selection Favors Imitation of Parents', *Current Anthropology* 49: 307–16.

Manski, C. 1993. 'Identification of Endogenous Social Effects: The Reflection Problem', *Review of Economic Studies* 60: 531–42.

————.2007. *Identification for Prediction and Decision.* Cambridge: Harvard University Press.

Nabhan, G.P. and S. St. Antoine. 1993. 'The Loss of Flora and Faunal Story: The Extinction of Experience', in S.R. Kellert and E. Wilson (eds), *Biophilia Hypothesis.* Washington, DC: Island Press, pp. 229–50.

Ohmagari, K. and F. Berkes. 1997. 'Transmission of Indigenous Knowledge and Bush Skills among the Western James Bay Cree Women of Subarctic Canada', *Human Ecology* 25: 197–222.

Reyes-García, V., T. Huanca, V. Vadez, W. Leonard and D. Wilkie. 2006. 'Cultural, Practical, and Economic Value of Wild Plants: A Quantitative Study in the Bolivian Amazon', *Economic Botany* 60: 62–74.

Reyes-García, V., E. Kightley, I. Ruiz-Mallén, N. Fuentes-Pelaez, K. Demps, T. Huanca and M.R. Martínez-Rodríguez. 2010. 'Schooling and Local Ecological Knowledge: Do they Complement or Substitute Each Other?', *International Journal of Educational Development* 30: 305–13.

Reyes-García, V., J.L. Molina, J. Broesch, L. Calvet, T. Huanca, J. Saus, S. Tanner, W.R. Leonard and T.W. McDade. 2008b. 'Do the Aged and Knowledgeable Men Enjoy More Prestige? A Test of Predictions from the Prestige-bias Model of Cultural Transmission', *Evolution and Human Behavior* 29: 275–81.

Reyes-García, V., V. Vadez, T. Huanca, W. Leonard and T. McDade. 2007. 'Economic Development and Local Ecological Knowledge: A Deadlock? Data from a Native Amazonian Society', *Human Ecology* 35: 371–77.

Reyes-García, V., V. Vadez, N. Martí-Sanz, T. Huanca, W. Leonard and S. Tanner. 2008a. 'Ethnobotanical Knowledge and Crop Diversity: Evidence from a Native Amazonian Society', *Human Ecology* 36: 569–80.

Richerson, P. and R. Boyd. 2005. *Not by Genes Alone: How Culture Transformed Human Evolution*. Chicago: University of Chicago Press.

Ross, N., D. Medin, J. Coley and S. Atran. 2003. 'Cultural and Experiential Differences in the Development of Folkbiological Induction', *Cognitive Development* 18: 25–47.

Ruddle, K. and R. Chesterfield. 1977. *Education for Traditional Food Procurement in the Orinoco Delta*. Berkeley: University of California Press.

Shaeffer, R.H. 1996. *Social Development*. Cambridge, MA: Blackwell.

Sternberg, R., C. Nokes, P. Geissler, R. Prince, F. Okatcha, D. Bundy and E. Grigorenko. 2001. 'The Relationship between Academic and Practical Intelligence: A Case Study in Kenya', *Intelligence* 29: 401–18.

Stross, B. 1973. 'Acquisition of Botanical Terminology by Tzeltal Children', in M.S. Edmonson (ed.), *Meaning in Mayan Languages*. The Hague: Mouton, pp. 107–41.

Vadez, V., V. Reyes-García, L. Apaza, E. Byron, T. Huanca, W. Leonard, E. Pérez and D. Wilkie. 2004. 'Does Integration to the Market Threaten Agricultural Diversity? Panel and Cross-sectional Evidence from a Horticultural-foraging Society in the Bolivian Amazon', *Human Ecology* 32: 635–46.

Vygostky, L. 1978. *Mind and Society: Development of Higher Psychological Processes*. London: Harvard University Press.

Weisner, T.S. and R. Gallimore. 1977. 'My Brother's Keeper: Child and Sibling Caretaking', *Current Anthropology* 18: 169–90.

Whiting, B.B. and J.W. Whiting. 1975. *Children of Six Cultures*. Cambridge: Harvard University Press.

Wolff, P., D. Medin and C. Pankratz. 1999. 'Evolution and Devolution of Folkbiological Knowledge', *Cognition* 73: 177–204.

Zarger, R. 2002. 'Acquisition and Transmission of Subsistence Knowledge by Q'eqchi' Maya in Belize', in J.R. Stepp, F.S. Wyndham and R. Zarger (eds), *Ethnobiology and Biocultural Diversity*. Athens, GA: International Society of Ethnobiology, pp. 592–603.

Zarger, R. and J.R. Stepp. 2004. 'Persistence of Botanical Knowledge among Tzeltal Maya Children', *Current Anthropology* 45: 413–18.

Zent, S. 1999. 'The Quandary of Conserving Ethnoecological Knowledge: A Piaroa Example', in T. Gragson and B. Blount (eds), *Ethnoecology: Knowledge, Resources, and Rights*. Athens, GA: University of Georgia Press, pp. 90–128.

Chapter 8

PROCESSUAL PERSPECTIVES ON TRADITIONAL ENVIRONMENTAL KNOWLEDGE

CONTINUITY, EROSION, TRANSFORMATION, INNOVATION

Stanford Zent

Introduction

Questions as to how and why traditional environmental knowledge (TEK) evolves were neglected issues in ethnoecological research until two decades ago. Since then, there has been a prodigious expansion of studies focusing on the dynamic properties of TEK systems from a processual perspective: their origins, transmission, transformation, diffusion, hybridization, erosion, extinction, resilience and revitalization (Ohmagari and Berkes 1997; Hunn 1999; Zent 1999; Ellen et al. 2000; Brodt 2002; Ross 2002; Zarger 2002; Zarger and Stepp 2004; Carlson and Maffi 2004; Butler 2006; Alexiades 2009; Heckler 2009b). This paradigm shift can be linked to a wider public discourse that portrays TEK as an increasingly valuable yet vanishing intellectual resource. The useful applications of TEK are recognized in rural development, bioprospecting, food security, health care, biodiversity conservation, climate change assessment and science education, to mention a few. However, it is widely perceived that the culturally distinctive, place-based knowledges and practices of many indigenous peoples and rural folk societies are declining rapidly as a consequence of modernization, development and environmental change. The quandary of how to preserve seemingly fragile and dwindling local knowledges has provided a major stimulus for the vigorous growth of TEK research. While much of this research has been geared to applied projects (e.g. participatory technology development, use-based conservation), another stream is guided by a more conceptual and analytical goal set: to understand better the dynamic processes of TEK persistence or loss, replication or modification, as well as the sociocultural and ecological factors that cause them. Analysis of these issues through systematically recorded, richly contextualized data is seen to contribute to more effective interventions or policy decisions. To the extent that this is true, it may be said that this research direction blurs the line between academics and activism.

The political consciousness implicit in a processual perspective on TEK is grounded in an explicit sense of history. A research position that incorporates time and transformation into its epistemological framework seems justified if we consider that there are so few places left in the world that are insulated from global currents of social and environmental change. Many of the erstwhile 'traditional' societies that are the preferred subjects of ethnoecological research are going through lifestyle-shaking transitions, such as population growth and crowding, migration, land encroachment, habitat degradation, biological invasions, climate change, new epidemiological risks, war and civil unrest, shift from subsistence to market economies, breakdown of common property regimes, imported technologies, formal schooling, literacy, biomedicine, electronic mass media, cultural imperialism, religious conversion, and language shift, among others. In consequence, the interactions between human groups, biota and ecosystems are undergoing drastic transformations even as local communities apply and adapt their ancestral ethnoecological knowledge and practices to cope with shifting life conditions. A historical approach points our attention to macro–micro connections: the dynamic interplay between large-scale institutional forces such as markets, government programmes or social movements, and the responses and agencies of small-scale societies. Such responses may entail modifications in the perception, valuation, extraction, utilization and management of natural resources (Zerner 1994; Peluso 1992). Diachronic analysis of local trends in resource relationships viewed against the background of larger historical milieus help to reveal the determining factors (Zent 1999; Sowerine 2004). A better understanding of these trajectories and the causes underlying them should be taken into account when planning interventions, not only because options for behavioural modification are circumscribed by the same set of selection pressures, but also because local attitudes and dispositions to adopt innovations are shaped as much by former ethnoecological habits as by the availability of new technologies and management styles.

While much recent research on the dynamic aspects of TEK has an applied purpose, especially in its application in the context of development or conservation programmes, its theoretical impact is less clear. Although there have been notable attempts to reconceptualize the field of indigenous/local knowledge in the light of historical and translocal data (Ellen and Harris 2000; Sillitoe 2002; Heckler 2009a), in view of the rapidly expanding empirical database this task of theoretical revision is still work in progress. One of the themes running throughout much recent work is the universality and constancy of change. This insight calls into question all-too-common portrayals of TEK as 'ancient' knowledge that is perfectly adapted to a particular habitat. However, the case can also be made that TEK, or at least a significant portion of it, is deeply rooted in the past (see 'Continuity' section below). Even though the results of processual research establish that the normal state of local knowledge is change, this same record shows that change is not everywhere uniform or unidirectional. Instead, we find complex and often divergent patterns of knowledge loss and gain, persistence and modification. While many indigenous groups and their knowledge systems are no doubt experiencing irreversible historical transitions, the speed and scale of change vary considerably between groups and places. Despite (or because of) the wealth of data, we still do not possess a very good synthetic understanding of this complexity, or what accounts for it. One way forward is to make a comparative and integrative assessment, looking for recurrent patterns or tendencies. This chapter begins this assessment through a review of the literature and key findings about the dynamic properties of TEK. My purpose is to peer beneath the surface of particular case histories to provide a glimpse of what Gould (1986: 64) calls the 'nomothetic undertones'. The main themes considered here are continuity, erosion, transformation and innovation.

Continuity

Attempts to delineate the field and subject matter of TEK have tended to construct it in oppositional terms to Western scientific knowledge (Howes and Chambers 1980; Kloppenberg 1991; DeWalt 1994; see discussions in Antweiler 2004; Menzies and Butler 2006; Heckler 2009a). One of the primary distinctions made between the two involves the dimension of time depth or historical continuity. Indigenous knowledge is often characterized as being inherently long lived. Thus it is developed through the slow accumulation of information gained by long-term experience and residence in a given locality, which is passed from generation to generation by traditional means of cultural transmission. Scientific knowledge, by contrast, is considered to be much more dynamic and provisional due in part to its sceptical, competitive, open-ended and context-free nature. Another important contrast concerns the spatial scale at which they operate. Indigenous knowledge is rich in detail about a particular local environment but it has less validity or utility outside its native context. Science purports to discover universal facts and theories that can be transferred intact from one location to another, and hence its spatial field of operation is much larger, potentially global (Inglis 1993; Berkes 1993; Hunn 1993). In short, the temporal extension of TEK is relatively large while its spatial extension is relatively small. From an ecological perspective, these dimensional attributes appear to be logically connected in the sense that progressive learning of and adjustment to site-specific environmental conditions over extended time periods confers an endemic quality to ethnoecological language or knowledge (Maffi 1999; Hunn 2001).[1] Meanwhile the presence of human populations and their activities may bring about significant modifications of local landscapes (Balée and Erickson 2006). In view of this mutual influence, some writers assert that indigenous groups and their knowledge-practice systems 'coevolve with their environment' (Berkes 1999: 150; cf. Dasmann 1988). Thus TEK is commonly represented as an evolved adaptive strategy that is perpetuated with only gradual modifications over time, assuming of course that other cultural and ecological parameters remain stable.

Empirical support for the *longue durée* vision of TEK is not hard to find. Little more than a cursory review of the archaeological, ethno-historical and ethnological literature is sufficient to turn up plenty of documented examples where indigenous technologies, economic patterns, resource items and, by implication, associated knowledges have survived for extremely long periods. Archaeological and palaeo-ecological research carried out in different settings has uncovered techno-economic sequences spanning from hundreds to thousands of years. Notable examples include: Ifugao rice terrace farming (> 500 years) (Acabado 2010), East African cattle herding (~ 5,000 years) (Blench and MacDonald 2000), landscape management by 'fire-stick farming' in aboriginal Australia (≥ 5,000 years) (Kohen 1995) and stone toolkits of prehistoric hunters in South-East Asian rain forests (10,000 years) (Hutterer 1988). More direct evidence of TEK durability can be inferred from case studies showing similarities between past and present knowledge systems – for instance, contemporary Itza Maya tropical agroforestry and classic Maya agriculture

(Atran 1993), or hunting techniques and prey species of present-day Pygmy groups and prehistoric populations of the Congo (Mercader 2003). Another indicator of TEK persistence, even in the face of migration and environmental change, can be found in the homologous ethnoecological traits shared by different cultural groups that have descended from a common ancestor. Areal case studies of this phenomenon are available for Tupians in Amazonia (Balée 2000), Bantus in central Africa (Vansina 1990), and Austronesians in Oceania (Kirch and Green 1987), among others.

In spite of the many impressive examples of the deep ethnoecological timelines that could be cited, in recent years greater awareness of the dynamic situations and contexts of TEK in the modern world has led some analysts to question its historical status (Agrawal 1995; Berkes 1999; Menzies and Butler 2006). One of the main problems with representations that emphasize the antiquity of TEK is that they sometimes imply the absence of change, or ignore its active properties (Butler 2006). This distortion is especially pronounced when simplistic, essentializing rhetoric is employed, whether coming from pejorative or idealistic positions. In both scholarly and popular works, indigenous knowledge is often polemicized as either anachronistic 'primitive thought' (Hallpike 1980) or as esteemed 'timeless wisdom' (Snively and Corsiglia 2001; Davis 2009). Although such constructs may appear to be diametrically opposed, they coincide in projecting an image of knowledge as fixed and frozen in time. However, this static and ahistorical viewpoint is giving way to a more flexible and parsed perspective of it as simultaneously encompassing elements of continuity as well as change. Berkes (1999: 8), for example, has written that it is 'both cumulative and dynamic, building on experience and adapting to changes' (cf. Johnson 1992; Menzies and Butler 2006). Hunn (1993: 13) notes that 'new ideas and techniques may be incorporated ... but only if they fit into the complex fabric of existing practices and understandings'. In view of its polygenetic, heterochronic make-up, when we speak of temporal continuity here we are referring to continuity in a partial and relative sense. Vansina's (1990: 258) comment that 'tradition is a moving continuity' is apposite.[2] For Sahlins, 'tradition in modern times does not mean stability so much as a distinctive way of changing' (Sahlins 1992: 21; 1994).[3] Among other things, this means that the historical transformations of local cultural systems, presumably including ethnoecological knowledge, following contact with global systems, manifest a dialectical quality: continuity in change/change in continuity. In view of the ambiguity regarding the ancestry of TEK, some authors suggest dropping the 'traditional' label altogether, or qualifying its meaning to admit the syncretic blend of older and more current elements (Berkes 1999; Ellen and Harris 2000; Warren 2004).

Recent theories of cultural transmission provide insights into the tendency of TEK to vary and change even as it is reproduced across space and time. The customary modes of TEK transmission are usually oral communication, behavioural demonstration, observation and imitation (Johnson 1992; Grenier 1998; Ellen and Harris 2000; Zarger 2010). The corresponding educational style is defined as informal (takes place outside the classroom), active (learning by doing) and holistic (i.e. integrated with other aspects of social life). According to population models of this process, vertical transmission constitutes the dominant mode of cultural transmission when the social and physical environment remains stable (Boyd and Richerson 1985; Bock 2010). In this scenario, social learning is the automatic result of teaching and imitation, and the corpus of knowledge acquired by antecedent generations will be passed on relatively intact to subsequent generations. Meanwhile, alternative sources of information, such as horizontal transmission (i.e. diffusion) and trial and error (i.e. innovation), are more costly and hence disadvantageous under stable conditions. However, models inspired by psychology now recognize that previously acquired knowledge also undergoes modification as a result of noise and inefficiency in the transmission process. Atran (2001a) observes that discrete units of cultural information are rarely copied with absolute fidelity, and the constant 'mutation or drift' of such information during communication is the source of endless creative variation. He argues that the process of cultural transmission occurs more by inference than by imitation. Small differences in the internalized inferential structure (i.e. propositional content, rule interpretations) between individuals lead to different outcomes, which explains why imperfect replication is the norm and not the exception.[4]

Ingold (2001) proposes a developmental approach to transmission that envisages the reproduction of cultural representations in the context of organism–environment interaction. The process of copying is described as 'not of information transmission but of guided rediscovery' which involves 'a mixture of imitation and improvisation' (Ingold 2001: 141). Elders or peers may teach what things to pay attention to, but every person must still go out and learn it anew by direct contact and participation in the environment (cf. Bates 2009). Variations arise out of the particulars of this developmental process.

Contributing Factors

If TEK is recognized as having a mixed constitution, consisting of parts that are more 'sedimented' alongside parts that have a shallower time depth, then this raises the questions of which parts are more likely to persist and what factors contribute to this tendency. One of the paramount factors identified here is language, since many observers regard language vitality to be a crucial ingredient in knowledge preservation (see 'Erosion' section below). Knowledge codified in language is easier to transmit and therefore more likely to be passed from generation to generation (Sterponi 2010). The most obvious examples are folk plant and animal terminologies, but other environmental domains are inscribed in the lexicon as well, like place names, landscape classifications, soil types, climatic phenomena and seasonal changes. Ecological knowledge may also be encoded in grammatical categories (noun classifiers, gender markers) and in forms of discourse (myths, folktales, songs, prayers, invocations, proverbs, idioms and metaphors) (Maffi 1999; Nettle and Romaine 2000; Zent 2009). Of course, language is also prone to change, even when shift and endangerment are not an issue, and cultural factors may influence which words or morphemes are retained and which are not. Berlin has compared ethnobotanical nomenclatures in related Mayan languages and found that the names of cultivated plants and medicinal plants are more likely to be conserved. From this he extracts the general rule that long-term lexical retention is a function of cultural salience (Berlin et al. 1973; Berlin 1999).

Besides language, the continuity of TEK is affected by cognitive, cultural and ecological factors. Influence from the cognitive side comes from the innate, mental modular structures that predispose the human mind to perceive, categorize and reason about the biological world in certain ways. Although still controversial, there is considerable evidence to suggest that the domain of folk biological classification exhibits certain universal principles (e.g. taxonomic organization, privilege of generic-species rank, presumption of underlying essence), and these principles are determined by domain-specific cognitive architecture (Berlin 1992; Atran and Medin 2008). According to Atran and Medin (2008), this does not imply complete and unmediated determination of the surface taxonomic form and content by the deep mental module, but rather the latter interacts with cultural and environmental factors to produce the former. Thus the empirical specificity and scope of a particular taxonomic system, and the inductive operations based on it, vary with people's cultural background and with their level of contact and experience with the biological world. However, the innate module imposes constraints on the way that information is processed and the resulting cultural representations that are subject to this type of processing – in this case, the folk biological taxonomies – are more resistant to variation from external influences and hence 'most apt to survive within a culture over time'. This internal constraint on ethnobiological variation and change extends not only to the taxonomic structure but also to the categorical substance, since certain biological groups and morpho-behavioural attributes (e.g. perceptually or ecologically salient ones) are privileged for recognition by the cognitive apparatus. For this reason, the semantic-referential content of folk taxonomies tends to be stable (though not static) within cultures, showing high levels of inter-informant agreement and historical longevity (Atran and Medin 2008: 117–18).[5]

Given the close connection and integration of TEK with its cultural and ecological context (Ellen and Harris 2000), it might be expected that this larger context figures as a primary determinant of the tendency towards change or stasis. Considering that the vast majority of recorded examples of TEK loss or transformation take place in situations marked by momentous changes in the surrounding social and natural environment, we might draw the corollary that TEK is more likely to persist in situations where cultural and ecological systems remain stable. What characteristics might account for such stability? Small-scale tribal and peasant societies that are still relatively isolated and independent from industrial civilization are considered to be paragons of cultural conservatism (Bodley 1990). From a socio-logical standpoint, these kinds of society are characterized by a social structure based mainly on kinship, a high level of social cohesion, personal relationships among members, common beliefs and values, and similar occupations and lifestyle. Such features are conservative in the sense that they promote conformism and inhibit deviation from past tradition (cf. Redfield 1941).[6] From a developmental per-spective, intergenerational TEK persistence is directly dependent on the maintenance of traditional subsistence activities (Hunn 1999) and of customary modes of social interaction that bring novices into contact with more knowledgeable others in appropriate learning con-texts (Lave and Wenger 1991).

Types of ecological knowledge embedded or implicated in formal-ized aspects of culture, such as ritual, myth, taboo, cultural symbols or beliefs, and social institutions, are more likely to be retained in the collective memory over time. Such formalization imposes repeti-tion, and hence retention, by sanctioning adherence to precedence (Hobsbawm and Ranger 1983).[7] Among the Desana Indians of the Colombian Amazon, patterns of exploiting wild animals and plants are regulated by ritual behaviours, beliefs in bush spirits and shamanic wisdom and practices (Reichel-Dolmatoff 1976). The codification and coordination of ecological knowledge and practice in different institutional spheres of social life resembles what some analysts refer to as a 'cultural script'. A script is 'an internalized plan used by people [for] carrying out and interpreting routine activities' (Schank and Abelson 1977). Alcorn and Toledo (1998) deconstruct the enduring Mesoamerican *milpa* (maize-dominant agriculture) as a multi-dimensional script or process. Besides embodying a set of cultivation techniques, the *milpa* script is transmitted to children and sustained by means of cultural and religious beliefs, folk-tales and festival events. While it is questionable whether TEK in and of itself constitutes a type of script, or predetermined plan of action (Richards 1989; see 'Innovation' section), in any case the extent to which ritualized and institutionalized forms of TEK are faithfully reproduced is tied to the fate of these coordinate cultural domains. The broader the cultural base of the script, the more durable and resistant it is to environmental disruptions such as new economic demands or technological introductions (Alcorn and Toledo 1998; Folke et al. 1998).

A stable ecosystem is widely regarded as a necessary, but not always a sufficient, precondition for the maintenance of TEK (Berkes and Folke 1998; Florey 2009: 27). Although the notion of ecological stability is somewhat fuzzy, varying according to the scale, the variable(s) used to define it and the type of ecosystem or community to which it is applied, in the human ecology literature it generally refers to a local environment where the human population is more or less in balance with resources, other populations and external factors (e.g. climate). With the rise of a non-equilibrium paradigm of ecology (Botkin 1990), stability is understood more as a matter of resilience (i.e. ability of the system to absorb disturbance and still persist) rather than of constancy (i.e. steady-state conditions). Local knowledge and management systems that are successful over the long term are those that achieve sustainable extraction of natural resources, where sustainability is understood as not challenging critical ecological thresholds. Disturbance is allowed to enter but at a scale that does not compromise the basic structure and behaviour of the ecosystem and the services it provides (Folke et al. 1998). Those types or aspects of knowledge and practice which contribute integrally to the maintenance of sustainable resource management and the resilience of the social-ecological system as a whole are those which are most likely to be retained throughout the life of the system. These include any number of management practices based on ecological knowledge (e.g. those related to environmental monitoring, species or habitat protection, resource or land rotation, harvest restrictions, and diversity management) as well as social mechanisms (e.g. land and resource tenure, stewardship roles, community assessments, taboos and sanctions) and cultural values (e.g. notions of sharing, reciprocity, respect, sacredness, identity) behind management practices (Folke et al. 1998: 418).[8]

While a historicized perspective of TEK naturally foregrounds its evolutionary tendencies and properties, this same historical mindset obliges us to recognize that continuity between past and present is one of its fundamental active properties. Although social and ecological systems are inherently dynamic and therefore predisposed to change, nonetheless there is always some degree of continuity within the change and vice versa. The question of what changes and what remains the same seems to be just as much a matter of research design and priority, especially the time frame employed, as it is a self-evident property of the knowledge system itself. The empirical and theoretical material reviewed in this section suggests that some aspects of TEK may be rightly regarded as ancient and other aspects may be relatively new. The continuity and survival of traditional knowledge and practice was seen as being closely tied to the (relative) stability of the cultural and ecological systems in which they are embedded. But what happens to TEK when the surrounding environment does not remain stable? In recent years a growing number of researchers have focused their attention on the question of TEK change, including the perceived problem of erosion.

Erosion

Much of the research being done on TEK from a historical–processual perspective is framed by a keen awareness of traditional knowledge erosion in the modern world. The notion that TEK is declining at an unusually rapid rate really began as a policy-aimed discourse formulated in terms of the same crisis rhetoric that was employed to publicize the critical situations of biodiversity extinction and language endangerment. In 1991, *Time* magazine ran a cover titled 'Lost Tribes, Lost Knowledge'. The headline story warns that as native cultures die out or are absorbed into modern civilization, the rest of humanity loses out on their valuable wisdom (Linden 1991: 32–40). The argument that TEK constitutes an endangered resource attracted more attention when it could be shown that this degenerative trend was not merely analogous to the loss of biological species or endemic languages, but was rather closely linked to it. Thus, Schultes (1994) replayed the metaphor of 'burning the library' to describe the twin destruction of Amazonian forests and the rich biodiversity they contain, and of the aboriginal cultures of Amazonian peoples and their expert botanical and phytochemical knowledge. Maffi (1999, 2001, 2005), among others, makes the case for the close and interdependent relationship between linguistic, cultural and biological diversity. Hence reduction of diversity in one realm often means reduction in another.

The success of this awareness campaign can be measured in terms of the rising prominence of TEK in key policy instruments, especially those dealing with global environmental governance and indigenous rights. In the environmental arena, several influential policy documents explicitly recognize the vital contribution that local and indigenous knowledge and resource management systems can make to environmental conservation efforts, while acknowledging that such systems are being threatened by current development and therefore require special protections; see for example the World Commission on Development and the Environment Report (United Nations 1987), the Convention on Biological Diversity (United Nations 1992) and the Millennium Ecosystem Assessment (UNEP 2006). Similar themes are developed in the indigenous rights literature. Here we find that traditional knowledge is deeply valued by indigenous people for many aspects of their lives, including their economic security, health, education, social institutions, identity, spirituality and self-determination, and therefore they assert their inalienable right to keep and exercise it (Posey 1999: 555–601).

A variation of the erosion thesis was developed to describe (and critique) the changing state of environmental consciousness among people in our global urbanized society. Pyle (1993) coined the phrase 'extinction of experience' to convey the loss of intimate, hands-on contact and experience with the natural world that is rampant today among urban and suburban dwellers. Because of their estrangement from wild green spaces, many people are typically apathetic towards environmental concerns. The 'extinction of experience' concept was developed further by Nabhan (1998a), who used it to explain the impoverished level of environmental knowledge displayed by most young people in the United States today, even the progeny of former cultures of habitat. His research among indigenous, Mexican and Anglo groups in the Sonoran Desert region of Arizona found a huge difference in the ability of children to name or identify native plants and animals in comparison with their parents or grandparents. He attributes this generation gap to diminished contact with the desert ecosystem in people's daily lives as well as lack of exposure to folk cultural traditions that are sources of ecological knowledge transmission. Louv (2006) contends that the collective physical and mental detachment from the natural environment has progressed to the point where it even constitutes a pathological condition, which he labels 'nature-deficit disorder'.

While the idea of TEK erosion has become firmly ingrained in policy and public discourses, the message arising from its scientific

study is less clear cut. In the last few decades there has been a proliferation of well-designed and well-executed case studies that examine
the loss or change of local ecological knowledge and provide a firmer
empirical ground for evaluating the extent and depth of this tendency. This body of work has succeeded in taking us well past anecdotal
proofs and generic proclamations about causes or consequences (cf.
Plotkin 1988; Linden 1991), but it has also complicated our overall
picture and thus raised new questions about how to interpret the
mixed results. A reading of the literature reveals that TEK loss or
erosion is indeed a recurrent and widespread phenomenon but also
that there is considerable variation and inconsistency across different
biocultural settings. Whereas some investigations confirm erosion of
TEK in response to cultural or economic globalization forces, others
report persistence in the face of surrounding change (Kristensen
and Lykke 2003; Lykke et al. 2004; Zarger and Stepp 2004) and still
others highlight the rapid acquisition of new forms of TEK (Guest
2002; Byg and Balslev 2004). Even where available data indicate that
knowledge is declining, a close look at each case shows that no two
look the same. The issue of divergence needs to be addressed, but first
we should establish just how extensive the problem of TEK erosion is.

The large number of independent case studies that report recent or
ongoing TEK erosion, or present data consistent with this conclusion,
provide compelling evidence that this process is occurring on a global
scale. Moreover, it has been documented at numerous sites distributed
among many different national, cultural and biogeographic contexts.
Viewed at a national scale, we find indications of this trend occurring
in: India (Navchoo and Buth 1990; Cruz García 2006), Nepal (Olsen
and Helles 1997), Bhutan (Tenzin 2006), Indonesia (Caniago and
Siebert 1998; Florey and Wolff 1998), Malaysia (Jarvie and Perumal
1994), Brunei (Voeks and Nyawa 2001), Thailand (Anderson 1986;
Wester and Yongvanit 1995; Somnasanc and Moreno-Black 2000),
Papua New Guinea (Case et al. 2005), Solomon Islands (Baines
and Hviding 1993), Vanuatu (Spriggs 1993), Federated States of
Micronesia (Lee et al. 2001), Algeria (Volpato et al. 2009); Guinea-
Bissau (Frazão-Moreira 2001), South Africa (Shackleton et al. 2002;
Malaza 2003), Mozambique (Matavele and Habib 2000), Sudan
(Katz 1989), Tanzania (Luoga et al. 2000), Kenya (Sternberg et al.
2001), Madagascar (Byg and Balslev 2001), Canada (Ohmagari
and Berkes 1997; Haruyama 2004; Turner and Turner 2008; Bates
2009), U.S.A. (Zepeda and Hill 1995; Nabhan 1998b; Nolan and
Robbins 1999; Griffin 2001; O'Brien 2010), Mexico (Benz et al. 2000;
Ross 2002; Ross and Medin 2005), Guatemala (Girón et al. 1991;
Comerford 1996; Atran 2001b), Honduras (Godoy et al. 1998), Brazil
(Begossi et al. 1993; Figueiredo et al. 1993; Shanley and Rosa 2004;

Voeks and Leony 2004; Monteiro et al. 2006), Bolivia (Reyes-García et al. 2005, 2007), Peru (Boster 1986; Phillips and Gentry 1993; Putsche 2000; Rocha 2005), Colombia (Galeano 2000; Marulanda 2005), Ecuador (Byg and Balslev 2004), Argentina (Ladio and Lozada 2003, 2004; Estomba et al. 2006), Venezuela (Zent 1999, 2001, 2009; Hoffman 2003), Surinam (Zalocusky and Short 2007), Italy (Edwards et al. 2005), Spain (Gómez-Baggethun et al. 2010) and Russia (Crate 2006). The biogeographic settings where this is happening encompass grasslands, deserts, woody savannas, tropical rain forests, swamp forests, temperate forests, boreal forests, circum-polar zones, high mountains, low mountains, coastal zones, coral atolls, and volcanic islands. The economic types include farmers, hunters, collectors, trappers, foragers, fisherfolk, pastoralists, and mixed combinations of these. In consideration of the great quantity and diversity of parallel case studies, it is safe to conclude that TEK erosion stands out as a mega-trend affecting many people in the world today.

Moving down in scale, however, we can observe many differences from one place to the next in the details of what domains or types of knowledge are most vulnerable, the rate of loss or change, the socio-demographic groups most affected and the causal or conditioning factors. It is not unusual to find contrasting impacts, erosive in one place, augmentative in another, attributed to the same variables (e.g. school attendance). Examples of TEK persistence, despite more general social or ecological change, pose a challenge to the notion that erosion is a universal process. Zarger and Stepp (2004) did a restudy of plant naming ability among Tzeltal Mayan children of a community that had been studied thirty years before by Stross (1973). Even though the locality had undergone various socioeconomic changes during this time interval, the researchers found no significant differences between the two datasets. The inconsistent results, revealed by way of a cross-cultural, multi-sited perspective, would seem to indicate that while powerful global forces such as market expansion or linguistic colonization may have a widespread erosional effect, this is not inevitable and culture- and site-specific factors also determine the outcome.

Another possible reason for the observed inconsistency is that many different research designs and methods have been used. The ways that knowledge is defined and measured, the sampling strategy, the variables included in the study, and the analytical procedures chosen influence research results and conclusions. Most studies of TEK variation and change are limited to single communities or ethnic groups, or occasionally encompass more than one community but in close vicinity. Furthermore, they have focused on particular, often narrowly defined, knowledge domains to the exclusion of others. For instance, the vast majority of studies on 'ethnobiological' change have dealt exclusively with plant knowledge whereas very few have explored animal knowledge. Some studies are concerned only with formal knowledge (e.g. inventories of plants and their uses), which are acquired earlier in life (Zarger 2010), while others have focused on practical skills (e.g. subsistence tasks), that take longer to master (Bock 2010).[9] The method of scoring or quantifying a person's or group's knowledge varies a great deal from one study to the next (Hoffman and Gallaher 2007). It is rare to find research reports in which exactly the same method, scope and sampling strategy has been applied at more than one site, and in the few cases where a comparative analysis has been undertaken it is usually ad hoc and entails comparing and contrasting one's results with those obtained from an independent study. Another source of incongruence is that very few field studies are longitudinal, and therefore are not based on true time-series data. The vast majority rely on transversal observations and infer diachronic processes of knowledge change by creatively interpreting synchronic patterns of knowledge variation and the co-variation of these patterns with contextual variables that are considered to be indicators of the general acculturation process (Zent and Zent 2011). In sum, lack of methodological uniformity inhibits comparability and constitutes the main impediment for a more refined and theoretical understanding of the complex and varied empirical reality of TEK loss or change.

Conditioning Variables

A variety of social and ecological variables have been identified as causing or conditioning the sharp decline of traditional knowledge and practices. Some of the recurrent ones (i.e. reported more than once) include: language shift, formal education, transition to market economy, occupational change, new technologies, settlement pattern shift, interethnic contact, habitat degradation, availability of Western medicines or health clinics, religious belief, change in values, and access to and dependence on modern media. However, the effects of these in terms of knowledge retention or change, and with respect to the domains or types of knowledge that are responsive to them, vary considerably across the different study sites.

The fate of local language is regarded as crucially important for the survival of TEK because much information about the environment and subsistence practices is encoded in language (Nettle and Romaine 2000; Maffi 2001; Bates et al. 2009). Because language itself is adapted over time to particular habitats (Mühlhäusler 1996), many of the place-indexed meanings attached to lexical and grammatical forms do not translate easily into exogenous majority languages, and thus the loss of language usually means a loss of knowledge (Bernard 1992; Woodbury 1993). By the same token, abrupt abandonment of hereditary knowledge and behaviour may be accompanied by irreversible language shift or decay, which is seen as distinct from the normal processes of language change (Hill 2001). Although children may be regularly exposed to an indigenous language, they still may not pick up vernacular names of local plant and animal taxa if they no longer engage in traditional activities or get 'hands-on experience' with their surrounding environment (Nabhan 1998b; cf. Hill 2001). Thus language is often looked upon as a particularly sensitive indicator, whether as cause or consequence, of knowledge erosion.

The process of replacing the local language with a national language often begins in school. Some argue that informal modes of learning, such as those employed in the acquisition of TEK, are often impacted negatively where formal education is instituted (Mosha 2000; Bates et al. 2009). However, empirical research reviewed here shows inconsistent results with respect to this relationship. Several studies reported school achievement or attendance as negatively impacting types of TEK acquisition (Wester and Yongvanit 1995; Zent 1999; Sternberg et al. 2001; Grigorenko et al. 2004; Voeks and Leony 2004; Rocha 2005; Cruz García 2006). In other studies, schooling is positively associated with higher knowledge (Byg and Balslev 2004; Reyes-García et al. 2007) or shows no correlation (Godoy et al. 1998; Guest 2002). Where the relationship is negative, it is explained as being due to the fact that time spent in school detracts from the time children can devote to subsistence and other traditional activities, or leads to devaluation of traditional knowledge (Sternberg et al. 2001; Cruz García 2006). Where the relationship is positive, it is interpreted as being the result of more opportunities to interact with people from other groups and gain exposure to their knowledge (Reyes-García et al. 2005).

The expansion of market economy into traditional societies is thought to be a major force altering local people's livelihoods and associated competencies (Santos et al. 1997; Putsche 2000; Godoy 2001; Souto 2009). The transition from subsistence to market economy impacts TEK by fostering economic specialization, substitution of local natural and crafted products by imported ones, and less pooling of knowledge and resources (Godoy et al. 2005). However, the specific effect of market integration on ecological knowledge depends on the type of activities that people engage in while producing for the market, their degree of dependence on those activities, and their technological sources. People occupied with the extraction of non-timber forest products for sale, or even logging, may retain more knowledge than do cash-cropping farmers or wage labourers. Meanwhile, the knowledge of those whose commercial activity is confined to a small range of natural products may become more narrowly specialized in comparison to those whose activities are geared for subsistence as well as sale (Godoy et al. 1998; Shanley and Rosa 2004; Lawrence et al. 2005). Among communities affected by the commercialization of timber and non-timber forest products, it has been observed that the market exerts a significant influence on species' quantitative importance values such that the more highly ranked species are those which tend to have commercial value (Pinedo-Vasquez et al. 1990; Shanley and Rosa 2004; Lawrence et al. 2005). Conversely, non-commercial species for such groups rate lower importance values and thus are less salient. In some places, market expansion is accompanied by technological innovation that in turn alters former practices and knowledge. A study among rural communities in south-western Spain discovered abrupt loss of traditional agricultural knowledge in association with recent agricultural intensification, while traditional livestock farming was little affected (Gómez-Baggethun et al. 2010).

Another major agent of TEK erosion is Western medicine and medical technology, whose influence is felt most directly in the domain of ethnomedical knowledge (Phillips and Gentry 1993; Plotkin 1993; Cox 2000; Vandebroek et al. 2004; Case et al. 2005). Although locally obtained, natural medicinals continue to be important for many rural communities, in a number of areas the rich aboriginal ethnopharmacopoea is nevertheless diminishing from collective memory as a result of health care modernization and other factors (Furtado et al. 1978; Figueiredo et al. 1993; Phillips and Gentry 1993; Caniago and Siebert 1998; Galeano 2000; Matavele and Habib 2000; Ugent 2000; Ghimire et al. 2004; Voeks and Leony 2004; Case et al. 2005; Estomba et al. 2006; Monteiro et al. 2006; Zent and Zent 2007). Local manifestations of this trend include a gap between younger and older adult knowledge of traditional medicines as well as the rarity or disappearance of specialist community healers (Begossi et al. 2002; Case et al. 2005; Lozada et al. 2006; Monteiro et al. 2006).

The decline in ecological knowledge and use is sometimes attributed to ecosystem degradation and species extinction, which in turn are linked to changes in settlement pattern, population growth and greater pressure on local resources. In some places, higher indices of introduced versus native plants are found precisely on deforested lands or next to urban areas. Here it is the loss of species on which local knowledge is based rather than a loss of interest that better explains TEK erosion (Shanley and Rosa 2004; Lykke et al. 2004).

A few studies have pointed to changing values and beliefs as being an important reason for TEK erosion. For example, certain types of resource use and associated knowledge may be consciously avoided (and forgotten) because of the social stigma attached to them (Caniago and Siebert 1998; Voeks and Nyawa 2001; Cruz García 2006). A classic case of this is when the authority and prestige of native healers are discredited by missionaries and their fundamentalist religious teachings, thus causing over time a loss of specialized ethnomedical knowledge (Case et al. 2005). In numerous indigenous communities, television and the internet have effectively become the primary source of nature-related learning for children. The problem is that most of the information conveyed refers to non-local environments and their components (Nabhan 1998b; cf. Pergams and Zaradic 2008; O'Brien 2010).

To summarize, there are multiple social and environmental factors that contribute to TEK erosion, but the presence and influence of each varies from place to place. Although such factors are often treated separately, it is important to recognize that they do not work in isolation but rather concurrently, as distinguishable but interrelated facets of the same overall process of change. For example, the role played by Western medicines and health clinics in TEK erosion goes beyond merely replacing traditional remedies as health care options, since they are also linked with other factors, including population growth, migration, sedentarization, trade, religious proselytism and changes in values (Etkin et al. 1990; Anyinam 1995; Vandebroek et al. 2004). Among the Piaroa of the Venezuelan Amazon, the establishment of schools, biomedical health clinics and other services in frontier zones, first by missionaries and later by the state, has encouraged downriver migration, settlement nucleation, interethnic contact and acculturation in a large proportion of the population since the 1970s. Some of the collateral outcomes of this process have been population crowding, market integration, land-cover alteration, natural resource depletion, more frequent contacts with urban populations, and more fluency in the Spanish language. All of these interrelated processes may be directly or indirectly associated with observed trends of ethnobotanical knowledge decline among adolescents and young adults (Zent 1993, 1997, 1999).

In view of the complex interactions between multiple socioenvironmental variables in modern contexts, we are confronted with the prospect that the sorts of variables reviewed above really represent proxies for more fundamental variables. Two things about the learning process stand out when one reviews the literature on TEK transmission: its experiential character, and the holistic character of experience. The first tells us that TEK is learned not only by verbal instruction but by means of direct contact, experience, observation, and participation in activities. The second refers to the idea that learning is embedded and integrated with all aspects of sociocultural life, and hence what one needs to learn is reinforced simultaneously in multiple institutional contexts: economic, political, moral, aesthetic, religious, and so on. Consistent with this line of thought, Wolff and Medin (2001) identify two kinds of change as the primary causes of TEK devolution: lack of contact with nature, and lack of cultural support. Thus the shift from rural to urban settings may result in a significant decrease in people's contact with the natural world and this in turn may bring about a decline in knowledge. This effect is either compounded or mitigated by cultural support, which has to do with the degree to which a society promotes a particular area of knowledge in the course of everyday life. Declines in cultural support, like declines in exposure to the natural world, could lead to devolution. While Wolff and Medin's devolution hypothesis offers a potentially fresh approach to studying the problem of erosion, the macro-variables of contact with nature and cultural support may take different forms and be difficult to measure.

After two decades of expanding research on TEK from a processual perspective, much has been learned about the tendencies and causes of local knowledge erosion. We now have enough evidence to assert that it is no longer just a disturbing hypothesis in need of empirical verification. On a global scale, it appears that many indigenous and local peoples are confronting similar processes of acculturation, language shift, economic reorientation, land insecurity and habitat change, and as a result their traditional knowledge systems are also under assault. However, at a smaller scale, by contrast, the picture is varied and complex. It was suggested that greater coherence among methodological approaches – for example, the application of standardized or at least comparable methods in different sites, and consideration of the interactions among contextual variables – would be needed to close the gap between global and local levels of analysis. Another gap that needs to be closed is the dire shortage of truly diachronic research. Without time-series data collected over long time spans, it will be impossible to tell whether observed trends really indicate knowledge erosion or whether they reflect background rates of change.

Transformation

Intergenerational changes of cultural knowledge cannot always be described as a simple case of loss, for as some items and classes of knowledge are being lost, others are surely being added. For instance, the colonial-era transition from a farming to a foraging lifestyle among certain Amazonian groups was accompanied by the attrition of formal ethnobotanical taxonomies and agroecological knowledge (Balée 1992, 1999) but also by the augmentation of substantive knowledge (e.g. of phenological states and ecological relations) in reference to forest plants (Rival 2009). In that sense, it would be more accurate to characterize the change process as one of 'replacement' or 'transformation' instead of mere 'loss' (cf. Ellen and Harris 2000; Alexiades 2009).[10] Therefore a valid critique of the erosion or devolution model of TEK change is that exclusive attention on the deficit side amounts to a unidimensional and hence partial perspective. Not only does this ignore whatever novel or exogenous elements are being acquired, it also exposes a static and passive conception of how the knowledge system operates in practice. This is especially evident when the focus is on assessing the impact of global society on small-scale cultural groups. In many such cases, local knowledge is treated as a pristine isolate which is assumed to have been whole, stable and independent prior to its debilitation or disruption from outside influences.

A perspective that would unreflexively interpret knowledge change as erosion comes close to recapitulating outdated and now discredited formulations of the acculturation concept in which contact between a dominant culture (Western industrial society) and a subordinate one (native society) is depicted as resulting in the deculturation and eventually the total cultural assimilation of the latter. The classic acculturation model can be faulted on several counts. For one thing, it tends to portray the diffusion of cultural traits from donor to receiver groups in asymmetrical terms and thereby loses sight of the bilateral exchange of information and the mutual processes of change resulting from the cross-cultural encounter (Schaub 2008). Secondly, it is based on a particulate model of culture as an agglomeration of distinct traits, and does not treat sociocultural practices and institutions as being structurally and functionally integrated. Therefore, it misses out on the disintegrative or restructuring aspects of culture change (Steward 1967). Thirdly, it rests on false assumptions about the (prior) autonomy and isolation of human societies (Murphy 1964). Fourthly, it treats the minority population as a passive recipient of the majority culture, and does not recognize that responses to cultural contact are active and variable, ranging from forms of acceptance and accommodation to resistance and appropriation (Sahlins 1992). Many of these criticisms can also be applied to analyses of TEK change preoccupied with loss.

In this section we review some of the research issues and findings regarding the more positively transformative aspects of TEK change. The notion of transformation implies reorganization in overall cultural or structural arrangements that results in a distinct form but at the same time maintains a significant amount of continuity with the prior form (Kapferer 1997). This broad definition subsumes a number of different processes and mechanisms. The mechanisms most relevant for the present discussion include diffusion, hybridization and migration. In so far as they concern TEK change, these topics have not been studied as intensively as the problem of erosion, maybe because finding reliable evidence is not as simple and straightforward.

Diffusion

Although development agencies have been actively involved in disseminating scientific technology to rural farmers or transferring indigenous technical knowledge across different sites (Warren et al. 1995), outside of this modern context the issue of diffusion has not hitherto figured prominently in research on TEK change. This seems surprising because there is an abundance of published information about aboriginal or preindustrial technological diffusion across time and space. If one accepts the maxim that traditional technology is 'knowledge-intensive' (Glick 1997: 466), then we can also infer that the spread of material culture implies not only the transfer of artefacts but also the know-how associated with their production along with the activity contexts for which the artefacts form a working part. In that sense, patterns of technological diffusion can be interpreted as indicators of historical and prehistorical TEK change. A good example of this is Dole's (1969) distributional analysis of techniques for preparing manioc flour in South America, from which she was able to reconstruct the spread, intensification and disintensification of manioc cultivation throughout the continent. In a similar vein, vestiges of the biogeographic origins and dispersal of plant domesticates offer insights into the movements of agroecological knowledge in the past (e.g. Stone 1984; Brücher 1990; Yen 1991). Although the exact mechanisms or motives (e.g. trade, population migration, colonization) of technological dispersals in antiquity can only be imagined, ethnobiological diffusion nonetheless stands out as one of the prime movers of human sociocultural evolution. This thesis is developed by Crosby (1972), who demonstrates how the exchange of biological material and production systems between continents following European discovery of the New World changed the demographic, technological and cultural face of the world. The far-reaching effects of this process can be appreciated even in regions remote from the active frontiers of colonization. The introduction of the sweet potato into highland New Guinea about 350 years ago, for instance, quickly displaced traditional crops and was followed by a series of technical innovations – such as tilling, ridging, ditching and draining – that set in motion a dynamic phase of agricultural intensification, population growth and sociocultural change (Brookfield and Padoch 1994). Bennett and Prance (2000) identified more than two hundred botanical species that were originally introduced by European colonizers which are being used today in the pharmacopeias of different indigenous groups scattered across the jungles and mountains of northern South America.

In addition to the distribution of plants and animals outside their native ranges, more direct evidence of TEK diffusion can be discerned in borrowed ethnobiological terms and taxa, in shared technologies for subsistence activities, food processing and crafts, and in overlapping resource management strategies (Turner et al. 2003). The sharing of names for plants and animals among neighbouring but linguistically unrelated groups is taken as proof positive of past adoption (Austerlitz 1968; Van den Eynden et al. 2004).[11] The exchange and absorption of folk knowledge between groups in contact with each other has also been explored by comparing the ethnobotanical inventories and use patterns of indigenous versus non-indigenous groups. Some non-indigenous or immigrant groups display large inventories of useful plants that compare favourably with the inventories of indigenous groups occupying similar biomes (Pinedo-Vasquez et al. 1990; Phillips et al. 1994; Rossato et al. 1999; Galeano 2000; Lawrence et al. 2005). In south-western Brazil, Campos and Ehringhaus (2003) discovered not only that non-native folk communities had picked up indigenous knowledge of the use of palms, but also that 20–30 per cent of the uses cited by the indigenous groups were recently acquired through contact with the colonists. A similar result was obtained by Alexiades and Peluso (2009) in their study of Ese-Eja ethnomedicine in the Bolivian Amazon. As a direct result of contact with mestizo rubber tappers and integration into the regional extractive economy since the last century, the Ese-Eja acquired knowledge of a large number of medicinal plants, and the pragmatic use of herbal medicines came to dominate therapeutic action at the expense of the more ancestral and esoteric shamanistic curing.

Turner et al. (2003) analysed patterns of intercultural overlap of ethnoecological knowledge (e.g. hunting and fishing techniques, basketry styles, canoe-making skills) among Canadian aboriginal tribes. Their research suggests that diffusion was most intensive in the border regions of different cultural groups, which they refer to as 'cultural edges'. Similar to the concept of ecological edge, a cultural edge is a transitional zone where natural and manufactured products of diverse regions and ecosystems are shared and redistributed when people from different cultural groups come together and interact on a sustained and habitual basis. Besides exchanging goods, they also trade concepts, skills, stories, songs, dances, religious ideas, names and vocabularies. Thus cultural edges constitute biocultural hot spots of diverse products, technologies and knowledges.

The reports of TEK diffusion reviewed here, involving the transfer of diverse types and domains of knowledge in different cultural and environmental contexts, suggest the pervasiveness of this process throughout human history and geography. The evidence of knowledge flow across permeable cultural boundaries effectively shows that local knowledge systems are not discrete or closed to surrounding influences and thus are not entirely *sui generis* or autonomous in terms of their development. If overlap and connectedness are common conditions, then this raises the question of how far and deep the connections go. Agrawal (1995) contends that indigenous or local knowledge is more closely linked with global science than many people suppose. The following section takes up this issue.

Hybridization

Hybridization is a concept sometimes linked with diffusion in discussions of local knowledge. In the participatory development literature, hybridization refers to the goal of integrating indigenous knowledge with global science, as well as to horizontal transfers of traditional wisdom between local communities, in order to improve locally managed farming, forestry and rangeland systems or other grassroots enterprises (Forsyth 1996; Gupta 1997; Thomas and Twyman 2004). Constructivist perspectives have used the concept of 'hybrid knowledges' (or 'hybrid cultures/natures') to describe the process by which local groups appropriate and negotiate diverse knowledges or discourses in the context of political action (e.g. affirm cultural identity, press land claims) vis-à-vis translocal actors. This use frame rejects the categorical distinction between 'local' and 'global' as independent epistemic traditions and instead constructs local knowledge as a provisional, fragmentary, situated and heterogeneous field of meanings/uses which moves back and forth between ideas stemming from one's own cultural heritage and ideas drawn from transcultural sources according to the expediency of particular circumstances (Escobar 1995; Nygren 1999; Guivant 2003). An appropriate example of politically motivated hybrid knowledge would be community-based, counter-mapping endeavours which combine local knowledge of landscape and territory with methods of scientific cartography for the purpose of asserting land claims (Peluso 1995; Toledo Maya 1997; Zent et al. 2004).

Other researchers concur that a sharp dichotomy between global science and local knowledge is perverse, and instead emphasize the manifold linkages and interpenetrations among multiple knowledge domains which occupy different points along a continuum from more local to more global systems (Brodt 2002; Sillitoe 2002, 2007). From a multidimensional, interactional and spectral point of view, a hybrid knowledge system displays a complex blend of concepts and practices of diverse origins that may be differentially distributed within a society according to social or economic statuses as well as personal experience. Brodt (2002), for example, shows how groups and individuals in a rural district in India exhibit different understandings and techniques for tree farming, which range from orientations more steeped in local folk knowledge to orientations more influenced by external scientific knowledge. In an increasingly globalized world, it should not surprise anyone that elements of global science manage to penetrate local knowledge systems, but it should also be understood that transplanted ideas and institutions are rarely copied perfectly. Instead, they are usually modified, more or less radically, by the receivers to suit their specific situation, a process that has been referred to as 'indigenization' (Kassam 2002; cf. Sahlins 1994). Etkin et al. (1990) describe the 'indigenization of pharmaceuticals' among the Hausa of Nigeria, who have not merely accepted pharmaceuticals as an alternative to indigenous medicine but have converted them into a subclass of indigenous medicine by reinterpreting their therapeutic value according to the logic of Hausa nosology. For example, erythromycin capsules, just like certain plants, are given to fortify the blood because they are red.[12]

Iskander and Ellen (2007) adhere to a narrower interpretation of hybridization in their study of the innovative incorporation of the leguminous tree *Paraserianthes falcataria* into the swidden cultivation system of the Baduy people of West Java. The Baduy decided to adopt the interplanting of the staple crop rice and the fallow crop *Paraserianthes* when they noticed that it resembled other existing crops in terms of its soil revitalization properties and saw that it could be easily integrated into existing farming practices. The authors clarify that it is not simply the incorporation of this tree and associated knowledge that qualifies this as a genuine case of hybridization but rather the generation of original knowledge through a synthesis of preexisting and newly introduced understandings acquired from the Indonesian forestry department.

The theoretical value of studies of knowledge hybridization is that they highlight the dynamic and interconnected make-up of different knowledge systems ranging from the global to the local. By exposing these connections and the renovations of traditional know-how and practice stimulated by them, the view that localized, culturally embedded knowledge systems have developed autonomously and apart from surrounding knowledge systems is undermined. In particular, this work advises that the historical trajectories of formal science and informal local knowledge need to be brought into closer alignment. A balanced assessment of this history admits that information flows not only from the written pages of science to the oral and enacted texts of local wisdom but also that folk knowledge has enriched the development of science (Agrawal 1995; Sillitoe 2007). Through the prism of hybrid knowledges, contact and communication with global science stands out as a potent generator of intellectual creativity and diversity precisely at the local level rather than as an eliminator of it.

Migration

The fashioning of TEK in the context of human migration represents a special case of transformation that is somewhat akin to the process of allopatric speciation in biological organisms. Although immigrant populations are often regarded as having relatively unsophisticated ecological knowledge and therefore were formerly underappreciated as worthy subjects of ethnoecological study, a recent wave of research focused precisely on these groups is proving that they offer a potentially rich field for studying the dynamics of TEK change (Nesheim et al. 2006; Pieroni and Vandebroek 2007a; Alexiades 2009). As Pieroni and Vandebroek (2007b: 3) point out, people who move into a new environment or society 'do not come empty-handed'. They are accompanied by their cultural traditions, world-views, values, knowledges, technologies and, in some cases, plant and animal resources. But the places in which immigrants settle are often very different from their place of origin, which means that they are confronted with unfamiliar social, economic or biophysical environments. This situation may not be compatible with simply recreating their former lifestyle in the new place of residence and instead they may be compelled to alter and adapt their customary habits, including their recognition and use of natural resources. The clash between old and new ways can be represented as theoretically opposite strategies – conservatism (i.e. identity reinforcement) versus adaptation (i.e. cultural assimilation) – but the reality of what migrants actually do probably lies somewhere in-between (Pieroni and Vandebroek 2007b: 4). The choice between retaining, abandoning or modifying certain ethnoecological knowledges and practices will depend on diverse factors related to the interface established between the incoming group and the host society, as well as the affordances and constraints presented by the physical environment. Given the dynamics and diversity inherent to the migration context, it offers an ideal laboratory for studying the mechanics of TEK transformation as well as the environmental drivers that shape and structure this process.

Ethnobiological research among contemporary immigrant populations shows considerable variation in terms of the nationalities or ethnic backgrounds of the migrant groups, the social and ecological context(s) where they have settled, the circumstances of the migration history and reasons why they moved, and the changing states and trends of TEK. If one commonality feature stands out it is that people are not merely passive responders to environmental forces encountered, and the transformation of knowledge systems that are implanted into a new habitat does not always follow a predictable path. The case of the displaced Sahrawi people, who fled foreign conquest and armed rebellion in their native Western Sahara and now live in refugee camps in Algeria, illustrates how traditional ethnomedical knowledge is perpetuated, albeit in a modified form, as an expression of political resistance. The refugees continue to use the traditional plant and animal-part remedies as a way of maintaining the connection between cultural identity, traditional resources and their homeland, but they have had to develop new social and economic strategies for obtaining them (Volpato et al. 2009). By contrast, rapid turnover of ethnobotanical knowledge was observed among a multiethnic migrant community in Guatemala made up of people who moved from the highlands to the lowlands to escape civil war and then moved several more times during the past generation. Most of their present plant knowledge was picked up at different locations during this period of itinerant resettlements. Men have learned more about the plants native to their current lowland forest habitat and this advantage is accounted for by the fact that their principal occupations – house building, timber cutting and non-timber forest product extraction – entail the use of numerous forest species (Nesheim et al. 2006).

Research on the ethnobotany of transnational immigrant communities living in large urban areas shows that their patterns of plant usage reinforce ethnic ties within a multicultural context (Balick et al. 2000; Nguyen 2003). For example, Dominican immigrants in New York City have moved to another country and enjoy access to modern biomedicine but still make extensive use of herbal medicines and other traditional healing techniques, many of which are imported from their home country and sold in small shops called *Botánicas*. Although there is considerable overlap of ethnomedical knowledge between rural communities in the Dominican Republic and the urban community in New York, there are also some notable differences. In the urban community, some traditional herbals have disappeared due to lack of availability or loss of cultural practices, while others have been added, especially those that are considered treatments for ailments that are not common in the Dominican Republic (e.g. high cholesterol, diabetes). The therapeutic choices of urban immigrants have also become more diversified in that they make use of remedies and healers stemming from different cultural traditions (Ososki et al. 2007; Vandebroek et al. 2007).

One of the main reasons why the ethnoecology of human migration offers such a unique perspective for studying the dynamic properties of TEK is that the movement of people and their traditional knowledge from one place to another implies a radical change not only in the structure and content of the knowledge system but also in the relationship between this system and its local environmental context. Considering that this relationship is often mentioned as one of the defining features of indigenous or local knowledge (Ellen and Harris 2000), we are interested in understanding more about the influence of dynamic environmental variables on knowledge formation (and vice versa) over time. The general situation of migrating knowledges simulates the formation process in fast-forward motion. The question of formation looks in two directions: (1) how is TEK deformed (i.e. what is lost or degraded) when the connection between it and its place of origin is broken, and (2) how is TEK reformed (i.e. what is added or reconfigured) when it is transported to a new setting. One of the most effective methods for studying the changes that occur as a result of migration is to make controlled comparisons between ecological knowledge and practices in the homeland and those found in the immigrant landscape (Nguyen 2003; Ososki et al. 2007; Vandebroek et al. 2007).

Innovation

The capacity of prescientific humans to discover or invent new knowledge and technology was long ignored by scientists who considered that such people were culturally programmed to follow traditional customs without deviating from 'the way it has always been done'. This impression was especially ingrained in evaluations of traditional agriculture from a scientific point of view (Rhoades and Bebbington 1995).

Farmers in tribal or peasant societies were reputed to be notoriously conservative and resistant to change. From a development standpoint, they were treated as passive recipients of new technology that was introduced by external promoters rather than as active innovators on their own (Schultz 1964). Curiously enough, the image of the superstitious, tradition-bound indigenous or peasant farmer who had survived intact into the industrial age contrasted starkly with the image depicted by archaeologists of the more progressive neolithic farmer in ancient times who was credited with domesticating more than five hundred plant species and spreading his inventions across continents (Braidwood 1967). Various theories were proposed to make sense of this apparent paradox: the natural limitations imposed by marginal environments; the strict conformity demanded by cultural scripts and peer pressure; the lack of economic incentive to change due to the high level of efficiency already achieved; the aversion to risk and uncertainty associated with new production strategies; and the lack of investment and infrastructural support by the state (Johnson 1972; Rhoades and Bebbington 1995). Other explanations placed the blame on the inability of scientific experts to recognize informal forms of technological ingenuity when they see them (Gupta 1989). The 'invisibility' of innovation in traditional agriculture could also be attributed to the very small-scale and scattered nature of changes, which meant they were imperceptible to outsiders (Richards 1985). The representation of peasant farmers as essentially conservative and conformist helped to perpetuate the popular misconception that traditional farming was timeless and unchanging (Richards 1985; Stone 2004).

By the 1970s, perceptions of traditional agriculture began to undergo a drastic revision, with the accumulation of research on local farming systems from an ethnoecological perspective and with the rise of participatory development. This viewpoint stressed the technical and ecological rationalities of traditional farming practices and the role of farmers as active, on-site participants in the research and development process. Researchers started taking notice of the experimental inclinations and capabilities of traditional farmers, and reflected on the implications of small-scale innovative behaviour for managing development (Johnson 1972; Howes and Chambers 1979; Biggs and Clay 1981; Rhoades 1989). Johnson (1972) maintained that individuality and low-risk experimentation are commonplace in traditional agriculture. He saw variability as a necessary ingredient for adaptive change, and experimentation as a step towards adaptive modification of the environment. Biggs and Clay (1981) distinguished informal from formal research and development. In the informal sector, farmers are continually engaged in experimentation and innovation, and have the advantage of basing their experiments on intimate knowledge of the local environment. Richards (1985) demonstrated that indigenous agricultural experiments are frequently more successful than experiments based on ex-situ scientific methods and understandings. Rhoades (1989) observed that typically farmers do not just simply adopt new agricultural technology recommended by scientists and extension agents but instead adapt it by selecting and testing certain elements from technological packages in order to solve problems or goals which they themselves define. In the wake of these influential position papers, interest in local agricultural innovation as a research topic and as a positive force for rural development has grown enormously (Scoones and Thompson 1994; Reij and Waters-Bayer 2001; Bentley 2006; Leitgeb and Vogl 2010).

Agricultural Experimentation

Innovation is understood here as the creation of new knowledge or the novel application of old knowledge that leads to new ways of doing things (cf. Spielman et al. 2008). From a systems perspective, innovation depends not only on generation of new information but also on the diffusion, acceptance and use of that information among other people (Leitgeb and Vogl 2010). Much of the published work that qualifies under this definition and involves some form of TEK focuses on informal agricultural experimentation. In this context, experimentation refers to the research or exploratory operations that farmers carry out with their crops, animals, lands and organizational modes to learn more about their environments and perform more effectively. Empirical descriptions of farmer experiments encompass a wide variety of specific applications ranging from purely technical to socioeconomic considerations. These include: choice of crop and animal types, selection of crop varieties and animal breeds, seed preparation and storage, grafting, cropping techniques and patterns, fertilizer application, green manuring, weed control, water control, pest management, fallow management, afforestation, machine and tool invention, labour organization, land tenure arrangements, market strategies, secondary product manufacture, and off-farm employment (Richards 1985; Chambers et al. 1989; Moock and Rhoades 1992; Scoones and Thompson 1994; Warren et al. 1995; Reij and Waters-Bayer 2001; Bentley 2006; Kummer et al. 2008).

Rhoades and Bebbington (1995) identify three basic motivations for agricultural experiment: curiosity, problem solving and adaptation. Experimentation out of curiosity may be defined as trying out something new and different just for the sake of seeing what will happen. It may be motivated by personality, boredom or a predisposition to exercise the imagination (Rhoades and Bebbington 1995; Bentley 2006; Kummer et al. 2008). Potato farmers in the Lake Titicaca region of Peru experiment with seed (instead of clones) to see if new varieties will arise, and it has been hypothesized that this practice is a primary reason for the enormous diversity of potato cultivars in the Andes (Rhoades and Bebbington 1995).

Problem-solving experiments are those designed to seek practical solutions to old and new problems. One of the most challenging and common problems faced by farmers is environmental change, whether that means unpredictable, short-term fluctuations in growing conditions or more long-term shifts in ecological, economic or technological conditions. This general factor has been identified as one of the leading drivers of experimentation, as farmers attempt to cope with the disruptions caused by delayed rainfall, outbreak of weevil infestation, a new crop disease, progressive soil erosion, exotic species invasions, introduction of modern varieties, improved tool design, falling crop prices, rising fuel costs, deregulation of international markets, rising consumer demand for certain products, road construction, population growth, labour migration and a host of other surrounding constraints and opportunities (Stolzenbach 1994; Rhoades and Bebbington 1995; Stone 2004; Kummer et al. 2008). In consideration of the large number of variables that potentially affect agricultural operations and the inherent variability of many of them, the practice of smallholder agriculture might be regarded as one big, never-ending experiment (Stolzenbach 1994; Stone 2004). This is basically what Richards (1989) means when he says that indigenous agriculture is better understood as a constantly improvised performance rather than a preconceived plan. Thus West African smallholders are constantly altering and adjusting their cultivation decisions in response to even minor variations in weather, predation, labour supply and market conditions, and decisions taken at one time affect later decisions throughout the cultivation cycle and beyond (see also Millar 1994).

Adaptation experiments involve the testing of unknown technology in familiar environments, known technology in unknown environments or unknown technology in unknown environments. This is one of the most common types of experiment among agriculturalists who have obtained new crop varieties or other technologies from exogenous sources (Millar 1994; Bentley 2006). A celebrated example involves the adoption of diffused light potato storage, promoted by the International Potato Centre. Many farmers exposed to this idea did not simply copy it but tinkered with the method to fit in with existing practices, site-specific conditions and cultural preferences (Rhoades and Booth 1982). Adaptive experimentation is also common among migrant groups who have moved into a new biome. In the early 1980s, migrants from the Andean highlands in Peru founded an agricultural colony in the lowland Amazonian district of Yurimaguas. By virtue of self-run experiments, they were able to establish wet rice cultivation, a first for the Upper Amazon (Rhoades and Bidegaray 1987).

Research on the process of informal agricultural experimentation has yielded insights into the epistemology of indigenous knowledge and its generation. One of the key issues is whether and to what extent folk and scientific epistemologies coincide (Stolzenbach 1994; Cleveland and Solieri 2002). The opinions of experienced observers of farmer experiments diverge in regard to the correspondence question. On the one hand, there are researchers who play up the differences. Stolzenbach (1994) distinguishes the 'adaptive rationality' of farmers from the formal rationality of scientists. The former is seen as a continuous interaction among visions, experiences and experiments. For farmers, local knowledge is tacit (i.e. experiential, intuitive, practical, unformalized) and is acquired through 'reflection-in-action' (i.e. a continuous process of observation and adjustment while performing the craft of farming). Millar (1994) concurs that execution, analysis and use of results are overlapping phases in farmer experimentation that relies on intuition, careful observation, skills and experience acquired over time, common sense and practical know-how. Juma (1987, cited in IDS Workshop 1989) contends that the local process of plant breeding is based on a distinctive epistemology that is uniquely tied to the particular culture and socio-ecological context. Bentley (2006) affirms that folk experiments are indeed experiments, but they are not science because they are not written down and (usually) disregard standard procedures of scientific method (e.g. consistent protocol, control groups, numerical data, formal treatments). On the other hand, there are authors who highlight that many of the basic rational design elements found in scientific research are also present in farmer-directed research. These elements include: empirical observation, concept formation, hypothesis testing, controlled comparisons (i.e. control versus experimental applications), validation, experiment replication, peer critique, step-wise amplification of the experiment, and further observation and evaluation of the results under a wider set of conditions (Rhoades 1987, Bebbington 1994; Richards 1994; McCorkle and McClure 1995; Rhoades and Bebbington 1995; Cleveland and Soleri 2002). Cleveland and Soleri (2002) claim that farmers are similar to scientific plant breeders in that they develop theoretical knowledge about plant varieties and their habits that includes hypotheses about causal relationships and forms the basis of predictions and plans. The assumptions of both farmer and breeder also appear to be constrained by the specific kinds of genotypes and environments with which they have firsthand experience.

The emerging viewpoint from this discussion seems to be that there is no sharp epistemological division with respect to how farmers and scientists go about gathering information and conducting their experiments, but they often do not share the same interpretative frameworks and therefore display differences in the way they read their research results. The distinction becomes further blurred if we consider that most rural smallholders nowadays have had some kind of exposure to scientific concepts or methods through formal education, farmer field schools, extension agents, seed vendors, agricultural researchers and access to printed or electronic media (Brodt 2002). Bentley (2006) observes that many folk experiments are in fact inspired by new ideas that originate from exogenous sources, and that contact with development agencies is associated with greater levels of experimentation.

The results of experiments conducted by individual farmers are often freely shared among other members of the community or passed along to neighbouring communities, thus amplifying their overall impact. The dissemination of innovation usually takes place via informal social networks. The relevant contexts include: personal visits to relatives or friends, village meetings, social get-togethers, collective labour activities, marketplaces, ceremonial affairs and festivals. Rural development researchers have observed that these informal means of communication are much more effective for spreading innovative knowledge and behaviour than more formal institutions (McCorkle and McClure 1995; Hanyani-Mlambo and Hebinck 1996; Wu and Pretty 2004).[13] Meanwhile empirical studies of the diffusion of agricultural innovations point to the primacy of social influences over environmental learning for determining adoption trends. Thus, people tend to adopt new technology based on whether their social peers or high-status members of their community are doing so, rather than evaluating for themselves the costs/benefits of adoption versus non-adoption (Henrich 2001; Stone 2007).

Non-agricultural Innovation

In comparison to all that has been written about agricultural innovation, the research on innovation in non-agricultural domains of TEK is remarkably meagre and vague. It is very rare to find studies that give more than cursory treatment to this topic, and these usually occur in the context of investigations with other priorities. One of the few exceptions to this pattern of neglect is the work of Berkes (1998, 1999), who discusses cases of new knowledge development involving different subsistence or commercial resource activities such as trapping, hunting, fishing, logging, charcoal making, sea urchin collecting and sea moss cultivation. A recurrent theme in his work is that local communities develop effective common property mechanisms for regulating the extraction of natural resources after a period of uncontrolled harvesting of natural resources has caused depletion of the resource supply.

On the island of St Lucia, haphazard cutting of wood for charcoal production under an open-access arrangement from 1960 to 1985 caused severe degradation of the mangroves where this activity took place. But then the charcoal producers got together and organized a more cooperative and stable tenure framework that led to more sustainable management and recuperation of the mangrove. The creation of new ecological knowledge in this and other contexts is interpreted by Berkes as an entirely normal process that exemplifies the principle of 'adaptive management'. According to this concept, ecosystems are always changing, and resource management institutions, of which traditional knowledge forms a part, respond to feedbacks from these changing states by adjusting and evolving until another state of equilibrium is reached.

A small but growing body of ethnobotanical research has also begun to investigate the innovation and evolution of ethnomedicine, particularly in regard to the knowledge and use of medicinal plants (Nolan 1998; Palmer 2004a, 2004b; Heckler 2007). The cultural domain of ethnomedical knowledge is highly sensitive to environmental change, especially where epidemiological factors are concerned, because it is a vital resource for the maintenance or restoration of human health. Comparative and historical research in Amazonia and Polynesia suggests that ethnopharmacopoeas were renewed and augmented in the space of a few generations following contact with colonizing populations and their infectious diseases (Whistler 1992; Davis 1995). A plausible explanation of the post-contact growth of phytomedicinal knowledge is that traditional healers became 'active scientific experimenters' as an adaptive response to invasion by exogenous pathogens (Davis 1995). Palmer's (2004a) account of the evolution of the native Hawaiian pharmacopoea from the early contact period to the present (1838–2002) is consistent with this conclusion. The proportional representation of traditional medicinal plants (of endemic, indigenous and Polynesian origin) declined, while that of newly introduced plant species increased gradually, such that the latter now constitute 45 per cent of the current inventory. The conspicuous presence of exotic species in the composition of ethnopharmacological inventories recorded from other regions of the world indicates that experimentation with herbal medicines is widespread (Rossato et al. 1999; Begossi et al. 2002; Albuquerque 2006; Estomba et al. 2006; Rocha Silva and Andrade 2006).

One of the general conclusions that can be drawn from the literature on the innovation of traditional knowledge and technology is that independent invention is probably more common than usually supposed, and therefore at least part of the creative impetus for TEK evolution in a given place comes from within the local social group itself. In this light, innovation constitutes an important source of internal cognitive and behavioural variation that, subject to cultural transmission mechanisms and environmental selection pressures, can lead to significant changes in the overall knowledge/practice system. At the same time, however, the line between innovation and transformation, whether originating from endogenous or exogenous sources, is not always clear-cut since many innovations are stimulated by contact with outsiders. In any case, environmental change stands out as a key driver of innovation, where the environment is understood in a broad sense as referring to dynamic biophysical or socioeconomic factors. Considering the pervasive and perpetual nature of environmental change, it is not hard to see why so-called traditional knowledge and management systems are being reinvented and renovated all the time.

Conclusion

The data and insights generated by processually minded research are changing the way we think about TEK, especially in regard to its ontological form, origins, longevity, stability, adaptability, distribution, composition and uniqueness. Synchronic approaches to the study of TEK effectively represent knowledge as an abstract object (i.e. a delimited corpus of interrelated terms, categories and meanings) whereas the diachronic perspectives reviewed in this chapter view it more as a contextualized process or set of processes (i.e. the variable cognitive representations and embodied practices that structure and inform interactions between people and their environments in specific settings at certain moments in time) (cf. Borofsky 1994). In other words, knowledge is conceptualized not as a static entity but rather its shape and substance are indefinite, flexible, and perpetually in flux through time and space (Ellen and Harris 2000; Sowerine 2004). This viewpoint calls into question cherished essentialist conceptions of TEK as something that is inherently timeless, bounded, emplaced, collective and coherent. The common perception that folk knowledge constitutes ancient, or extremely long-lived, wisdom that has been handed down through countless generations is modified by a more dynamic view of it as adapting and adjusting rather quickly to changing environmental conditions. Instead of being a system closed to outside influences, it is treated as being open to contact and exchange of information with other knowledge systems. The notion of local knowledge as being entirely unique to, and deeply rooted in, a particular place is moderated to admit that it consists of a distinct combination of endogenous as well as exogenous elements. The idea that TEK corresponds to a shared, homogeneous body of understandings held in common by a given society is supplanted by recognition of considerable variation across individuals, groups and social statuses. The image of the knowledge system as a fixed, internally coherent set of signs and meanings that provide instructions for action gives way to a sense of knowledge as something more fluid and indeterminate that manifests itself in different ways according to situational variables. It should be emphasized that the conceptual revisions summarized here are not being presented in order to advocate the replacement of one set of essentialisms with another, but rather to make the point that notions of what TEK is or ought to be have become much more complex, qualified, relativistic and contested in the light of histori-cally informed research.

Acknowledgements

The author wishes to thank Roy Ellen for his superb editorial as-sistance and guidance, Christian Vogl and Anja Nygren for sending their work relevant to the topic, Egleé Zent for her nonstop encour-agement, and IVIC for material support.

Notes

1. The notion of endemism has been applied to cultures or languages in much the same way as it has been used for plants or animals – that is, as denoting the quality of being geographically restricted and hence rare overall. Nabhan (1995: 2) introduced the notion of *ethnobiological endemism* to convey the 'unique ways of classifying and using local plants found nowhere else in the world'. Hunn (2001: 126, 129) has written about 'endemic culture', describing people who 'preserve a rich tradition of environmental knowledge' and whose 'way of life is tightly bound to that small piece of the earth's surface they call home', and 'endemic languages', qualified as those that 'have a specialized attachment to and dependence on restricted local habitats'. Milton's (1991) comparative analysis of the subsistence habits of small indigenous populations of the Brazilian Amazon provides some insight into how such endemism may be perpetuated. These groups occupy similar habitats but display varying suites of resources, which amounts to ecological niche differentiation. Such differentiation serves to mark social boundaries between neighbouring ethnic groups, and such boundaries in turn help to maintain cultural diversity at a very small scale.
2. The same author elaborates further that, given the inevitability of environmental change and consequent discrepancy of cognitive reality from physical reality, periodic renewal in some aspects of TEK is necessary to keep it alive (Vansina 1990).
3. Sahlins' thesis is that local (non-Western, non-industrial) peoples are able to negotiate the process of cultural contact and assimilation into the expanding world system on their own cultural terms. Thus they do not merely adopt exogenous goods, customs and institutions in a passive manner but rather reinterpret them according to the autochthonous system of meaning and value. Therefore what appears to be radical cultural change and assimilation from an external point of view may look more like cultural continuity and differentiation from the inside.

4. This theory seems to be based largely on Atran and collaborators' research analysing intercultural and inter-informant variations in folk biological inductive reasoning behaviour, especially in regard to drawing inferences about ecological relationships and category-relatedness. Such differences may be attributed to variables in the learning landscape, such as: exposure to role models and their stories, prior learning experience, intelligence, motivation, selective attention and preexisting values (Atran and Medin 2008: 215–19).

5. Elsewhere Atran (1999: 120–21) expands on this line of reasoning as follows:

    The universal character of folkbiological taxonomy does not mean that folkbiological categories are culturally irrelevant. On the contrary, inso- far as they reflect a cognitively biased, phenomenal appreciation of the surrounding environment, they help to set the constraints on life that make culture possible. It is little wonder then that folkbiological taxono- mies tend to be among the most stable, widely distributed, and conserva- tive structures in any culture. Once set into place, such a structure would likely survive even catastrophic historical upheaval to a clearly recog- nizable degree. Ancient and contemporary Maya societies would be no exception. Even with the social order and cosmological system sundered, the folkbiological structure would persist as a cognitive basis for cultural survival under two conditions: first, there must be significant biological continuity in the ecological distribution of species; second, there must be significant linguistic continuity with the dialect that first encoded the knowledge.

    In support of this argument, he notes that following the Spanish conquest of the Izaj Maya in 1697, 'the Itzaj cosmological system was destroyed, Itzaj folkbiological knowledge – including taxonomic competence and practical application – remains strikingly robust'.

6. The informed reader will notice that this statement is based somewhat on Redfield's (1941) portrayal of folk society and its imputed resistance to deviating from the established social and moral order. While Redfield's model has been amply analysed and criticized (see for example Miner 1952), nevertheless the correlation of the different traits mentioned here has not been one of these points of contention. As Miner (ibid.: 535) observes, 'If, considering all known societies, there is shown to be no general tendency for the elements of the type to co-occur, then obviously the ideal type is not valid. So far as the writer knows, no one has claimed that the general tendency does not exist.'

7. That formalized cultural (or national) traditions may be invented or revised periodically as befits social or political demands, as Hobsbawn and Ranger (1983) argue, does not diminish the fact that such formalization, to the extent it routinizes or legitimizes existing arrangements, is instrumental in perpetuating the status quo.

8. The entire list of 'socio-ecological practices and mechanisms for resilience and sustainability' presented by Folke et al. (1998: 418) is too long to reproduce here and therefore the reader is advised to consult the original article for more complete information.

9. According to Zarger's research (2010), the bulk of plant taxonomic knowledge is acquired by the end of early adolescence (< 13 years old) whereas Bock (2010) reports that peak abilities for some types of subsistence skills, such as mondongo nut processing among San women or hunting prowess by Ache men, are not attained until well into adulthood (35–40 years old).

10. This point also raises some crucial questions. What is the quality of the new knowledge that is substituted or added? Is it comparable in terms of empirical

accuracy, detail and effectiveness to the former information that has been discarded or altered? Is it compatible with sustainable use of resources and biodiversity preservation? If high-quality information is replaced by low-quality information, then it seems reasonable to speak of 'erosion' as the net effect.

11. Where this kind of lexical borrowing has been documented, the names that successfully cross linguistic boundaries are usually lent by the more ancestral residents to the newcomers and refer to organisms that are completely unknown or unlike any that are found in the latter's former territorial range.

12. The notion of 'knowledge indigenization' as discussed here bears a close affinity to what Kroeber called 'stimulus diffusion' (or 'idea diffusion'), which he defines as 'a new pattern of growth initiated by precedent in a foreign culture' (Kroeber 1940: 20). The basic idea with this type of diffusion, as with indigenization or hybridization of knowledge, is that the receiving culture adopts an idea from another culture but infuses it with content and purpose of its own, thereby creating something new with it.

13. The study by Wu and Pretty (2004) in Shaanxi province, China, highlights the crucial link between social communication and farmer innovation. Farmers in this region rely heavily on informal networks to share technology-learning information. The researchers demonstrate effectively that households that are more socially connected in terms of greater household communication networks, technology learning groups, and inter-village links are more likely to adopt new farming technologies (and have higher incomes).

References

Acabado, S.B. 2010. 'The Archaeology of the Ifugao Agriculture Terraces: Antiquity and Social Organization'. Ph.D. dissertation. The University of Hawai'i at Manoa.

Agrawal, A. 1995. 'Dismantling the Divide between Indigenous and Scientific Knowledge', *Development and Change* 26: 413–39.

Albuquerque, U.P. 2006. 'Re-examining Hypotheses Concerning the Use and Knowledge of Medicinal Plants: A Study in the Caatinga Vegetation of NE Brazil', *Journal of Ethnobiology and Ethnomedicine* 2: 30.

Alcorn, J.B. and V.M. Toledo. 1998. 'Resilient Resource Management in Mexico's Forest Ecosystems: The Contribution of Property Rights', in F. Berkes and C. Folke (eds), *Linking Social and Ecological Systems: Management Practices and Social Mechanisms for Building Resilience.* Cambridge: Cambridge University Press, pp. 216–49.

Alexiades, M.N. (ed.). 2009. *Mobility and Migration in Indigenous Amazonia: Contemporary Ethnoecological Perspectives.* Oxford: Berghahn Books.

Alexiades, M.N. and D.M. Peluso. 2009. '"Plants of the Ancestors", "Plants of the Outsiders": Ese Eja History, Migration and Medicinal Plants', in M.N. Alexiades (ed.), *Mobility and Migration in Indigenous Amazonia: Contemporary Ethnoecological Perspectives.* Oxford: Berghahn Books, pp. 220–48.

Anderson, E.F. 1986. 'Ethnobotany of Hill Tribes of Northern Thailand. II. Lahu Medicinal Plants', *Economic Botany* 40: 442–540.

Antweiler, C. 2004. 'Local Knowledge Theory and Methods: An Urban Model from Indonesia', in A. Bicker, P. Sillitoe and J. Pottier (eds), *Investigating Local Knowledge: New Directions, New Approaches.* Aldershot: Ashgate Publishing, pp. 1–34.

Anyinam, C. 1995. 'Ecology and Ethnomedicine: Exploring the Links between Current Environmental Crisis and Indigenous Medical Practices', *Social Science and Medicine* 40: 321–29.

Atran, S. 1993. 'Itza' Maya Tropical Agroforestry', *Current Anthropology* 34: 633–700.

_____.1999. 'Itzaj Maya Folkbiological Taxonomy: Cognitive Universals and Cultural Particulars', in D.L. Medin and S. Atran (eds), *Folkbiology*. Cambridge: The MIT Press, pp. 119–203.

_____.2001a. 'The Trouble with Memes: Inference versus Imitation in Cultural Creation', *Human Nature* 12: 351–81.

_____.2001b. 'The Vanishing Landscape of the Peten Maya Lowlands', in L. Maffi (ed.), *On Biocultural Diversity: Linking Language, Knowledge, and the Environment*. Washington, DC: Smithsonian Institution Press, pp. 157–74.

Atran, S. and D. Medin. 2008. *The Native Mind and the Cultural Construction of Nature*. Cambridge: The MIT Press.

Austerlitz, R. 1968. 'Native Seal Nomenclatures in South-Sahalin', in J.K. Yamagiwa (ed.), *Papers of the CIC Far Eastern Language Institute*. Ann Arbor, MI: Panel on Far Eastern Language Institutes of the Committee on Institutional Cooperation, pp. 133–41.

Baines, G. and E. Hviding. 1993. 'Traditional Environmental Knowledge for Resource Management in Marovo, Solomon Islands', in N.W. Williams and G. Baines (eds), *Traditional Ecological Knowledge: Wisdom for Sustainable Development*. Canberra: Centre for Resource and Environmental Studies, National Australian University, pp. 56–65.

Balée, W. 1992. 'People of the Fallow: A Historical Ecology of Foraging in Lowland South America', in K.H. Redford and C. Padoch (eds), *Conservation of Neotropical Forests: Working from Traditional Resource Use*. New York: Columbia University Press, pp. 35–57.

_____.1999. 'Mode of Production and Ethnobotanical Vocabulary: A Controlled Comparison of Guajá and Ka'apor', in T. Gragson and B. Blount (eds), *Ethnoecology: Knowledge, Resources, Rights*. Athens, GA: University of Georgia Press, pp. 24–40.

_____.2000. 'Antiquity of Traditional Ethnobiological Knowledge in Amazonia: The Tupí-Guaraní Family and Time', *Ethnohistory* 47(2): 399–422.

Balée, W. and C.L. Erickson. 2006. *Time and Complexity in Historical Ecology*. New York: Columbia University Press.

Balick, M., F. Kronenberg, A.L. Ososki, M. Reiff, A. Fugh-Berman, B. O'Connor, M. Roble, P. Lohr and D. Atha. 2000. 'Medicinal Plants Used by Latino Healers for Women's Health Conditions in New York City', *Economic Botany* 54(3): 344–57.

Bates, P. 2009. 'Learning and Inuit Knowledge in Nunavut, Canada', in P. Bates, M. Chiba, S. Kube and D. Nakashima (eds), Learning and *Knowing in Indigenous Societies Today*. Paris: UNESCO, pp. 95–105.

Bates, P., M. Chiba, S. Kube and D. Nakashima (eds). 2009. *Learning and Knowing in Indigenous Societies Today*. Paris: UNESCO.

Bebbington, A. 1994. 'Indigenous Agricultural Knowledge Systems, Human Interests, and Critical Analysis: Reflections on Farmer Organization in Ecuador', *Agriculture and Human Values* 8(1–2): 14–24.

Begossi, A., N. Hanazaki and J. Tamashiro. 2002. 'Medicinal Plants in the Atlantic Forest (Brazil): Knowledge, Use, and Conservation', *Human Ecology* 30(3): 281–99.

Begossi, A., H.F. Leitão-Filho and P.J. Richerson. 1993. 'Plant Uses in a Brazilian Fishing Community (Buzios Island)', *Journal of Ethnobiology* 13: 233–56.

Bennett, B.C. and G.T. Prance. 2000. 'Introduced Plants in the Indigenous Pharmacopoeia of Northern South America', *Economic Botany* 54: 90–102.

Bentley, J.W. 2006. 'Folk Experiments', *Agriculture and Human Values* 23: 451–62.

Benz, B.F., J. Cevallos, F. Santana, J. Rosales and S. Graf. 2000. 'Losing Knowledge about Plant Use in the Sierra de Manantlan Biosphere Reserve, Mexico', *Economic Botany* 54: 183–91.

Berkes, F. 1993. 'Traditional Ecological Knowledge in Perspective', in J.T. Inglis (ed.), *Traditional Ecological Knowledge: Concepts and Cases*. Ottawa: International Program on Traditional Ecological Knowledge and International Development Research Centre, pp. 1–9.

_____.1998. 'Indigenous Knowledge and Resource Management Systems in the Canadian Subarctic', in F. Berkes and C. Folke (eds), *Linking Social and Ecological Systems: Management Practices and Social Mechanisms for Building Resilience*. Cambridge: Cambridge University Press, pp. 98–128.

_____.1999. *Sacred Ecology: Traditional Ecological Knowledge and Resource Management*. Philadelphia: Taylor and Francis.

Berkes, F. and C. Folke. 1998. 'Linking Social and Ecological Systems for Resilience and Sustainability', in F. Berkes and C. Folke (eds), *Linking Social and Ecological Systems: Management Practices and Social Mechanisms for Building Resilience*. Cambridge: Cambridge University Press, pp. 1–25.

Berlin, B. 1992. *Ethnobiological Classification: Principles of Categorization of Plants and Animals in Traditional Societies*. New Jersey: Princeton University Press.

_____.1999. 'Lexical Reflections on the Cultural Importance of Medicinal Plants among Tzotzil and Tzeltal Maya', in T. Gragson and B. Blount (eds), *Ethnoecology: Knowledge, Resources, Rights*. Athens, GA: University of Georgia Press, pp. 12–23.

Berlin, B., D. Breedlove, R.M. Laughlin and P.H. Raven. 1973. 'Cultural Significance and Lexical Retention in Tzeltal-Tzotzil Ethnobotany', in M.S. Edmonton (ed.), *Meaning in Mayan Languages*. Janua Linguarum (All Series), Ser. pract. 158. The Hague: Mouton, pp. 143–64.

Bernard, R. 1992. 'Preserving Language Diversity', *Human Organization* 51(1): 82–89.

Biggs, S.D. and E. Clay. 1981. 'Sources of Innovation in Agricultural Technology', *World Development* 9: 321–36.

Blench, R.M. and K.C. MacDonald (eds). 2000. *The Origins and Development of African Livestock: Archaeology, Genetics, Linguistics and Ethnography.* London: UCL Press.

Bock, J. 2010. 'An Evolutionary Perspective on Learning in Social, Cultural and Ecological Context', in D.F. Lancy, J. Bock and S. Gaskins (eds), *The Anthropology of Learning in Childhood.* Walnut Creek, CA: AltaMira Press, pp. 11–34.

Bodley, J.H. 1990. *Victims of Progress.* Third Edition. Mountain View, CA: Mayfield Publishing.

Borofsky, R. 1994. 'On the Knowledge and Knowing of Cultural Activities', in R. Borofsky (ed.), *Assessing Cultural Anthropology.* New York: McGraw-Hill, pp. 331–48.

Boster, J.S. 1986. 'Exchange of Varieties and Information between Aguaruna Manioc Cultivators', *American Anthropologist* 88(2): 428–36.

Botkin, D.B. 1990. *Discordant Harmonies: A New Ecology for the Twenty-First Century.* Oxford: Oxford University Press.

Boyd, R. and P. Richerson. 1985. *Culture and the Evolutionary Process.* Chicago: University of Chicago Press.

Braidwood, R.J. 1967. *Prehistoric Men.* Glenview, IL: Scott, Foresman and Co.

Brodt, S.B. 2002. 'Learning about Tree Management in Rural Central India: A Global-local Continuum', *Human Organization* 61: 58–67.

Brookfield, H. and C. Padoch. 1994. 'Appreciating Agrodiversity: A Look at the Dynamism and Diversity of Indigenous Farming Practices', *Environment* 36(5): 1–17.

Brücher, H. 1990. 'Difusión Transamericana de Vegetales Útiles del Neotrópico en la Época Pre-Colombina', in D.A. Posey and W.L. Overal (eds), *Ethnobiology: Implications and Applications.* Vol. I. Belem: Museu Paraense Emilio Goeldi, pp. 265–83.

Butler, C. 2006. 'Historicizing Indigenous Knowledge', in C.R. Menzies (ed.), *Traditional Ecological Knowledge and Natural Resource Management.* Lincoln: University of Nebraska Press, pp. 107–26.

Byg, A. and H. Balslev. 2001. 'Diversity and Use of Palms in Zahamena, Eastern Madagascar', *Biodiversity and Conservation* 10: 951–70.

—————.2004. 'Factors Affecting Local Knowledge of Palms in Nangaritza Valley, Southeastern Ecuador', *Journal of Ethnobiology* 24(2): 255–78.

Campos, M.T. and C. Ehringhaus. 2003. 'Plant Virtues are in the Eyes of the Beholders: A Comparison of Known Palm Uses among Indigenous and Folk Communities of Southwestern Amazonia', *Economic Botany* 57(3): 324–44.

Caniago, I. and S.F. Siebert. 1998. 'Medicinal Plant Economy, Knowledge and Conservation in Kalimantan, Indonesia', *Economic Botany* 52: 229–50.

Carlson, T. and L. Maffi (eds). 2004. *Ethnobotany and Conservation of Biocultural Diversity.* Advances in Economic Botany Series, Vol. 15. Bronx, NY: The New York Botanical Garden Press.

Case, R.J., G.F. Pauli and D.D. Soejarto. 2005. 'Factors in Maintaining Indigenous Knowledge among Ethnic Communities of Manus Island', *Economic Botany* 59: 356–65.

Chambers, R., A. Pacey and L.A. Thrupp (eds). 1989. *Farmer First: Farmer Innovation and Agricultural Research*. London: Intermediate Technology Publications.

Cleveland, D.A. and D. Soleri. 2002. 'Indigenous and Scientific Knowledge of Plant Breeding: Similarities, Differences and Implications for Collaboration', in P. Sillitoe, A. Bicker and J. Pottier (eds), *Participating in Development: Approaches to Indigenous Knowledge*. ASA Monographs 39. London and New York: Routledge, pp. 206–34.

Comerford, S.C. 1996. 'Medicinal Plants of Two Mayan Healers from San Andres, Petén, Guatemala', *Economic Botany* 50: 327–36.

Cox, P. 2000. 'Will Tribal Knowledge Survive the Millennium?', *Science* 287: 44–45.

Crate, S. 2006. 'Elder Knowledge and Sustainable Livelihoods in Post-Soviet Russia: Finding Dialogue across the Generations', *Arctic Anthropology* 43(1): 40–51.

Crosby, A.W. 1972. *The Colombian Exchange: Biological and Cultural Consequences of 1492*. Westport, CT: Greenwood Press.

Cruz García, G.S. 2006. 'The Mother–Child Nexus: Knowledge and Valuation of Wild Food Plants in Wayanad, Western Ghats, India', *Journal of Ethnobiology and Ethnomedicine* 2: 39.

Dasmann, R.F. 1988. 'Towards a Biosphere Consciousness', in D. Worster (ed.), *The Ends of the Earth*. Cambridge: Cambridge University Press, pp. 277–88.

Davis, E.W. 1995. 'Ethnobotany: An Old Practice, A New Discipline', in R.E. Schultes and S. von Reis (eds), *Ethnobotany: Evolution of a Discipline*. Portland, OR: Dioscorides Press, pp. 40–51.

———.2009. *The Wayfinders: Why Ancient Wisdom Matters in the Modern World*. Toronto: House of Anansi Press.

DeWalt, B.R. 1994. 'Using Indigenous Knowledge to Improve Agriculture and Natural Resource Management', *Human Organization* 53(2): 123–31.

Dole, G. 1969. 'Techniques of Preparing Manioc Flour as a Key to Culture History in Tropical America', in A.F.C. Wallace (ed.), *Men and Cultures: Selected Papers of the Fifth International Congress of Anthropological and Ethnological Studies*. Philadelphia: University of Pennsylvania Press, pp. 241–48.

Edwards, S., S. Nebel and M. Heinrich. 2005. 'Questionnaire Surveys: Methodological and Epistemological Problems for Field-based Ethnopharmacologists', *Journal of Ethnopharmacology* 100: 30–36.

Ellen, R.F. and H. Harris. 2000. 'Introduction', in R. Ellen, P. Parkes and A. Bicker (eds), *Indigenous Environmental Knowledge and its Transformations*. Amsterdam: Harwood Academic Publishers, pp. 1–33.

Ellen, R.F., P. Parkes and A. Bicker (eds). 2000. *Indigenous Environmental Knowledge and its Transformations*. Amsterdam: Harwood Academic Publishers.

Escobar, A. 1995. *Encountering Development: The Making and Unmaking of the Third World*. Princeton: Princeton University Press.

Estomba, D., A. Ladio and M. Lozada. 2006. 'Medicinal Wild Plant Knowledge and Gathering Patterns in a Mapuche Community from Northwestern Patagonia', *Journal of Ethnopharmacology* 103: 109–19.

Etkin, N.L., P.J. Ross and I. Muazzamu. 1990. 'The Indigenization of Pharmaceuticals: Therapeutic Transitions in Rural Hausaland', *Social Science and Medicine* 30(8): 919–28.

Figueiredo, G.M., H.F. Leitão-Filho and A. Begossi. 1993. 'Ethnobotany of Atlantic Forest Coastal Communities: Diversity of Plant Uses in Gamboa (Itacuruça Island, Brazil)', *Human Ecology* 21: 419–30.

Florey, M. 2009. 'Sustaining Indigenous Languages and Indigenous Knowledge: Developing Community Training Approaches for the 21st Century', in P. Bates, M. Chiba, S. Kube and D. Nakashima (eds), *Learning and Knowing in Indigenous Societies Today*. Paris: UNESCO, pp. 25–37.

Florey, M. and X.Y. Wolff. 1998. 'Incantations and Herbal Medicines: Alune Ethnomedical Knowledge in a Context of Change', *Journal of Ethnobiology* 18(1): 39–67.

Folke, C., F. Berkes and J. Colding. 1998. 'Ecological Practices and Social Mechanisms for Building Resilience and Sustainability', in F. Berkes and C. Folke (eds), *Linking Social and Ecological Systems: Management Practices and Social Mechanisms for Building Resilience*. Cambridge: Cambridge University Press, pp. 414–36.

Forsyth, T. 1996. 'Science, Myth and Knowledge: Testing Himalayan Environmental Degradation in Thailand', *Geoforum* 27: 375–92.

Frazão-Moreira, A. 2001. 'As Classificações Botânicas nalu (Guiné-Bissau): Consensos e Variabilidades', *Etnográfica* 5(1): 131–55.

Furtado, L.G., R.C. Souza and M.E.V. Berg. 1978. 'Notas Sobre o Uso Terapêutico de Plantas Pela População Cabocla de Manaparim, Pará', *Boletim do Museu Paraense Emilio Goeldi, ser. Antropologia* 70: 1–31.

Galeano, G. 2000. 'Forest Use at the Pacific Coast of Chocó, Colombia: A Quantitative Approach', *Economic Botany* 54: 358–76.

Ghimire, S.K., D. McKey and Y. Aumeeruddy Thomas. 2004. 'Heterogeneity in Ethnoecological Knowledge and Management of Medicinal Plants in the Himalayas of Nepal: Implications for Conservation', *Ecology and Society* 9(3): article 6.

Girón, L.M., V. Freire, A. Alonzo and A. Cáceres. 1991. 'Ethnobotanical Survey of the Medicinal Flora Used by the Caribs of Guatemala', *Journal of Ethnopharmacology* 34: 173–87.

Glick, T. 1997. 'Technology', in T. Barfield (ed.), *The Dictionary of Anthropology*. Oxford: Blackwell, pp. 464–66.

Godoy, R. 2001. *Indians, Markets, and Rain Forests: Theory, Methods, Analysis*. New York: Columbia University Press.

Godoy, R., N. Brokaw, D. Wilkie, D. Colón, A. Palermo, S. Lye and S. Wei. 1998. 'On Trade and Cognition: Markets and the Loss of Folk Knowledge among the Tawahka Indians', *Journal of Anthropological Research* 54: 219–33.

Godoy, R., V. Reyes-García, E. Byron, W. Leonard and V. Vadez. 2005. 'The Effect of Market Economies on the Well-Being of Indigenous Peoples and on Their Use of Renewable Natural Resources', *Annual Review of Anthropology* 34: 121–38.

Gómez-Baggethun, E., S. Mingorría, V. Reyes-García, L. Calvet and C. Montes. 2010. 'Traditional Ecological Knowledge Trends in the Transition to a Market Economy: Empirical Study in the Doñana Natural Areas', *Conservation Biology* 24(3): 721–29.

Gould, S.J. 1986. 'Evolution and the Triumph of Homology, or Why History Matters', *American Scientist* 74(1): 60–69.

Grenier, L. 1998. *Working with Indigenous Knowledge: A Guide for Researchers.* Ottawa: International Development Research Centre.

Griffin, D. 2001. 'Contributions to the Ethnobotany of the Cup'it Eskimo, Nunivak Island, Alaska', *Journal of Ethnobiology* 21(2): 91–127.

Grigorenko, E.L., E. Meier, J. Lipka, G. Mohatt, E. Yanez and R.J. Sternberg. 2004. 'The Relation between Academic and Practical Intelligence: A Case Study of the Tacit Knowledge of Native American Yup'ik People in Alaska', *Learning and Individual Differences* 14(4): 183–207.

Guest, G. 2002. 'Market Integration and the Distribution of Ecological Knowledge within an Ecuadorian Fishing Community', *Journal of Ecological Anthropology* 6: 38–49.

Guivant, J. 2003. 'Pesticide Use and Risk Perception: An Analysis from the Laboratory Fields', *International Journal of Sociology of Agriculture and Food* 11: 41–51.

Gupta, A.K. 1989. 'Scientists' Views of Farmers' Practices in India: Barriers to Effective Interaction', in R. Chambers, A. Pacey and L.A. Thrupp (eds), *Farmer First: Farmer Innovation and Agricultural Research.* London: Intermediate Technology Publications, pp. 24–30.

————.1997. 'The Honey Bee Network: Linking Knowledge-rich Grassroots Innovations', *Development* 40(4): 36–40.

Hallpike, C.R. 1980. *The Foundations of Primitive Thought.* Oxford: Oxford University Press.

Hanyani-Mlambo, B.T. and P. Hebinck. 1996. 'Formal and Informal Knowledge Networks in Conservation Forestry in Zimbabwe', *Indigenous Knowledge and Development Monitor* 4(3): 1–8.

Haruyama, T. 2004. *Nature of Traditional Ecological Knowledge Loss.* www. ps.ritsumei.ac.jp/assoc/policy_science/112/11212.pdf.

Heckler, S. 2007. 'Herbalism, Home Gardens, and Hybridization: Wõtïhã Medicine and Cultural Change', *Medical Anthropology Quarterly* 21(1): 41–63.

————.2009a. 'Introduction', in S. Heckler (ed.), *Landscape, Process and Power: Re-evaluating Traditional Environmental Knowledge.* New York: Berghahn Books, pp. 1–18.

———— (ed.). 2009b. *Landscape, Process and Power: Re-evaluating Traditional Environmental Knowledge.* New York: Berghahn Books.

Henrich, J. 2001. 'Cultural Transmission and the Diffusion of Innovations: Adoption Dynamics Indicate that Biased Cultural Transmission is the Predominate Force in Behavioral Change', *American Anthropologist* 103(4): 992–1013.

Hill, J. 2001. 'Dimensions of Attrition in Language Death', in L. Maffi (ed.), *On Biocultural Diversity: Linking Language, Knowledge, and the Environment.* Washington, DC: Smithsonian Institution Press, pp. 175–89.

Hobsbawm, E. and T. Ranger. 1983. *The Invention of Tradition.* Cambridge: Cambridge University Press.

Hoffman, B. and T. Gallaher. 2007. 'Relative Cultural Importance Indices in Quantitative Ethnobotany', *Ethnobotany Research and Applications* 5(1): 201–18.

Hoffman, S. 2003. 'Arawakan Women and the Erosion of Traditional Food Production in Amazonas, Venezuela', in P.L. Howard (ed.), *Women and Plants: Gender Relations in Biodiversity Management and Conservation*. London: Zed Books, pp. 258–72.

Howes, M. and R. Chambers. 1979. 'Indigenous Technical Knowledge: Analysis, Implications and Issues in Rural Development: Whose Knowledge Counts?', *IDS Bulletin* 10(2): 6–11.

————.1980. 'Indigenous Technical Knowledge: Analysis, Implications and Issues', in D. Brokensha, D.M. Warren and O. Werner (eds), *Indigenous Knowledge Systems and Development*. Lanham, MD: University Press of America, pp. 323–34.

Hunn, E. 1993. 'What is Traditional Ecological Knowledge?', in N. Williams and G. Baines (eds), *Traditional Ecological Knowledge: Wisdom for Sustainable Development*. Canberra: Centre for Resource and Environmental Studies, National Australian University, pp. 13–15.

————.1999. 'The Value of Subsistence for the Future of the World', in V.D. Nazarea (ed.), *Ethnoecology: Situated Knowledge/Located Lives*. Tucson: University of Arizona Press, pp. 23–36.

————.2001. 'Prospects for the Persistence of "Endemic" Cultural Systems of Traditional Environmental Knowledge: A Zapotec Example', in L. Maffi (ed.), *On Biocultural Diversity: Linking Language, Knowledge, and the Environment*. Washington, DC: Smithsonian Institution Press, pp. 118–32.

Hutterer, K. 1988. 'The Prehistory of Asian Rain Forests', in J.S. Denslow and C. Padoch (eds), *People of the Tropical Rain Forest*. Berkeley: University of California Press, pp. 63–72.

IDS Workshop. 1989. 'Farmers' Knowledge, Innovations, and Relation to Science', in R. Chambers, A. Pacey and L.A. Thrupp (eds), *Farmer First: Farmer Innovation and Agricultural Research*. London: Intermediate Technology Publications, pp. 31–38.

Inglis, J.T. (ed.). 1993. *Traditional Ecological Knowledge: Concepts and Cases*. Ottawa: International Program on Traditional Ecological Knowledge and International Development Research Centre.

Ingold, T. 2001. 'From the Transmission of Representations to the Education of Attention', in H. Whitehouse (ed.), *The Debated Mind: Evolutionary Psychology versus Ethnography*. Oxford: Berg, pp. 113–53.

Iskander, J. and R. Ellen. 2007. 'Innovation, "Hybrid" Knowledge and the Conservation of Relict Rainforest in Upland Banten', in R. Ellen (ed.), *Modern Crises and Traditional Strategies: Local Ecological Knowledge in Island Southeast Asia*. Oxford: Berghahn Books, pp. 133–42.

Jarvie, J. and B. Perumal. 1994. 'Ethnobotanical Uses and Loss of Knowledge Concerning Forest Trees among some Iban in Sarawak', *Tropis* 3: 155–62.

Johnson, A. 1972. 'Individuality and Experimentation in Traditional Agriculture', *Human Ecology* 1(2): 149–59.

Johnson, M. 1992. *Lore: Capturing Traditional Environmental Knowledge*. Ottawa: Dene Cultural Institute and International Development Research Centre.

Juma, C. 1987. 'Ecological Complexity and Agricultural Innovation: The Use of Indigenous Genetic Resources in Bungoma, Kenya'. Unpublished paper for the Workshop on Farmers and Agricultural Research: Complementary Methods, Institute of Development Studies, 26–31 July.

Kapferer, B. 1997. 'Social Change', in T. Barfield (ed.), *The Dictionary of Anthropology*. Oxford: Blackwell, pp. 428–29.

Kassam, A. 2002. 'Ethnotheory, Ethnopraxis: Ethnodevelopment in the Oromia Regional State of Ethiopia', in P. Sillitoe, A. Bicker and J. Pottier (eds), *Participating in Development: Approaches to Indigenous Knowledge*. ASA Monographs 39. London and New York: Routledge, pp. 64–81.

Katz, C. 1989. 'Herders, Gatherers and Foragers: The Emerging Botanies of Children in Rural Sudan', *Children's Environments Quarterly* 6(1): 46–53.

Kirch, P.V. and R.C. Green. 1987. 'History, Phylogeny, and Evolution in Polynesia', *Current Anthropology* 28(4): 431–56.

Kloppenberg, J. 1991. 'Social Theory and the De/Reconstruction of Agricultural Science: Local Knowledge for an Alternative Agriculture', *Rural Sociology* 56: 519–48.

Kohen, J.L. 1995. *Aboriginal Environmental Impact*. Sydney: UNSW Press.

Kristensen, M. and A.M. Lykke. 2003. 'Informant-based Valuation of Use and Conservation Preferences of Savanna Trees in Burkina Faso', *Economic Botany* 57: 203–17.

Kroeber, A.L. 1940. 'Stimulus Diffusion', *American Anthropologist* 42(1): 1–20.

Kummer, S., F. Leitgeb and C.R. Vogl. 2008. 'Changes as Triggers and as Results of Farmers' Experiments: Examples of Organic Farmers in Austria', in B. Dedieu and S. Zasser-Bedoya (eds), *Empowerment of the Rural Actors: A Renewal of Farming Systems Perspectives*. Clermont-Ferrand: INRA SAD, pp. 413–22.

Ladio, A.H. and M. Lozada. 2003. 'Comparison of Wild Edible Plant Diversity and Foraging Strategies in Two Aboriginal Communities of Northwestern Patagonia', *Biodiversity and Conservation* 12: 937–51.

_____.2004. 'Patterns of Use and Knowledge of Wild Edible Plants in Distinct Ecological Environments: A Case Study of a Mapuche Community from Northwestern Patagonia', *Biodiversity and Conservation* 13: 1153–73.

Lave, J. and E. Wenger. 1991. *Situated Learning: Legitimate Peripheral Participation*. Cambridge: Cambridge University Press.

Lawrence, A., O.L. Phillips, A.R. Ismodes, M. López, S. Rose, D. Word and J. Farfan. 2005. 'Local Values for Harvested Forest Plants in Madre de Dios, Peru: Towards a More Contextualised Interpretation of Quantitative Ethnobotanical Data', *Biodiversity and Conservation* 14: 45–79.

Lee, R.A., M.J. Balick, D. Lee Ling, F. Sohl, B.J. Brosi and W. Raynor. 2001. 'Cultural Dynamism and Change – An Example from the Federated States of Micronesia', *Economic Botany* 55(1): 9–13.

Leitgeb, F. and C.R. Vogl. 2010. 'Farmers' Experiments and Innovations and their Contribution to Cuba's Agricultural Innovation System', *Workshop 1.8: Knowledge Systems, Innovations and Social Learning in Organic Farming.* http://ifsa.boku.ac.at/cms/fileadmin/ Proceeding2010/2010_WS1.8_LeitgebVogl.pdf

Linden, E. 1991. 'Lost Tribes, Lost Knowledge', *Time* 138(12): 32–40.

Louv, R. 2006. *Last Child in the Woods: Saving Our Children from Nature-Deficit Disorder.* Chapel Hill, NC: Alonquin Books of Chapel Hill.

Lozada, M., A. Ladio and M. Weigandt. 2006. 'Cultural Transmission of Ethnobotanical Knowledge in a Rural Community of Northwestern Patagonia, Argentina', *Economic Botany* 60(4): 374–85.

Luoga, E.J., E.T.F. Witkowski and K. Balkwill. 2000. 'Differential Utilization and Ethnobotany of Trees in Kitulanghalo Forest Reserve and Surrounding Communal Lands, Eastern Tanzania', *Economic Botany* 54: 328–43.

Lykke, A.M., M.K. Kristensen and S. Ganaba. 2004. 'Valuation of Local Use and Dynamics of 56 Woody Species in the Sahel', *Biodiversity and Conservation* 13: 1961–90.

McCorkle, C.M. and G. McClure. 1995. 'Farmer Know-how and Communication for Technology Transfer: CTTA in Niger', in D.M. Warren, L.J. Slikkerveer and D. Brokensha (eds), *The Cultural Dimension of Development: Indigenous Knowledge Systems.* London: Intermediate Technology Publications, pp. 323–32.

Maffi, L. 1999. 'Linguistic Diversity', in D.A. Posey (ed.), *Cultural and Spiritual Values of Biodiversity.* London: Intermediate Technology Publications, pp. 21–35.

————.2001. 'Linking Language and Environment: A Coevolutionary Perspective', in C.L. Crumley (ed.), *New Directions in Anthropology & Environment.* Walnut Creek, CA: AltaMira Press, pp. 24–48.

————.2005. 'Linguistic, Cultural, and Biological Diversity', *Annual Review of Anthropology* 34: 599–617.

Malaza, M. 2003. 'Modernization and Gender Dynamics in the Loss of Agrobiodiversity in Swaziland's Food System', in P.L. Howard (ed.), *Women and Plants: Gender Relations in Biodiversity Management and Conservation.* London: Zed Books, pp. 243–57.

Marulanda, S.C. 2005. 'Transmission and Transformation of Traditional Environmental Knowledge in Indigenous Communities from the Amazon and the Peten: Cultural and Generational Variations'. Ph.D. dissertation, University of Illinois at Urbana-Champaign. Ann Arbor, MI: University Microfilms International.

Matavele, J. and M. Habib. 2000. 'Ethnobotany in Cabo Delgado, Mozambique: Use of Medicinal Plants', *Environment, Development and Sustainability* 2: 227–34.

Menzies, C.R. and C. Butler. 2006. 'Understanding Ecological Knowledge', in C.R. Menzies (ed.), *Traditional Ecological Knowledge and Resource Management.* Lincoln: University of Nebraska Press, pp. 1–17.

Mercader, J. 2003. 'Foragers of the Congo: The Early Settlement of the Ituri Forest', in J. Mercader (ed.), *Under the Canopy: The Archaeology of Tropical Forests.* New Brunswick, NJ: Rutgers University Press, pp. 93–116.

Millar, D. 1994. 'Experimenting Farmers in Northern Ghana', in I. Scoones and J. Thompson (eds), *Beyond Farmer First*. London: Intermediate Technology Publications, pp. 160–64.

Milton, K. 1991. 'Comparative Aspects of Diet in Amazonian Forest Dwellers', *Philosophical Transactions of the Royal Society*, Series B. 334: 253–63.

Miner, H. 1952. 'The Folk-Urban Continuum', *American Sociological Review* 17(5): 529–37.

Monteiro, J.M., U. Paulino de Albuquerque, E. Machado de Freitas Lins-Neto, E. Lima de Araújo and E.L. Cavalcanti de Amorim. 2006. 'Use Patterns and Knowledge of Medicinal Species among Two Rural Communities in Brazil's Semi-arid Northeastern Region', *Journal of Ethnopharmacology* 105: 173–86.

Moock, J.L. and R.E. Rhoades (eds). 1992. *Diversity, Farmer Knowledge, and Sustainability*. Ithaca, NY: Cornell University Press.

Mosha, R.S. 2000. *The Heartbeat of Indigenous Africa. A Study of Chagga Educational System*. New York: Garland Publishing.

Mühlhäusler, P. 1996. *Linguistic Ecology: Language Change and Linguistic Imperialism in the Pacific Rim*. London: Routledge.

Murphy, R.F. 1964. 'Social Change and Acculturation', *Transactions of the New York Academy of Sciences* 26: 849.

Nabhan, G.P. 1995. 'Losing Species, Languages and Stories: Cultural and Environmental Change in the Binational Southwest', *The Seedhead News* 51: 1–2.

————.1998a. *Cultures of Habitat: On Nature, Culture, and Story*. Washington, DC: Counterpoint.

————.1998b. 'Passing on a Sense of Place and Traditional Ecological Knowledge between Generations: A Primer for Native American Museum Educators and Community-based Cultural Education Projects', *People and Plants Handbook* 4: 30–33.

Navchoo, I.A. and G.M. Buth. 1990. 'Ethnobotany of Ladakh, India: Beverages, Narcotics, Food', *Economic Botany* 44(3): 318–21.

Nesheim, I., S.S. Dhillion and K.A. Stolen. 2006. 'What Happens to Traditional Knowledge and Use of Natural Resources when People Migrate?', *Human Ecology* 34: 99–131.

Nettle, D. and S. Romaine. 2000. *Vanishing Voices: The Extinction of the World's Languages*. Oxford: Oxford University Press.

Nguyen, M.L.T. 2003. 'Comparison of Food Plant Knowledge between Urban Vietnamese Living in Vietnam and in Hawai'i', *Economic Botany* 57(4): 472–80.

Nolan, J.M. 1998. 'The Roots of Tradition: Social Ecology, Cultural Geography, and Medicinal Plant Knowledge in the Ozark-Ouachita Highlands', *Journal of Ethnobiology* 18(2): 249–69.

Nolan, J.M. and M.C. Robbins. 1999. 'Cultural Conservation of Medicinal Plant Use in the Ozarks', *Human Organization* 58: 67–72.

Nygren, A. 1999. 'Local Knowledge in the Environment Development Discourse: From Dichotomies to Situated Knowledges', *Critique of Anthropology* 19(3): 267–88.

O'Brien, C.M. 2010. 'Do They Really "Know Nothing"? An Inquiry into Ethnobotanical Knowledge of Students in Arizona, USA', *Ethnobotany Research & Applications* 8: 35–47.

Ohmagari, K. and F. Berkes. 1997. 'Transmission of Indigenous Knowledge and Bush Skills among the Western James Bay Cree Women of Subarctic Canada', *Human Ecology* 25(2): 197–222.

Olsen, C.S. and F. Helles. 1997. 'Medicinal Plants, Markets, and Margins in the Nepal Himalaya: Trouble in Paradise', *Mountain Research and Development* 17: 363–74.

Ososki, A., M.J. Balick and D.C. Daly. 2007. 'Medicinal Plants and Cultural Variation across Dominican Rural, Urban, and Transnational Landscapes', in A. Pieroni and I. Vandebroek (eds), *Traveling Cultures and Plants: The Ethnobiology and Ethnopharmacy of Human Migrations*. Oxford: Berghahn Books, pp. 14–38.

Palmer, C.T. 2004a. 'The Inclusion of Recently Introduced Plants in the Hawaiian Ethnopharmacopoeia', *Economic Botany* 58(Supplement): S280–S293.

————.2004b. '*Plantago* spp. and *Bidens* spp.: A Case Study of Change in Hawaiian Herbal Medicine', *Journal of Ethnobiology* 24(1): 13–31.

Peluso, N.L. 1992. 'The Political Ecology of Extraction and Extractive Reserves in East Kalimantan, Indonesia', *Development and Change* 49(4): 49–74.

————.1995. 'Whose Woods are These? Counter-mapping Forest Territories in Kalimantan, Indonesia', *Antipode* 27(4): 383–406.

Pergams, O.R.W. and P.A. Zaradic. 2008. 'Evidence for a Fundamental and Pervasive Shift away from Nature-based Recreation', *Proceedings of the National Academy of Sciences* 105: 2295–300.

Phillips, O., and A.H. Gentry. 1993. 'The Useful Plants of Tambopata, Peru: II. Additional Hypothesis Testing in Quantitative Ethnobotany', *Economic Botany* 47(1): 33–43.

Phillips, O., A.H. Gentry, C. Reynel, P. Wilkin and C. Gálvez-Durand. 1994. 'Quantitative Ethnobotany and Amazonian Conservation', *Conservation Biology* 8: 225–48.

Pieroni, A. and I. Vandebroek (eds). 2007a. *Traveling Cultures and Plants: The Ethnobiology and Ethnopharmacy of Human Migrations*. Oxford: Berghahn Books.

————.2007b. 'Introduction', in A. Pieroni and I. Vandebroek (eds), *Traveling Cultures and Plants: The Ethnobiology and Ethnopharmacy of Human Migrations*. Oxford: Berghahn Books, pp. 1–13.

Pinedo-Vasquez, M., D. Zarin, P. Zipp and J. Chota-Inuma. 1990. 'Use Values of Tree Species in a Communalm Forest Reserve in Northeast Peru', *Conservation Biology* 4: 405–16.

Plotkin, M.J. 1988. 'Ethnobotany and Conservation in the Guianas: The Indians of Southern Suriname', in F. Almeda and C. Pringle (eds), *Tropical Rainforests: Diversity and Conservation*. San Francisco: California Academy of Sciences, pp. 87–109.

————.1993. *Tales of a Shaman's Apprentice: An Ethnobotanist Searches for New Medicines in the Amazon Rainforest*. New York: Viking.

Posey, D. (ed.). 1999. *Cultural and Spiritual Values of Biodiversity*. London: Intermediate Technology Publications.

Putsche, L. 2000. 'A Reassessment of Resource Depletion, Market Dependency, and Culture Change on a Shipibo Reserve in the Peruvian Amazon', *Human Ecology* 28(1): 131–40.

Pyle, R.M. 1993. *The Thunder Tree: Lessons from an Urban Wildland*. Boston: Houghton Mifflin.

Redfield, R. 1941. *The Folk Culture of Yucatan*. Chicago: The University of Chicago Press.

Reichel-Dolmatoff, G. 1976. 'Cosmology as Ecological Analysis: A View from the Rain Forest', *Man* (N.S.) 11(3): 307–18.

Reij, C. and A. Waters-Bayer (eds). 2001. *Farmer Innovation in Africa: A Source of Inspiration for Agricultural Development*. London: Earthscan.

Reyes-Garcia, V., V. Vadez, E. Byron, L. Apaza, W.R. Leonard, E. Pérez and D. Wilkie. 2005. 'Market Economy and the Loss of Folk Knowledge of Plant Uses: Estimates from the Tsimane' of the Bolivian Amazon', *Current Anthropology* 46(4): 651–56.

Reyes-Garcia, V., V. Vadez, T. Huanca, W.R. Leonard and T. McDade. 2007. 'Economic Development and Local Ecological Knowledge: A Deadlock? Quantitative Research from a Native Amazonian Society', *Human Ecology* 35(3): 371–77.

Rhoades, R.E. 1987. *Farmers and Experimentation*. Agriculture Administration (Research and Extension) Discussion Paper No. 21. London: Overseas Development Institute.

————.1989. 'The Role of Farmers in the Creation of Agricultural Technology', in R. Chambers, A. Pacey and L.A. Thrupp (eds), *Farmer First: Farmer Innovation and Agricultural Research*. London: Intermediate Technology Publications, pp. 3–9.

Rhoades, R.E. and A. Bebbington. 1995. 'Farmers Who Experiment: An Untapped Resource for Agricultural Research and Development', in D.M. Warren, L.J. Slikkerveer and D. Brokensha (eds), *The Cultural Dimension of Development: Indigenous Knowledge Systems*. London: Intermediate Technology Publications, pp. 296–307.

Rhoades, R.E. and P. Bidegaray. 1987. *Land Use and Cropping Strategies in the Peruvian Jungle*. Lima: International Potato Center.

Rhoades, R.E. and R. Booth. 1982. 'Farmer-back-to-Farmer: A Model for Generating Acceptable Agricultural Technology', *Agricultural Administration* 11: 127–37.

Richards, P. 1985. *Indigenous Agricultural Revolution: Ecology and Food Production in West Africa*. Boulder, CO: Westview Press.

————.1989. 'Agriculture as a Performance', in R. Chambers, A. Pacey and L.A. Thrupp (ed.), *Farmer First: Farmer Innovation and Agricultural Research*. London: Intermediate Technology Publications, pp. 39–43.

————.1994. 'Local Knowledge formation and validation: the case of rice production in Central Sierra Leone', in I. Scoones and J. Thompson (ed.), *Beyond Farmer First*. London: Intermediate Technology Publications, pp. 165–69.

Rival, L. 2009. 'Towards an Understanding of the Huaorani Ways of Knowing and Naming Plants', in M.N. Alexiades (ed.), *Mobility and Migration in Indigenous Amazonia: Contemporary Ethnoecological Perspectives*. Oxford: Berghahn Books, pp. 47–68.

Rocha, J.M. 2005. 'Measuring Traditional Agro-ecological Knowledge: An Example from Peasants in the Peruvian Andes', *Field Methods* 17(4): 356–72.

Rocha Silva, A.J. and L.H. Cavalcante Andrade. 2006. 'Cultural Significance of Plants in Communities Located in the Coastal Forest Zone of the State of Pernambuco, Brazil', *Human Ecology* 34(3): 447–65.

Ross, N. 2002. 'Cognitive Aspects of Intergenerational Change: Mental Models, Cultural Change, and Environmental Behavior among the Lacandon Maya of Southern Mexico', *Human Organization* 61: 125–38.

Ross, N. and D.L. Medin. 2005. 'Ethnography and Experiments: Cultural Models and Expertise Effects Elicited with Experimental Research Techniques', *Field Methods* 17(2): 131–49.

Rossato, S.C., H.D.F. Leitão-Filho and A. Begossi. 1999. 'Ethnobotany of Caiçaras of the Atlantic Forest Coast (Brazil)', *Economic Botany* 53: 387–95.

Sahlins, M. 1992. 'The Economics of Develop-man in the Pacific', *Anthropology and Aesthetics* 21: 13–25.

_____.1994. 'Goodbye to Tristes Tropes: Ethnography in the Context of Modern World History', in R. Borofsky (ed.), *Assessing Cultural Anthropology*. New York: McGraw-Hill Inc., pp. 377–94.

Santos, R.V., N.M. Flowers, C. Coimbra and S. Gugelmin. 1997. 'Tapirs, Tractors, and Tapes: The Changing Economy and Ecology of the Xavante Indians of Central Brazil', *Human Ecology* 25(4): 545–66.

Schank, R. and R. Abelson. 1977. *Scripts, Plans, Goals and Understanding*. New York: Wiley.

Schaub, M.H. 2008. *Transitions in Acculturation: The Psycho-social Adjustments of American Immigrants*. Netherlands: Tilburg University.

Schultes, R.E. 1994. 'Burning the Library of Amazonia', *The Sciences* 34(2): 24–31.

Schultz, T. 1964. *Transforming Traditional Agriculture*. New Haven, CT: Yale University Press.

Scoones, I. and J. Thompson (eds). 1994. *Beyond Farmer First*. London: Intermediate Technology Publications.

Shackleton, S.E., C.M. Shackleton, T.R. Netshiluvhi, B.S. Geach, A. Balance and D.H.K. Fairbanks. 2002. 'Use Patterns and Value of Savanna Resources in Three Rural Villages in South Africa', *Economic Botany* 56: 130–46.

Shanley, P. and N.A. Rosa. 2004. 'Eroding Knowledge: An Ethnobotanical Inventory in Eastern Amazonia's Logging Frontier', *Economic Botany* 58: 135–60.

Sillitoe, P. 2002. 'Participant Observation to Participatory Development: Making Anthropology Work', in P. Sillitoe, A. Bicker and J. Pottier (eds), *Participating in Development: Approaches to Indigenous Knowledge*. London: Routledge, pp. 1–23.

_____.2007. 'Local Science vs. Global Science: An Overview', in P. Sillitoe (ed.), *Local Science vs. Global Science: Approaches to Indigenous Knowledge in International Development*. Oxford: Berghahn Books, pp. 1–22.

Snively, G. and J. Corsiglia. 2001. 'Discovering Indigenous Science: Implications for Science Education', *Science Education* 85(1): 6–34.

Somnasanc, P. and G. Moreno-Black. 2000. 'Knowing, Gathering and Eating: Knowledge and Attitudes about Wild Food in an Asian Village in Northeastern Thailand', *Journal of Ethnobiology* 20(2): 197–216.

Souto, T. 2009. 'Ethnobotanical Knowledge and Forest Reliance of Three Rural Non-Indigenous Communities that Reside in the Lower Caura River, Southern Venezuela'. Ph.D. dissertation. University of Hawai'i at Manoa.

Sowerine, J.C. 2004. 'The Socio-ecological Landscape of Dao Traditional Botanical Medicine: A Tradition in Process', in T. Carlson and L. Maffi (eds), *Ethnobotany and Conservation of Biocultural Diversity*. Advances in Economic Botany Series. Bronx, NY: The New York Botanical Garden Press. pp. 235–62.

Spielman, D.J., J. Ekboir, K. Davis and C.M.O. Ochieng. 2008. 'An Innovation Systems Perspective on Strengthening Agricultural Education and Training in Sub-Saharan Africa', *Agricultural Systems* 98(1): 1–9.

Spriggs, M. 1993. 'The Current Relevance of Ethnohistorical and Archaeological Systems', in N.W. Williams and G. Baines (eds), *Traditional Ecological Knowledge: Wisdom for Sustainable Development*. Canberra: Centre for Resource and Environmental Studies, National Australian University, pp. 109–14.

Sternberg, R.J., C. Nokes, P. Wenzel Geissler, R. Prince, F. Okatcha, D.A. Bundy and E.L. Grigorenko. 2001. 'The Relationship between Academic and Practical Intelligence: A Case Study in Kenya', *Intelligence* 29: 401–18.

Sterponi, L. 2010. 'Learning Communicative Competence', in D.F. Lancy, J. Bock and S. Gaskins (eds), *The Anthropology of Learning in Childhood*. Walnut Creek, CA: AltaMira Press, pp. 235–59.

Steward, J.H. 1967. 'Perspectives in Modernization: Introduction to the Studies', in J.H. Steward (ed.), *Three African Tribes in Transition. Volume I of Contemporary Change in Traditional Societies*. Urbana: University of Illinois Press, pp. 1–56.

Stolzenbach, A. 1994. 'Learning by Improvization: Farmers' Experimentation in Mali', in I. Scoones and J. Thompson (eds), *Beyond Farmer First*. London: Intermediate Technology Publications, pp. 155–59.

Stone, D. (ed.). 1984. *Pre-Colombian Plant Migration*. Papers of the Peabody Museum of Archaeology and Ethnology, Vol. 76. Cambridge, MA: Harvard University Press.

Stone, G. 2004. 'Biotechnology and the Political Ecology of Information in India', *Human Organisation* 63(2): 127–40.

———.2007. 'The Birth and Death of Traditional Knowledge: Paradoxical Effects of Biotechnology in India', in C. McManis (ed.), *Biodiversity and the Law: Intellectual Property, Biotechnology and Traditional Knowledge*. London: Earthscan, pp. 207–38.

Stross, B. 1973. 'Acquisition of Botanical Terminology by Tzeltal Children', in M.S. Edmonson (ed.), *Meaning in Mayan Languages*. The Hague: Mouton, pp. 107–41.

Tenzin, K. 2006. 'Quantitative Ethnobotany and Variation in Local Knowledge: A Case for Farmers from the Punakha District in Western Bhutan'. Master's thesis. Cornell University.

Thomas, D.S.G. and C. Twyman. 2004. 'Good or Bad Rangeland? Hybrid Knowledge, Science, and Local Understandings of Vegetation Dynamics in the Kalahari', *Land Degradation and Development* 15: 215–31.

Toledo Maya Cultural Council. 1997. *Maya Atlas: The Struggle to Preserve Maya Land in Southern Belize*. Berkeley, CA: North Atlantic Books.

Turner, N., I.J. Davidson-Hunt and M. O'Flaherty. 2003. 'Living on the Edge: Ecological and Cultural Edges as Sources of Diversity for Social-ecological Resilience', *Human Ecology* 31(3): 439–60.

Turner, N. and K. Turner. 2008. '"Where our women used to get the food": Cumulative Effects and Loss of Ethnobotanical Knowledge and Practice. Case Study from Coastal British Colombia', *Botany* 86: 103–15.

Ugent, D. 2000. 'Medicine, Myths and Magic: The Folk Healers of a Mexican Market', *Economic Botany* 54: 27–43.

UNEP. 2006. 'Millennium Ecosystem Assessment', in C.J. Cleveland (ed.), *Encyclopedia of Earth*. Washington, DC: Environmental Information Coalition, National Council for Science and the Environment.

United Nations. 1987. *Report of the World Commission on Environment and Development*. General Assembly Resolution 42/187, 11 December 1987.

———.1992. *Convention on Biological Diversity*. http://www.cbd.int/doc/legal/cbd-en.pdf

Vandebroek, I., M.J. Balick, J. Yukes, L. Durán, F. Kronenberg, C. Wade, A.L. Ososki, L. Cushman, R. Lantigua, M. Mejía and L. Robineau. 2007. 'Use of Medicinal Plants by Dominican Immigrants in New York City for the Treatment of Common Health Conditions: A Comparative Analysis with Literature Data from the Dominican Republic', in A. Pieroni and I. Vandebroek (eds), *Traveling Cultures and Plants: The Ethnobiology and Ethnopharmacy of Human Migrations*. Oxford: Berghahn Books, pp. 39–63.

Vandebroek, I., J. Calewaert, S. De Jonckheere, S. Sanca, L. Semo, P. Van Damme, L. Van Puyvelde and N. De Kimpe. 2004. 'Use of Medicinal Plants and Pharmaceuticals by Indigenous Communities in the Bolivian Andes and Amazon', *Bulletin of the World Health Organization* 82: 243–50.

Van den Eynden, V., E. Cueva and O. Cabrera. 2004. 'Of "Climbing Peanuts" and "Dog's Testicles": Mestizo and Shuar Plant Nomenclature in Ecuador', *Journal of Ethnobiology* 24(2): 279–306.

Vansina, J. 1990. *Paths in the Rainforests: Toward a History of Political Tradition in Equatorial Africa*. Madison: University of Wisconsin Press.

Voeks, R.A. and A. Leony. 2004. 'Forgetting the Forest: Assessing Medicinal Plant Erosion in Eastern Brazil', *Economic Botany* 58(Supplement): S294–S306.

Voeks, R.A. and S. Nyawa. 2001. 'Healing Flora of the Brunei Dusun', *Borneo Research Bulletin* 32: 178–95.

Volpato, G., A.A. Emhamed, S.M.L. Saleh, A. Broglia and S. di Lello. 2009. 'Procurement of Traditional Remedies and Transmission of Medicinal Knowledge among Sahrawi People Displaced in Southwestern Algerian Refugee Camps', in A. Pieroni and I. Vandebroek (eds), *Traveling Cultures and Plants. The Ethnobiology and Ethnopharmacy of Human Migrations*. Oxford: Berghahn Books, pp. 245–69.

Warren, D.M. 2004. 'The Role of Indigenous Knowledge Systems in Facilitating Sustainable Approaches to Development: An Annotated Bibliography', in G. Sanga and G. Ortalli (eds), *Nature Knowledge: Ethnoscience, Cognition, and Utility*. New York: Berghahn Books, pp. 317 30.

Warren, D.M., L.J. Slikkerveer and D. Brokensha (eds). 1995. *The Cultural Dimension of Development: Indigenous Knowledge Systems*. London: Intermediate Technology Publications.

Wester, L. and S. Yongvanit. 1995. 'Biological Diversity and Community Lore in Northeastern Thailand', *Journal of Ethnobiology* 15: 71–87.

Whistler, W.A. 1992. *Polynesian Herbal Medicine*. Lawai: National Tropical Botanical Garden.

Wolff, P. and D.L. Medin. 2001. 'Measuring the Evolution and Devolution of Folk-biological Knowledge', in L. Maffi (ed.), *On Biocultural Diversity: Linking Language, Knowledge and the Environment*. Washington, DC: Smithsonian Institution Press, pp. 212–27.

Woodbury, A.C. 1993. 'A Defense of the Proposition, "When a Language Dies, a Culture Dies"', in R. Queen and R. Barrett (eds), *SALSA I: Proceedings of the 1st Annual Symposium about Language and Society*, Texas Linguistic Forum 33, pp. 101–29.

Wu, B. and J. Pretty. 2004. 'Social Connectedness in Marginal Rural China: The Case of Farmer Innovation Circles in Zhidan, North Shaanxi', *Agriculture and Human Values* 21: 81–92.

Yen, D.E. 1991. 'Polynesian Cultigens and Cultivars: The Question of Origin', in P.A. Cox and S.A. Banack (eds), *Islands, Plants, and Polynesians: An Introduction to Polynesian Ethnobotany*. Portland: Dioscorides Press.

Zalocusky, K.A. and P.C. Short. 2007. *Environmental Education as a Fulcrum for Consilience in Conservation Efforts*. Conference of the North American Association of Environmental Education. Virginia Beach, VA.

Zarger, R. 2002. 'Acquisition and Transmission of Subsistence Knowledge by Q'eqchi' Maya in Belize', in J.R. Stepp, F.S. Wyndham and R.K. Zarger (eds), *Ethnobiology and Biocultural Diversity: Proceedings of the Seventh International Congress of Ethnobiology*. International Society of Ethnobiology. Athens, GA: University of Georgia Press, pp. 593–603.

_____.2010. 'Learning the Environment', in D.F. Lancy, J. Bock and S. Gaskins (eds), *The Anthropology of Learning in Childhood*. Walnut Creek, CA: AltaMira Press, pp. 341–69.

Zarger, R. and J.R. Stepp. 2004. 'Persistence of Botanical Knowledge among Tzeltal Maya Children', *Current Anthropology* 45(3): 413–18.

Zent, E.L., S. Zent and L. Marius. 2004. 'Autodemarcando la Tierra: Explorando las Ideas, los Árboles y Caminos Hotï', *Boletín Antropológica* 59(2): 313–38.

Zent, S. 1993. 'Donde no hay Médico: Las Consecuencias Culturales y Demográficas de la Distribución Desigual de los Servicios Médicos Modernos entre los Piaroa', *Antropológica* 79: 41–84.

————.1997. 'Reinventando los Sistemas de Atención Médica para las Comunidades Indígenas: El Papel de las Medicinas Tradicionales', in J. Chiappino and C. Ales (eds), *Del Microscopio a la Maraca*. Caracas: Editorial Ex Libris, pp. 339–49.

————.1999. 'The Quandary of Conserving Ethnobotanical Knowledge: A Piaroa Example', in T. Gragson and B. Blount (eds), *Ethnoecology: Knowledge, Resources, Rights*. Athens, GA: University of Georgia Press, pp. 90–124.

————.2001. 'Acculturation and Ethnobotanical Knowledge Loss among the Piaroa of Venezuela: Demonstration of a Quantitative Method for the Empirical Study of TEK Change', in L. Maffi (ed.), *On Biocultural Diversity: Linking Language, Knowledge, and the Environment*. Washington, DC: Smithsonian Institution Press, pp. 190–211.

————.2009. 'Traditional Ecological Knowledge (TEK) and Biocultural Diversity: A Close-up Look at Linkages, Delearning Trends, and Changing Patterns of Transmission', in P. Bates, M. Chiba, S. Kube and D. Nakashima (eds), *Learning and Knowing in Indigenous Societies Today*. Paris: UNESCO, pp. 39–58.

Zent, S. and E.L. Zent. 2007. 'On Biocultural Diversity from a Venezuelan Perspective: Tracing the Interrelationships among Biodiversity, Culture Change, and Legal Reforms', in C. McManis (ed.), *Biodiversity and the Law: Intellectual Property, Biotechnology & Traditional Knowledge*. London: Earthscan/James and James Publishers, pp. 91–114.

————. 2011. 'Ethnobiological Methods for Ethnomycological Research: Quantitative Approaches', in A. Cunningham and X. Yang (eds), *Mushrooms in Forests and Wildlands: Resource Management Values and Local Livelihoods*. London: Earthscan, pp. 61–85.

Zepeda, O. and J. Hill. 1995. *Papago Dialect Survey*. Unpublished manuscript. Tucson, AZ: University of Arizona.

Zerner, C. 1994. 'Through a Green Lens: The Construction of Customary Environmental Law and Community in Indonesia's Maluku Islands', *Law and Society Review* 28(5): 1079–122.

Chapter 9

TRANSMITTING PENAN BASKETRY KNOWLEDGE AND PRACTICE

Rajindra K. Puri

Introduction

Basketry is an important handicraft industry for poor forest-dependent peoples. It requires a vast array of knowledge – of plants, dyes, tools – and laborious practical tasks and skills, such as harvesting, processing and weaving. Where baskets are used for domestic purposes, for carrying and storage, they may be quickly substituted with store-bought manufactured cloth and plastic products. If basket production survives it is often only as an art form or as souvenirs for tourists, so the number of basket makers may shrink together with the knowledge and skills required for its continuity. Thus, it is claimed that global capitalism and a modernizing 'develop-mentalism' insidiously subverts age-old traditions and contributes to homogenization of societies and the loss of biocultural diversity (Godoy et al. 2005; Maffi 2005). But this does not happen everywhere, and more attention needs to be given to the economic and cultural uses and meanings of these products which show considerable inertia to change and which continue to drive local economies that serve to maintain traditional knowledge and production, albeit with adaptations and innovations. This is certainly the case for the Penan Benalui people of the Kayan-Mentarang area of East Kalimantan, Indonesian Borneo, who continue to harvest wild stands of rattan and make plant-based dyes for the numerous basket products that they use, trade and sell everyday, despite the presence of cheap and easily available substitutes. This chapter describes Penan basket making and the way it is simultaneously adapting to new circumstances while still maintaining continuity with past traditions. The explanation for this continuity resides in the complex intersections of processes of cultural transmission and the sociocultural and economic contexts in which they occur. Of particular importance is the way in which Penan egalitarianism opens up the possibilities for simultaneous transmission and transformation of basketry practices between and within the generations.

Anthropology of Knowledge

Before describing this study of Penan basketry knowledge, I want to briefly explain how I conceptualize both knowledge and its transmission, and in doing so touch on some of the recent literature from anthropology and ethnobiology.

Studies of knowledge and knowing sit at the heart of social and cultural anthropology, yet, as Marchand (2010: S3) has recently observed, 'the majority of anthropological analyses stop short of providing satisfying explanations (or approximations) of how learning, knowing and practice actually occur, take shape, and continually transform *with* situated bodies and minds'. In the special edition of the *Journal of the Royal Anthropological Institute* (JRAI) which Marchand edits, many of the authors argue that knowledge is never simply transmitted from person to person, generation to generation or culture to culture; knowledge is 'made' in a process of shared production '*between* people and *with* the world' (ibid.). Likewise, following Ingold (2011: 238), anthropologists 'make' their knowledge *with* the people that are their hosts, friends and teachers, in the well-described process of participant observation, including *active* participant observation (Nelson 1969, 1973), which may involve deep immersion in those practices under study as an apprentice, and eventually as a practitioner themselves. What we learn is very much contingent upon whom we are with, how we are taught or what we are allowed to see and experience, and under what conditions (environmental, social, psychological) we happen to experience this process. In order to advance our understanding of these 'situated and inter-subjective practices in "making knowledge"', Marchand (2010: S7) argues for a more interdisciplinary approach to the study of knowing and learning, incorporating in addition to a more engaged ethnography (that may include apprenticeship), insights and methods from phenomenology, anatomy and neurosciences, conventional psychology, and the cognitive sciences. He also advocates more attention to individual life-histories (or, 'lifelines' *sensu* Rose 1998; see also Ingold 2007) in order to demonstrate the way that particular minds, bodies and environments interact to produce unique individuals. Of course, we know that when examined closely, all individuals are a unique result of the dialectal interaction of genes and environment, the biological and the

sociocultural, nature and nurture. But, we also know that, by definition, many traditions (e.g. in crafts, music, dance, myth and ritual)
are shared and endure; so then, how do these lifelines of individuals,
family members, residents and citizens interact to co-produce these
shared practices and enduring bodies of knowledge?

Perhaps even more vexing is the way egalitarian societies, such
as those found in many of the world's extant hunter-gatherer populations, manage to perpetuate traditions despite an often anarchic
social structure based on values of independence, freedom and
mobility, while being devoid of obligations to conform, and lacking
kinship lineages, political hierarchies and other coercive authorities (Gibson and Sillander 2011). Such is the case with the formerly
nomadic Western Penan of central Borneo's mountains and tropical
forests (Needham 1972; Brosius 1991; Puri 2005), who, despite set-
tling down into villages, taking up rice agriculture and becoming
more integrated into a market economy and a more socially stratified Indonesian society, have maintained their egalitarian ethos and
many of their traditional practices and material culture.

Ethnobiological Approaches to Knowledge Transmission

By knowledge transmission, ethnobiologists usually mean the learning and teaching of environmental knowledge between and among
generations. Knowledge is conceived of as abstract representations in
the mind that bear some resemblance to the naturalistic reality they
are said to represent, and may include facts, truths and principles
(Gregory 1987 in Puri 2005: 15; see also Barth 2002, cf. Sillitoe
2010). Knowledge includes the *knowing of things* (facts), as well as
knowing how to use those facts. It includes both verbal and non-verbal
(or tacit) kinds of knowledge, and both theoretical (i.e. known but not
used) and practical (i.e. enacted or instantiated) knowledge (see Ellen
and Harris 2000). Local environmental knowledge is substantively
concerned with biotic and abiotic entities and their relationships, including humans and their activities, but is also intimately related to
other cultural domains, such as religious and medical belief systems,
social structures and linguistic forms and expressions. 'Due to its
multi-dimensional and interconnected nature, the demarcation of environmental knowledge from other kinds of cultural-based knowledge
is somewhat ambiguous and arbitrary, and in many societies implies
a conceptual imposition that has no meaning for local members' (Zent
and Maffi 2008: 15).

With regard to practical aspects of environmental knowledge, in
my own work on hunting knowledge (Puri 1994; Puri 2005) and here
on basket-making knowledge (Puri et al. 2004), I have distinguished
physical or kinesthetic skills (such as throwing spears, stalking, or

shaving rattan strips for weaving) from managerial skills (such as organizing production and dealing with contingencies), and have labelled these 'behavioural' and 'performance' knowledge. Both are types of practical knowledge, often non-verbal and tacit, but also involving verbal instructions (for learning behavioural skills) and verbal explanations (for decisions made in the course of an activity). In this conceptualization of knowledge there is no strict distinction between knowledge (as text) and practice (cf. Berkes 1999), for what one needs to 'know' in order to hunt is certainly not limited to the names of animals or fruit trees, or myths and stories about other hunts, or instructions about how one should attempt to find and capture prey. Hunting and basketry knowledge, like most environmental knowledge, is embedded in activity, and can be defined in terms of a sequenced set of tasks (or a taskonomy *sensu* Dougherty and Keller 1982), in which the declarative, the behavioural and the performative are integrated (Puri 2005). With regard to knowledge transmission, 'declarative, behavioural and performance' knowledge forms can be thought of as cultural, in the sense of being, for the most part, socially learned and transmitted.

This definition of culture derives in part from biological models of social learning, cultural evolution and cultural transmission (Durham 1991: 155–56; see also Lumsden and Wilson 1981; Cavalli-Sforza and Feldman 1981; Boyd and Richerson 1985; Reyes-García et al. 2004) that pre-date recent interest in the transmission of ethno-biological knowledge (see below). These biological models often define culture as the process of social learning, rather than the content (norms, values, beliefs) or substantive knowledge that is being transmitted and learned. In contrast to individual learning, anything that is shared through mechanisms of transmission is considered cultural, and what is shared is assumed to be useful and adaptive – maladaptive knowledge is, however, expected, and may even be propagated if its impact is too subtle or long term to be detected, or if it serves individual or group ambition. The dominant conceptual framework is the 'dual inheritance model', whereby culture is seen as a second non-genetic inheritance system of traits and behaviours that are selected based on 'cultural fitness' – that is, according to values, beliefs and norms particular to a society or group (Cavalli-Sforza and Feldman 1981; Boyd and Richerson 1985). Random (i.e. stochastic) factors are also accounted for in this model, such that cultural variants may 'drift' along with factors such as fluctuating population sizes in a manner directly analogous to that of genetic drift (Bentley et al. 2004). Cultural knowledge can be transmitted from parents to children (vertical), among peers (horizontal), and between non-parental members of older generations (such as uncles, aunts, grandparents) and children (oblique) (Cavalli-Sforza and Feldman 1981). Vertical transmission is believed to be the most conservative, horizontal transmission allows for the spread of new ideas quickly in a population, and oblique transmission, perhaps, ensures continuity down and across the generations, especially for knowledge concerning infrequent events (migrations, epidemics, weather extremes), and in contexts where other pathways have been lost. Of course, some traits are transmitted along multiple pathways, while others are limited to one or another (Cavalli-Sforza and Feldman 1981).

Cultural transmission is biased directly or indirectly to favour certain variants that are perceived to be better, according to culturally specific criteria. Teaching directly biases (or favours) transmission of knowledge that teachers want or are compelled to teach. However, success may depend on the social composition of the event: parent to child, peer to peer, one to one, one to many, or many to one – all have varying degrees of success. Intelligence, social status, wealth, fame and prejudice are all factors that influence the likelihood that an idea or bit of knowledge is going to be passed from teacher(s) to student(s), and remembered and acted upon. The motivation of the student is clearly an important factor as well, as all teachers and even some students will admit. Richerson and Boyd (2005: 164) describe three indirect biases that affect transmission: conformist bias, such as peer pressure among youths; content bias, such as demonstration plots, which affect perceived advantages; and prestige bias, favouring knowledge or cultural traits that elevate statuses. Thus, what eventually is learned or acquired by students, youth in general, or indeed any person in society, is the result of these interacting biases. Transmission of culture and knowledge by social learning is a complex process, one that also interacts with individual learning and biological predispositions all taking place in a particular social-ecological context.

Other anthropological research on the nature of knowledge has suggested that not all shared knowledge can be transmitted and learned in the same way (Bloch 1991; Barth 1995; Puri 2005). For instance, we in the West distinguish universities for 'book learning' from technical schools for 'experiential learning' or on-the-job-training in trades. And some ethnobiologists are considering transmission mechanisms such as 'enskilment' that do not necessarily require intentional teaching or a social environment, and instead rely on contextual factors to create the environment for individual learning of what is essentially shared, cultural knowledge (Ingold 2000; Ellen 2009). Finally, the social process of validating and accepting individual learning and innovation is critical to understanding the dynamic nature of knowledge in today's contexts (Ellen et al. 2000). Thus, the dual inheritance model offers an important framework upon which to build a more ethnobiologically informed model of cultural transmission that recognizes the multidimensionality and interrelated aspects of knowledge described above.

Ethnobiological interest in knowledge transmission has increased in the last few decades (Hewlett and Cavalli-Sforza 1986; Inglis 1993; Ohmagari and Berkes 1997; Wilbert 2002; Zarger 2002; Nakashima 2005; Puri 2005; Reyes-García et al. 2007, 2009; Reyes García et al. and Zent, this volume), in part as a response to newly recognized threats to local and indigenous knowledge, which had only recently been 'rediscovered' and identified as an important resource for rural development (e.g. crop development, pest management), health care (e.g. medicinal plants), biological conservation (sustainable use practices) and cultural survival, among others (Plotkin 1988; Chambers et al. 1989; Inglis 1993; Warren et al. 1995; Sillitoe 1998; Posey 2000; Sillitoe et al. 2002). There are, however, several important studies that foreshadowed its emergence, some of these derive from an earlier concern among anthropologists with explaining variation in cultural knowledge and practices (Harris 1968: 585; Gardner 1966; Sankoff 1971; Pelto and Pelto 1975; Dougherty 1979), which led to a view of culture as a 'partially shared and socially patterned knowledge pool' (Strauss and Quinn 1997; Zent and Maffi 2008: 17), where social patterning was assumed to be a result of knowledge acquisition and transmission processes.

Ethnobotanists and others began to investigate variation in what were assumed to be culturally homogenous, if not universal, systems of animal and plant classification (Hays 1974; Hunn 1975; Ford 1976; Gardner 1976; Ellen 1979; Boster 1986). At first, an 'omniscient informant' was invoked to attribute a cultural system of classification that encompassed variation, rather than explaining it. Hays (1976: 505) critiqued this drive towards a 'composite' model, claiming 'ethnographers have for too long considered informants' disagreements and variable behaviour as a source of frustration, inevitable but regrettable, in their search for "authoritative" informants who will reveal *the* culture'. His work among the Ndumba of Papua New Guinea demonstrated that lexical knowledge of plants varied by age and sex, with barely 80 per cent of total plant nomenclature being shared among his ten principal informants (Hays 1974). Young adults identified fewer plant voucher specimens, as did women, when compared to men. The very marked geographical and economic division of labour meant that men had much more knowledge of forest plants, while women's knowledge was focused on garden and village plants. The relationship between adults' knowledge and that of their children was only anecdotally examined, so Hays could not draw any conclusions concerning transmission processes that might underlie the variation. Boster's study (1986) of Aguaruna classification of manioc varieties is the classic modern study that demonstrated the relationship between variation in knowledge, social relationships and transmission processes; he also pioneered the use of quantitative methods of analysis in ethnobotany to demonstrate these relationships. Most recently, the Tsimane' Amazonian Panel Study (TAPS) in Bolivia has rigorously analysed cultural transmission of ethnobotanical knowledge and skills, and demonstrated the important role of oblique pathways for transmission (Reyes-García et al. 2009; Reyes-García et al. this volume; for reviews of ethnobiological studies of transmission, see Zent and Maffi 2008 and Reyes-García et al. 2007).

The study discussed here was one of a number conducted by ethnobiologists at the University of Kent as part of a project on 'Interactive Methods for Studying Environmental Knowledge Transmission' (Ellen 2007, 2009; Novellino 2007, 2009; Vougioukalou 2006). Among the methods developed and tested in the field were plant identification tasks *in situ* along designated plant trails (Robinson 2003; Fitzpatrick 2004; see also Stross 1973 and Zarger and Stepp 2004), in homegardens (Vogl et al. 2004) and *ex situ* using voucher specimens and images on laptop computers, which is described below (Puri et al. 2004). Identification tasks have been shown to be an important means of comparing individuals' knowledge of a domain, where the ability to identify an object is taken as a proxy for general knowledge of the domain, especially for comparing the differences between age classes and generations (Reyes-García et al. 2007). When combined with questions about use (theoretical and substantive) and other methods for studying the instantiation of knowledge in everyday tasks, these tests can help to identify changes in knowledge over time, which may result from changes to the processes of cultural transmission. The case below describes these methods in greater detail and illustrates their significance in explaining Penan basketry knowledge and its transmission.

Penan Benalui

The Penan Benalui, also known as Penan Menalui, Penan Badeng and Penan Lurah, are a subgroup of the Western Penan (*sensu* Needham 1972). They migrated from Sarawak (Malaysia) to the upper Lurah River (East Kalimantan, Indonesia) around 1895. From an initial population of probably between 50 and 100, this group has grown to over 450 in six settlements, including the site for this study, Long Lameh Baru, a new settlement of over 200 Penan on the banks of the Bahau River just upriver from the Kenyah Bakung village of Long Apan Baru (Figure 9.1).

Penan traditional economic life involved hunting, collection of fruit and other wild foods, sago processing, and trade in non-timber forest products (Needham 1972; Brosius 1991; Puri 2005). In the

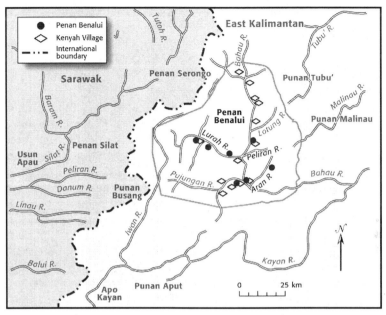

Figure 9.1. Map of settlement area of Penan Benalui, Kecamatan Pujungan, Kabupaten Malinau, East Kalimantan, Indonesian Borneo. Long Lameh is on the Aran River, while Long Lameh Baru ('new') is on the Bahau River just upstream from the confluence of the Aran and the Bahau. (Source: Puri 2005)

1960s, a process of sedentarization began among the Penan Benalui, and by the mid-1970s most Penan had begun to settle in villages and to adopt gardening and rice swidden agriculture, either on their own or in the villages of the Kenyah (Puri 2005). Christian missionaries, Indonesian health officials, bureaucrats, teachers and military personnel have all attempted to influence the Penan during this period of transition, with varying degrees of success. The increased use of high-powered outboard engines, large boats and air transport have reduced the travel time to and from the coastal cities. Not surprisingly, there has been a corresponding increase in the volume and diversity of trade products reaching the area. While the area is subject to a boom–bust cycle in the extraction of various non-timber forest products (Sellato 2001), including damar (resin of *Agathis borneensis*), rattan and gaharu (see Momberg et al. 2000), the Penan have always, as far they know, been able to trade rattan baskets, mats, meat and other animal products to neighbouring farming communities.

While initially exclusive trading partners of the Kenyah Badeng, Penan Benalui families have since the 1930s moved in and out of settlements and economic relationships with various Kenyah swidden farming communities. They have allied themselves continually with the most powerful of the Kenyah leaders in the area. Recently, and as the power of the local political system wanes, they have established trading relations with Indonesian officials, such as the subdistrict chief or *camat*, the local military and police officers as well as wealthy down-river merchants. These new patrons sponsor Penan forest product collecting expeditions and commission basketry products and metalwork, much like the Kenyah chiefs of the past.

The effects of these relationships on Penan social organization has been debated (Sellato 1993), with some authors arguing that perhaps the Penan are not as politically egalitarian as has been claimed for most hunter-gatherer groups in South-East Asia and elsewhere (Gibson and Sillander 2011). Thus, there have always been elder male leaders in Penan groups that brokered these relationships (Sellato 2001) and benefited materially and socially, although most incoming material goods would be shared or were available for all to use. Even today, there are Penan who claim they are, or are descended from, 'maren', the equivalent of the Kenyah farmers' 'paren' class, the aristocratic elites that ruled over these stratified societies (Whittier 1978). These same Penan 'leaders' may claim at least prestige and some status, and seem to be the ones that get positions in the government-supported village political leadership, but such positions do not grant increased power to influence other individuals' decisions.

Despite this, it is important to note that disputes among the Penan can be long and vociferous when it comes to decisions that affect income or access to material goods. Leaders are expected to be honest and fair, and any hint of impropriety is pounced on, often by the women, who are unafraid to voice their concerns over perceived inequities. It is the case that, historically, disputes might have been settled by outside parties, such as patron traders or *paren* leaders, or more usually the group would split, with disputing leaders taking their families and followers off to establish new communities. The Penan of Long Lameh Baru had to have their Head of School, from the Lun Dayeh ethnic group, help to negotiate and distribute royalties and fees paid to the community by a logging company that logged parts of their ancestral lands. Neighbouring farmers that were holding Penan debts negotiated directly with the Head of School to have their debts settled before any money was distributed to the Penan. Such patron–client relationships are nothing new, but often it was simply goods and forest products that exchanged hands, and there was little interference by patrons in the distribution of trade items or in any other affairs of the community. While egalitarianism remains a valued marker of Penan identity, it is clear that the influences of the market economy are beginning to erode practices such as sharing or reciprocal exchange, which is becoming increasingly monetized (see Godoy et al. 2005). Households are beginning to exhibit marked differences in wealth, as indicated by the presence of durable goods such as televisions, generators, boats and chainsaws, but whether these changes will affect the political ethos of egalitarianism remains to be seen.

While most Penan families clear and plant rice swiddens, every year some fields will be abandoned in the first few weeks in favour of more immediately rewarding activities, such as hunting, sago processing, fruit collecting and trading of forest products for rice and other foods. Some families say that their swiddens are too far from their homes, while others complain that there is not enough time or labour available to both provision the family and work in the fields. Swidden gardens produce some maize, beans and cucumbers. Near their homes, the Penan families plant manioc gardens. These homegardens occasionally include taro, sweet potato or yam; some families also have papaya and banana trees. Wild animals and fish provide almost all of the animal protein and fat in their diet, with a small amount coming from the occasional chicken. When in the Kenyah villages, the Penan were regular participants in schools, churches, sports, feasts and other community activities. They were often hired by the Kenyah to provide meat for festivals. Penan also traded meat, fruit, raw rattan, baskets, mats, the aromatic wood *gaharu* (Momberg et al. 2000), animal products, and steel and wooden tools in exchange for rice, garden produce, medicines, clothes and other manufactured goods.

Throughout this history, basketry has remained an important component of the Penan economy and cultural identity, essential for subsistence and a reliable and prestige product for exchange. Unfortunately, both of these functions are potentially threatened by island-wide changes to the environment, primarily deforestation but also forest conversion, and the introduction of potentially substitutable manufactured goods, such as plastic and cloth bags, containers and packs. New social institutions and mechanisms of cultural transmission – such as church, school and, increasingly, mass media – are simultaneously displacing older practices and challenging Penan values with regard to their traditional plant-based crafts. Yet, as already mentioned, basketry remains popular and important in Penan livelihoods and is still highly regarded by most outsiders. The study reported on in this chapter sought to understand why this might be so and how knowledge and practices necessary to maintain this activity are transmitted and learned, both between and within the generations.

Studying Cultural Transmission

The most common way to study cultural transmission is to conduct a cross-sectional analysis of the trait (or knowledge domain) of interest, and infer processes of transmission and acquisition that have led to the observed distribution (as in Boster 1986; Reyes-García et al.

2004; Reyes-García et al. 2007; Zent and Maffi 2008). Typically, the presence or absence of a trait is compared among age sets to determine if indeed there has been transmission of the trait/knowledge in question between generations: loss of knowledge among younger age sets implies cultural changes, whereas similar knowledge implies maintenance of cultural processes of transmission. Of course, researchers must control for the fact that older people generally know more than younger people by virtue of having lived longer. In this research, and elsewhere, evidence of variation in knowledge was gathered by simple comparisons of informants' responses to identification tasks. As already mentioned, the ability to identify and name biotic taxa, either in situ or ex situ, is but one kind of ethnobiological knowledge that is of interest, primarily because it is often taken as a proxy for an individual's total corpus of environmental knowledge. Knowing *what* knowledge(s) is being transmitted then is the first step in these approaches, including recognizing that different forms of knowledge (e.g. declarative versus tacit) are likely to be represented differently and thus transmitted and learned differently.

Given the shallow time depth of such studies, it is often very difficult to observe actual transmission events or follow individuals for very long to see from whom and how they learn. Usually, researchers observe what they can and then interview informants to elicit a life-history account containing their sources and means of acquiring the knowledge of interest (Hewlett and Cavalli-Sforza 1986).

A longitudinal study (such as a panel study, see Vadez et al. 2004) that tracks an individual's personal history is potentially the most accurate way to document transmission processes, but the research costs are high and there is often a need for institutional support to ensure continuity and secure data over the length of the study. Repeat studies of knowledge distribution are an intermediate strategy for studying change over time, although they may not occur as frequently as in a panel study, and there is still the problem of having to infer the processes that have led to changes, or indeed maintained stasis, over the interval (Zarger and Stepp 2004; van Etten 2006; see also Zent and Maffi 2008: 33).

In researching Penan basket-weaving knowledge, a set of mixed methods (quantitative and qualitative) were used to: (1) document the full complement of knowledge required to make a rattan basket, (2) document any instances of learning or teaching of this knowledge, (3) document life-histories of basket makers to infer transmission processes, and (4) understand the distribution of knowledge across the study community as a result of transmission and learning events and processes. These methods included the use of video to record the collection and processing of materials as well as the weaving of baskets from start to finish. Recorded activities were shown to respondents with the aim of eliciting additional information on the knowledge content of the filmed activities. More standard ethnobotanical methods included an inventory of baskets present in all households, life-history interviews with basket makers, mapping locations of rattan stands and the collection of voucher specimens for all plant resources used, identification of rattan specimens by children, and identification of basket types and decorative motifs by a sample of adults and children. The research was conducted with the assistance of Dr Johan Iskandar and Mr Rimbo Gunawan of the Institute of Ecology, Padjajaran University, Bandung (see Puri et al. 2004; Puri n.d.).

Penan Basketry Knowledge and its Transmission

This section summarizes and discusses some of the research findings concerning the character of Penan basketry knowledge, how some of that knowledge is distributed, and the processes and mechanisms of transmission that may have led to both variability and continuity of knowledge and practice. A more detailed presentation of some of the research results is to follow elsewhere (Puri n.d.).

What is Penan Basketry Knowledge?

Asking this question to Penan basket makers in Penan is nigh impossible, since there is no name for the generic category of 'basket' (see also Ellen 2009). Instead, people refer to particular baskets or other woven objects (Table 9.1).

Most are familiar with the Indonesian term *anjat*, which could refer to all baskets, but in the villages of the Pujungan it usually just refers to the decorative drawstring *bukui*, the iconic Penan basket in great demand by neighbours and tourists (Figure 9.2). When pushed, Penan basket makers suggested they could use *anyaman* ('something woven', from *manyam* 'to weave'), but this was never heard in typical conversation.

'Knowledge' is as difficult to pin down, there being no easy translation in Penan; nor is there familiarity with the Indonesian *pengetahuan* ('knowledge'), although *mojam* ('to be knowledgeable or smart') can be used to ask 'who knows?' (*Siran mojam?*). It is also a mouthful to ask 'what do you need to know to make a *bukui?*' Usually, the response is much the same as if you had asked the more instrumental question, 'how do you make a *bukui?*' (*Kona ko' mano' bukui?*). The Penan will quickly, and without too much thought, list a series of tasks that need to be completed to produce a basket (Table 9.2).

Table 9.1 Baskets and other woven objects, other than textiles, known to the Penan

Basket type	English description
Bukui tanyung	Tight weave decorative drawstring basket
Bukui sulok	Loose weave drawstring basket
Bukui gang	Simple drawstring basket
Gai	Simple basket with straps, for firewood
Kiva kelokung	Frame pack with sides
Kiva vai	Frame pack with woven sides, Kenyah farmer style
Kiva kebalik	Frame pack with fine weaving (rare)
Kiva tegalo	Frame pack without sides
Kiva bukui	Pack made from *bukui tanyung* (new)
Kerian	Small container (sometimes called *buan*)
Kitong	Multiple-compartment container (new)
Mak borat	Sleeping mat from rattan (aka *borat*)
Mak reu'	Sleeping mat from *Pandanus* sp.
Mak bidu	Mat
Taing	Mat for drying and storing rice
Jan	Mat for sago processing
Rak kiva	Clothes shelves (new)
Ingen	For harvesting rice
Ba' anak	For carrying babies
Tapan	For cleaning/winnowing rice
Ayu tilam	Carpet beater (new)

Figure 9.2. *Bukui tanyung* basket made by Penan Benalui of Long Lameh Baru, 2004. Photo by R.K.Puri.

Table 9.2 Penan tasks for making a *bukui tanyung*

Penan tasks	English gloss
Pita lakeu	Look for rattan
Mosek	Bend the cane to remove the outer covering
Memetih	To dry the cane
Memilah	To split the cane in two
Menyalet lakeu	To further split the canes
Mojet	To cut the sharp edges off the cane strips, using a penat jet knife
Mokih	To thin the cane strips by removing the soft pith
Mengadeng	To dye the strips, usually black
Mulat	To make the rings (ulat) at the top from which the basket is woven
Metum ulat	To fasten the rings together
Manyam alih podeng	To weave the upper part of the basket
Manyam sala'	To weave the large motifs characteristic of the middle part
Mano' lotuk bukui	To make the bottom of the basket
Mano' vy	To make the straps
Mano' kisiu	To make the rings that guide the drawstring
Mano' iten	To make the lower string
Mano' taneng	To make the upper drawstring

Each task can then be broken down into subtasks, many of which have specific knowledge requirements that are described by Penan in terms of their content and form. For example, in collecting rattan canes from the forest (*pita' lakeu*), young men must learn where to find clumps of rattan; they must be able to identify the correct kind of rattan, and assess its quality and whether it is mature enough to be harvested. Then they have to be able to pull the cane from the canopy, knock the spiny cane sheath off, cut the cane from the clump and canopy, cut the harvested cane into appropriate lengths, recognize and discard damaged bits, bundle it and carry it home. There may also be some rattan management activities associated with these tasks, such as clearing away competing plants, marking a plant as reserved (*molong*), pruning clumps or even inserting the remainder of cut rattan canes into the ground to prevent disease killing off the whole clump. How to recognize and deal with contingencies requires another set of related tasks: for example, how to respond to a break in the cane, or what to do if the cane gets stuck in the tree canopy (Figure 9.3).

Similar taskonomies exist for processing collected rattan and then weaving and assembling the various parts of the basket, again consisting of a set of generic activities broken down into very specific 'behavioural' skills, such as *mojet* (shaving off the sharp edges of the split cane using the *penat jet* knives) and *mokih* (thinning the rattan strips by shaving the soft inner pith). Other tasks have a more 'declarative' content, such as knowing the names of the various motifs (*sala'*), and the number and configuration of black and white rattan strips that are required to weave them (*manyam sala'*).

The sequence of tasks is somewhat flexible at certain points, but certainly at a generic level, collection, processing and weaving must occur in sequence, although the time intervals between them can vary significantly. The ability to manipulate the sequence of modular tasks, as well as the tasks themselves, perhaps due to contingencies such as changes in availability of raw materials or labour, the scheduling of other activities or changes in needs and demands, is a good example of 'performance' knowledge in the basket-making

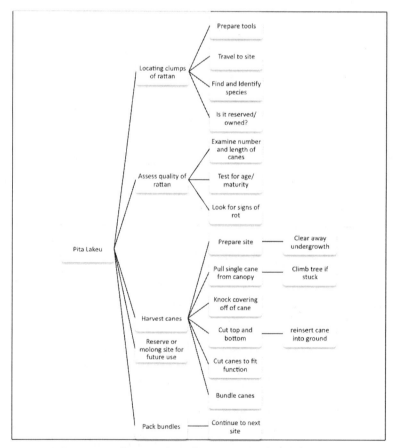

Figure 9.3. Penan taskonomy for collecting rattan from forest, 2004.

process. The Penan speak of being able to *atur* ('arrange' or 'order') the process of making a basket, a skill they say that comes with age and experience.

With regard to knowledge processes, amongst these tasks are those that can be described as solely 'knowledge acquisition' tasks, such as when rattan collectors speak with their elders or others about where to go to get certain species of rattan. However, most tasks involve the application or instantiation of 'declarative' and 'behavioural' knowledge to physically accomplish some aspect of making a basket. Most tasks can also function as 'knowledge trans-mission' events when novices accompany experts or simply take an interest in those activities that are often public, taking place in common spaces or in homes that are open for all in the community to wander in and out. Still other tasks that novices may engage in on their own may provide the context for individualized knowledge acquisition and innovation. While Penan rattan collectors recog-nize that elders can explain (*bara'*) where to find rattan and how to collect it (in a theoretical sense, even though they may be too old to engage in these tasks anymore), all will admit that knowing and doing are difficult to separate, and that to know something well (to be *mojam*) is to be able to do it well, consistently and under varying circumstances.

Of course, not all baskets are equal; some are considered 'better' (*jiyen*) and thus reflect higher skill, or talent, of the basket maker. As one might expect, young novice basket makers produce simpler, and often smaller, versions. While differences related to the func-tional qualities of baskets are minor and seldom commented upon, the aesthetics of the decorative *bukui tanyung* and the sleeping mats (*borat*) are noticed and often discussed, especially when they are being sold. It seems the general consensus is that *bukui* and *borat* that are *halus* ('fine') are considered to be of greater value. This fine-ness is due to the slenderness and narrowness of the *wat*, the cane strips that are dyed and woven into the various designs. The nar-rower and thinner the *wat*, the softer and more pliable is the basket, but this requires very careful shaving so as not to slice the strip into pieces. The trade-off is with strength, which is reduced as the wat become thinner and more fragile; but then these days the baskets and mats are made for show and sale to the local elite and the tour-ists. The baskets are probably never going to be used to carry heavy loads from the forest, nor the sleeping mats ever slept on, as they are often framed and hung on walls.

The thinner the *wat*, the more *ulat* ('rings' that the *wat* are attached to) can be used to make a *bukui*, and thus the more complex, detailed and fine the motifs that can be woven into the basket. A *bukui tanyung* may have between 39 and 59 *ulat*, with the latter being necessary for large motif designs such as *sala' baraka* ('belaka motif') and *sala' odo kelunan* ('human motif', borrowed from neighbouring Kenyah people). These complicated designs require the correct number of *ulat* or the repeating motif will overlap (described as *ganjil*, 'uneven') (Figure 9.4). Novice basket makers are often faced with this problem, especially when they scale up from smaller motifs that repeat more frequently (such as *sala' ujep* or 'bamboo shoot motif'). While most will learn with experience and some tutelage how to weave more complicated designs without error, some informants claimed that you have to have a certain mindset to be a good weaver of motif designs: 'some have it, while others just don't!' I will return to this topic when I discuss expertise below.

So, following the conceptual framework introduced above, Penan basketry knowledge thus encompasses declarative, behavioural and performance forms of knowledge that comprise a sequence of modular tasks, beginning with identification and location of plant resources, management practices, harvesting and processing of the raw materials; and ending with the weaving and construction and either utilization or commercialization of the basket. And as we will see below, this knowledge can vary from basket maker to basket maker, as a result of preference for making certain baskets or due to personal talent and experience.

Who Knows What?

It is now widely accepted that knowledge in a group is segmentary and fragmented; that is, people's competences in domains vary (e.g. basket weavers know more motif designs), and no one person has knowledge of an entire domain (no basket weaver knows all the motif designs) (Ellen and Harris 2000). Typically, variation in knowledge is found along such dimensions as age, sex, formal education, occupation, wealth or income, to name but a few; thus, only women know how to weave *bukui* baskets and, at least in practice, only men know how to make the *kiva* backpacks. These distributions of knowledge may be explained in terms of the social processes of learning (i.e. cultural transmission

Figure 9.4. Motifs used in Penan *bukui tanyung*. Clockwise from left: *sala' odo kelunan, sala' beraka, sala' punan aput* with overlap mistake at right. Photo by R.K.Puri.

that is affected by the beliefs, norms and values held by the group); for instance, apprentices learn occupational knowledge from mentors, mothers teach daughters about motifs and weaving *bukui*, and men take their sons into the forest to collect rattan. Changes in these pathways of learning and transmission are thus seen as proximate causes of change in knowledge, whether loss or gain, and can be affected by a large number of underlying causes. Recent concern with knowledge loss among indigenous peoples has focused attention on these underlying causes, but of course loss, innovation and transformation have always been inherent characteristics of knowledge systems: every time a master craftswoman dies, pathways of transmission shift and knowledge is surely lost. Zent and Maffi's (2008: 40) recent review identified the following variables that have been correlated with, or suggested as, contemporary causes of variation and change in environmental knowledge across study populations:

> formal education, parental schooling, language shift, bilingualism, market involvement, imported technology, occupational focus, wealth, land availability, public economic assistance, sedentism, habitat degradation, useful species extinction, distance to forest or town, migration, travel, interethnic contact, availability of Western medicines or health clinics, religious belief, and values change.

Such a wide-ranging set of change factors emphasizes the complexity involved in understanding knowledge distribution and transmission. In addition, my own experience with hunters, forest product collectors and basket weavers (Puri 2005), as well as university students, suggests that changes in the social processes of knowledge transmission do not have uniform impact across groups because they ultimately interact with individual capabilities, motivations and experiences. Thus, what people know is not just down to what they are taught or exposed to, but reflects a more complex and personal causal history that includes social, cultural, political, economic, ecological and psychological factors, as neatly captured in the idea of individual 'lifelines' (Rose 1998; Ingold 2007).

With regard to this study of Penan cultural transmission, we documented variation in knowledge of basket making for the purposes of examining intergenerational change and continuity. We developed six different methods to document variation in knowledge (see Puri et al. 2004; Puri n.d.): (1) participant observation and video documentation of four rattan-collecting expeditions; (2) video documentation of the making of three baskets, a *kiva*, a *bukui tanyung* and a *gai*; (3) an identification task of rattan types with boys and men; (4) an inventory of all baskets and woven products to find out who made what, when and for what purpose; (5) a computer-assisted identification task of basketry types; and (6) a computer-assisted identification task of motif types. For the last two tasks, we used photos of existing baskets and motifs found in the village, and added pictures of baskets and motifs taken from museum and private collections of Bornean basketry to assess continuity and loss in terms of basket types and motif designs. Many of these baskets came from other ethnic groups in Borneo and were for the most part unfamiliar to the Penan basket makers, but there was clear indication of continuity in design and motifs with Penan baskets that had been collected in the 1950s in Sarawak (Arnold 1959).

Here, I present results from the analysis of the inventory of baskets (4) and the identification exercise with basket motifs (6); but first some general comments on the division of labour in basket-making tasks, alluded to above. Given the thesis that knowledge is embedded in tasks, the fact that men and women engage in distinctly different tasks for making different kinds of baskets implies an important segmentation in Penan basketry knowledge and thus in the pathways and possible means of learning and transmitting that knowledge. Thus, men almost always collect rattan and make kiva backpacks, women almost always process the cut canes, collect materials for the dye, dye the rattan strips and weave the decorative baskets (*bukui tanyung*) and sleeping mats (*mak borat*). Other baskets that men have been known to make include the very simple loosely plaited drawstring baskets (*bukui soluk* and *bukui geng*) and rice storage baskets (*ingen*). Women can also make these, and probably could make all of the woven objects listed above if need be (Table 9.3).

We inventoried all twenty-two households in Long Lameh Baru (total Penan population of 212), and discovered 99 baskets and other woven objects (such as mats and packs), 93 of which were completed, and 82 of which were made by forty living residents and one recently deceased resident of the community (the remaining twelve came from six Penan living in other communities). Table 9.3 shows the sixteen kinds of object found, and the sex of their makers, where known. Men made 30 objects (about 30 per cent), of nine kinds, usually completing all tasks required themselves. They made all the heavy-duty packs. Women seldom collected rattan, but usually completed all other tasks in making 67 objects (about 70 per cent), of twelve kinds. Seven types of basket were made exclusively by women, four were made exclusively by men, and they both made five. The inventory shows the wide diversity of baskets being made in the village today – evidence of the continuity of knowledge and practice. The major income earners, *bukui tanyung* and *borat*, were made exclusively by women, while the *bukui tanyung* was the most frequently seen basket, despite being the most economically valuable. It is likely that many of the newer ones would have been sold or traded soon after the study was completed.

Table 9.3 Inventory of baskets and woven objects by sex of maker, for ninety-seven objects found in Long Lameh Baru, August 2004.

Basket Type	Made by men	Made by women*
Bukui tanyung	0	25
Bukui sulok	8	1
Bukui gang	4	4
Gai	1	7
Kiva kelokung	11	0
Kiva vai	1	2
Kiva bukui	1	0
Kitong	0	1
Kerian	0	6
Mak borat	0	10
Jan	0	3
Rak kiva	2	0
Ingen	1	5
Ba' anak	0	2
Tapan	0	1
Ayu tilam	1	0
Totals	30	67

*Typically women will prepare the materials and weave these objects, while the rattan will have been collected by men.

In fact, there appears to be a high turnover of baskets overall, with most being less than a year or two old, and only one over five years old. The Penan claimed that there is such a high demand for baskets and mats, especially the decorative ones, that they are almost always claimed or sold very quickly. Some mentioned that they struggle to hold on to them for their own use, since the need for cash is often pressing. It is also the case that with continuous use outside in the forests and fields, many rattan products will not last more than a year or two, exceptions being the rice storage baskets (*ingen*), the heavier packs (*kiva kelokung*) and some new products for storing clothes and other items indoors (*rak kiva*, a shelving unit for clothes).

Table 9.4 shows the breakdown of basket makers by age and sex for eighty objects made by residents of Long Lameh Baru. Basket makers comprised 16 per cent of the total population (nineteen women and fourteen men), and included a few unmarried youths, adults (parents) and elders (grandparents), with the elder women being the most numerous and most productive. All but three households had baskets (mean of 4.5), and all but four had basket makers (mean of 1.6). I can conclude then that the practice was widespread across the community, not at all a specialized craft of a few experts.

Table 9.4 Number of baskets and basket makers (in parentheses) classed by age and sex for Long Lameh Baru.

	Male	Female	Totals
Youth	1 (1)	2 (2)	3 (3)
Adult	16 (8) H	18 (8) HHHH	34 (16)
Elder	10 (5) HH	33 (9)* HHHH	43 (14)
Totals	27 (14)	53 (19)	80 (33)

* One deceased basket maker included; H = Expert

But there are experts, at varying ages and for both sexes, that are widely recognized for their skill at producing beautiful, fine and high quality objects. They are said to have nimble dexterous fingers that allow them to work quickly (and thus be productive), produce complex motif designs (without overlap), and are said to have a 'mind for making baskets', referring to their understanding of the numerical complexity of patterns. Of the thirty-three basket makers identified in Long Lameh, three males and eight females were identified by others as being experts, including one young mother about twenty-five years old (Table 9.4). She had been brought up in a household of full-time professional basket makers, and started making baskets at the age of ten, which is relatively early for Penan women. She made four of the twenty-five *bukui tanyung* inventoried, and allowed us to film her weaving a fifth. She was by no means perfect and had one basket with an overlapping mistake, but she explained that she was still learning and experimenting, and so sometimes made mistakes.

The experts turned out to be the most prolific, having at least three and as many as eight baskets in circulation in the village during the inventory. They claim to always be working on something, some being specialists in one or two types, others being versatile and able to produce many kinds. They are also responsible for all the latest innovations in objects and designs, such as the *rak kiva* and *kitong*, which are storage items whose design is based on a clever adaptation of the *kiva kelokung* pack (see Table 9.1 for other new objects).

With regard to motifs, expert women used more motifs in their *bukui tanyung* baskets, and seemed to know more about them, so a comparison of the motifs on these baskets was made to determine how similar baskets were to each other, and how similar baskets makers were in the way they combined motifs. The methods and details of this analysis are to be published elsewhere (see Puri n.d.), but some of the findings can be discussed here. It was expected that the baskets of mothers and daughters would share similar combinations of motifs because the daughters might be instructed directly by mothers, perhaps using one of their own baskets as a model. The assumption was that daughters learn primarily from their mothers. If this were always true, we might find family- or household-specific designs, somehow symbolic or representative of that lineage. The other possibility was that we would find novices with baskets similar to experts, because they were choosing to imitate the perceived best baskets in the community. The sample size was small (25 baskets made by 17 basket makers from 13 households, who together used 28 motif designs), and represents only a moment in time. Clearly a longitudinal study of basket designs would be needed to test these hypotheses in a more robust manner. However, the results are interesting; they show a wide diversity of basket designs, both in terms of the number and type of motifs included. Every basket is unique. One had just one motif in red, an innovation mimicking the plaid design found on Javanese men's sarongs. Others had almost a dozen different motifs, making for a dizzying stack of bands on these cylindrical baskets. There are some similarities though: a core of three motifs tend to be found on most baskets (*ali* 'line', *ali pudung* 'standing lines', *lipan* 'centipede'), usually woven first and considered to be the simplest and easiest to make. After these, the possible inclusion and combination of motifs is huge. The large central panel is indicative of expertise, as this is where the larger, more difficult and newer motifs are usually placed; most beginners will stick with some variant of *sala' punan aput*, a black and white diamond design borrowed from the Punan Aput (Figure 9.4). In this collection we also had a newly created motif, not yet named (Figure 9.6), but based on the popular *lut zio'*, an 'S' shaped design (Figure 9.2). Perhaps unexpected in an artistic tradition, there seemed to be positive reinforcement for innovations and even a bit of competition among women to come up with new motifs and make more beautiful objects, which could be sold at higher prices too.

Analysis of grandmother-mother-daughter baskets showed no obvious patterns of similarity. Many informants confirmed that these motifs are just for decoration and are neither individually nor in combination indicative of households, villages or ethnic group identity. We did come across two pairs of similar baskets, in both cases a young novice's basket was similar to that of an elder expert, albeit from a different household. While we have no evidence that these older baskets were copied by the novices, it is quite common to see young girls learning to make some of their first baskets by copying another's. Several basket makers claimed that once a novice no longer needs a model then they can be called *mojem* ('knowledgeable'). Given the lack of proprietorship of motifs and designs, and the easy accessibility of other baskets, it is not surprising that any basket can serve as a model or inspiration. So while many daughters may be taught or supervised by their mothers at the earliest stages of learning, it is clear that once they learn the basics, they are then free to imitate or adapt anyone else's designs.

Since the baskets themselves showed no clear evidence of patterned transmission, we also conducted an identification task of motifs to see if it was present in this aspect of basketry knowledge. We had noted that there appeared to be synonyms for some motifs, and some disagreement on the names of others. Some of this variation was clearly due to perceptual differences in viewing motifs, some of which are reversible images that can be seen in either the positive or negative (Figure 9.5). We thought that this variation might be patterned according to transmission processes, and so compared the pattern of agreement in responses rather than assessing whether identifications were correct or not. We then analysed the data in terms of the similarity of responses of related individuals, especially those claimed to be teachers or students.

We also wanted to see if knowledge of motif names was indicative of a basket maker's status as expert or beginner. We included men and boys in the exercise, even though only women make basketry objects using motifs, to see if this knowledge was also a proxy for their recognized status, as well as several who claimed not to be basket makers. Again, the details of this exercise will be published elsewhere (Puri n.d.), but some of the findings can be reported here. The identification exercise, conducted with thirteen women and five men, showed some consensus in the names of motifs, certainly for the easier and more common motifs, but less so for rarely used or seen ones. As expected, there was disagreement over motifs with reversible designs. Also as expected, the experts knew more of the motifs and agreed on their names, but only if they were makers of *bukui tanyung*, while some specialists in other basket types did poorly, and those who did not make baskets identified the fewest and were most different to the group consensus. One woman elder who is considered an expert, but no longer does much weaving because of her poor eyesight, had difficulty identifying motifs on the computer screen. One elder male expert in producing unadorned rice baskets (*ingin*), was largely in agreement with the women experts when he knew a name, including some older rare ones, but made a couple of mistakes and failed to identify a third of the motifs. With

Figure 9.5. Reversible motif in Penan basketry, identified as either *maten manok* 'bird's eye' or *kelekung* 'up and down'. Photo by R.K.Puri.

regard to our first objective, comparing the pattern of agreement in responses did not reveal obvious clusters based on kinship or household membership. In several cases, teachers and students (irrespective of whether male, female, or closely related) showed little agreement in their responses. Experts came not from just one family or household; they and the knowledge of motifs and the abilities to weave them, were distributed throughout the community. Overall, expertise was a good predictor of competence in this task, while age, residence and kinship were not (Puri n.d.).

If there are continuities in basket-making knowledge and practice within lineages of women then perhaps they are much more subtle, such as in the posture and kinesthetic of the weaving of the rattan itself, or the contexts in which weaving takes place (time of day, location in house, etc.). We do not have the data to test this, but my observations suggest that even when daughters claim to have been taught by their mothers, they watch, and may even help, most other basket makers long before they begin to learn themselves. It seems more likely that baskets, motifs and knowledge are widely distributed throughout the community due to its predominantly egalitarian ethos, where most material objects, though claimed by someone, are freely shared, and where production takes place in the open for all to see and imitate if they wish.

How Do They Know?

How does this seemingly random distribution of knowledge and practice arise among the Penan of Long Lameh Baru? In order to answer this question, I will describe some of the contexts and means of learning and teaching, and then analyse data on the pathways of transmission as reported by respondents. There are no formal institutions for learning basketry, such as schools or apprenticeships; rather learning takes place in informal contexts, by direct instruction and coaching, imitation (of baskets being made as well as completed ones), and experiential learning on one's own. Despite their importance to daily subsistence and economic exchange, basket making is usually taken up by young adults once they have married and have to establish a household of their own. If not in school, Penan girls are betrothed by the age of 13 or so, and then married and having children by 15; meanwhile, their husbands are often older by two to five years. Based on interviews with fourteen female basket makers, the average reported age for starting was 14.2 years (range from 10 to 18); while for six male basket makers it was 17.1 years (range from 10 to 25). Typically, young couples stay with one set of parents, although the others are often nearby, and begin to take a more active role in hunting, fishing, gardening, gathering, cooking, and other tasks, and distance themselves from their former playmates and other children. Girls will sit with their mothers, aunts and elders while they work – watching, helping and eventually being prodded to try for themselves. Boys tend to spend more time with their peers alone, hunting and working in the forest collecting rattan and other forest products. They too will observe elder men making the packs and loose string bags (*bukui sulok*), sometimes in the forest itself, before asking for help in getting started. Of course, no one is forced to learn, the Penan can cajole and argue, but in the end it is up to these young adults to take the initiative. Many start by helping an adult or elder: drying and stripping the rattan cane, collecting leaves and clay for dye, and making the various parts of the baskets. Then, they will start one of their own, asking for help and being supervised, often rather casually, by the same or even another adult. The girls will often use other baskets as models to learn the way to weave the more complicated motifs for the central panel. There were varying reports on how long it takes to learn to be a basket maker. Some said a year or so, while others thought that the basics for making the simpler baskets and packs (*gai, bukui sulok, kiva* etc.) could be learned in a week. But they do recognize that this learning period can vary, as some people catch on quicker, while others just do not have, or may never really get, the mindset for it.

For most adults that have busy schedules, basket making often takes place at midday, when it is too hot outside to work and when children are napping, and after dinner, usually by lamplight before bedtime. Rainy days in the wet season may also result in gatherings of several women to weave and socialize at the same time; men may do the same when on forest expeditions. If a particular goal arises, such as a need for cash to pay for a journey to the nearby town to buy supplies or, more rarely, to visit the hospital downriver, women will begin to work full time to produce as many *bukui tanyung* baskets or *borat* mats as they can. On the other hand, experts and those that see themselves as professional basket makers, whether men or women, seem to be always working, often intensely and with great concentration, which, I would argue, creates an atmosphere that attracts attention and inspires others.

Initial discussions suggested a fairly straightforward vertical transmission of basket-making knowledge from parents to children, but interviews with individual basket makers revealed a much more complex and unpredictable set of transmission pathways. Table 9.5 below summarizes the reported initial teaching sources of a sample of men and women in Long Lameh Baru. Note that there is an absolute sexual division, with men reporting only male teachers and women reporting only female teachers. Also, it is assumed that these are the primary teachers, but that others may have been influential at the same time or while becoming a proficient basket maker. Today's basket makers keep an eye on each other's work and are borrowing and innovating as a result.

Table 9.5 Relationship of teachers of basket makers in Long Lameh Baru

Kin relationship	Men (n=11)	Women (n=17)
Father/Mother (F/M)	1	6
Stepfather/Mother	0	1
Uncle/Aunt (FB,MB/FZ,MZ)	3	0
Brother/Sister (B/Z)	1	1
Cousin (e.g. FBS or MZD)	1	2
In-law (e.g. WF or HM,HMZ)	0	2
Grandparent (e.g. FF or MM)	1	0
Great Uncle/Aunt (e.g. FFB or MMZ)	1	1
Second Cousin (e.g. FFBSS)	1	0
Second Uncle/Aunt (e.g. FFBS or MMZD)	3	3
Self taught	1	0
Unknown	0	1

What is striking is the wide variety of sources of knowledge for basket makers. Only one out of eleven men had been taught by their fathers, the rest by various male relations, sometimes because fathers had died or because they were themselves not competent basket makers. Their uncles (FB or MB) and fathers' cousins (e.g. FFBS) were more influential among this group. One elder who specializes in rice storage baskets (*ingin*), which he sells to the Kenyah farmers in neighbouring villages, claimed to have taught himself by simply copying their baskets. By contrast, almost a third of women claimed to have been taught by their mothers. Their mother's cousins were also influential, as were in-laws (e.g. HM, HMZ) for those that moved into their new husband's home. Given the huge differences in the ages of siblings (sometimes as many as ten children born over twenty years), its difficult to correlate kin relationships with age sets, so it makes little sense to talk about vertical, horizontal or oblique transmission of basketmaking knowledge using kinship terms alone. Of course, beginners are taught by their elders (usually one primary teacher), and once the basics have been learned they may be influenced by peers as well as elders, but often peers may in fact be uncles and elders may be siblings and cousins. In general, transmission appears to be contingent on oblique pathways much more than originally anticipated.

The data hides the fact that one teacher can be represented more than once, having multiple relationships with basket makers. Among these women, one now-deceased basket maker was highlighted several times as the most influential for the village, having been a grandparent's sister (e.g. MMZ) or a parent's cousin (e.g. MMZD) to several informants who have since taught some of the newest generation of basket makers. Many of the men also pointed to her as the most expert of all basket makers in living memory. But this does not imply a convergence of influences back to some apical ancestor of all basket makers; there are several other 'ancestors' that can be traced through the life-histories of students and teachers, not to mention the influence of women marrying into the village from the two other main communities of Penan in the area, and the effects of travel and trade on baskets and motif designs.

There is also information and innovation coming from a variety of sources outside the community, as well as being generated internally, sometimes driven by friendly rivalry to produce more beautiful baskets (Figure 9.6). Sources include neighbouring Kenyah villages, other Penan groups from other districts (such as the Punan Aput of the Kayan Hilir), manufactured trade goods (such as blankets and sarongs, purses and folders), and Timorese labourers working in the logging industry.

Figure 9.6. New Penan basketry objects and motifs borrowed or innovated. From top left clockwise: Javanese carpet beater (*ayu tilem*); clothes shelves (*rak kiva*); innovative storage (*kitong*); file folder (*kedandian*); Javanese plaid blanket design; innovative snake design based on *lutsio'*; *sala' lutsio'* design borrowed from Kenyah basket maker. Photos by R.K.Puri.

On the other hand, some designs and basket types have been lost (Figure 9.7), either due to loss of knowledge or simply due to a lack of interest in expending the effort to produce complicated types, such as the *kiva kebalik*. No example of this *kiva* was available to be photographed, but it was said to have smaller and more intricate looping of thin rattan canes for the walls of the pack, which requires much more effort and a high degree of skill.

To summarize the results, Penan basketry knowledge encompasses declarative, behavioural and performance forms of knowledge that comprise a sequence of modular tasks, beginning with identification and location of plant resources, management practices, harvesting and processing of the raw materials; and ending with the weaving and construction and either utilization or commercialization of the basket. Based on the inventory of extant baskets and woven objects in the community, almost all known basket types are still being produced, demonstrating the continuity of the practice and the widespread knowledge of basket making across most households. There are many basket makers, of both sexes and a wide range of ages; basket making begins after marriage, but while they are still in their teens. Pathways to learning vary significantly, being sometimes vertical, sometimes horizontal (with respect to age or kin), and perhaps more often oblique. Novices may learn by imitating any number of basket makers or finished baskets, as there are no set rules or discernable patterns that govern transmission pathways. Hence, knowledge of motifs is not patterned according to household or family lineage. Experts know more and are more likely to agree on names of motifs, but expertise is not confined to just elders or women. Some experts are specialists and thus may not

Figure 9.7. Penan basket designs that are rare or no longer used. Photos by R.K.Puri.

have such a breadth of basketry knowledge as those who produce a wider range of basket types. Because of such a variety of pathways and opportunities for learning and borrowing, and with the freedom to produce baskets as they wish, every motif-decorated basket and mat is unique. Perhaps with longer study of basket production and closer observation of transmission or learning events, a more patterned transmission process might be discovered, but based on this preliminary work there appears to be an open, creative and anarchic process to basket making among the Penan.

Conclusion

Despite there being twenty-two households, sheltering as many as forty-four nuclear families, cultural transmission of Penan basketry knowledge is not confined to genealogical lines or domestic groups or households; knowledge is flowing across the small community quite freely, across and between generations, in a seemingly random process. This free movement of knowledge is facilitated by an egalitarian social structure based on sharing, a compact settlement pattern with open access to all houses, and of course, the fact that most people can acquire the basic knowledge and skills to produce at least some types of basketry which are needed for most subsistence practices and exchange (barter as well as for cash). Decorative baskets and mats appear to have been an exchange item for many ethnic groups across Borneo, including the Penan Benalui, who claim they have always traded rattan baskets, first for other goods and now, as well, for cash. Yet there is little overt competition among basket makers for this trade, nor is there secrecy concerning new designs or innovative basketry types. Perhaps open and easy access to rattan resources and a seemingly limitless demand for their baskets contribute as much as their egalitarian social structure to this non-competitive attitude, but this remains a question for future research.

A broader approach to Penan ethnobiological knowledge and its transmission in basketry, as well as in hunting, sago processing, forest product collecting and swidden gardening, showed that very young children clearly have little choice but to follow their parents. But once five or six years of age, children often have the freedom to decide whether to participate or not in activities such as food procurement (primarily hunting, gathering and gardening), forest product extraction (for cash and barter) and tool and craft production, although many are easily drawn into trying these activities by encouragement from parents, siblings and friends (Puri 2005). Despite an ethos of political egalitarianism, one cannot deny the usually less-than-subtle power of elders and parents to guide other group members in collective activities. Peer pressure to some extent is exerted on Penan boys to participate in activities such as hunting, rattan and fruit collecting, play and sports. It turns out that young Penan girls also may feel peer pressure to produce 'beautiful' rattan baskets and other handicrafts that are the trademark of Penan and other hunter-gatherer groups throughout Borneo. But more often, young men and women are driven to learn the basic skills of daily life by the simple necessity to provide food and materials for their own families' to survive independently. Thus, as was described above, once a couple marry, they then actively seek out assistance with learning to make baskets, packs and other tools necessary for provisioning their families. A culture of sharing allows for variation in competence or circumstance among individuals in these egalitarian groups, whereby experts in daily activities (e.g. hunting or gardening) as well as specialists (e.g. in blacksmithing, basketry or healing) will emerge. Those who are too ill or old to work also benefit from sharing obligations. So cultural transmission among egalitarian hunter-gatherers is perhaps less problematic than it at first seems, although it is less structured and prescribed than in ranked societies and among trade guilds and professions.

References

Arnold, G. 1959. *Longhouse and Jungle: An Expedition to Sarawak.* London: Chatto and Windus.

Barth, F. 1995. 'Other Knowledge and Other Ways of Knowing', *Journal of Anthropological Research* 51: 65–68.

————.2002. 'An Anthropology of Knowledge', *Current Anthropology* 43: 1–18.

Bentley, R.A., M.W. Hahn and S. Shennan. 2004. 'Random Drift and Culture Change', *Proceedings of the Royal Society of London B* 271: 1443–50.

Berkes, F. 1999. *Sacred Ecology: Traditional Ecological Knowledge and Resource Management.* Philadelphia: Taylor and Francis.

Bloch, M. 1991. 'Language, Anthropology and Cognitive Science', Man (N.S.) 26: 183–94.

Boster, J.S. 1986. 'Exchange of Varieties and Information between Aguaruna Manioc Cultivators', *American Anthropologist* 88(2): 428–36.

Boyd, R. and P.J. Richerson. 1985. *Culture and the Evolutionary Process.* Chicago: University of Chicago Press.

Brosius, J.P. 1991. 'Foraging in Tropical Rain Forests: The Case of the Penan of Sarawak, East Malaysia (Borneo)', *Human Ecology* 19(2): 123–50.

Cavalli-Sforza, L. and M.W. Feldmann. 1981. *Cultural Transmission and Evolution: A Quantitative Approach.* Princeton, NJ: Princeton University Press.

Chambers, R., A. Pacey and L.A. Thrupp (eds). 1989. *Farmer First: Farmer Innovation and Agricultural Research.* London: Intermediate Technology Publications.

Dougherty, J.W.D. 1979. 'Learning Names for Plants and Plants for Names', *Anthropological Linguistics* 21: 298–315.

Dougherty, J.W.D. and C.M. Keller. 1982. 'Taskonomy: A Practical Approach to Knowledge Structures', *American Ethnologist* 9: 763–74.

Durham, W. 1991. *Coevolution: Genes, Culture and Human Diversity.* Stanford, CA: Stanford University Press.

Ellen, R.F. 1979. 'Omniscience and Ignorance: Variation in Nuaulu Knowledge, Identification and Classification of Animals', *Language in Society* 8: 337–59.

_____.2007. 'Indonesia, the Moluccas (South Central Seram)', in D. Novellino and F. Ertug (eds), 'Baskets of the World: The Social Significance of Plaited Crafts', in F. Ertug (ed.), *Proceeding of the IVth International Congress of Ethnobotany* (21–26 August 2005), Yeditepe University. Istanbul: Zero Prod. Ltd, pp. 640–42.

_____.2009. 'A Modular Approach to Understanding the Transmission of Technical Knowledge: Nuaulu Basket-making from Seram, Eastern Indonesia', *Journal of Material Culture* 14(2): 243–77.

Ellen, R.F. and H. Harris. 2000. 'Introduction', in R.F. Ellen, A. Bicker and P. Parkes (eds), *Indigenous Environmental Knowledge and its Transformation: Critical Anthropological Perspectives.* London: Harwood, pp. 1–33.

Ellen, R.F., P. Parkes and A. Bicker (eds). 2000. *Indigenous Environmental Knowledge and Its Transformations: Critical Anthropological Perspectives.* London: Harwood.

Etten, J. van. 2006. 'Changes in Farmers' Knowledge of Maize Diversity in Highland Guatemala, 1927/37–2004', *Journal of Ethnobiology and Ethnomedicine* 2: 12. Online at http://www.biomedcentral.com/content/pdf/1746-4269-2-12.pdf

Fitzpatrick, I. 2004. 'A study of recognition, transmission, and use of wild-food plants in two Wichi communities of the Argentine Chaco'. MSc dissertation. Canterbury, UK: School of Anthropology and Conservation, University of Kent.

Ford, R.I. 1976. 'Communication Networks and Information Hierarchies in Native American Folk Medicine: Tewa Pueblos, New Mexico', in W. Hand (ed.), *American Folk Medicine.* Berkeley: University of California Press, pp. 143–57.

Gardner, P.M. 1966. 'Symmetric Respect and Memorate Knowledge: The Structure and Ecology of Individualistic Culture', *Southwestern Journal of Anthropology* 22: 389–415.

_____.1976. 'Birds, Words, and a Requiem for the Omniscient Informant', *American Ethnologist* 3: 446–68.

Gibson, T. and K. Sillander (eds). 2011. *Anarchic Solidarity: Autonomy, Equality and Fellowship in Southeast Asia.* Yale Southeast Asia Studies Monograph 60. New Haven, CT: Yale Southeast Asia Studies.

Godoy, R.A., V. Reyes-García, E. Byron, W. Leonard and V. Vadez. 2005. 'The Effect of Market Economies on the Well-being of Indigenous Peoples and on their Use of Renewable Natural Resources', *Annual Review of Anthropology* 34: 121–38.

Harris, M. 1968. *The Rise of Anthropological Theory*. New York: Thomas Y. Crowell.

Hays, T.E. 1974. 'Mauna: Explorations in Ndumba Ethnobotany', Ph.D. thesis. Seattle: University of Washington.

————.1976. 'An Empirical Method for the Identification of Covert Categories in Ethnobiology', *American Ethnologist* 3: 489–507.

Hewlett, B. and L. Cavalli-Sforza. 1986. 'Cultural Transmission among Aka Pygmies', *American Anthropologist* 88: 922–43.

Hunn, E.S. 1975. 'The Tenejapa Tzeltal Version of the Animal Kingdom', *Anthropological Quarterly* 48(1): 14–30.

Inglis, J. (ed.). 1993. *Traditional Ecological Knowledge: Concepts and Cases*. Ottawa: IPTEK-IDRC.

Ingold, T. 2000. *The Perception of the Environment: Essays on Livelihood, Dwelling and Skill*. Oxford: Routledge.

————.2007. *Lines: A Brief History*. Oxford: Routledge.

————.2011. *Being Alive: Essays on Movement, Knowledge, Description*. Oxford: Routledge.

Lumsden, C.J. and E.O. Wilson. 1981. *Genes, Mind and Culture*. Cambridge: Harvard University Press.

Maffi, L. 2005. 'Linguistic, cultural and biological diversity'. *Annual Review of Anthropology* 29: 599–617.

Marchand, J. 2010. 'Making Knowledge: Explorations of the Indissoluble Relation between Minds, Bodies, and Environment', in T.H.J. Marchand (ed.), *Making Knowledge*. Journal of the Royal Anthropological Institute Special Issue 2010, pp. S1–S21.

Momberg, F., R.K. Puri and T. Jessup. 2000. 'Exploitation of Gaharu and Conservation Efforts in the Kayan-Mentarang National Park, East Kalimantan, Indonesia', in C. Zerner (ed.), *People, Plants, and Justice*. New York: Columbia University, pp. 259–84.

Nakashima, D. 2005. *Safeguarding the Transmission of Local & Indigenous Knowledge of Nature*. UNESCO Working Document. Paris: UNESCO.

Needham, R. 1972. 'Punan-Penan', in F. LeBar (ed.), *Ethnic Groups of Insular Southeast Asia, Vol.1*. New Haven, CT: Human Relations Area Files Press, pp. 176–80.

Nelson, R.K. 1969. *People of the Northern Ice*. Chicago: University of Chicago Press.

————.1973. *Hunters of the Northern Forest*. Chicago: University of Chicago Press.

Novellino, D. 2007. 'Weaving Traditions from Island Southeast Asia: Historical Context and Ethnobotanical Knowledge', in F. Ertug (ed.), *Proceeding of the IVth International Congress of Ethnobotany* (21–26 August 2005), Yeditepe University. Istanbul: Zero Prod. Ltd, pp. 317–26.

————.2009. 'From Museum Collections to Field Research: An Ethnographic Account of Batak Basket-weaving Knowledge in Palawan Island, Philippines', *Indonesia and the Malay World* 37(108): 203–24.

Ohmagari, K. and F. Berkes. 1997. 'Transmission of Indigenous Knowledge and Bush Skills among the Western James Bay Cree Women of Subarctic Canada', *Human Ecology* 25(2): 197–222.

Pelto, P.J. and G.H. Pelto. 1975. 'Intra-cultural Diversity: Some Theoretical Issues', *American Ethnologist* 2: 1–18.

Plotkin, M.J. 1988. 'Ethnobotany and Conservation in the Guianas: The Indians of Southern Suriname', in F. Almeda and C. Pringle (eds), *Tropical Rainforests: Diversity and Conservation*. San Francisco: California Academy of Sciences, pp. 87–109.

Posey, D.A. (ed.). 2000. *Cultural and Spiritual Values of Biodiversity: A Complementary Contribution to the Global Biodiversity Assessment*. London: IUCN and Intermediate Technology Publications.

Puri, R.K. 1994. 'A Deadly Dance of Deception: Hunting Knowledge of the Penan Benalui of East Kalimantan, Indonesia'. Paper presented at 3rd Biennial International Conference of the Borneo Research Council, Pontianak, West Kalimantan, Indonesia.

————.2005. *Deadly Dances in the Bornean Rainforest: Hunting Knowledge of the Penan Benalui*. Leiden: KITLV Press.

————.n.d. 'Expertise in Basketmaking'. Manuscript in preparation.

Puri, R.K., J. Iskandar and R. Gunawan. 2004. 'Interactive Methods for the Study of Transmission and Acquisition of Environmental Knowledge: Rattan and Baskets in East Kalimantan'. Final Report submitted to Indonesian Institute of Sciences (LIPI), Jakarta.

Reyes-García, V., J. Broesch, L. Calvet-Mir, N. Fuentes-Peláez, T.W. McDade, S. Parsa, S. Tanner, T. Huanca, W.R. Leonard, M.R. Martínez-Rodríguez, and TAPS Bolivian Study Team. 2009. 'Cultural Transmission of Ethnobotanical Knowledge and Skills: An Empirical Analysis from an Amerindian Society', *Evolution and Human Behavior* 30: 274–85.

Reyes-García, V., N. Marti, T. McDade, S. Tanner and V. Vadez. 2007. 'Concepts and Methods in Studies Measuring Individual Ethnobotanical Knowledge', *Journal of Ethnobiology* 27(2): 182–203.

Reyes-García, V., V. Vadez, E. Byron, L. Apaza, W. Leonard, E. Pérez and D. Wilkie. 2005. 'Market Economy and the Loss of Ethnobotanical Knowledge: Estimates from Tsimane' Amerindians, Bolivia', *Current Anthropology* 46: 651–56.

Richerson, P.J. and R. Boyd. 2005. *Not by Genes Alone*. Chicago: Chicago University Press.

Robinson, F. 2003. 'Distribution and transmission of traditional botanical knowledge in the changing social environment: a study of a Kenyah-Dayak community in interior Borneo'. MSc dissertation. Canterbury, UK: School of Anthropology and Conservation, University of Kent.

Rose, S. 1998. *Lifelines: Biology, Freedom and Determinism*. London: Penguin Press Science.

Sankoff, G. 1971. 'Quantitative Analysis of Sharing and Variability in a Cognitive Model', *Ethnology* 10: 389–408.

Sellato, B.S. 1993. 'The Punan Question and the Reconstruction of Borneo's Culture History', in V.H. Sutlive (ed.), *Change and Development in Borneo*. Williamsburg, VA: Borneo Research Council, pp. 47–81.

————.2001. *Forest, Resources and People in Bulungan: Elements for a History of Settlement, Trade, and Social Dynamics in Borneo, 1880–2000*. Bogor, Indonesia: CIFOR.

Sillitoe, P. 1998. 'The Development of Indigenous Knowledge', *Current Anthropology* 39(2): 223–52.

————.2010. 'Trust in Development: Some Implications of Knowing in Indigenous Knowledge', *Journal of the Royal Anthropological Institute* 16(1): 12–30.

Sillitoe, P., A. Bicker and J. Pottier (eds). 2002. *Participating in Development: Approaches to Indigenous Knowledge.* ASA Monographs 39. London and New York: Routledge.

Strauss, C. and N. Quinn. 1997. *A Cognitive Theory of Cultural Meaning.* Cambridge: Cambridge University Press.

Stross, B. 1973. 'Acquisition of Botanical Terminology by Tzeltal Children', in M.S. Edmonson (ed.), *Meaning in Mayan Languages.* The Hague: Mouton, pp. 107–41.

Vadez, V., V. Reyes-García, R. Godoy, E. Byron, L. Apaza, W. Leonard, E. Pérez and D. Wilkie. 2004. 'Does Integration to the Market Threaten Agricultural Diversity? Panel and Cross-sectional Evidence from a Horticultural-foraging Society in the Bolivian Amazon', *Human Ecology* 32: 635–46.

Vogl, C. R., B. Vogl-Lukasser and R.K. Puri. 2004. 'Tools and methods for Data Collection in Ethnobotanical Studies of Homegardens'. *Field Methods* Vol. 16(3): 285–306.

Vougioukalou, S.A. 2006. 'Weaving Knowledge and Weaving Plants in the Cook Islands: What Will Survive the 21st Century?', in F. Ertug (ed.), *Proceeding of the IVth International Congress of Ethnobotany* (21–26 August 2005), Yeditepe University. Istanbul: Zero Prod. Ltd, pp. 327–34.

Warren, M.D., L.J. Slikkerveer and D. Brokensha (eds). 1995. *The Cultural Dimension of Development.* London: Intermediate Technology Publications.

Whittier, H.L. 1978. 'The Kenyah', in V.T. King (ed.), *Essays on Borneo Societies.* London: Oxford University Press, pp. 92–122.

Wilbert, W. 2002. 'The Transfer of Phytomedical Knowledge among the Warao', in J.R. Stepp, F.S. Wyndham and R.K. Zarger (eds), *Ethnobiology and Biocultural Diversity.* Athens, GA: International Society of Ethnobiology, pp. 336–50.

Zarger, R.K. 2002. 'Acquisition and Transmission of Subsistence Knowledge by Q'eqchi' Maya in Belize', in R. Stepp, F. Wyndham and R.K. Zarger (eds), *Ethnobiology and Biocultural Diversity.* Athens, GA: International Society for Ethnobiology, pp. 593–603.

Zarger, R.K. and J.R. Stepp. 2004. 'Persistence of Botanical Knowledge among Tzeltal Maya Children', *Current Anthropology* 45(3): 413–18.

Zent, S. and L. Maffi. 2008. 'Final Report on Indicator No. 2: Methodology for Developing a Vitality Index of Traditional Environmental Knowledge (VITEK) for the Project "Global Indicators of the Status and Trends of Linguistic Diversity and Traditional Knowledge"'. Terralingua. Online at http://www.terralingua.org/projects/vitek/VITEK_Report.pdf, accessed 29 May 2011.

Chapter 10

PLANT EXCHANGE AND SOCIAL PERFORMANCE

IMPLICATIONS FOR KNOWLEDGE TRANSFER IN BRITISH ALLOTMENTS

Simon Platten

Introduction

The exchange of plant material is ubiquitous amongst allotment plot holders and the social networks of which they are a part. On almost any British allotment site it is possible to identify many of the various kinds of exchange that have received attention in the anthropological literature, and also some of the distinctive social features of exchange systems that motivate material transfers, such as the recounting of the exchange histories of particular plant varieties, and the presence of pivotal individuals at the centre of redistributive and micro-political networks (Ellen and Platten 2011). While it is clearly beyond the remit of this chapter to cover all forms of exchange that are prevalent on British allotment sites, I shall focus here on the distribution of what I shall call 'early growth plant material', namely seedlings, cuttings and offsets (but excluding seeds and tubers). I shall use this focus as a means of describing how contemporary allotment practice is transmitted between individuals through instruction. I thereby reinforce the theoretical point that in the context of human cultural transmission at least, what we might very loosely describe as an individual 'transmission event', or transmission process, is in fact part of a transaction or series of transactions. It must therefore be understood as situated within a complex set of rules and norms of social exchange. I shall use mainly qualitative ethnographic case study data from the Leverhulme British Homegardens Project, the fieldwork for which was conducted primarily at two Kentish allotment sites between 2007 and 2010.

Defining the British Allotment

Literally, the word 'allotment' means 'portion', though in Britain the word is more commonly associated with small-scale cultivation. Allotment sites are essentially large fields portioned into smaller plots, which are then rented to tenants for a minimal fee for the explicit purpose of growing food. Allotments are arguably a special case of 'homegarden' within the range found in the British Isles.

By far the majority of homegardens, whether in rural, urban or peri-urban settings, are directly adjacent to dwellings. Allotments, by contrast, are geographically detached from the homes of the people who work them. They are, as such, perceived as a survival from an older system of land tenure, the roots of which reach into the common property regimes that existed prior to the seventeenth century. Each plot within an allotment site is measured according to an old English unit called a rod, perch or pole, depending upon where you are in Britain. Most plots are currently ten rods in size, which is equal to 253 square metres or one sixteenth of an acre. Allotment sites containing these plots vary in size and may contain any number of plots, from single figures to many hundreds, although most sites seem to have between fifty and two hundred. Many sites were initially on the edge of towns and cities but have since been absorbed into completely urban landscapes, creating often seemingly incongruous green spaces within otherwise built-up areas. In other cases the allotment sites are still on the fringes of settlements and form a transitional space between urban and agricultural land use.

Allotment sites are usually owned by local government authorities, though some are provided by private landlords. Those sites that are owned by local councils are protected and governed according to statutory legislation that, amongst other things, prohibits their use as market gardens. Although some sale of surplus produce is allowed, cultivation for the explicit purpose of sale is prohibited: allotment produce is assumed to be destined for use by members of the household who cultivate it and their close social network. The day-to-day management of these sites is often transferred to a committee of plot holders, democratically selected by their fellows on that particular site. Whilst there is national legislation, many allotment sites also have additional rules often peculiar to their locality, which may further restrict the use of plots. For example, whilst general legislation allows the keeping of livestock, with chickens being particularly popular, many sites will prohibit animals of all kinds. Similarly, there are often additional rules governing tree crops and field shelters or sheds (Crouch and Ward 1997). The current motivations of allotment holders foster conditions that are ideal for the conservation of bio-cultural resources. The plant material held within allotment systems is diverse, and maintained by communities of allotment plot holders who are, I suggest, bound by mutually reinforcing exchanges of plant material, knowledge, and productive horticultural practice. This is the context in which knowledge transmission takes place.

Allotments and Food Security

At the turn of the twentieth century allotments became increasingly incorporated into town planning as a direct result of the uptake of the garden city concept (Wiltshire et al. 2000). During both the First and Second World Wars the number of allotments grew enormously as the general public were encouraged to provide for as much of their subsistence needs as they could. Throughout this period allotments and vegetable plots made a very real contribution to the food security of the nation. In the First World War, more areas of land were opened up as allotments, in particular some held by the railways. The number of allotments was dramatically increased again during the Second World War in order to enhance the country's food security. Allotment provision reached its peak in the mid-1940s, with approximately 1.5 million plots across England and Wales (Crouch and Ward 1997).

In the immediate postwar period the number of allotments declined as parks and similar areas of land reverted to their previous functions. The number of allotment plots continued to decline, particularly after 1950. It is likely that the increasing efficiency of commercial agriculture lessened the demand for allotments as markets were better able to provide food security, although the use of allotment land for new housing and other development was also suspected (Crouch and Ward 1997; Wiltshire et al. 2000). In 1969 the Thorpe Report (HMG 1969) was commissioned to investigate the reasons for the decline in allotment plot holding. Whilst allotment land had indeed been taken for other uses, there were additional reasons for the decrease in the number of plots, namely the rise in popularity of other leisure activities coupled with an increase in the standard of living more generally. In short, increased prosperity had taken the economic necessity out of allotment cultivation and been replaced by recreational and other aspirational lifestyle motivations. The Thorpe Report recognized that allotment gardening was important as a leisure pursuit in its own right, and sought to promote allotments further by an attempted re-branding of them as 'leisure gardens', more in keeping with similar traditions in other parts of northern Europe (Wiltshire et al. 2000). However, this had rather limited success, perhaps because in Britain the concept of 'leisure garden' failed to capture some vital values of the allotment movement, namely hard work, independence and self-provisioning.

In the mid-1970s, allotments enjoyed a brief revival due to the rising popularity of self-sufficiency reflected in 'The Good Life', a television situation comedy satirizing both its ideals and practice. Nevertheless, the general trend over the latter half of the twentieth century was one of slow decline in the number of allotment plots until the mid-1990s. Since then, however, there has been a steady increase in the demand for allotment plots as a means of producing fresh, organically grown, local food. This demand seems to have accelerated exponentially over the last decade, perhaps due to extensive media coverage.

When the number of allotment sites was in decline more and more land was taken for other, more profitable, and higher priority uses (Wiltshire et al. 2000: 204). However, by 2009 – at the time of the Kent-based British Homegardens Project – the allotment movement in Britain was in the throes of an enthusiastic revival on a very large, though not unprecedented, scale. Vegetables have become fashion-able, and their seeds are outselling those of flowers from garden centres and mail order suppliers (HTA 2008). The National Trust has spearheaded a campaign for greater allotment provision by opening up areas of land for new plots. There has been an explosion of coverage across all media platforms expounding the benefits of 'growing your own'. These developments seem to be rooted in changing attitudes more generally to carbon-based fuel use. During interviews carried out in 2007, many plot holders cited the excessive 'food miles' that supermarket food had often travelled as one of their reasons for grow-ing their own. Associated with transportation over huge distances are food storage conditions, and the kinds of varieties that store well, both of which plot holders say have a distinct influence on the taste of supermarket-bought vegetables. From all allotment holders in East Kent so far surveyed, the most common reason mentioned for grow-ing their own food is the superior taste and otherwise unavailable quality of the food that they can produce themselves.

Dramatic increases in the cost of fuel and transportation has prompted a number of policy makers and lobbyists to consider na-tional food security in a new light. In July 2008, the Department for Environment, Food and Rural Affairs (DEFRA) produced a discussion paper concerning the food security of the U.K. in a global context. We now have people such as Tim Lang (President of Garden Organic) urging us to 'Dig for Victory' again, this time to win a certain degree of independence from international food transportation chains. There has also been renewed parliamentary interest in allotments, and the publication of an updated version of 'Growing in the Community: A Guide to Best Practice Allotment Provision and Management' by the Local Government Association (LGA 2009). From a grass-roots level, allotments and 'growing your own' have become high on the agenda for 'transition-town' groups concerned with the local effects of peak oil: in 2008 all local transition groups were encouraged to run or participate in local seed-saving events.

In the first instance the media were responding to public demand, but by 2009 they appeared to be nourishing it and, to some extent, directing it. There are currently nineteen different gardening- and allotment-orientated magazines on the shelves of Canterbury's retail outlets alone. Gardening has been big business in the U.K. for much of the second half of the twentieth century, and commercial enterprises have not been slow off the mark to take advantage of a renewed public appetite for productive gardening. Placed in the midst of this melee are television celebrities such as chef Jamie Oliver, gardener Alan Titchmarsh and chef turned small-holding enthusiast Hugh Fearnley-Whittingstall, all of whose endorsements of particular vegetable varieties during television appearances have had an impact upon the varieties of vegetables some people purchase and grow. Alan Titchmarsh has his own range of commercially available organic seeds, and the seed merchant Franchi go as a far as telling you on their website in which episode of Jamie Oliver's latest series their particular varieties were featured. Such media fervour has led many speculators to suggest that the allotment has shifted from being the domain of the older working-class male and is rapidly becoming the 'terroir' of the middle classes.

The British Homegardens Project is showing, along with other indicators, that, perhaps unsurprisingly, the U.K. allotment as a green-tinged badge of middle-class identity is as much a stereotype as the Arthur Fowler image (a character in the television soap opera *Coronation Street*) of a previous era. These stereotypes are, by and large, held by non-plot-holders, or perhaps I should say they are not held by long-term plot holders.

Nevertheless, there has been a significant change in the demographic profile of plot holders over the first decade of the twenty-first century. Older plot holders agree that there are a great deal more women keeping their own plots than in previous years, and more younger families and people from different ethnic backgrounds are also becoming involved. This is an observation supported by Buckingham (2005) who also notes that it is only in the mid to late twentieth century that women have not been at least equally present working on allotment gardens. The current demand for plots has outstripped supply, and many allotment sites that used to have problems with overgrown and unused plots now have long waiting lists. The results of the changes described above are twofold. Firstly, freedom from market limitations, coupled with a lack of economic necessity to motivate growing, fosters conditions in which horticultural curiosity can flourish unrestrained and in which biological diversity is not only maintained and manipulated, but also actively increased. Where the usual application of 'food security' relates primarily to its presence or absence, its application within current allotment discourse is more sophisticated. Plot holders are concerned with the quality and diversity of the plant material that they grow. They do not wish to support market models of provision that continue to simplify and erode these basic components. They also want to be secure in the detailed knowledge of the provenance of their food, avoiding where possible various aspects of its pollution.[1]

Secondly, there has been an influx of new plot holders who have very little practical gardening experience. Many have gained preliminary knowledge from television programmes, magazines and books that they try to instantiate with the expectation of immediate results. Experienced plot holders see this as a problem, as often these new plot holders have no realistic idea of the amount of time and hard work they need to spend working the soil before it will look like the gardens seen on television and in magazine photographs. There is consequently a high turnover of new plot holders.

Thinnings

In the back room of the pub after one of the quarterly meetings of an allotment association committee, I raised the subject of generosity with fellow committee members. I had been talking to a couple earlier that day who had recently taken on a plot on the site and I mentioned how they were struck by the generosity of their fellow allotment holders. Several other plot holders had come up to speak to them while they were clearing weeds, and they had been given some raspberry canes and some cabbage seedlings. The couple had found their introduction to what they recognized as 'the allotment community' thoroughly heart warming. They were impressed by the welcome they had received and said it had 'restored their faith in human nature'. Romanticized as their interpretation of events seemed to be, I too was caught up in the idea of allotment solidarity, egalitarianism and sharing, and this obviously came across in my tone of voice when I mentioned it to the committee members in the pub, all of whom were long-standing plot holders on the allotment site and all experienced gardeners. At first there was a short but noticeably embarrassed silence followed by:

> Jenny: 'What you have to remember, is that you always sow more than you need. Some might not come up, so I always sow more, and then when they all come up I plant the good ones and the rest I don't want.'

> Colin: 'Yes, I just gave them the thinnings, I didn't want to compost them.'

> Brian (grinning broadly): 'Here you are on about those "social factors" again – all this time I just thought I was growing vegetables' (general laughter).

Evidently there is a rather more pragmatic underpinning of allotment altruism than is apparent to most newcomers to an allotment site. Central to ideas expressed later in this chapter are different conceptions of reciprocity and gift exchange. The exchange of early growth plant material clearly operates simultaneously on different levels, the perception of actors involved fluctuating between folk categories of exchange perhaps best viewed as points along a continuum of reciprocity (Sahlins 1974; Davis 1992).

Good allotment keeping invariably creates a surplus of plant material, and not just of seedlings thinned from an initially cautious sowing. Plants have a habit of growing and space is often limited. Perennials may need to be divided, suckers and offsets need to be removed, self-propagating volunteers grubbed up. Looking across the allotment site as a whole, some of this material is composted, but the majority is otherwise distributed. If the recipients of such a surplus are actively selected then this is certainly of anthropological interest, more so if there is incongruence in the interpretation of the transaction between giver and recipient.

Centre and Periphery: Implications for Plant Diversity

At present in the British Isles the majority of foodstuffs are commodified and exchanged through market transactions, making the market place the central exchange mechanism. Allotments as a source of food production are generally viewed as part of the periphery of agricultural and horticultural production in Britain. Food that is produced from allotments is primarily for household consumption, or is circulated within a close social network. Exchanges between plot holders are rarely monetized. Large-scale agricultural production in Britain has undergone considerable simplification over the last fifty years in terms of the alpha diversity[2] employed by individual farmers. With the rise in the power of the supermarkets, breeding programmes for vegetable and fruit crops have been increasingly directed towards uniformity, appearance, and durability in transportation and storage. These changes have been largely market driven. In short, commercial varieties are selected according to their shelf appeal, with people who grow their own food often stating that this has been at the expense of flavour.

Continuity and Change

At first glance, an observer of the contemporary allotment scene might think that it is perhaps reminiscent of agricultural organization within the manorial system, or at least a biased selection of several characteristics of medieval strip farming. Land under strip-farming cultivation consisted of larger common fields divided into narrow strips, with each peasant household claiming several strips of land across the manor estate or common land. These pieces of land provided for the subsistence needs of their cultivators. Within the strip farming system, neighbouring strips would grow the same crop so as to facilitate cooperation with respect to ground preparation, crop rotation, sowing and harvesting. Allotments are akin to strip farms in that a community of people divide and work a single field, and also in the way that the day-to-day maintenance of the allotment site might be collectively organized. Humphries (1990) argues that there has been a continuous historical drift from a generalized production strategy founded upon common property prior to the seventeenth century, towards specialized capitalist production in the twentieth. Her assertion is that this drift began in earnest with the parliamentary enclosure of common lands in the eighteenth and nineteenth centuries. A look at the historical and political ecology of land use in Britain at this time indicates that allotments and their predecessors, 'guinea gardens' or 'potato gardens', have been far from peripheral but rather have played a central role in changing the character of land use and political order (Archer 1997).

Throughout, however, allotments have remained on the periphery of market exchange. Such positions give cultivators a certain amount of liberty to choose the kinds of plants that they wish to grow, embedding individual idiosyncrasies and personal identity within the plant inventories of allotment plots. Like the marginal cultivators described for various other parts of the world by Nazarea (2005), allotment plots and plot holders provide a refuge for landraces and horticultural knowledge impossible within the mainstream of commercial cultivation. Contemporary allotments are manifestations of individual horticultural choices. They are highly individualistic in their crop and crop variety content, as well as in their aesthetic appearance, despite the existence of an overlapping repertoire in the kinds of crops grown and in gardening styles. Where independence may have previously been demonstrated through provision for individual household subsistence needs, it is now also, and perhaps to a greater extent, expressed through unique planting patterns and approaches to cultivation. This notion of self supporting individualism within a community is an important feature of the current allotment ethic, and one that resonates strongly with common perceptions of precapitalist community subsistence and organization. The exchange of produce and plant material in this context is an indication that a gardener has produced a surplus – a proxy for a certain amount of gardening skill. The exchange of plant material in particular defines the allotment community, and I shall argue, contributes significantly to its continuation through knowledge transmission.

The Spring Plant 'Giveaway'

The onset of the growing season is marked by great activity on the allotment site. Beds are dug, cane structures are built for beans, last-minute manure is spread. Experienced plot holders wait in anticipation of the last frost, commune around the allotment shop or each other's sheds, and try to reach consensus over the best time to plant potatoes (some have already planted a few just in case). Many of their summer crops have been sown under glass or in polytunnels, potting sheds and greenhouses, either on their plots or directly adjacent to their houses, ready to be brought on site in fairer weather. By Easter the first surplus seedlings are being offered around, and the giveaway reaches a peak in May.

The similarity between the early and mid twentieth century peaks in allotment holding and the present peak is the emphasis on self-provisioning. As with other examples of homegardens, ecologically implicit is an anthropogenic, small-scale, resilient, food-producing ecosystem maintained by one or two individuals. Here the allotment, as with many tropical homegardens, builds upon the recognized qualities of complex extant ecosystems as a means of mimicking their resilience. Since much has been made of the 'ecosystem services' provided by the biological diversity found in homegardens, there seems little need to reiterate it here; suffice to say that diversity, and thus redundancy, is taken as the key to continuity of harvestable produce across fluctuating and varied ecological conditions (Geertz 1963; Beckerman 1983; Boster 1983; Nazarea 1998, 2005; Maffi 2001; Brookfield et al. 2002; Brookfield et al. 2003; Kumar and Nair 2004; Eyzaguirre and Linares 2004).

From this point of view there are distinct systemic advantages in increasing plant diversity within a plot. The sowing of more than you need is a lesson learned as soon as some of your seeds fail to germinate. However, it is not simply a risk averse strategy for coping with potentially poor seed viability. With the recognition that there are others in the immediate proximity engaged in the same activity comes an opportunity for an economy of scale. Seed packets invariably contain more seeds than a single plot holder is likely to want to grow in any one season. Since seed viability declines with age it is best to use new seed each year if possible. Rather than individuals sowing each and every variety and crop type they may want to grow, time and money can be saved by specializing. A surplus of favourite varieties can be swapped with established exchange partners or given away to others. If enough plot holders give away their surplus, quite a range of local favourites can be obtained during the giveaway period as a means of increasing plot diversity. The process is illustrated in the following case study.

Giving and Swapping: Plot Holder 1

Brian is aged sixty, and he has three allotment plots. He has had one of these for eleven years and has managed to gain the others over the last five to six years. Brian has been growing vegetables since he was a child and says that he has been gardening for forty-five years. He joined the RAF in his teens and worked as an engineer. This was the only period in his life when he has not had a vegetable garden. He left the RAF and joined the National Health Service to work as a computer system administrator. During this time the allotment became particularly important for him: 'Before (retirement), it was really important for stress (relief). I would come up and take it out on the soil, it was great for that.'

He enjoys the hard work because the rewards are tangible; there is a great deal of satisfaction to be had from digging. Now that he is retired he thinks of allotment keeping as his job – a job that keeps him fit, healthy and active as well as providing him with fresh food for the table. It is also a job that his fellow plot holders say he is very good at. Brian is known across the site as a source of good gardening knowledge. He is generous with his time and his planting material. On one of his plots he has a greenhouse and a small asparagus bed; the rest of the plot is dedicated entirely to raspberries. He is the primary source of raspberry canes on the allotment site as the variety he grows has proliferated abundantly each year and many have to be grubbed up. Rather than compost the excess he gives them away to fellow plot holders, in particular those who have just taken on plots: 'Well its good isn't it, they fill the plot up, gives them a bit of encouragement.'

The fruit he keeps he eats fresh or preserves. He has a couple of arrangements with friends – one provides him with preserving jars in return for some of the jars filled with raspberries, another runs a pub and will barter the fruit for beer during the summer months. He has a similar swapping arrangement with a plot neighbour, and each year they both grow tomatoes; Brian will grow 'Ailsa Craig' and his friend will grow 'Big Boy', then they swap some plants with each other to increase the number of varieties they grow on their own plots. Brian tries to grow at least two varieties of most of his vegetables. He says that it is necessary with vegetables like sweetcorn, as sometimes one will fail to produce or will do badly. He sticks to a trusted variety and then experiments with another. He sows most of his seed direct in the ground rather than transplanting. He tries to give his thinnings away whenever possible and will be given surplus plants by others, although he does not accept all that he is offered. Brian is quite proud of the fact that he does not have to buy any vegetables at any time of the year and can grow more than enough to put into store to last him through the winter. He saves seed from squash and beans, and swaps some seed with his plot neighbours.

In the above account, Brian engages in exchanges that may be separated in their anthropological treatment. On each occasion Brian exchanges one beer for a beer-sized portion of raspberries. The items exchanged are non-identical; an exchange rate has been established and both parties recognize that the raspberries are a substitute for currency. By any reasonable reckoning this may be initially interpreted as 'barter'. The exchange of tomato plants is an established and annual exchange of half a dozen plants that Brian relies upon as a source of planting material. Both parties have a similar level of gardening experience, reflected perhaps in the equivalence and reliance placed upon the annual exchange. A previous year his friend did not plant enough 'Big Boy' and had planted more 'Alicante' instead, a variety that Brian had also sown that year. As a result Brian was a little short on variety within his tomato plants, though in 2008 things were back to normal. This is a balanced reciprocal exchange that contains enough elements of the spirit of the gift for it to be termed an immediate 'balanced reciprocal gift exchange', or in the allotment vernacular, a 'swap'. The jars of preserved raspberries are more problematic: Brian receives the jars in batches, as and when they are collected by his friend over the year, but he does not keep track of how many jars he has received or how many full jars he returns.

There is a degree of necessity within these exchanges. Experienced gardeners, specializing in particular varieties and then swapping with others, build the level of diversity they require for their own cultivation. However, in allotment swaps, none would identify the connotations of negative reciprocity associated with barter. Interestingly, the same is also true of the exchange of beer for raspberries in our case study. Brian could, for example, easily pay for his beer with cash rather than raspberries. In fact, his use of raspberries, and the pub owner's acceptance of them, tempers the negative reciprocity of the commercial context and highlights aspects of the exchange being more akin to 'the gift'. To view barter purely in terms of negative reciprocity is liable to result in the underestimation of its significance (Humphrey and Hugh-Jones 1992: 2–3). Plant material is, after all, inalienable, and is in fact a particularly appropriate medium of exchange in this regard. The degree of care and attention paid to the plant material is both apparent and tangible before and after an exchange takes place, and in the case of edible harvests it is physically consumed at a later date. In the instance above, what could be described as barter bears more resemblance to another 'swap'. As Strathern (1992) suggests, the emphasis when looking at barter of this kind should not be placed upon the items exchanged, the exchange rate established or the frequency of transaction, but on the recognition by exchange partners that there is the potential for an exchange of some form between them, and therefore upon the relationship between the parties concerned. 'Swapping', then, is the emphasis of aspects of community and sociality over the relative impersonality of the market.

Brian frequents his plots most days even if only briefly, and during the summer months harvesting and processing becomes a full-time occupation. From being on site, Brian is on familiar terms with most of the other plot holders, both established and those just beginning. Any surplus seedlings or thinnings he offers to people he thinks might be interested in them – people he knows have not got similar seedlings themselves, in particular those just beginning allotment cultivation. Brian tries to be as encouraging as possible with new plot holders and is keen to give advice along with planting material. He has also put planting guides up on the allotment association website. Taken at face value, Brian's actions with regard to the early growth plant material he gives away appear to be an example of generalized reciprocity as conceived by Sahlins (1974), or altruism as conceived by Davis

(1992). He says that he does not often receive planting material from inexperienced plot holders, because, unsurprisingly, most are not organized enough to produce surplus plant material. Although there is a considerable amount of 'swapping' between experienced gardeners, there is still a general bias in the flow of surplus plant material from experienced gardeners to less experienced gardeners.

Teaching and Learning Allotment Best Practice: Plot Holder 2

Recognition of this flow from experienced practitioner to novice was voiced by another plot holder, Bob, on another allotment site, and he is the subject of our second case study. The following is taken directly from my field notes.

> I bumped into Bob on site and he asked me how I was off for onion sets as he had some show onion sets going spare and I should come along to his shed. Bob used to grow for vegetable shows along with a friend of his, but over the last few years he has lost interest and now grows exclusively for the dinner table. In the end he gave me 19 'Kelsea' exhibition onion sets, five different tomato varieties (one 'Inca', one 'Sweet Olive', one 'Red Alert', one 'Legend', two 'Arctic Plenty'). He also gave me 6–7 iceberg lettuce seedlings, 19 marigolds, and two handfuls of mixed gladioli bulbs. All he would accept in return was some runner bean seed. He normally has his own seed that he grows on and off and which he got from an old guy years ago who had bred it himself – but he has lost the seed for the moment and does not want to miss the runner bean planting window. We talked about tomatoes – he grows six or so varieties each year, this year he has five main plants of 'Gardeners Delight'. 'These are my "bankers", then I grow 3–4 other varieties just to try them out – to see if any can push out my Gardeners Delight'.

I commented that with all the plants that I was being given by everybody I would have the most diverse plot on site – he said that was a good thing as that was what it was all about. I asked him if he saved his own seed – he said yes. 'The worst thing is the seed you get nowadays. You get 30 cauliflower all ready on Tuesday the 13th December. The old seed was better, 'cos each plant would do its own thing.'

I thanked him for his generosity as he helped me carry all the plants back to our plot – he said that I was welcome and that it was because he remembered when he first started growing. 'When I was first learning about growing, for the first 4–5 years, when I had the first plot of my own when I just got married, I remember there was an old guy on the plot next door, he kept me going, he would keep giving me all this stuff and say "it's just surplus, surplus". I think that is the way allotments should be.'

Both Brian and Bob were reluctant to accept return exchanges for the plant material they gave away to less experienced gardeners, unless it was something that they absolutely wanted, and then there was an apparent preference for seed over seedlings. One reason for this was that, as they were both experienced gardeners, they already had all their planting material organized. Bob later elaborated upon his comment that his older plot neighbour 'kept him going'. When Bob was just learning to garden, he had not got the hang of timing his preparation and sowing, and so was often just finishing his soil preparation by the time others were planting seedlings which he had not even sown yet. At other times his seeds had failed for one reason or another of his own doing and he was left with nothing to plant. In these instances the gifts of surplus plants and thinnings allowed him to catch up a little and not miss 'the window' for planting out certain crops. In doing so, this enabled him to harvest some produce, which he found rewarding and which kept him coming back to the allotment plot.

The 'Spring plant giveaway' acts as a lesson to plot newcomers who receive plant material. It informs them of the local planting timetable, a timetable consisting of windows of planting opportunity, within which specific plantings are fixed according to a combination of individual rules of thumb and consensus found during plotside conversation. What is clear to inexperienced gardeners is that when surplus is available, the experienced gardeners have already planted, and one should note the need to be better prepared for the next year in order to mimic their success. The kinds and varieties of plants given away also says a great deal about tried-and-tested crops for the local conditions, and of course the favourites of particular plot holders. Receiving such plant material enables newcomers to progress through the season learning more about caring for the plants as the plants grow. Without the plant material provided during the giveaway period, novices would not necessarily have the same quality or quantity of plant material to 'practise' with.

Given that experienced gardeners were once learning themselves, and were, like Bob, 'taught' by the generosity of the experienced gardeners of the time, it is easy to understand their reluctance to receive reciprocal gifts of plant material from more inexperienced gardeners. For more experienced gardeners, being able to be generous with planting material is the completion of a transaction started years before when they were given seedlings. What appears to inexperienced gardeners as generalized reciprocity is the balancing of the help they received themselves when starting to garden. The ability to complete such an exchange is also an acknowledgement that their own gardening skills have progressed. Importantly it is also a means for experienced plot holders to reinvest in their horticultural community and contribute directly to its perpetuation. Seed material is exempt from these transactions, I suggest, because of its evident dormancy. Seedlings and other early growth plant material are clearly alive and ready to go. In this way experienced gardeners are 'priming' a novice's plot for them; giving them a spring-loaded learning mechanism as it were, to see what they can do with it. If they are any good they can learn how to load it next year.

Whilst some gardeners, like Bob, consciously acknowledge this process, others do not, yet still conform to the model of allotment generosity. On several occasions different plot holders termed the giving away of seedlings as 'recycling'. This is an interesting recognition of a reciprocal exchange perhaps initiated a generation before, when they were themselves inexperienced gardeners. Conventional recycling, of course, would be the composting of the surplus thinnings on the experienced plot holders own plot so as to retain the nutrients bound up in the plant material. However, the emphasis in 'recycling' is upon gardening knowledge, and maintaining a community that uses it, not nutrients. It is upon the plot holder's recognition of a process of learning over time and a need to pass on knowledge to a new generation for the community to continue, and upon the lifecycle of the gardener and the recycling of their knowledge in order to perpetuate horticultural skill. Such a 'cultural model' (as per Holland and Quinn 1987) requires the apparent generalized reciprocity of experienced gardeners, and its acceptance by novices, in order to persist. In the terms of the language of performance, there is a generosity 'script' accompanying plot-holder identity, and numerous codes surrounding planting material. Each exchange is a kind of code, or public demonstration, signifying to others recognition of the script (Horton 2003).

Continuity in the Transmission of Knowledge

Although plot holders do not discuss it in these terms, what we have here is an example of a rather common interface between agency and structure, whereby actors who are motivated by social and immediately pragmatic stimuli, perform in ways that have systemic and ecological consequences that they are not necessarily aware of. Givers of plant material focus on generosity, on sharing exciting new plant material, on improving their growing skills, and demonstrating their skills to others. Novice plot holders who are receivers of plant material welcome the generosity, are frustrated that they cannot reciprocate what they see as a single transaction of gift exchange, attach value to the origins of plant material and talk about 'help' and 'learning' from those who have given material to them. They learn the rules of allotment performance, the acceptance of plant material from more experienced gardeners and the obligation to help others who are learning. This is a much more embedded and interactive process of learning and knowledge transmission than is suggested in unrealistic media portrayal of 'learning to garden'. The reality is that allotment keeping is rooted in community, physical labour and a degree of patience. These are factors that perhaps do not make 'good television' and are perhaps difficult to express in a condensed and limited time slot.

The exasperation of experienced plot holders regarding allotment gardening in the media is understandable. The knowledge transmission pathway is frustrated by unrealistic expectations about the length of time it is necessary to spend on site. Often new plot holders, particularly those who end up not lasting more than a year, do not even spend sufficient time on site to enable them to be offered help or planting material. Paradoxically some even refuse help when it is offered, seeing the comments of experienced gardeners as interference with the labour they appreciate needs to be done. For many of the new influx of younger plot holders, the allotment has to fit around a working week. This has an impact both on the amount of time they can spend on the plot and on the amount they are able to socialize with fellow plot holders when there. At an extreme, one family new to keeping an allotment gave up their plot after three weeks as it became clear to them that they would not have time to do the necessary work:

> We can only get there maybe one day a week at the weekend, and if one of us is there looking after the kids only one of us can really do any work, and then the old-boys (the older men) come up and want to chat all the time, and you have to chat otherwise it's rude isn't it, so it is impossible. (PW, ex-'plot holder' 2008)

Conclusion

The delayed balancing of reciprocity by experienced plot holders shakes at the foundations of interpretations of plant exchange, which either do not take a diachronic perspective upon contemporary exchange relationships, or which emphasize the material components of the exchange. If experienced allotment plot holders have a universal 'debt' to pay, one that obligates them to reinvest continually in their community of practice, then their 'exchange rate' on a transaction-by-transaction basis will appear forever skewed. The ethnography of exchanging early growth plant material leads us to the 'scripts' described above, which combined constitute a cultural model of allotment-holding best practice, but which is almost certainly not limited to the allotment. Once recognized, the value of generosity is extended by gardeners to cover plant produce, as well as plant material. This, at least, goes some way towards explaining the exuberant generosity in the distribution of produce often held as a hallmark of allotment plot holders, but also ascribed to the moral economy of British gardening more generally. Produce even pervades other spheres of economic exchange, as exemplified by our raspberry and beer 'swapping'. Hand in hand with this generosity go other emergent properties of the knowledge transmission process which are of current interest to policy makers in the U.K., such as community building, local resilience and, of course, food security. If, as DEFRA publications suggest, a further increase in enthusiasm in Britain for 'growing one's own' is going to be policy lead, simply increasing its media profile is likely to prove unsatisfactory and at worst counterproductive unless greater recognition is placed on the fact that gardening is also a social activity. To meet with any success, greater attention needs to be paid to how plant material is exchanged and to existing knowledge embedded within established social networks.

In the context of the theoretical purposes of this book, this chapter not only emphasizes the importance of a particular kind of 'situated' learning (Lave and Wenger 1991; Lave 1993), but shows how the specificities of a particular domain of cultural practice (allotment gardening) influence knowledge transmission. Moreover, it shows how much cultural transmission is mediated and reinforced by processes of social interaction and bonding that do not in themselves have an explicit instructional component, and that this takes place through physical transactions which provide opportunities for learning about gardening, not least in providing 'quality plant material to practise with'. As to how we understand the directionality of transmission, the example of allotment associations suggests that while knowledge undeniably moves from the more experienced to the less experienced, this process is not institutionalized as we might expect from, say, an apprentice model (Coy 1989), while it is similarly difficult to characterize the direction of movement in terms of simple contrasts between 'vertical', 'horizontal' and 'oblique' (e.g. Hewlett and Cavalli-Sforza 1986), at least at the level of dense ethnographic description.

Acknowledgements

The British Homegardens Project is hosted by the School of Anthropology and Conservation at the University of Kent, and the 2007–10 phase was funded by the Leverhulme Trust (5/00 236/N). The project seeks to investigate the agrodiversity, local knowledge and economic significance of gardening within allotment and other homegardens in the U.K. Data gathered as part of this project include interviews, garden maps, plant inventories, and other material provided through participant observation. The data on retail outlets and publications were assembled by Dr Rachel Kaleta.

Notes

1. By pollution I mean both symbolic and physical contaminants. Pollution can often, of course, be seen as a mixture of both of these (Leach 1972; Jaffe and Dürr 2010). For example, whilst high levels of pesticide residue might be considered poisonous, found at lower levels the food concerned might be deemed fit for human consumption. There are many people who would still consider lower levels of chemical residues to have physically 'poisoned' their food, whereas advocates of chemical use might classify this as purely symbolic pollution. 'Food miles', or the distance foodstuffs have travelled between production and consumption, might also be seen as symbolically polluting the food transported (whilst contributing to the physical pollution of the atmosphere through carbon dioxide emissions), and consequently have an effect upon consumer food choices.

2. Whittaker (1972) describes a framework for the understanding of species diversity employing the concepts of alpha-, beta- and gamma-diversity. Alpha-diversity is generally considered to be the species richness of a particular habitat or ecosystem.

References

Archer, J.E. 1997. 'The Nineteenth-century Allotment: Half an Acre and a Row', *The Economic History Review, New Series* 50(1): 21–36.

Beckerman. S. 1983. 'Does Swidden Ape the Jungle?', *Human Ecology* 11: 1–13.

Boster, J.S. 1983. 'A Comparison of the Diversity of Jivaro Gardens with the Tropical Forest', *Human Ecology* 11: 47–68.

Brookfield, H., C. Padoch, H. Parsons and M. Stocking. 2002. *Cultivating Biodiversity: The Understanding, Analysis and Use of Agrodiversity*. London: ITDG Publishing.

Brookfield, H., H. Parsons and M. Brookfield (eds). 2003. *Agrodiversity: Learning from Farmers across the World*. Tokyo: United Nations University Press.

Buckingham, S. 2005. 'Women (Re)construct the Plot: The Regen(d)eration of Urban Food Growing', *Area* 37(2): 171–79.

Coy, M. (ed.). 1989. *Apprenticeship: From Theory to Method and Back Again.* Albany, NY: State University of New York.

Crouch, D. and C. Ward. 1997. *The Allotment: Its Landscape and Culture.* Nottingham: Five Leaves.

Davis, J.H.R. 1992. *Exchange.* Buckingham: Open University Press.

Department for Environment, Food and Rural Affairs. 2008. 'Ensuring the UK's Food Security in a Changing World' retrieved 2 May 2009 from http://www.defra.gov.uk

Ellen, R. and S. Platten. 2011. 'The Social Life of Seeds: The Role of Networks of Relationships in the Dispersal and Cultural Selection of Plant Germplasm', *Journal of the Royal Anthropological Institute (N.S.)* 17: 563–84.

Eyzaguirre, P.B. and O.F. Linares (eds). 2004. *Home Gardens and Agrobiodiversity.* Washington, DC: Smithsonian Books.

Geertz, C. 1963. *Agricultural Involution.* Berkeley: University of California Press.

Her Majesty's Government. 1969. *The Thorpe Report, Departmental Committee of Inquiry into Allotments.* London: Ministry of Land and Natural Resources.

Hewlett, B.S. and L.L. Cavalli-Sforza. 1986. 'Cultural Transmission among Aka Pygmies', *American Anthropologist* 88(4): 922–34.

Holland, D. and N. Quinn (eds). 1987. *Cultural Models in Language and Thought.* Cambridge: Cambridge University Press.

Horticultural Trade Association. 2008. Annual Report.

Horton, D. 2003. 'Green Distinctions: The Performance of Identity among Environmental Activists', in B. Szerszynski, W. Heim and C. Waterton (eds), *Nature Performed: Environment, Culture and Performance.* Oxford: Blackwell, pp. 63–77.

Humphries, J. 1990. 'Enclosures, Common Rights, and Women: The Proletarianization of Families in the Late Eighteenth and Early Nineteenth Centuries', *The Journal of Economic History* 50(1): 17–42.

Humphrey, C. and S. Hugh-Jones 1992. 'Introduction: Barter Exchange and Value' in C. Humphrey and S. Hugh-Jones (eds), *Barter, Exchange and Value: An Anthropological Approach.* Cambridge: Cambridge University Press, pp. 1–20.

Jaffe, R. and E. Dürr. 2010. 'Introduction: Cultural and Material Forms of Urban Pollution', in E. Dürr and R. Jaffre (eds), *Urban Pollution: Cultural Meanings, Social Practices.* New York and Oxford: Berghahn Books, pp. 1–29.

Kumar, B.M. and P.K.R. Nair. 2004. 'The Enigma of Tropical Homegardens', *Agroforestry Systems* 61: 135–52.

Lave, J. 1993. 'Situated Learning in Communities of Practice', in L.B. Resnick, J. Levine and S. Teasley (eds), *Perspectives on Socially Shared Cognition.* Washington, DC: American Psychological Association, pp. 63–82.

Lave, J. and E. Wenger. 1991. *Situated Learning: Legitimate Peripheral Participation.* Cambridge: Cambridge University Press.

Leach, E.R. 1972. 'Anthropological Aspects: Conclusion', in P.R. Cox and J. Peel (eds), *Population and Pollution: Proceedings of the Eighth Annual Symposium of the Eugenics Society, London 1971.* London and New York: Academic Press, pp. 37–43.

Local Government Agency. 2009. *Growing in the Community: A Good Practice Guide for the Management of Allotments.* London: LGA.

Maffi, L. (ed.). 2001. *On Biocultural Diversity: Linking Language, Knowledge and the Environment.* Washington, DC: Smithsonian Institution Press.

Nazarea, V.D. 1998. *Cultural Memory and Biodiversity.* Tucson: University of Arizona Press.

————.2005. *Heirloom Seeds and their Keepers: Marginality and Memory in the Conservation of Biological Diversity.* Tucson: University of Arizona Press.

Sahlins, M.D. 1974. *Stone Age Economics.* London: Tavistock Publications.

Strathern, M. 1992. 'Qualified Value: The Perspective of Gift Exchange', in C. Humphrey and S. Hugh-Jones (eds), *Barter, Exchange and Value: An Anthropological Approach.* Cambridge: Cambridge University Press, pp. 169–92.

Whittaker, R.H. 1972. 'Evolution and Measurement of Species Diversity', *Taxon* 21: 213–51.

Wiltshire, R., D. Crouch and R. Azuma. 2000. 'Contesting the Plot: Environmental Politics and the Urban Allotment Garden in Britain and Japan', in P. Stott and S. Sullivan (eds), *Political Ecology: Power, Myth and Science.* London: Edward Arnold, pp. 203–17.

Chapter 11

THINKING LIKE A CHEESE

TOWARDS AN ECOLOGICAL UNDERSTANDING OF THE REPRODUCTION OF KNOWLEDGE IN CONTEMPORARY ARTISAN CHEESE MAKING

Harry G. West

Introduction

My observations on the way in which knowledge is reproduced among contemporary artisan cheese makers start with reflections on the artisan category and its constituent other, industrial cheese makers. These two categories shade into one another, but a fundamental difference of philosophy distinguishes them as abstract types. I find Aldo Leopold's famous essay, 'Thinking Like a Mountain' (Leopold [1949] 1987), apropos to this philosophical difference. Leopold tells the story of the elimination of wolves from the American prairie landscape that he inhabited in the 1930s. To dairy farmers, whose herds these animals sometimes preyed upon, the only good wolf was a dead wolf. To hunters, like the young Leopold, wolves were rivals; he confesses that he and his companions reasoned 'that because fewer wolves meant more deer, that no wolves would mean hunters' paradise' (ibid.: 130). An older and wiser Leopold recollects in the essay, however, that with the complete disappearance of wolves from the range, the deer population indeed rose dramatically, but that these unchecked herds overgrazed the range, with disastrous consequences for the rangeland, subsequently for the deer population, and ultimately for dairy farmers and their animals. Leopold castigates dairy farmers and deer hunters for their singular, self-interested focus on wolves. Stewardship of the range, he argues, requires thinking not *about*, nor even *as*, only one species, but instead more holistically – in his words, 'thinking like a mountain' which 'understands' the value of wolves, along with every other element, in its complex ecology. Referring to Thoreau's dictum, 'In wildness is the salvation of the world', Leopold concludes, 'Perhaps this is the hidden meaning in the howl of the wolf, long known among mountains, but seldom perceived among men' (ibid.: 133).

Industrial cheese makers, it would seem, think rather like Leopold's dairy farmers and deer hunters. To maximize the predictability of their productive process and the consistency of their product, and to minimize any potential hazards, they seek to eliminate threatening variables wherever possible. The scale of industrial cheese production generally requires that milk be sourced from numerous and, often, distant dairies, increasing the likelihood that supplies will be contaminated with pathogens such as *Tubercles bacillus*, *Escherichia coli*, *Salmonella*, *Brucella melitensis*, *Staphylococcus aureus*, *Campylobacter*, or *Listeria monocytogenes*. To mitigate such hazards, industrial cheese makers pasteurize their milk. They homogenize their milk as well to ensure uniform levels of fat and protein. To prevent their milk, and subsequently their cheese, from interacting with a broader natural environment after pasteurization, they work in virtually sterile rooms, with stainless steel vats and utensils. They follow unchanging recipes that dictate exact temperatures at particular phases in the productive process and exact levels of humidity in each room through which their product passes (see also Paxson 2010: 444). Industrial cheese makers' attempts to simplify the ecology of cheese making produce ironic effects, however. Pasteurization eliminates pathogens from the milk, but it also eliminates the very bacteria upon which cheese making depends. Industrial cheese makers must consequently reintroduce bacteria into the milk in the form of a 'starter culture' – bacteria isolated and reproduced in laboratory conditions. Just as large agricultural fields planted in one crop are highly susceptible to pest invasion, starter cultures are highly vulnerable to bacteriophage – virus particles that attack and destroy bacteria – and so industrial cheese makers must rotate starter cultures in order to stave off the collapse of the simple micro-ecology that is their cheese. Whereas the indigenous micro-flora in raw milk generally out-compete pathogenic bacteria from milking parlour to serving plate – constituting an immune system of sorts for raw milk cheeses – industrial cheese is also relatively more defenceless against pathogens to which it may be exposed after pasteurization, increasing stakes in the maintenance of hygiene from production and processing to sale and consumption.

The approach of the artisan cheese maker is markedly different from that of the industrial cheese maker. Rather than seeking to eliminate variables, artisan cheese makers embrace – even celebrate – some degree of variability. Whereas industrial cheese makers seal off their productive process from the surrounding environment, artisan producers seek to engage actively with their environment. In the course of production, their cheeses may interact with the microflora in wooden tools, straw aging mats, or cave walls, not to mention in their bare hands. They generally work with raw, unhomogenized milk. According to enthusiasts, the broader spectrum of bacteria in unpasteurized milk gives rise to more complex flavours in artisan cheese. As the composition of the artisan cheese maker's raw materials and the environment in which she works changes from season to season, from day to day, even from morning milking to afternoon milking, so too must the productive process. Artisan cheese makers and those who celebrate their work often speak of their dynamic relationship with a broader ecology in terms of 'terroir'. As with wines, it is said that cheeses partake of and reflect the environment in which they are made in defining ways. Different natural environments favour different breeds of animal, whose milk may differ substantially from one another. Distinctive soil composition gives rise to a distinctive palate of grasses and wild flowers on which animals feed, lending taste to the milk (enthusiasts suggest that the flowers in bloom when an animal grazes can be tasted in the cheeses made from her milk). Different patterns of heat and humidity lend themselves to the production of different kinds of cheeses, from pasture to dairy to aging room to shop floor. Mould spores in the air, in the grass, and on cave walls, also give rise to signature tastes and textures in an artisan cheese (this compared with industrial mould-ripened cheeses onto which laboratory-produced moulds are sprayed).

Those who use the term terroir assert that, along with the many variables in a cheese maker's ecology, the artisan herself constitutes a component of terroir. Accordingly, inhabitants of a particular place learn over time how best to work within its distinctive parameters – how to coax the best results out of its natural endowment – and they pass this distinctive, traditional knowledge from generation to generation. But those who use the terroir concept tell us very little about how this cultured ecology and these artefacts of human invention are actually 're-membered' (meaning both sustained in memory, and manufactured once more) – in other words, how they are preserved through time and transmitted from one cheese maker to another. If industrial cheese makers think like Leopold's deer hunters and dairy farmers, do artisan producers think like Leopold's mountain? If terroir constitutes the relevant ecology of artisan cheese making, do artisan cheese makers 'think like a terroir'? If terroir is reproduced in microcosm in an artisan cheese, does an artisan cheese maker 'think like a cheese'? If so, what exactly does this mean? In what follows, I explore this question by considering the stories of two cheese makers with whom I have spent time in the course of my fieldwork.

Resonating with Terroir

Joe Schneider was born in Syracuse, New York in the United States. He studied agricultural sciences at Cornell University before moving to the Netherlands, where he met an enterprising Turkish immigrant who was making cheese for sale mostly to the Turkish diaspora there. Joe's interest was piqued. He helped his new friend to set up a small cheese plant in an Amsterdam warehouse, but after a taste of industrial cheese making in an urban setting, he became interested in a different kind of cheese making – one that included the farm, the animals, and the milking parlour. He decided to travel the country, 'teaching [himself] how to make cheese' by visiting farmhouse cheese makers and making cheese with them: 'I just begged, "Can I come and make cheese with you?" So they said, "Yeah". And that's how I learned.'

Joe also learned through his growing contacts that farmhouse cheese making was on the rise in England, and so he and his wife moved to Sussex, where Joe found work as a cheese maker on a biodynamic farm. He was subsequently recruited to make cheese for Daylesford, where his cheeses won several awards. Following this, Randolph Hodgson, owner of Neal's Yard Dairy (the most important cheesemonger in the United Kingdom), proposed that Joe partner with him to fill a void on the British cheese plate by producing a blue-veined full-cream cheese from raw cows' milk. The project was an archaeological one of sorts. Following the Second World War, the production of Stilton – England's best loved blue cheese – became increasingly industrial, with producers opting to use pasteurized milk. By the 1990s, no one was making Stilton from raw milk, and Randolph hoped that, together with Joe, they might create a Stilton-style cheese with the deeper flavours that he remembered Stilton once delivering. Joe remembered Randolph's pitch when he spoke with me in December 2006:

> Randolph said, 'Do you know Stilton hasn't been made on a farm since the 1930s?' So all of a sudden you get this picture of, like, wow, here's this cheese, it's considered the 'King of English cheeses', and really, in it's current manifestation, it's a mere shadow of its former self. We don't even know what that former self was now. There are a handful of people who have an accurate memory of what unpasteurized Stilton tasted like in the 80s, and nobody's had it since. And nobody's had farmhouse Stilton since the 30s. So it just ticked all my boxes as a cheese maker.

Joe signed on to the project and oversaw the construction of his own cheese room on the Collingthwaite Farm on the edge of the village of Cuckney in Nottinghamshire. He began making the new cheese – which he and Randolph decided to call Stitchelton – in October 2006. The first batches reached maturity for the Christmas market at the end of the year. 'Re-membering' the Stiltons of the past has not been a simple task, however. Paul Connerton (Connerton 1989: 72) has written:

> We preserve versions of the past by representing it to ourselves in words and images. Commemorative ceremonies are pre-eminent instances of this. They keep the past in mind by depictive representations of past events. They are re-enactments of the past, its return in a representational guise which normally includes a simulacrum of the scene or situation recaptured. Such re-enactments depend for much of their rhetorical persuasiveness ... on prescribed bodily behaviour. But we can also preserve the past deliberately without explicitly re-presenting it in words and images. Our bodies, which in commemorations, stylistically re-enact an image of the past, keep the past also in an entirely effective form in their continuing ability to perform certain skilled actions ... Many forms of habitual skilled re-membering illustrate a keeping of the past in mind that, without ever adverting to its historical origin, nevertheless re-enacts the past in our present conduct. In habitual memory the past is, as it were, sedimented in the body.

Connerton (1989: 72–73) goes on to distinguish between two distinct types of practices, namely 'inscribing practices' (through which information is conveyed by means of storing it for later retrieval) and 'incorporating practices' (through which information is stored in and imparted by bodily activity).

Joe sought to rediscover raw milk Stilton through both inscribed and incorporated mnemonics. Of the former, there were basic recipes – that clearly 'prescribed bodily behaviour' to use Connerton's words – even if most of the existing Stilton makers were guarded about specific details of their productive processes. Of the latter, there were experienced cheese makers – bearers of a 'continuing ability to perform certain skilled actions', in Connerton's words – who Joe looked upon as potential mentors. Joe told me:

> When I thought about it, I thought, I've never done this – blue cheese. But the thing I really felt confident about was the support I had around me, the knowledge I could tap into. A lot of people know how to make Stilton. Some of them even remember how to make raw milk Stilton. So, I felt like if I'm lacking in the technical acumen, I've got resources to dip into: we have Randolph in terms of what does it taste like and look like; Colston Bassett (one of the smaller industrial producers, and the last to make raw

milk Stilton), in terms of the technicalities of it; even Ernie Wagstaff, who was the last chap to make [raw milk Stilton, at Colston Bassett] – we could ask him. So that filled me with confidence that we'd be able to succeed. I wouldn't be on my own. It wasn't an unknown quantity. There were people out there who knew the tradition and could pass it on – as long as they were willing.

Willingness, it turned out, was not the problem. Joe reported: 'To get us started, the chaps at Colston Bassett really helped us'. But his account of this help betrayed the limitations of such assistance, even as Joe recognized its value:

> They were instrumental in terms of helping us, and then in terms of coming back later, when I had gotten enough experience under my belt and I could understand more about the nuances of it to make some sort of quantum leaps. After I got through the mechanics of it, and I could understand some subtleties, they came back and we'd talk about it some more, and we spent a few days, and that really helped me in terms of ... that 'transmission of knowledge' [a term I had used previously in our conversation].

But Joe concluded by admitting: 'It's so true, there's pretty good technical resources out there in terms of books and courses and everything but, until you get stuck in it, and you start translating what you know into your materials, there's so much of it that you can't glean from those resources.' He addressed this issue more specifically on another occasion:

> If you look at the maturing rooms – if you look at the books, if you talk to people, they said, 'you need 90 per cent humidity and this tempera-ture', so I plugged that into my design. And it didn't work! So what's going on? So I walk in and think, 'I think this is too much humidity' or 'It's too close, I don't have enough airflow'. So you look in the book and it says, 'Good airflow needed'. What does that mean?! So you have great big fans blowing across and now the cheese is drying out. So, let's turn those fans down. That's the sort of struggle that we went through.

In the dialogue between 'Theory' and 'Practice' (entitled *Art of the Earth*) written by the sixteenth-century Huguenot potter Bernard Palissy, Practice says to Theory:

> Even if I used a thousand reams of paper to write down all the accidents that have happened to me in learning this art, you must be assured that, however good a brain you may have, you will still make a thousand mis-takes, which cannot be learned from writings, and even if you had them

in writing, you would not believe them until practice has given you a thousand afflictions. (In Smith 2004: 103)

Palissy's words underscore the importance of individual experience in learning a craft. But Joe's early difficulties making Stitchelton could not be attributed solely to his lack of experience, for even his mentors would have been unable simply to 're-member' the Stilton of the past on the Collingthwaite Farm. Joe's 'thousand afflictions' – or, as he described it, 'getting stuck in it' – had much to do with terroir. He was making a Stilton-style cheese in a different context from any of his predecessors. The context in which he was working was a unique constellation of soil, pasture, climate, herd, cheese room, and aging room, unlike that known by any Stilton maker before him. His predecessors knew a similar range of variables, but Joe's variables *varied differently* from theirs. *His* experience with these variables would necessarily be part of what *he* would have to know in order to know how to make a Stilton-style raw milk cheese in *his* cheese room. He alone could learn this unique cheese making ecology – an ecology of which he *himself* was part.

Joe's method – his way of coping with 'a thousand afflictions' – has been, in part, 'scientific'. He works to a recipe, albeit an ever-changing one, first adapted from Stilton recipes available to him, and subsequently adjusted to reflect lessons learned through experience. Throughout 'the make' (as cheese makers call their productive process), he carefully monitors, among other things: the temperature of the milk when the rennet is added; the time after renneting when the curd is cut; the acidity level of the curd when it is removed from the draining tray, milled, and placed in cylinders called hoops; and the temperature and humidity in the rooms in which the cheeses are dried and aged. He keeps thorough records of these measures, along with sensory 'data' he gathers at various stages in the make, and refers back to these as he evaluates the quality of his cheeses when they finally mature some two to three months later. His description of this 'scientific' practice reveals its complexity and limitations, however:

> So you're looking at this huge giant vat of curd and by the end of it you've got this very good sense of: well, this end was soft, but it got harder here, maybe because that's thicker; the whey ran a bit there; ah, this one's under-salted – a very complex picture. And I gotta walk over to this piece of paper and distil all that complex *feeling* into a word. So, you'll say, 'soft', right? So twelve weeks later [when the cheese has matured], when I'm looking at the make sheet, it's like, 'Oh, yeah, soft curd', but all the complexity of that understanding is gone, because I can't carry that.

In reference to all of the 'data' that he observes in the course of a day in the cheese room, Joe told me, 'There's nowhere to write it, nowhere to record it. It would be, you know, ideal, if every day you made a piece of cheese, you put everything down there.' But then he pointed out that even if he had all of these data, no formula exists to plug them into telling him what conclusions to draw from them. There are far too many variables in artisan cheese making, and the scope of their variation is far too great, to permit for such an 'equation'.

According to Joe, a singular focus on any one variable – reminiscent of Leopold's focus on wolves – is simply not possible in artisan cheese making. He told me that, in the first year of making Stitchelton, he tried to eliminate a bitter taste by reducing the amount of starter culture he was using, but that this adjustment actually caused his cheeses to shrink in size. He and his customers were happy with the taste of these new cheeses, but wanted cheeses of the original, larger size. But merely putting more curd into the hoops would not have solved this new problem – it may even have created a new problem – as the improved taste of the cheeses was bound up not only with the reduction of starter culture, but also with the changing ratio of salt to curd volume in the smaller cheeses. So along with more curd, Joe had to add more salt to each hoop.

Because he cannot isolate any single variable, Joe has to see each one in the context of his entire cheese-making ecology. He told me:

> If you could look inside my head, every day when I'm walkin' around the place makin' cheese, the background information that I'm tryin' to take in, ya' know, goes right from: 'who's milking?; where have the cows been?; are they out?; what time of year it is?; which milk is it?; is it older milk?; is it this morning's milk?; what's the temperature outside?' – because I know that air's going to be going into the maturing rooms, and on a wet day humidity's going to be going up and on a dry day humidity's going to be going down. So all these sorts of background bits and pieces that you just sort of file away in your head – that helps you make a decision later.

Decision making, as Joe described it to me, entails not only tinkering, but holding tinkering in a broader context, such as he did in the case discussed above when adjustment to the amount of starter produced changes that required him to change the amount of salt. He zooms in on an issue, but then zooms out again to see the issue, and his engagement with it, in the context of the whole in which the background information in his head is relevant. In his words, 'you make an educated guess, or a calculation, or whatever – how much salt you want to put in it – it's sort of, you know, some maths and a little bit of luck. And you throw it in, and now you've got to wait all over [until the cheese matures] and go through the experience again.' Speaking of a dialectic between 'narrowing' and 'widening', he said, 'You never make a perfect cheese every time, right, so you're constantly doing that back and forth, adjusting things.'

Key to this dynamic, he told me, is a measured response to variability:

> What I find useful as a cheese maker is the patience and confidence of ignoring blips ... So if you're looking at acidity, and you think 'I'll try this', ah, and it goes off the scale, you know. But a young cheese maker might go 'Oh that was completely wrong, I'll go this way', and then it swings the other way. But sometimes there's that experience, like, 'Hmm, that seems a bit strange to me, but I think I'll just stick with what I'm doing, and watch it over a few goes, and see how it reacts.'

He told me that he adjusts the amount of starter, as well as the amount of rennet he uses, with the changing seasons, but that he does so gradually, incrementally, allowing himself 'to make two or three bad batches instead of knee-jerking ... knowing that those things happen in cheese making and you don't react at the first sort of feedback you get that's not right; you wait a minute, because the cheese and the milk and everything that happens in the day – it is multi-variant, and you can't be confident that that one little thing's the problem'. According to Joe, each of the variables has a 'bandwidth' within which he tries to hold them, while at the same time recognizing that adjusting one may push another one out of the desirable range until yet another is adjusted. A good cheese maker eventually finds a set of parameters that, together, generally work well, within which such fine-tuning can take place.

Navigating this constantly shifting array of contextual variables requires an approach similar to that described by Ingold – a sort of 'wayfaring' through unknown space (Ingold 2010). Of course, when things are going badly, wayfaring can feel more like 'groping in the dark'. The early days of inventing a new cheese – or reinventing an old one – may entail throwing out a lot of failed cheeses, although Joe rarely had to do this with early batches of Stitchelton, despite expecting to need to. In time, however, the successful cheese maker develops a 'knack' for his terroir – an intangible way of understanding its dynamics and engaging with them. Elsewhere, Ingold (2001: 136) describes a woodsman selecting a tree to fell and deciding where to place the notch so as to bring the tree down where he wants:

> To observe him doing this ... is to watch as he paces the woods, casting his eyes over different trees, sizing them up. In other words, it is to observe him, feeling his way, in an environment, towards a goal that is conceived in anticipation of a future project ... [T]he 'plans' that the woodsman arrives at through this activity in no sense specify or determine the

movements that follow, or the circumstances attending them, in all their concrete detail. What they do, rather, is to place him in a position of readiness, from which to launch into the subsequent project with a reasonable chance of success.

Understanding such 'workmanship', Ingold tells us, requires an 'ecological approach', built upon the premise that 'human knowledgeability is not founded in some combination of innate capacities and acquired competence, but in *skill*'. He tells us, 'The movement of the skilled practitioner ... is continually and fluently responsive to perturbations of the perceived environment' (Ingold 2001: 135). In other words, Ingold tells us, 'the perceptual system of the skilled practitioner *resonates* with the properties of the environment'. He writes: 'The accomplished woodsman ... looks around him for guidance on where and how to cut: he consults the world, not a picture in his head. The world, after all, is its own best model' (Ingold 2001: 142). Like Ingold's woodsman, Joe constantly surveys his environment, attuned to the many changing elements within it, from pasture to milking parlour, to cheese room, to aging room. His plans change with his changing perceptions of these changing elements. His thoughts 'resonate' with the weather, the grass, the milk, the curd and, finally, the cheese. He works in 'real time', and his 'taskscape' (both Ingold's terms, ibid.) is his terroir and, in microcosm, his cheese (see also Paxson 2010: 444–45). He thinks not only about his cheese, but also with it – dare we say, *like* it. For his cheese is 'its own best model'.

Learning from a Cheese

The second case I present reveals in greater detail just what it means for 'the perceptual system of the skilled practitioner [to *resonate*] with the properties of the environment,' as Ingold would say, or, to paraphrase Leopold, for a cheese maker to 'think like a cheese'. The Bellonte farm is situated in a hamlet called Farges in the Saint-Nectaire commune of the Puy-de-Dôme department, located in the Auvergne region of central France. At least eight generations of Bellontes have lived in Farges, making Saint-Nectaire cheese from the milk of their own cows. Members of all three living generations work on the farm, which is now owned by three brothers and one sister of the middle generation: Bernard (now retired), Pierre (who manages the herd), Alphonse (who manages the cheese room and the farm shop complex that includes a restaurant and visitors' centre, about which more later), and Marie-France (who runs a shop in the village of Saint-Nectaire where she sells '*produits locaux*', including cheese made on the family farm).

The father of these four siblings, Émile, had retired when I first started visiting the farm in 2004, and has since passed away, while their mother, Bernadette, continues to lend a hand in the stables and in the cheese room. Bernard's wife, Annie, and Pierre's wife, Doudoune, are the principal cheese makers. All nine members of the next generation – mostly in their late teens and early twenties during the years I visited the farm – have worked in the stables, and/or in the cheese room, the farm shop, the restaurant, or the visitors' centre, and many continue to do so.

In the simplest sense, the Bellontes have learned to make cheese from their forebears. Annie and Doudoune have 'taught' their children as well as their nieces and nephews, just as Bernadette 'taught' them, and Emile's mother 'taught' her. But the way in which the Bellontes speak of learning belies the notion that knowledge was simply passed on to them like an object from hand to hand. For the Bellontes, learning to make cheese has been a much more diffuse process, at once far simpler and far more complex than being 'taught' by anyone. When I asked Alphonse how and why he became a cheese maker, he answered me only by saying: 'I fell into it ... I was born into it.' When I asked Doudoune how she came to make cheese, her answers betrayed a similar sense of happenstance: 'I married Pierre'; 'to earn a living'; 'you have to enjoy it'; and 'it's not a bad life'. Everyone on the Bellonte farm, it would seem, 'fell into cheese making' – everyone was 'born into it', or 'married into it'. Each of them came of age in a world where dairying and cheese making were taken-for-granted facts of life. Each spent time in the stable and in the cheese room long before they sought to learn, and long before others sought to teach them. By the time they might have started learning, they seemingly already knew. They rarely ever asked how to do something, and rarely were they explicitly told.

The way in which the Bellontes de-accentuated person-to-person interaction in favour of a more environmental conception of the learning process harbours more complexity than first meets the eye, however. They did not simply become cheese makers for having lived in a place where cheese was made. Their terroir did not possess them like a spirit possessing an unconscious host. Instead, they and their family members played an active role in their learning to make cheese. But their casual disregard of formal tutelage and learning bore within it a deeper truth: in their experience, adepts and novices are not the only agents at work in the reproduction and transmission of knowledge, and they may in fact interact rather little, if at all, in the re-membering of a cheese. Instead, many of the crucial interactions in their re-membering Saint-Nectaire have been with other elements in their cheese making ecology.

A closer look at a few of these reveals a great deal about how, for the Bellontes, 'the world [or more specifically, their cheese] is its own best model'. A crucial moment in cheese making on the Bellonte farm, as in most cheese rooms, is the removal of the curd from the vat and its placement in a 'form' (incidentally, the term (originally in Latin) from which Romance language words for cheese such as the Italian *formaggio* and the French *fromage* derive). At this moment, the qualities – along with the quality – of the curd are generally the object of shared interest for everyone in the cheese room, for much about the characteristics of the final cheese can be discerned in the curd. Curd, however, is not merely an *object* of collective inquiry and, eventually, of shared knowledge. Nor is good curd simply the result of good cheese making knowledge. As cheese makers stand over the vat, curd is a *means* by which knowledge of cheese making is actually transmitted. But how? While the Bellontes possess a vocabulary with which to talk about the curd (moist, dry, fragile, hard, etc.), they rarely used this and, when they did, it was insufficient for their purposes. The transmission of cheese making knowledge by means of the curd was more than just a matter of *communication* between the Bellontes *about* the curd. Ingold (1992: 53) has written: 'Acting in the world is the practitioner's way of knowing it, thus the acquisition of environmental knowledge is inseparable from productive practice'. To illustrate this, he tells the story of his father showing him mushrooms in the woods. He tells us that his father was not communicating information by way of the mushrooms, but instead introducing him to them and inviting him to engage with them (Ingold 2000: 21). Similarly, the Bellontes learned about good curd by *engaging* with it. Their engagement with the curd entailed more than even Ingold's analysis suggests, however. It was not only a question of being *shown* (Ingold 2000: 21) the curd (rather than merely being told about it); it was not only a question of 'following what other people do ... watch[ing], feel[ing], or listen[ing] to the movements of the expert, and seek[ing] through repeated trials to bring [one's] own bodily movements into line with those of [one's] attention so as to achieve the kind of rhythmic adjustment of perception and action that lies at the heart of fluent performance' (Ingold 2001: 141). The Bellontes engaged with the curd by *making* it, *touching* it, *feeling* it, *pressing* it in the form, and what is more by perceiving how *it* felt, how *it* behaved in their hands, and how *it* stitched together and aged into a cheese.

Alfred Gell's discussion of objects and agency is useful here, if also insufficient. According to Gell, objects can exercise agency. For example, landmines do something: they explode; they kill people. Similarly, in the Bellonte cheese room, curd was not merely a medium through which adept and novice communicated, or engaged, with one another. Curd *did* things. It sometimes squished and gave off whey, it sometimes broke apart too easily, and it sometimes held together well in the form. It was from these *actions of the curd* far more than from being shown or being told about it that the Bellontes ultimately learned what was right and what was wrong about curd. Working with the curd, they learned from the curd itself. It could, of course, be weeks before the quality of the curd revealed itself, in the maturing caves and, finally, on the shop counter or on the restaurant plate. Learning from the curd was therefore a fragmented, disjointed process. But it was a learning process that was held together, in the experience of the Bellontes, by the curd/cheese itself as it moved through time and space, *doing* one thing or another.

Gell (1998: 20–21, 222–23) argues that the agency of objects – whether landmines, paintings, or curd – is always 'secondary' to the human actor whose 'primary agency' initiates and animates it, or is, in other words, 'distributed' through it. Objects, according to Gell, only bear the traces of the intentional, agentive acts of those who create them, and it is these acts, he tells us, that may be discerned by those who later engage with an object and experience how it has intervened in a 'causal milieu' – that is to say, altered 'the way things are'. He tells us that objects are not in and of themselves 'self-sufficient agents'. Writing specifically of art objects, he concludes: 'the kinds of agency which are attributed to art objects (or indexes of agency) are inherently and irreducibly social in that art objects never (in any relevant way) emerge as agents except in very specific social contexts' (Gell 1998: 17). The Bellontes appreciate well the importance of the social context that surrounds a cheese from the vat to the shop floor to the dining table, and they spend far too much time caring for their cheeses to consider them 'self-sufficient'. But for the Bellontes, the agency of their cheeses was more than a mere trace of the agency of their maker, to be discerned by those who later engaged with them. Often, in fact, the person who made the cheese was the one who later engaged with it, whether pressing it into the form, turning it in the ageing cave, or cutting it for sale on the farmshop counter. If the agency of their cheeses was ultimately only their own, the Bellontes would have been reading their own acts to themselves much of the time as they engaged with their cheeses. Rather, for them, what was discerned in moments of working with the curd, and with the cheeses it became, was more than the intentions of the maker – it was the behaviour of the curd, and later the cheese, itself. And it was largely from this behaviour that the Bellontes learned to reproduce Saint-Nectaire cheese as well as they did. For the Bellontes – as for most artisan cheese makers I have worked with – the line between the primary agency of people and the secondary agency of objects is considerably blurrier than Gell suggests.

Most cheese makers and enthusiasts speak of their cheeses as 'living things'; refrigerating them, they warn customers, will 'slow their metabolism', while wrapping them in cling film or sealing them in an airtight container will 'suffocate them'. Of course, cheese is not an organism, but it is an ensemble of things, some of which *are* organisms – some of which *are* living things in the conventional biological sense. And the agency of these things, and of the entire ensemble, is rather more autonomous than Gell would admit (see also Paxson 2008). Even if Bernadette's forebears only dimly perceived the living entities that inhabited their cheeses, it was in large measure through interaction with *them* that they learned their craft and through engagement with *them* that the knowledge of Saint-Nectaire was reproduced and transmitted through time. By way of illustration, until quite recently Saint-Nectaire makers ripened and renneted their milk, and cut their curd, in a barrel-shaped vat called a *baste*, which was made of a local hardwood. A good baste might last for decades before its leaks could no longer be repaired and it had to be replaced. Following the acquisition of a new baste, a cheese maker would generally notice that her curd was not right and that, subsequently, her cheeses would fail to mature properly. Through generations, Saint-Nectaire makers sustained their belief that the baste itself played an *active* role in cheese making – a belief eventually confirmed by microbiologists who discovered that the baste's wooden surfaces harboured useful residual bacteria and served to enhance the milk's indigenous flora. With only a dim perception of this, cheese makers in the past struggled to get their cheeses right again after replacing a baste. 'Knowledge' of this problem – although not necessarily of what to do about it – was partially sustained among cheese makers between such debacles, but the dilemma it provoked was partially rediscovered anew with each crisis. Cheese makers, in fact, did not 'learn' how to rectify this problem from one another so much as they 'discovered' its solution from the action of the living entities with which they worked – in other words, from milk and bacteria and wood *doing what they do* while the cheese maker tinkered and time passed. The flora in the milk that they poured daily into their new bastes colonized the wood, and the cheese maker's problem was eventually resolved.

To give another example, Saint-Nectaire cheese has long been aged on pine boards in caves hewn from the rock of volcanic pumice. Only recently has it been discovered that the biochemistry of the wood (its resins, its tannins, etc.) presents a hostile environment for the growth of pathogenic bacteria. Saint-Nectaire makers aged their cheeses on pine boards for a host of reasons, including the way in which they absorbed excess moisture from the surface of the aging cheese. From time to time, however, a cheese maker departed from this practice.

If those who ate her cheeses became ill, she asked herself why, and if she returned to the use of pine boards and subsequently found that her cheeses were once more safe to eat, she stayed with this tested practice.

Given the multiplicity of 'objects' involved in making a cheese, indeed, the multiplicity of entities within a cheese, many of which can be said to act in one way or another, it is perhaps more useful to think of a cheese not as an object but instead as an 'assemblage'. Bennett (Bennett 2010: 23–24) builds on the work of Deleuze and Guattari (1987) to define an assemblage as follows:

> Assemblages are *ad hoc* groupings of diverse elements, of vibrant materials of sorts. Assemblages are living, throbbing confederations that are able to function despite the persistent presence of energies that confound them from within ... Assemblages are not governed by any central head: no one materiality or type of material has sufficient competence to determine consistently the trajectory or impact of the group. The effects generated by an assemblage are, rather, emergent properties, emergent in that their ability to make something happen ... is distinct from the sum of the vital force of each materiality considered alone. Each member and proto-member of the assemblage has a certain vital force, but there is also an effectivity proper to the grouping as such: an agency of the assemblage. And precisely because each member-actant maintains an energetic pulse slightly 'off' from that *of* the assemblage, an assemblage is never a stolid block but an open-ended collective, a 'non-totalizable sum'. An assemblage thus not only has a distinctive history of formation but a finite life span.

Echoing Bennett, cheese is a 'living, throbbing confederation' of milk fat and proteins, lactobacilli, rennet, salt, moulds and fungi, to name only the most basic elements. Each of these entities acts on the others, and as any cheese maker knows, the effects of this array of actions are anything but certain. Together, however, the vital forces of each of these component parts, the assemblage as a whole, adds up to something: a cheese – or at least the cheese maker hopes that this is the case. And this assemblage has a finite life span, coming of age in a glorious climax of flavour and, if not eaten, eventually 'going off'. This assemblage, of course, is made up of component assemblages, and is part of still other larger assemblages. 'Terroir' is one of the latter – a broader, encompassing assemblage whose component elements act, also, at the dimension of the cheese itself. The cheese maker herself is part of this broader assemblage – just as proponents of the terroir concept suggest – and she is perhaps even part of the assemblage that is the cheese, for without her agency, there would be no cheese (see also Paxson 2008: 25). But she alone does not 'determine the trajectory' of the whole. Other elements in the assemblage also contribute to this trajectory. As we have seen, many of the essential decisions in cheese making are ones that the individual cheese maker never makes; rather, it may be said, other elements in the assemblage contribute to the trajectory of the whole by doing what they do, unless the cheese maker deflects or overrides them (sometimes to desired effect and sometimes only to discover why she should not have done so).

If 'local knowledge' is often rendered explicit to individual cheese makers only when they depart from established practices and observe the negative consequences, one might conclude that much of the 'knowledge' of how to make a cheese lies in 'tradition', and that it is manifest in habitual practices that individual makers perform by rote, without reflection. To be sure, cheese-making knowledge transcends the individual. It transcends pairs of adepts and novices working together in the cheese room. It even transcends generations. But this begs the question: where does cheese-making knowledge reside then, and how is memory of a cheese sustained through time? Connerton's framework for understanding 'how societies remember' is of little help here, for as we have seen, to a significant degree, what is re-membered is not incorporated into the body of the individual cheese maker. In so far as recipes are insufficient for learning how to make a good cheese, nor is what is re-membered intentionally inscribed in codified form by one cheese maker for retrieval and decoding later by another. Ingold (2001: 133) is more useful here. He writes: 'It makes no sense to ask whether the capacity to climb lies with the climber or the ladder, or whether the capacity to play the piano resides in the pianist or the instrument. These capacities exist neither "inside" the body and brain of the practitioner nor "outside" in the environment.' Citing the work of Andy Clark (1997), he concludes, '[These capacities] are rather properties of environmentally extended systems that crosscut the boundaries of body and brain'. Building on this and revisiting Connerton, one might say that knowledge – or at least that which is re-membered in cheese making – is both *inscribed* into the assemblage as a whole by various agents and – in so far as the assemblage is a living throbbing entity – also *incorporated* into it. In other words, to a significant degree, the knowledge of cheese making resides in the interactive interstices between cheese makers and their broader ecologies – in terroirs comprising them and the other components of an assemblage, including soil, rain, grass, animals, milk, vats, bacteria, caves, moulds, shelves and fungi. These components may not themselves *think* – (their agency is manifest, for example, in their development rather than in their *thought*) – but the cheese maker must think *with* them, *through* them, or as Leopold would say, *like* the broader ecology that comprises them. The stuff of knowledge, then, is harboured in the interstices of this broader ecology like bacteria in a wooden vat. As much as recipes and master-apprentice dialogues, these interstices are the sites of the act of re-membering a cheese. In the words of Sarah Whatmore (2002: 162), 'The rhythms and motions of [such] inter-corporeal practices configure spaces of connectivity between more-than-human life worlds; topologies of intimacy and affectivity that confound conventional cartographies of distance and proximity, and local and global scales'. Reproducing a cheese – or, contributing decisively to its reproduction – thus requires a cheese maker to attune (Pickering 1995: 14) her thinking, as well as her practices, with the dynamics of this cheese making ecology and with the agentive potentialities of the entire cheese making assemblage.

Expanding Terroir

Thus far I have used the 'terroir' concept to advocate an ecological approach to understanding the transmission of knowledge in artisan cheese making. In the rest of this chapter, however, I wish to pick up Whatmore's suggestion that practices such as cheese making 'confound ... local and global scales' by arguing that the relevant ecology of a contemporary artisan cheese is a much larger assemblage than users of the terroir term generally recognize – that it transcends the vale, the county or the department, even the nation. One might conclude from my argument that the terroir assemblage is embedded in still larger assemblages – ones that comprise national, and even international, market linkages, as well as varied forms of national and international regulation and self-regulation. Instead I suggest that, so fundamental to the cultural ecology of cheese making today are these larger dimensions, so essential are they to the work of re-membering these cultured objects, that we might expand the terroir concept to include them.

I will focus on just three elements of this broader contemporary ecology of cheese making, beginning with the consumer. Those who use the terroir concept have long acknowledged the place within terroir of people. The 'traditional knowledge' of local producers is widely recognized as a key element in terroir. However, rarely if ever do those who celebrate terroir speak of the consumer. But if there is a 'taste of place' (Trubek 2008) that distinguishes *produits de terroir* – one that guides producers in certain directions, as opposed to others, as they seek to give expression to a specific natural endowment in their products – surely those who have eaten these products have played an important historical role in shaping this taste. Not long ago, inclusion of the consumer as an element of terroir would not have necessitated spatial expansion of the concept. This is not to suggest that terroir foods, along with those who have made and eaten them, have ever been sealed off from a broader world. We need look no further than our two examples to see that 'local products' have long travelled, often great distances: despite being made in the counties of Derbyshire, Nottinghamshire and Leicestershire, Stilton was in fact named after a town on the Great North Road in Huntingtonshire (now Cambridgeshire) because significant amounts of it were marketed there, not only to travellers but also to retailers who sold the cheese in London and beyond (Hickman 1995); and recognition of a cheese called Saint-Nectaire, and a corresponding productive 'tradition', may be traced to the presentation of a cheese from the region to Louis XIV by the Maréchal de France, Henri de La Ferté-Senneterre (a corruption of Saint-Nectaire), and subsequent demand for this prized commodity at Versailles and elsewhere in France. Notwithstanding such histories, in the past a much greater proportion of such products were consumed closer to their places of production. Not more than a century ago, the vast majority of producers of what are today called artisan foods themselves consumed much of what they made, and a substantial part of their 'surplus' was eaten by local residents such as the millers, masons, cobblers and seamstresses who also inhabited rural areas prior to the industrial revolution. But with industrialization and urbanization, rural societies have witnessed dramatic out-migration over the past century. Remaining farmers have often expanded farm sizes, and dairy farmers have increased herd sizes. Even if together today's 'artisan producers' make less cheese than their farmhouse forebears (although on average each makes far more than these predecessors), there remain even fewer 'local' people to buy what they wish to sell, and so they depend to a far greater extent upon extra-local consumers who, owing to mechanized transport, refrigeration and mass marketing, are now within reach. The preferences of these consumers – shaped as they are by the necessities and conveniences of modern life – have to a significant degree supplanted those of fellow village residents in the cultural ecology of contemporary cheese making.

The Bellonte case illustrates this well. I described Joe and Randolph's Stitchelton project above as an archaeological one of sorts; Alphonse Bellonte's project is quite literally archaeological. As a young man, Alphonse grew interested in a complex of caves on a portion of the farm that his father, Émile, had acquired from neighbours who left the village in 1962. Émile used the caves primarily to store disused farm equipment and bric-a-brac, as well as to age some wine and a bit of cheese. But in 1991, Alphonse convinced his father to allow him and an archaeologist friend to clear out and excavate the caves. The layers of sediment bore witness to the rich history not only of the caves but also of the region. They had been dug out of pumice deposited by the volcanic eruptions that gave birth to the Massive Central more than 3 million years ago. They were inhabited in the Middle Ages by those who quarried stone in the immediate vicinity for use in the construction of many of the region's Romanesque churches. During the French Revolution, the local vicar took refuge in the caves along with the relics of Saint Nectaire. In the aftermath of the phylloxera blight that ravaged vineyards elsewhere in France in the second half of the nineteenth century, vines were planted in large numbers for the first time in the Auvergne, and the caves were used for a time as wine cellars. Subsequently, they were used to age cheese. Alphonse envisioned yet another use for the caves. He had seen in his lifetime not only the decline of many craft industries in the Auvergne region but also the rise of tourism, including ski resorts, hiking trails, camp grounds, and spas built over long-famous hot springs. A great number of the local residents who remain in the region now work in the tourist industry, or combine farming or other trades with tourist activities such as hosting visitors on the farm. Alphonse decided he would use the caves to bring tourists, and income, to the Bellonte farm. With assistance from a specialist firm, Alphonse set up a small museum in the cave complex. An hour-long multimedia tour of the caves tells their story, and then directs visitors to the stables (where they can see the Bellonte herd of a hundred or so Montbéliard cows), the cheese room (where they can watch the Bellontes make cheese), and the farm shop (where they can buy cheese made on the farm, as well as other *produits locaux*). During the summers that I have visited the Bellonte farm, *Les Mystères de Farges* (as the museum is called) attracts dozens of car-fulls and several bus-loads of visitors a day, mainly from within France, but some also from across Europe and beyond. Building on this success, Alphonse opened a restaurant in a restored sheep barn adjoining the caves, serving up to 150 diners at a time, including corporate groups using the facility for away-day meetings.

During the peak tourist season, visitors buy most of the cheese made on the farm; subsequent mail orders from these same visitors take up some of the slack during the tourist off-season. As a consequence, the Bellontes sell most of their cheese direct to their customers, capturing more of the value of their labour than they would by marketing through other means. Alphonse's strategy has effectively reconnected the Bellonte farm with those who have left the region over the last century, if not literally (although in some cases visitors are actually those who once lived in the region) then at least figuratively (most tourists embrace the narrative of 'rediscovering' the life of 'their forebears' in the 'unspoiled' countryside). Regardless of whether or not these visitors actually are, or descend from, departed neighbours, they now stand in for these as a body of consumers whose tastes constitute part of the relevant cultural ecology of Saint-Nectaire cheese. In other words, as the chain linking the Bellontes to those who consume their cheese stretches, so too does the terroir assemblage. In the interface with these consumers, knowledge of cheese making, as well as the cheese itself, is continually reshaped. Thinking like a cheese has, for the Bellontes, necessarily implied thinking at the dimensions of the market nexus, where taste for their cheese is sustained and satisfied – where, as Alphonse would say, the 'living tradition' of Saint-Nectaire is given new lease. Tellingly, the Bellontes now talk more openly and more often about their cheese – how it is made, its defining characteristics, its desirable qualities – with the tourists who visit them than they do (or have ever done) amongst themselves. And the Bellontes now sell younger – and, by their own admission, 'blander' – cheeses than they did only a few years ago, as such cheeses travel better, whether in a suitcase stowed in the luggage compartment of a tour bus, or in the post. In other words, the Bellontes' repetitive re-membering of Saint-Nectaire for tourist consumption has subtly transformed their knowledge, and their cheese.

Consumers near and far have also been an element in the relevant ecology of Stitchelton. Savvy promotion and strong media interest in the project have created vigorous demand for the cheese, allowing it to be sold by a number of specialist cheesemongers in the United Kingdom and abroad. Most of the trade in Stitchelton is, however, handled by Neal's Yard Dairy, where the cheese occupies pride of place on the retail counter. Neal's Yard Dairy has played a central role in the late-twentieth-century revival of artisan cheeses in the United Kingdom and beyond, not only by supporting producers with technical advice and good prices, but also by educating consumers about the qualities of raw milk cheeses. When the company first opened, however, there were few artisan cheeses to sell, and it had considerable difficulty moving its own products over the counter as well, not only because customers were unfamiliar with good artisan cheeses but also because, by their own admission, Neal's Yard Dairy cheeses were simply not very good. The shop's practice of assertively offering customers a piece of cheese to taste was in those days less about getting them hooked on a good cheese than about getting someone to actually consume some of their product, and was usually followed by asking for critical commentary on the cheese. Neal's Yard Dairy has historically treated commentary – which over the years has become rather more positive – as a resource, at first using it to improve their own product line, and then, after the company ceased to make its own cheese, feeding it back to the producers whose cheeses they sell.

The customer has therefore always been prominent in the evaluation of good cheese at Neal's Yard Dairy. In Randolph's words, 'a cheese must be good on the customer's palate to be a good cheese'. To be sure, Stitchelton is a cheese borne of Randolph's desire to restore to the British cheese plate the tastes that he remembers raw milk Stilton once delivering. Together, Joe and Randolph seek to make a cheese 'more traditional' than one of Britain's most celebrated 'traditional' cheeses – more 'Stilton' than Stilton itself. And in principle, consumers have been sympathetic to the idea. Potential Stitchelton customers include the growing numbers who express anxiety about 'over-processed' industrial foods whose origins and methods of production seem unknown to them. Stichelton is both made by less intensive means (it is certified organic, and it is also 'handmade') and traceable to a farm, a region, and a regional history of cheese making. But the 'simple' reincarnation of raw milk Stilton has been impossible in the Stitchelton cheese room, not only because of the subtle differences in terroir described above, but also because Joe and Randolph must sell their cheese in a different world from that of raw milk Stilton makers of old. In order to succeed, Joe has had to produce a blue-veined, full-cream cow's milk cheese that competes with today's industrial Stiltons, not only through differentiation (e.g. by offering more complex flavours) but also through comparison (e.g. by matching their consistency and creaminess). As a result, the cheese that he makes unavoidably differs somewhat from raw milk Stiltons of the past, despite referring to them. And so it is, once more, in the interface with consumers and their expectations, that Stichelton is re-membered. Knowledge of how to make this cheese is reconstituted in the moment of its reproduction within the context of an enlarged terroir assemblage, including consumers who Joe must constantly keep in mind.

Also among the elements stretching the dimensions of the terroir assemblage today are 'geographical indications'. In 1411, King Charles VI of France famously decreed that only cheeses aged in the caves of Roquefort-sur-Soulzon could be sold by the name Roquefort; more than five hundred years later, in 1925, Roquefort cheese was granted the first ever French *Appellation d'Origine Contrôlée* (AOC). French law subsequently allowed producers of other products named after their place of production – at first mostly wines, and then cheeses – to apply for AOC status to protect them against competitors using their name while employing sub-standard methods or working in a different terroir. Other European nations followed suit and, in 1992, the European Union (EU) decreed that member states would recognize one another's geographical indications as well under a common Protected Designation of Origin (PDO) scheme. Widely recognized by consumers, and considered to be an assurance of both quality and tradition, geographical indications often gloss highly contentious struggles to define and capture the value of terroir. Because terroir comprises numerous elements, each of which vary differently through geographical space, and some of which vary significantly through time, drawing its boundaries is always a question of interpretation. If terroir is a story told to make sense of and to celebrate a product, then it is one that is told differently by different actors. The terroir stories giving foundation to geographical indication regimes therefore almost always protect some producers by excluding others. Who organizes the application for geographical indication status often determines not only who is included and who is excluded, but also which characteristics and methods of production are henceforth defined as proper to the product in question. Standardizing a product in this way generally entails many producers not only learning to re-member it somewhat differently, but also partially forgetting the ways in which they previously made it – obliterating at least some of the subtle variation that once defined a product landscape. Depending upon who ultimately controls the application for a geographical indication, it may in fact do less to protect 'tradition' (as defined by most) than to legitimate and facilitate transformation in tradition's name.

The Saint-Nectaire geographical indication bears evidence of bifurcated interests in the cheese, for it defines two different products: dairy Saint-Nectaire (*laitier*), and farmhouse Saint-Nectaire (*fermier*). The former is made from pasteurized milk in large commercial dairies, and the later from raw milk by farmstead producers. For each category, the *Syndicat du Fromage Saint-Nectaire – AOC* establishes production parameters. Any cheese sold by the name *Saint-Nectaire Fermier* must: be made in the delimited area, with milk collected in the area, whether in the morning or in the evening; be made immediately after milking; be made from 'uncooked' and semi-firm curd which has been pressed and salted; have a flowery rind with white, yellow or red mould; contain a minimum 45 per cent fat, and 52 per cent fat solids; and be circular, 21 centimetres in diameter, 5 centimetres high, and approximately 1.7 kilograms in weight. Since 1955, anyone wishing to market their cheeses as *Saint-Nectaire Fermier* has had to meet these requirements. This has led to a more uniform product, with the transformation of many previous variants of the cheese into this homogenous one. Along the way, many Saint-Nectaire producers have had to re-member the cheese differently than they did previously, harmonizing their productive practices with an assemblage that has included this new regulatory regime. At the same time, the Syndicat protocol has contributed to the transformation of the cheese by what it does *not* require. As its architects did not specify the breed of animal from whose milk Saint-Nectaire could be made, most producers today, including farmhouse producers, milk Holstein-Friesian cows, for they give considerably more milk, even if not as rich, than the Salers cows that most Saint-Nectaire makers kept in the past. Most also feed their animals at least in part on silage (not explicitly prohibited by the AOC, and therefore 'legitimated' by it), whereas before the AOC was established this was generally considered poor practice in the region.

Like Saint-Nectaire, Stilton is protected by a geographical indication – one of only a handful granted to British cheeses. Unlike Saint-Nectaire, Stilton has only one category. When application for PDO status was made in the mid-1990s, all of the existing Stilton producers – already members of an association – made their cheese from pasteurized milk, and they required this in the PDO specifications. Although this particular specification did not transform the production practices of any existing Stilton producers, it later prevented Joe and Randolph from calling their blue-veined full-cream cheese 'Stilton', despite the fact that it more closely resembled 'traditional' Stilton than did PDO Stiltons. Not to be thwarted, Joe and Randolph discovered that the original name of the town of Stilton, recorded in the eleventh-century Domesday Book, was Stitchelton, and by claiming this original name they implied that their cheese was the true heir of a regional cheese-making tradition. This story of a tradition deeper and truer than the 'official' (PDO) version of 'tradition' is essential to the way in which Joe and Randolph re-member their cheese, accentuating at once rupture and continuity with the past.

Hidden within the Stilton–Stitchelton divide is yet another element affecting how cheese-making knowledge is reproduced within the context of a broader assemblage – another entity of increasing relevance to the cultural ecology of contemporary artisan cheese making. It was in the wake of a health scare linked to Stilton cheese that Colston Bassett, the last Stilton maker to make some of its cheeses from raw milk, decided in 1989 to make only pasteurized milk cheeses. In recent decades, consumer safety concerns have become a prominent force in the artisan cheese trade. Since 1949, cheese made from raw milk cannot be marketed in the United States unless aged for at least sixty days, making virtually impossible the sale of raw milk soft cheeses, as well as many semi-soft and blue cheeses. In the late 1990s, the United Kingdom and the European Union each considered banning raw milk cheese production and sale. Following concerted protest by raw milk cheese makers (including large entities such as the Roquefort and Comté *syndicats*, and the Parmigiano-Reggiano *consorzio*, representing thousands of producers) as well as cheese mongers and consumers, the EU instead issued two directives establishing sanitary norms with which raw milk cheese makers would have to comply, and requiring them to monitor the safety of their own products. These directives were interpreted somewhat differently from country to country. In many countries, the strict and persistent enforcement of these norms, and attendant pressures on cheese makers to modernize their cheese rooms by tiling floors and walls, and by buying stainless steel vats and other equipment, pushed many out of cheese making. The Bellontes survived this offensive, but many of their neighbours and counterparts in many EU countries did not.

In the United Kingdom, the relatively small number of raw milk cheese makers were, in many ways, better organized in their response to these EU directives. The Specialist Cheesemakers Association (SCA) – a membership organization of small-scale U.K. cheese makers – developed and published a Code of Best Practice outlining safe methods of raw milk cheese production, and also held workshops on safe production to which cheese makers, as well as Environmental Health Officers, were invited. Individual cheese makers also began to implement the Hazards Analysis Critical Control Points (HACCP) method – developed by NASA to ensure the safety of foods produced for its astronauts – to help them to identify, monitor and control moments in their productive processes when contamination might occur. The initiatives of the SCA and individual cheese makers in Britain have contributed to a somewhat more congenial relationship between cheese makers and health inspectors. But these initiatives have also reconfigured the relevant ecology of cheese making, considerably altering the environment with which a cheese maker's perceptual system must resonate. As the measure of sanitary norms and the meeting of HACCP protocols occupies an ever more prominent place in the cheese room, it is with these data that cheese makers increasingly engage, whether in addition to, or instead of, sensory data such as the feel of the curd and the smell and taste of the aging cheese. While this too entails learning from the cheese itself, it involves the mediation of instruments and institutions that are arguably as much a part of the contemporary terroir assemblage as the pasture, the milk and the cave.

Reproducing Culture

Conceiving of consumers, geographical indications and health inspectors as component parts of the terroir of contemporary cheese making may stretch the 'terroir' term uncomfortably, but it reminds us that terroir has always been a human construct (used by different parties to different ends, but always to articulate and defend human interests), not to mention one that includes within its constituent elements human understanding and agency. Whereas a more conventional conception of terroir reminds us that the natural ecology plays a crucial role in sustaining human traditions such as cheese making, this expanded conception of the term safeguards against the notion that human culture is over-determined by this natural ecology – a notion that proponents of terroir have often been accused of holding. If terroir is an assemblage, it is one that comprises many elements, and many forms of agency, including 'cultures' both bacterial and human. If a cheese expresses its terroir, it too is animated by human and non-human agency. Reproducing the cultured practice of cheese making therefore entails acting with cognizance of a broader whole including many other elements – a complex ecology of cheese making that comprises everything from lactobacilli to supra-state bureaucracies; that is, culture on both micro and macro scales (see also Paxson 2008). Thinking like a cheese, it turns out, is not only a multi-variant project, but also a multi-scalar one – or, even, one that 'flattens' scales (Marston, Jones III and Woodward 2005). As such, it reminds us that culture itself is more than just a human project; that it is 'not governed by any central head', to borrow Bennett's words; that it is not simply transmitted from person to person, or from generation to generation; that we are never alone as we remember and reproduce our cultured world, even – perhaps especially – when we only dimly perceive its dynamics; and that we live in a 'more-than human' world, to use Whatmore's phrase, with which we must in significant measure harmonize our acts in order to reproduce ourselves.

Acknowledgements

The research upon which this chapter is based has been funded by the British Academy (LRG 45537). Draft versions of this paper were presented in the 'Transmission of Knowledge' seminar series at SOAS, University of London (31 January 2007); the Anthropology research seminar at the University of Kent (16 October 2007); and the Anthropology seminar at the Instituto de Ciências Sociais, Universidade de Lisboa (28 March 2008). I wish to thank Trevor Marchand, Roy Ellen, José Sobral, David Sutton, Christy Spackman, Sasha Cuerda and Heather Paxson for their constructive engagement with the piece.

References

Bennett, J. 2010. *Vibrant Matter: A Political Ecology of Things*. Durham and London: Duke University Press.

Clark, A. 1997. *Being There: Putting Brain, Body, and World Together Again*. Cambridge, MA: MIT Press.

Connerton, P. 1989. *How Societies Remember*. Cambridge: Cambridge University Press.

Deleuze, G. and F. Guattari. 1987. *A Thousand Plateaus: Capitalism and Schizophrenia*. Minneapolis: University of Minnesota Press.

Gell, A. 1998. *Art and Agency: An Anthropological Theory*. Oxford and New York: Clarendon Press.

Hickman, T. 1995. *The History of Stilton Cheese*. Stroud, Gloucestershire: Sutton Publishing.

Ingold, T. 1992. 'Culture and the Perception of the Environment', in E. Croll and D. Parkin (eds), *Bush Base, Forest Farm: Culture, Environment and Development*. London and New York: Routledge, pp. 39–56.

————.2000. *The Perception of the Environment: Essays in Livelihood, Dwelling and Skill*. London and New York: Routledge.

————.2001. 'From the Transmission of Representations to the Education of Attention', in H. Whitehouse (ed.), *The Debated Mind: Evolutionary Psychology versus Ethnography*. Oxford and New York: Berg, pp. 113–53.

————.2010. 'Footprints through the Weather-World: Walking, Breathing, Knowing', *Journal of the Royal Anthropological Institute* 16 (Supplement 1): 121–39.

Leopold, A. (1949) 1987. 'Thinking Like a Mountain', in *A Sand County Almanac, and Sketches Here and There*. New York: Oxford University Press, pp. 129–32.

Marston, S.A., J.P. Jones III and K. Woodward. 2005. 'Human Geography without Scale', *Transactions of the Institute of British Geographers* 30(4): 416–32.

Paxson, H. 2008. 'Post-Pasteurian Cultures: The Microbiopolitics of Raw-Milk Cheese in the United States', *Cultural Anthropology* 23(1): 15–47.

————.2010. 'Locating Value in Artisan Cheese: Reverse Engineering Terroir for New World Landscapes', *American Anthropologist* 112(3): 444–57.

Pickering, A. 1995. *The Mangle of Practice: Time, Agency, and Science*. Chicago: University of Chicago Press.

Smith, P.H. 2004. *The Body of the Artisan: Art and Experience in the Scientific Revolution*. Chicago: University of Chicago Press.

Trubek, A.B. 2008. *The Taste of Place: A Cultural Journey into Terroir*. Berkeley: University of California Press.

Whatmore, S. 2002. *Hybrid Geographies: Natures, Cultures, Spaces*. London and Thousand Oaks, CA: Sage.

Chapter 12

LINEAGES OF CULTURAL TRANSMISSION

Stephen Shennan

Over the last thirty years the idea that the processes producing cultural stability and change are analogous in important respects to those of biological evolution has become increasingly popular. According to this view, just as biological evolution is characterized by changing frequencies of genes in populations through time as a result of such processes as natural selection, so cultural evolution refers to the changing distributions of cultural attributes in populations, likewise affected by processes such as natural selection, but also by others that have no analogue in genetic evolution. The key impetus for this trend has been theoretical developments in the modelling of culture based on mathematical population genetics. However, this chapter aims to show that this is only one of several effectively Darwinian traditions that have existed within the anthropological disciplines, and that bringing together elements from these different traditions can provide important theoretical and methodological tools for the empirical study of cultural transmission in the material culture record.

Any process that is evolutionary in a Darwinian sense must involve an inheritance mechanism, since unless variation is transmitted there is nothing on which processes such as natural selection can act. That is to say, selection processes affect the probability that specific traits will be copied in the future; without transmission there is only phenotypic variation (cf. Boone and Smith 1998). In the case of culture, the inheritance mechanism is social learning – a mechanism linked to a definition of culture as 'information capable of affecting individuals' behaviour which they acquire from other members of their species through teaching, imitation and other forms of social transmission' (Richerson and Boyd 2005: 5). It has often been suggested that the definition of heritable cultural attributes is arbitrary and problematical (e.g. Weiss and Hayashida 2002), and implies the existence of cultural 'particles'. However, as a number of authors have shown, even continuous traits (i.e. physical measurements) can provide a perfectly satisfactory basis for the operation of Darwinian processes (e.g. Henrich and Boyd 2002; Eerkens and Lipo 2005; Henrich et al. 2008). O'Brien et al. (2010: 3797) provide an extensive and important discussion of units of transmission and offer a useful shorthand definition: 'Cultural traits are units of transmission that permit diffusion and create traditions – patterned ways of doing things that exist in identifiable form over extended periods of time.'

This definition usefully reminds us that, in some important respects, the cultural evolution perspective represents a revival of the culture history approach that characterized American anthropology in the early twentieth century, and Anglo-American archaeology for much longer, until its rejection in favour of various forms of functionalism, especially the systemic approach of the New Archaeology (e.g. Binford 1962). However, in contrast to the culture historians, as a result of the developments in cultural evolutionary theory, we now have the beginnings of a theoretical framework, and some specific models, for relating processes at the scale of daily activities and human lifetimes to the large-scale space–time distribution patterns of artefact types and inferred practices which are the particular focus of archaeologists.

What has not really been appreciated in the anglophone cultural evolution world, or indeed in that of its anglophone critics, is the extent to which its agenda has been paralleled within the French anthropological and sociological tradition, based on very different foundations. As Marsden (2000) has pointed out, the programme of cultural evolution, and in particular its memetic variant, was anticipated to a remarkable degree by the French sociologist and philosopher Gabriel Tarde at the end of the nineteenth century, who saw imitation, meant in the most general sense, as the basis of social life and human history:

> Self-propagation and not self-organisation is the prime demand of the social as well as of the vital thing. Organisation is but the means of which propagation, of which generative or imitative imitation, is the end. (Tarde 1903: 74)
>
> All resemblances of social origin in society are the direct or indirect fruit of the various forms of imitation – custom-imitation or fashion-imitation, sympathy-imitation or obedience-imitation, precept-imitation or education-imitation, native imitation, deliberate imitation, etc. (ibid.: 14)

Inventions involve the recombination of existing imitations, and their success or otherwise depends on the extent to which they are compatible with the existing prevalent set of imitations, including the power relations with which they are connected. Success is achieved through processes of competition and substitution of one imitation by another, or through 'accumulation', in which different imitations become linked to one another. As Marsden (2000) points out, some of Tarde's observations in particular strike a very modern chord:

> Let me conclude with the observation that the social peaks, the classes or nations which are most imitated by others, are those within which the greatest amount of reciprocal imitation goes on. Great modern cities are characterised by the intensity of their imitation of internal things; it is proportionate to the density of their population and to the multiform multiplicity of the relations of their inhabitants. (Tarde 1903: 239)

For Tarde (ibid.: Chapter IV) the two disciplines central to tracing the patterns of imitation were archaeology and statistics, because they ignored individuals and dealt with aggregates, statistics by choice and archaeology by necessity; but of the two archaeology was the more important because of the information it could provide about the outcome of imitation processes over long time-spans without the noise of short-term distractions.

Interestingly, Latour (2009) has also recently acknowledged the significance of Tarde's work, and in particular Tarde's ([1893] 1999) book *Monadologie et Sociologie*, as an ancestor of his own actor-network theory, not least because of the equal role he gave to non-human entities, including inanimate objects, as monads in his system. As Latour observes, this parallels the role that the properties of artefacts have in affecting their own future reproduction within at least some present-day Darwinian approaches (cf. Dennett 1995).

Of course, it was not Tarde's ideas that came to dominate French anthropology and sociology in the early twentieth century, but the entirely opposed ideas of Durkheim – hence the need for Tarde to be 're-discovered'. However, the Durkheimian tradition had its own branch that attached significance to cultural transmission and culture history, associated with Marcel Mauss and his concept of 'civilization'. This is much closer than Tarde's radical ideas to the sort of 'culture area' approach espoused by early-twentieth-century American anthropologists and their German predecessors of the 'Kulturkreis' school, but involved a key distinction between 'civilization' and 'society':

> The phenomena of civilisation … are by definition social phenomena of given societies. But not all social phenomena are, in the narrow sense of the term, phenomena of civilisation. There are indeed some phenomena

which are entirely specific to the society in question, which differentiate it and set it apart. ... it is better not to talk of civilisations when speaking of phenomena that are limited to a given society.

But even in the most isolated societies there exists a whole body of social phenomena which must be studied separately and in their own right, if one is to avoid errors or, more precisely, unwarranted abstractions. These phenomena all share one important feature: they are common to a larger or smaller number of societies and to a longer or shorter period in the past of these societies. They can be labelled 'phenomena of civilisation'.

These phenomena of civilisation are thus essentially international. ... They can therefore be defined, in opposition to the social phenomena which are specific to such and such society, as those social phenomena which are common to several societies, more or less related to each other; be it through prolonged contacts, through some permanent intermediaries, or through relationships from common descent. (Mauss 2006: 59–61)

But Mauss made another set of contributions to non-Darwinian foundations for the importance of cultural transmission, with his work on 'techniques of the body', a concept he created out of what had previously been a disconnected mass of miscellaneous facts:

[S]pecificity is characteristic of all techniques. An example: during the War I was able to make many observations on this specificity of techniques, e.g. the technique of digging. The English troops I was with did not know how to use French spades, which forced us to change 8,000 spades a division when we relieved a French division, and vice versa. This plainly shows that a manual knack can only be learned slowly. Every technique properly so-called has its own form. (Mauss 2006: 79)

What emerges very clearly from [lists of techniques previously given] is the fact that we are everywhere faced with physiopsychosociological assemblages of series of actions. These actions are more or less habitual and more or less ancient in the life of the individual and the history of the society. (Mauss 2006: 92)

Such ideas were to be greatly extended and developed, and placed in a much broader context, by the work of Leroi-Gourhan, who had been a student of Mauss. The wide-range of his contributions to an evolutionary approach in French anthropology and archaeology is impossible to summarize here (for a review and bibliography, see Audouze 2002), but two linked features may be identified here – the importance of memory and the idea of the *chaîne opératoire*:

Techniques are at the same time gestures and tools, organized in sequence by a true syntax which gives the operational series both their stability and their flexibility. The operational syntax is generated by memory and is born from the dialogue between the brain and the material realm. (Leroi-Gourhan 1993, pp. 114, 230–34, cited by Audouze 2002: 287)

The key word here is memory, which for Leroi-Gourhan had three different dimensions: (1) a very basic kind of biological memory associated with the unconscious operation of the central nervous system, and widespread in the living world; (2) memory acquired by individuals through experience, much more restricted in its distribution and far more developed in humans than other species, and in whom it is extended by (3) the knowledge that is transmitted by language (Audouze 2002: 293).

> Periodical operational sequences and exceptional operational sequences require lucid behaviour [in which language takes a dominant part]. But most of our lives are filled with semiautomatic stereotyped operational sequences that are transmitted through the family unit or youth peer groups. They form the basis of individual behavior within the ethnic group and give the strongest ethnic imprint to the individual. They are the necessary counterpart to freedom of behavior in exceptional circumstances. (Audouze 2002: 294, summarizing Leroi-Gourhan 1993: 227–33)

It is not clear why lucid behaviour should always or even often require language, as opposed to individual trial-and-error learning, but the key point here is the dominance of cultural transmission in affecting what people do most of the time, and thus the creation of specific, localized ways of doing things. Whether these must be 'ethnic' is another matter that it is not possible to go into here, except to note that they are not necessarily restricted to self-conscious identity groups, though they may be.

As Audouze (2002) makes clear, Leroi-Gourhan's ideas have had a profound influence on the study of techniques and technology in the French social sciences, through the creation of the *techniques et cultures* school and its associated journal, giving them an importance that they have long since lost in Anglo-American anthropology. For archaeologists of course the key point is that it is potentially possible to identify the existence of specific cultural traditions by identifying the *chaînes opératoires* that have been used to create specific artefacts, and this idea has had a profound influence on the French approach to prehistoric archaeology, especially to the study of stone tools, as any cursory examination of the literature will show. In order to achieve this aim it has developed a generalizing tradition of ethnoarchaeology that aims to 'correlate macro- and micro-features of the artefact with technical operations, defined in terms of techniques (physical modalities by which raw material is transformed) and manufacturing stage' in order to build general rules of inference that can be applied to the understanding of the archaeological record (Roux 2007: 156). Thus, Roux's study of potters in India showed that it required ten years of apprenticeship to become completely competent at the wheel-throwing of pottery, involving the mastery of a wide range of physical movements. It follows that if one can demonstrate the presence of wheel-thrown pots in the archaeological record it implies a high degree of craft specialization, because acquiring the required level of expertise is incompatible with spending a large amount of time carrying out other activities, and will therefore be limited in its distribution within a given society, associated with very specific transmission networks – a point of considerable importance (as we will see below). Even though this does not involve a simple process of imitation, but rather the acquisition of embodied skills, the fact that it takes a long time and that learning one complex set of skills effectively makes it very difficult to learn another, means that the creation and maintenance of traditions in this sort of area is more or less inevitable. They also channel innovation possibilities since, for example, specific new time-saving techniques are far more likely to be adopted if they are easy to learn, given the current set of traditional technical skills. Conversely, things that may not involve the learning of new skills, such as new decorative techniques, are potentially much more transferable horizontally, between individuals of the same generation.

Gosselain (2000) has proposed a similar general framework for inferring the nature of ceramic traditions. Thus, other things being equal, technical steps whose traces are visible on the vessels themselves and that are easy to carry out are also highly transmissible even in situations of quite superficial contact, and thus more prone to innovation, including ones that come from other media. Some other aspects of pottery production, like clay selection, extraction and processing, are also relatively straightforward technically and therefore relatively open to modification once learned. However, in these cases the technical processes cannot be simply 'reverse engineered' on the basis of seeing the finished product, so they will only be influenced by contact with others who work in this domain. Gosselain proposes that innovation in these areas will be less frequent and will be most likely when potters move and have to change their clay sources, or if they want to produce some new pottery type. Finally, there are the technical processes that correspond to Roux's (2007) skills, the mastery of specific sets of physical movements that are not only relatively invisible on the finished object but also take a great deal of practice to acquire and are therefore difficult to change. To acquire these involves long-lasting contact with a limited number of people, generally close relatives of a senior generation.

Gosselain (2000) then uses a comparative ethnographic study of pottery from Africa to assess whether these suggestions are supported. He shows that the large-scale distribution of different types of roulette decoration is related to geographic networks of relatively superficial contact, often linking unrelated populations, whereas the distribution of different vessel-forming techniques correlates, at least at a broad scale, with the distribution of different language families and their subdivisions, both learned once a generation and resistant to change.

Even though this francophone tradition has developed entirely separately from Anglo-American cultural evolution, and some of its present-day practitioners (e.g. Gosselain, in press) are strongly hostile to it, the parallels are obvious and their strengths are complementary. The foundations of recent work in cultural evolution, by which I mean in particular the dual inheritance theory tradition founded by Cavalli-Sforza and Feldman (1981) and Boyd and Richerson (1985), lie in mathematical population genetics, on the one hand, and in theoretical psychology on the other. Empirical studies have been slow to develop, at least partly because (by and large) the models look at the processes involved from the point of view of the human agents, not from that of the cultural attributes that are being transmitted, modified and selected. This perspective matters because these culturally transmitted features are the only data accessible to archaeologists, and often all that anthropologists have as well. In fact, they are the only direct data about past cultural traditions and the forces affecting them that we have available. Moreover, the agent-centred cultural evolutionary processes that represent the foundations of the theory are micro-scale ones: they occur at short time scales, at most a human generation but very often on a virtually day-to-day basis, and between individuals or small groups. The question for the archaeologists then becomes, to what extent is it possible to identify the action of the various cultural evolutionary processes on the basis of distributions of through-time variation in the past, given the often poor temporal resolution of the archaeological record and the enormous range of complex processes that have affected it?

In fact, even to demonstrate that a pattern of contemporary variation or one of continuity through time results from the operation of a cultural transmission process is not straightforward. Clearly, transmission implies continuity but continuity does not necessarily imply transmission. It might arise, for example, from the continuity of environmental conditions or of a particular function. To take one clearly documented example, through-time fluctuations in the proportional and absolute frequencies of wild and domestic animal bones at Neolithic sites in Switzerland probably did not relate to changing cultural preferences for hunting versus farming but to climatic fluctuations, because hunting became predominant at times of a cool, wet climate, which could be demonstrated by independent evidence. More subtly perhaps, the classic S-curve for the spread of innovations can be produced both by biased cultural transmission processes (Henrich 2001) and by the existence of differences in what people are prepared to pay for an innovation if the population concerned is economically stratified (Steele 2009).

This point is an example of a more general issue. For culture to be transmitted it must be defined as information, as for example in the definition by Richerson and Boyd above. However, as Lipatov et al. (2011) have recently emphasized, we cannot necessarily assume that the distribution of practices prevalent in a particular time and place corresponds to the distribution of ideas within a population, since those ideas, norms or preferences may be differentially expressed for other contextual reasons; in other words, the idea that there will always be a 'one-to-one correspondence between cultural information and human behaviour' (ibid.) is simply incorrect. Indeed, this is precisely the criticism that Binford made of traditional culture history in the early 1960s (Binford 1962), when he rejected what he called the 'aquatic' view of cultural behaviour and argued for a systemic view; in other words, what people do in particular cases is not simply dictated by their cultural norms but by contextual social and economic factors. A classic example of this phenomenon is Cronk's (2000) analysis of parental investment in male and female children by the Mukogodo in Kenya. Although in terms of their expressed values they subscribe to the idea, prevalent in the prestigious cattle-keeping patrilineal groups among which they live, that sons are more important than daughters, in practice they invest more in their daughters. This is because in general they are too poor in cattle to pay the bride price that sons need in order to marry, and so do better in terms of reproductive success by investing in daughters for whom a bride price will be paid. Thus, once again, the agent-centred cultural evolutionary models can tell us about the consequences of the operation of particular processes for distributions of ideas within populations, but the archaeologist, and very often the cultural anthropologist as well, has to deal with the 'inverse problem' of starting with a distribution of the results of practices and postulating the factors that produced it. Lipatov et al. (2011) address the question of accounting for changing frequencies of virilocal and uxorilocal marriage in early-twentieth-century Taiwan by modelling both the distribution of preferences for the different marriage types and the distribution of cost–benefit considerations which were changing as a result of economic development.

What other ways of addressing these issues are available to archaeologists? One route that gets us at least some of the way there in the case of artefacts is that of the French *techniques et cultures* school described above. The *chaîne opératoire* approach abstracts from artefact forms characteristic sequences of steps for the production of particular things in particular ways. It is reasonable to think that these 'recipes' represent the information that is transmitted, whether by imitation as such, or by various processes of 'scaffolded' learning. Moreover, given the practical nature of technical learning processes, it can be argued that there should be less of a disjunction between the distribution of norms and preferences and the distribution of practices than, for example, with marriage preferences, since even in the case of 'scaffolded' learning it is the practice itself that provides the basis for information transmission.

We can make other arguments about the probability or otherwise of a distribution of practices corresponding to a distribution of norms in a population, for example, on the basis of cultural drift. Following the logic of genetic drift, in cultural drift, variation is the result of random copying of cultural attributes, with some possibility of innovation, and the results of the process depend solely on the innovation rate and the effective population size, itself dependent on the scale of interaction. It is very unlikely that any individual act of copying, for example, of a ceramic decorative motif, will be random in terms of the model copied, but if everyone has their own reasons for copying one person rather than another, the result will be that there are no directional forces affecting what or who is copied. In such a case there is no basis for thinking that there will be a discrepancy between the preferences in the minds of craftspeople and what they actually produce because there is no force that could generate such a distinction. Unfortunately, it is increasingly clear that in many circumstances distributions that are compatible with neutrality are also compatible with the operation of various bias and selection processes (Mesoudi and Lycett 2009; Steele et al. 2010; Kandler and Shennan, submitted), but departures from neutrality can be identified and indeed it seems plausible to extend this argument even where other forces do exist, at least in certain circumstances. For example, if conformism plays a important role in the transmission of some cultural practice, then the distribution of models that naive individuals have available to them will reflect that, so it stretches credibility to imagine that the distribution of models in people's minds at any given time will be vastly different from that which is actually put into practice, because there would be no basis for acquiring them. More generally, Brantingham's recent Price Equation approach (2007, 2010a, 2010b) provides a basis for evaluating the relative strength of bias/selection forces and drift in accounting for changing frequencies of different practices in the archaeological record.

Despite the dangers of the 'aquatic' view of culture, the process of cultural transmission remains fundamental to understanding change, but it needs embedding in a systemic context. Roux's (2008) account of the apparently strange history of the production of wheel-fashioned pottery in the ancient Levant provides an excellent example of the importance of understanding the relevant *chaîne opératoire* and its implications for cultural transmission in explaining a situation which at first sight seems rather puzzling, since the production of wheel-fashioned pottery comes and goes twice before finally becoming permanently established. It is present in the Late Chalcolithic period, disappears in the subsequent initial Early Bronze Age, appears again in EB III, disappears in EB IV and finally takes off in the Middle Bronze Age. In this case there is no reason to envisage a radical disjuncture between the prevalence of the skill in the population and its expression in wheel-coiled vessels, since there would be no point in learning the skill if it were not to be used. Roux locates the explanation in the context of the practice and transmission of the craft. For the Chalcolithic period a study of the petrology of the pottery and the techniques used to make it, as well as the contexts in which it was found, indicated that only a few individuals made the bowls, that they moved around and that they were attached to elites. This restricted group of potters within which wheel coiling was transmitted was distinct from those much more numerous potters throughout the region who made the utilitarian pottery. The same is true of the EB III period, in that wheel coiling was restricted to a small number of specialists, whose potter's turntables are found in palace contexts. The result in both periods was a technical system that Roux characterizes as fragile and closed.

Fragility refers to the size of the network concerned. In a precise analogy with genetic drift, any practice that is restricted to a small number of individuals is vulnerable to loss as a result of external circumstances, regardless of its benefits (cf. Rivers 1926). The fact that the Late Chalcolithic and EB III potters using wheel coiling were few in number meant that the practice disappeared in the face of the socioeconomic collapses that ended the Chalcolithic and Early Bronze Age periods, because the transmission network was broken. In contrast, robust transmission networks are sufficiently large that they are not vulnerable to the effects of external historical events because even if part of the network is destroyed in one place it will survive elsewhere, and this is what happened in the Middle Bronze Age with the expansion of the wheel-coiling transmission network. Similar explanations have been offered for the coming and going of 'Upper Palaeolithic' cultural traits in Middle Stone Age Africa (Shennan 2001; Powell et al. 2009).

However, the size of the network in itself is only one element in the fragility or robustness of a given technical transmission system. One way in which it can expand is by the transfer of the technique to other areas of production than that in which it originally emerged. Again this did not happen in the Chalcolithic or Early Bronze Age. Wheel coiling remained restricted to a small circle of specialist potters who only used it to produce specific elite items. This changed in the Middle Bronze Age in the southern Levant, with the application of this innovative practice to an extensive range of different items in widespread use, in the context of the expansion of cities and the probable development of a market economy. Workshops using the wheel-coiling technique and producing a wide range of vessels gradually expanded, leading to the decline of domestic pottery production, which became restricted to the making of cooking vessels.

In cases where we know or can assume a great deal about social actors' goals and constraints, hypotheses can be more closely framed and the role of information transmission can at least in principle be more readily tested. Recently Charlton and colleagues (2009, 2010) have taken an evolutionary approach to understanding iron-smelting technology in a case study from north-west Wales. Here there can be no doubt about the goal (at least in general terms), and the conditions required to smelt iron successfully are well understood, arising as they do from universal properties of the materials involved. Again, there is every reason to believe that the distribution of actual practices should correspond to the distribution of norms and beliefs within the relevant population about the best way to smelt iron rather than conflict with it, as in the case of Mukogodo child rearing.

Once again though, the issue is first to identify patterns of cultural descent in the methods used and to distinguish variation arising from transmission from that relating, for example, to the local ore or fuel type; and then to characterize the forces affecting that variation, in a situation where, by the very nature of the process, there are only a limited number of successful solutions. The most informative source of information on the processes involved in past episodes of early iron production is chemical variation in the slags produced as a waste product. In this case then, the data are quantitative variations in the chemistry of chronologically ordered slag deposits and the inverse problem is as above: can we establish whether or not there is a signal of cultural descent in the chemical variation, and if so, what can we infer about the factors affecting transmission processes that produced it?

Charlton (2009) showed convincingly that a transmission signal could be identified. In terms of the forces acting on the technical knowledge and practices passed on from one iron producer to another, it is easy to imagine that there might be some more or less random variation in exactly what was done each time. It is also likely that there would be strong selection for those practices that were successful, although given the complexity of the process and its many stages it would not necessarily be easy to identify precisely what produced a successful smelt on any given occasion. From the point of view of the agents, it is thus likely that transmission would be affected by results bias; from the point of view of the smelting recipes this would be a process of natural selection, since recipes would be differentially reproduced depending on their ability to smelt iron successfully. The results of Charlton et al. (2010) showed that all changes related to furnace operation could be accounted for by a drift process, but that at a certain point, a second effective procedure was more or less accidentally discovered and a decision was taken to make use of the two distinct procedures, visible in different slag signatures. At the same time there were clear trends in the use of manganese-rich ores with better fluxing capabilities, and evidence of decreased variability in reducing conditions related to results bias: that is to say the iron makers consistently reproduced the airflow conditions that gave the best results for a given recipe. Ore variability, on the other hand, did not decrease through time and probably simply reflects the properties of the bog ore available. This complex process of the dissection of different factors affecting variation in the content of slags shows the way in which difficult archaeological inverse problems can be addressed.

Conclusion

Within the disciplines of archaeology and anthropology there are several different more or less independent academic lineages that have attached importance to cultural transmission, for a variety of different reasons. When we examine these lineages it becomes apparent that the present-day descendants of those traditions have much more in common with one another than some of the exponents of those traditions would like to believe. The connection between the ideas of memetics and those of Latour's actor-actant networks, with their emphasis on the active role of artefacts, is a good example. Similarly, the *chaîne opératoire* approach offers the most thoroughly developed way of tracing technical traditions and the changes within them in the archaeological record. In fact, the strengths of the francophone and anglophone traditions are complementary. The ethnoarchaeology of craft-learning skills provides a basis for distinguishing the factors relevant to the transmission of different types of attributes, as with the distinctions revealed by Gosselain between the distribution of decorative patterns and motor habits. The mathematical apparatus of cultural evolutionary theory provides the basis for establishing what happens when processes are iterated large numbers of times. Tracing the history of different *chaînes opératoires* and their implications in the past enables us to reconstruct culture histories and the factors affecting them, like the wheel-fashioned pottery production of the Levant, but in turn this work can be further developed by more extensive quantification to provide data for the testing of specific mathematical models.

References

Audouze, F. 2002. 'Leroi Gourhan: A Philosopher of Technique and Evolution', *Journal of Archaeological Research* 10: 277–306.

Binford, L.R. 1962. 'Archaeology as Anthropology', *American Antiquity* 28: 217–25.

Boone, J.L. and E.A. Smith. 1998. 'Is it Evolution Yet? A Critique of Evolutionary Archaeology', *Current Anthropology* 39: S141–S174.

Boyd, R. and P.J. Richerson. 1985. *Culture and the Evolutionary Process.* Chicago: University of Chicago Press.

Brantingham, P.J. 2007. 'A Unified Evolutionary Model of Archaeological Style and Function Based on the Price Equation', *American Antiquity* 72: 395–416.

———.2010a. 'Detecting the Effects of Selection and Stochastic Forces in Archaeological Assemblages', *Journal of Archaeological Science* 37: 3211–25.

———.2010b. 'The Mathematics of Chaînes Opératoires', in S.J. Lycett and P.R. Chauhan (eds), *New Perspectives on Old Stones: Analytical Approaches to Paleolithic Technologies.* New York: Springer, pp. 183–206.

Cavalli-Sforza, L.L. and M.W. Feldman. 1981. *Cultural Transmission and Evolution: A Quantitative Approach.* Princeton, NJ: Princeton University Press.

Charlton, M.F. 2009. 'Identifying Iron Production Lineages: A Case-study in North-west Wales', in S.J. Shennan (ed.), *Pattern and Process in Cultural Evolution.* Berkeley: University of California Press, pp. 133–44.

Charlton, M.F., P. Crew, T. Rehren and S.J. Shennan. 2010. 'Explaining the Evolution of Ironmaking Recipes – An Example from Northwest Wales', *Journal of Anthropological Archaeology* 29: 352–67.

Cronk, L. 2000. 'Female-biased Parental Investment and Growth Performance among the Mukogodo', in L. Cronk, N. Chagnon and W. Irons (eds), *Adaptation and Human Behavior.* New York: Aldine de Gruyter, pp. 203–22.

Dennett, D. 1995. *Darwin's Dangerous Idea.* London: Allen Lane, The Penguin Press.

Eerkens, J.W. and C.P. Lipo. 2005 'Cultural Transmission, Copying Errors, and the Generation of Variation in Material Culture and the

Archaeological Record', *Journal of Anthropological Archaeology* 24: 316–34.

Gosselain, O.P. 2000. 'Materializing Identities: An African Perspective', *Journal of Archaeological Method and Theory* 7: 187–217.

————.In press. 'Ça ne s'attrape pas, ça se pratique! Contours et Dynamique des Cultures Potières en Afrique', in F. Joulian (ed.), *Comment le Chimpanzé a Dérobé la Culture*. Paris: Editions de la Maison des Sciences de l'Homme.

Henrich, J. 2001. 'Cultural Transmission and the Diffusion of Innovations', *American Anthropologist* 103: 992–1013.

Henrich, J. and R. Boyd. 2002. 'On Modeling Cognition and Culture: Why Replicators are not Necessary for Cultural Evolution', *Journal of Cognition and Culture* 2: 87–112.

Henrich, J., R. Boyd and P. Richerson. 2008. 'Five Misunderstandings about Cultural Evolution', *Human Nature* 19: 119–37.

Kandler, A. and S.J. Shennan. 'A Non-equilibrium Neutral Model for Cultural Change'. Submitted.

Latour, B. 2009. 'Gabriel Tarde and the End of the Social', in P. Joyce (ed.), *The Social in Question: New Bearings in History and the Social Sciences*. London: Routledge, pp. 117–32.

Leroi-Gourhan, A. 1993. *Gesture and Speech*. Cambridge, MA: MIT Press.

Lipatov, M., M.J. Brown and M.W. Feldman. 2011. 'The Influence of Social Niche on Cultural Niche Construction: Modelling Changes in Belief about Marriage Form in Taiwan', *Philosophical Transactions of the Royal Society B* 366: 901–17.

Marsden, P. 2000. 'Forefathers of Memetics: Gabriel Tarde and the Laws of Imitation', *Journal of Memetics – Evolutionary Models of Information Transmission* 4. http://cfpm.org/jom-emit/2000/vol4/marsden_p.html

Mauss, M. 2006. 'Techniques of the Body', in N. Schlanger (ed.), *Techniques, Technology and Civilisation*. Oxford: Berghahn Books.

Mesoudi, A. and S.J. Lycett. 2009. 'Random Copying, Frequency-dependent Copying and Culture Change', *Evolution and Human Behavior* 30: 41–48.

O'Brien, M.J., R.L. Lyman, A. Mesoudi and T.L. VanPool. 2010. 'Cultural Traits as Units of Analysis', *Philosophical Transactions of the Royal Society B* 365: 3797–806.

Powell, A., S.J. Shennan and M.G. Thomas. 2009. 'Late Pleistocene Demography and the Appearance of Modern Human Behavior', *Science* 324: 1298–301.

Richerson, P.J. and R. Boyd. 2005. *Not By Genes Alone: How Culture Transformed Human Evolution*. Chicago: University of Chicago Press.

Rivers, W.H.R. 1926. *Psychology and Ethnology*. London: Kegan Paul, Trench, Trubner & Co.

Roux, V. 2007. 'Ethnoarchaeology: A Non-historical Science of Reference Necessary for Interpreting the Past', *Journal of Archaeological Method and Theory* 14: 153–78.

_____.2008. 'Evolutionary Trajectories of Technological Traits and Cultural Transmission: A Qualitative Approach to the Emergence and Disappearance of the Ceramic Wheel-fashioning Technique in the Southern Levant during the Fifth to Third Millennia BC', in M. Stark, B. Bowser and L. Horne (eds), *Breaking Down Boundaries: Anthropological Approaches to Cultural Transmission and Material Culture in Memory of Carol Kramer.* Tucson: University of Arizona Press, pp. 82–104.

Shennan, S.J. 2001. 'Demography and Cultural Innovation: A Model and some Implications for the Emergence of Modern Human Culture', *Cambridge Archaeological Journal* 11: 5–16.

Steele, J. 2009. 'Innovation, Diffusion and Travelling Waves', in S.J. Shennan (ed.), *Pattern and Process in Cultural Evolution.* Berkeley: University of California Press, pp. 163–74.

Steele, J., C. Glatz and A. Kandler. 2010. 'Ceramic Diversity, Random Copying, and Tests for Selectivity in Ceramic Production', *Journal of Archaeological Science* 37: 1348–58.

Tarde, G. (1893) 1999. *Monadologie et Sociologie.* Le Plessis Robinson: Institut Synthélabo.

_____.1903. *The Laws of Imitation.* New York: Henry, Holt and Co.

Weiss, K. and F. Hayashida. 2002. 'Kulturcrisis! Cultural Evolution Going Round in Circles', *Evolutionary Anthropology* 11: 136–41.

NOTES ON CONTRIBUTORS

James Broesch is a Post-Doctoral Research Fellow in the School of Population and Public Health at the University of British Columbia. He holds a PhD in Anthropology from Emory University, and recently completed a Robert Wood Johnson Foundation-Health and Society Scholar Fellowship at the University of Wisconsin-Madison. His research focuses on the transmission and acquisition of culture, and the intersection between culture and health. His most recent work incorporates methods and theory from anthropology, psychology, and sociology to operationalize and measure culture in population health research. Email: james.broesch@gmail.com

Mark Collard is Canada Research Chair and Professor in the Department of Archaeology at Simon Fraser University, British Columbia, Canada. He is also Director of Simon Fraser University's Human Evolutionary Studies Program (http://hesp.irmacs.sfu.ca/), and a Co-Director of the Centre for Human Evolution, Cognition and Culture (http://www.hecc.ubc.ca/), which is a joint venture between the University of British Columbia and Simon Fraser University. Professor Collard works on a number of topics in evolutionary anthropology, among which are the identification of species in the hominin fossil record, the reconstruction of primate phylogenetic relationships, and the estimation of body mass, stature and age from skeletal material. In addition, he is using methods and theory from evolutionary biology to investigate archaeologically and ethnographically documented patterns of material culture variation. Email: mcollard@sfu.ca

Alice Cowie is a postgraduate student at the Centre for Social Learning and Cognitive Evolution, School of Biology, University of St Andrews, Scotland. She gained her B.Sc. (Biology) from the University of Birmingham in 2007, and her M.Sc. (Animal Behaviour) from the University of Exeter in 2009. She is currently studying social learning in birds with Professor Kevin Laland. Email: ahc28@st-andrews.ac.uk

Roy Ellen is Professor of Anthropology and Human Ecology at the School of Anthropology and Conservation, University of Kent, Canterbury. His recent publications include *On the Edge of the Banda Zone* (University of Hawaii Press 2003), *The Categorical Impulse* (Berghahn 2006) and *Nuaulu Religious Practices: The Frequency and Reproduction of Rituals in a Moluccan Society* (KITLV Press 2012). Among his recent edited works is *Ethnobiology and the Science of Humankind* (Blackwell 2006). He is a Fellow of the British Academy and a member of its Council. He was President of the Royal Anthropological Institute between 2007 and 2011. Email: r.f.ellen@kent.ac.uk

Michael D. Fischer is Professor of Anthropological Science and Director of the Centre for Social Anthropology and Computing at the School of Anthropology and Conservation, University of Kent, Canterbury. He is a co-editor of *The Handbook of Cognitive Anthropology* (Wiley-Blackwell 2011), and his recent work includes investigating the impact of mobile social computing on culture and society, in publications such as 'Connected Individuation and PolySocial Reality in Communities' (*FutureInternet*), and the creation and transmission of new knowledge, following on from 'Cultural Dynamics: Formal Descriptions of Cultural Processes' in *Structure and Dynamics*. He is Editor for the Society for Anthropological Sciences and is on the Executive Board of the Human Relations Area Files. Email: mf1@kent.ac.uk

Tatyana Humle is a Lecturer in the School of Anthropology and Conservation (Durrell Institute of Conservation and Ecology) at the University of Kent, Canterbury. She is the author of several seminal publications on chimpanzee culture and behaviour, including 'Social Influences on Ant-dipping Acquisition in the Wild Chimpanzees of Bossou Guinea, West Africa' (*Animal Cognition* 2009), 'How are Army Ants Shedding New Light on Culture in Chimpanzees?' (in *Understanding Chimpanzees: The Mind of the Chimpanzee* 2010), and an edited book entitled *The Chimpanzees of Bossou and Nimba* (Springer-Verlag 2011). She is also on the executive committee of the Great Ape Conservation section of the IUCN and the GRASP-UNEP scientific commission. Email: t.humle@kent.ac.uk

Sarah E. Johns is a Senior Lecturer in Evolutionary Anthropology at the School of Anthropology and Conservation, and is Sub-Dean for the Faculty of Social Sciences at the University of Kent, Canterbury. Her research focuses on the variation of the age at first birth in humans, understanding life-history trade-offs in Western populations, and how public health policy and evolutionary theory can be integrated. Recent publications include: 'Red is Not a Proxy

Signal for Female Genitalia in Humans' (*PLoS ONE* 2012); 'Perceived Environmental Risk as a Predictor of Teenage Motherhood in a British Population' (*Health and Place* 2011); and 'Teenage Pregnancy and Motherhood: How might Evolutionary Theory Inform Policy?' (*Journal of Evolutionary Psychology* 2011). Email: s.e.johns@kent.ac.uk

Kevin Laland is a Professor of Biology at the Centre for Social Learning and Cognitive Evolution, School of Biology, University of St Andrews, Scotland. After completing his Ph.D. at University College London in 1990, he was awarded BBSRC and Human Frontier Science Program postdoctoral fellowships and a Royal Society University Research Fellowship, held at University of California Berkeley and Cambridge University. His research focuses on animal behaviour and evolution, particularly animal social learning, gene-culture co-evolution and niche construction, combining experimental and theoretical methods. He has authored ten books and nearly two hundred scientific articles, has been the recipient of over £8 million of grants, and is an elected Fellow of the Royal Society of Edinburgh. Email: knl1@st-andrews.ac.uk

Stephen J. Lycett is Senior Lecturer in Anthropology at the School of Anthropology and Conservation, University of Kent, Canterbury. Trained in both biological anthropology and archaeology, his work is multidisciplinary, and makes extensive use of evolutionary principles and quantitative methodologies. His major research interests focus on integrating the biological, cultural and technological aspects of evolution in humans, non-human primates and fossil hominins. He co-edited the volume *New Perspectives on Old Stones: Analytical Approaches to Palaeolithic Technologies* (Springer 2010) and is a member of the editorial board for *Journal of Archaeological Science*. Email: S.J.Lycett@kent.ac.uk

Alex Mesoudi is Reader in Anthropology in the Department of Anthropology at Durham University. He is the author of twenty-nine journal articles in such publications as *Behavioral and Brain Sciences*, *Evolution*, *Proceedings of the Royal Society B* and *Psychological Review*, and in 2011 of a book entitled *Cultural Evolution* for University of Chicago Press. He is Treasurer and Steering Committee Member of the European Human Behaviour and Evolution Association (EHBEA) and on the editorial board of the journal *PLoS ONE*. In 2012 he was the recipient of the Margot Wilson Award for best paper published in the journal *Evolution and Human Behavior*. Email: alex.mesoudi@durham.ac.uk

Tom Morgan is a doctoral student at the Centre for Social Learning and Cognitive Evolution, School of Biology, University of St Andrews, Scotland. He is interested in decision making in a social context, and the relationship between social learning and culture. He is co-author of 'The Biological Bases of Conformity' (with K.N. Laland, 2012) in *Frontiers in Neuroscience*, and of 'Cognitive Culture: Theoretical and Empirical Insights into Social Learning Strategies' (with L. Rendell, L. Fogarty, W. Hoppitt, M.M. Webster and K.N. Laland, 2011) in *Trends in Cognitive Sciences* 15: 68–76. Email: tjhm3@st-andrews.ac.uk

Nicholas E. Newton-Fisher is Senior Lecturer in Primate Behavioural Ecology at the School of Anthropology and Conservation, University of Kent, Canterbury. His research focuses on chimpanzees and the long-term study of the Sonso community (Budongo, Uganda). Publications include: 'Grooming Reciprocity in Wild Male Chimpanzees' (*Animal Behaviour* 2011); 'Paternity and Social Rank in Budongo Forest Chimpanzees' (*American Journal of Physical Anthropology* 2010); 'Wild Female Chimpanzees form Coalitions against Male Aggression (*International Journal of Primatology* 2006); 'The Relationship between Food Supply and Chimpanzee Party Size in the Budongo Forest Reserve, Uganda' (*International Journal of Primatology* 2000); and 'The Diet of Chimpanzees in the Budongo Forest' (*African Journal of Ecology* 1999). Email: n.e.newton-fisher@kent.ac.uk

Sean O'Neill is a postgraduate student in the Department of Archaeology at the School of Geosciences, University of Aberdeen, Scotland. He is also currently a Member of Cambridge University, based at the Fitzwilliam Museum. He is interested in complex hunter-gatherer societies, with a focus on technological evolution and innovation, in how these developments are socially constructed and then culturally transmitted, and in how they can be traced archaeologically. He is primarily working with dual-inheritance models on the Pacific Northwest Coast of North America, within an ethnographic present circa 1870–1900. Email: r01spo7@abdn.ac.uk

Simon Platten is an Honorary Research Fellow at the School of Anthropology and Conservation, University of Kent, Canterbury. He is currently Project Manager at Tamar Grow Local, a community interest company (CIC) which creates and supports local food provision in the Tamar Valley, Cornwall. At Kent he was a Leverhulme Research Fellow on the British Homegardens Project. Recent publications include (with Roy Ellen, 2011) 'The Social Life of Seeds: The Role of Networks of Relationships in the Dispersal of Plant Germplasm', *Journal of the Royal Anthropological Institute* 17(3): 563–84. Email: sjp10@kent.ac.uk

Rajindra K. Puri is Senior Lecturer in Environmental Anthropology and Director of the Centre for Biocultural Diversity at the School of Anthropology and Conservation, University of Kent, Canterbury. He has a long-term interest in the historical ecology and ethnobiology of a rainforest valley in Indonesian Borneo, working with Penan Benalui hunter-gatherers and Kenyah swidden agriculturalists, and applied conservation social science. His recent work has been on local adaptation to climatic variability and change in Borneo. He was also co-investigator on the ESPA project Human Adaptation to Biodiversity Change, 2010–2011, focused on southern Karnataka, India. He is author of *Deadly Dances in the Bornean Rainforest* (KITLV Press 2005) and co-editor with M. Pardo de Santayana and A. Pieroni of *Ethnobotany in the New Europe* (Berghahn Books 2010). Email: rkp@kent.ac.uk

Victoria Reyes-García is ICREA Professor at the Institut de Ciència i Tecnologia Ambientals of the Universitat Autònoma de Barcelona, Spain. Her research focuses on ethnoecology, indigenous peoples, biocultural diversity and local ecological knowledge. In 2010 she received a Starting Grant from the European Research Council (ERC) to study the returns of local ecological knowledge in three indigenous societies. Her recent co-authored publications include 'Home Gardens in Three Mountain Regions of the Iberian Peninsula: Description, Motivations for Gardening, and Financial Benefits' (*Journal of Sustainable Agriculture* 2012), and 'The Role of Ethnobotanical Skills and Agricultural Labor in Forest Clearance: Evidence from the Bolivian Amazon' (*Ambio* 2011). Her chapter is jointly authored with the TAPS (Tsimane' Amazonian Panel Study) Team based in Beni, Bolivia. Email: victoria.reyes@uab.cat

Stephen Shennan is Professor of Theoretical Archaeology and Director of the Institute of Archaeology at University College London. His publications include the books *Genes, Memes and Human History* (2002), *The Evolution of Cultural Diversity: A Phylogenetic Approach* (ed. with Ruth Mace and Clare Holden 2004), *Pattern and Process in Cultural Evolution* (ed. 2009), and *Innovation in Cultural Systems: Contributions from Evolutionary Anthropology* (ed. with M. O'Brien 2010). He was elected a Fellow of the British Academy in 2006 and was awarded the Rivers Memorial Medal of the Royal Anthropological Institute in 2010. Email: s.shennan@ucl.ac.uk

Jamshid J. Tehrani is Research Fellow in the Department of Anthropology at Durham University. His recent publications include 'Missing Links: Species, Artefacts and the Cladistic Reconstruction of Prehistory', in *Evolutionary and Interpretive Archaeologies – A Dialogue*

edited by E. Cochrane and A. Gardner (Left Coast Press 2011); 'Human Niche Construction in Interdisciplinary Focus', *Philosophical Transactions of the Royal Society* (2011, a special issue that he co-edited with J. Kendal and J. Odling-Smee); and 'Testing for Divergent Transmission Histories among Cultural Characters: A Study Using Bayesian Phylogenetic Methods and Iranian Tribal Textile Data' (*PLoS One*, with L.J. Matthews, F.M. Jordan and C.L. Nunn, 2011). Email: jamie.tehrani@durham.ac.uk

Harry G. West is Professor of Anthropology, and Chair of the Food Studies Centre, at the School of Oriental and African Studies, University of London. He is author of *Kupilikula: Governance and the Invisible Realm in Mozambique* (University of Chicago Press 2005) and *Ethnographic Sorcery* (University of Chicago Press 2007), as well as editor of four other volumes and author of numerous book chapters and journal articles. Email: hw16@soas.ac.uk

Stanford Zent is Investigador Asociado Titular and Jefe del Laboratorio de Ecología Humana at the Centro de Antropología, Instituto Venezolano de Investigaciones Científicas (IVIC) in Caracas, Venezuela. Twice (2000, 2003) he won the Venezuelan national prize for the best scientific paper, social science area, and he is co-author of a book that was named the best book of the year (2006), development category. Recent papers include: 'Jodï Horticultural Belief, Knowledge and Practice: Incipient or Integral Cultivation?' and 'Reflexiones sobre el Proyecto de Auto-Demarcación y EtnoCartografía de las Tierras y Hábitats Jodï y Eñepa'. In the past few years, he has been working on developing an indicator for measuring the vitality of traditional environmental knowledge (VITEK). Email: srzent@gmail.com

INDEX